Praise for *The Home for the Friendless*

I got lost in the wonderful world of memory, how the narrator at three years of age uses the language available to her, just as the narrator does at nine, fifteen, etc. It is crafted beautifully. I also loved being able to come along with someone who lived through some of America's most trying growing pains, just as she was fielding uncertainties about her surroundings, her mind and her body. Her gift in writing comes from an understanding of how stories should move, how sentences should flow, and of course the ability to draw from her past in order to present the reader with texture, pathos and so much humanity. I worried and prayed she'd dodge the pitfalls of poverty, loneliness, creepy strangers and parents who loved her, but who were derailed at times by their own circumstances and their own vulnerabilities. I enjoyed it so much.

— JOSHUA BRAFF, *The Unthinkable Thoughts of Jacob Green* and *Peep Show*

A wonderful reading experience. Poignant, brutally honest, sad, at times heart-breaking, and laughing-out-loud funny. Just as pearls are formed by grains of sand, Betty and her siblings were shaped by the adversity of hard times and a dysfunctional family with enough resolve to live life to the fullest.

— CHARLES D. HAYES, *September University: Summoning Passion for an Unfinished Life*

The Home for the Friendless is an engrossing reminder of how it was for some families during desperately poverty-stricken times. With compelling frankness, she takes us along with herself and her two siblings on their journey from tots to teenagers. What might have been a sad, sad story emerges as one of inspiration. It bestows upon its readers an affirming sense of family, hope, and those small but significant victories won by everyday fortitude. This book will bring a tear, but it will bring even more smiles, totally unexpected chortles, and no shortage of thoughtful wistfulness and longing for the good times and stalwart people of that era, despite its poverty.

— JOHN WATSON, Writer

Betty Auchard tells her amazing life story with purpose, humor, and no regret. Her tale is unique, yet universal, a collection of memories that expose her soul and will touch your heart.

— BETH MILLER, former Program Coordinator for the History Center of Cedar Rapids, IA

Praise for *Dancing in my Nightgown*

Dancing in My Nightgown: The Rhythms of Widowhood is also available in Spanish as *Bailando en mi camisón: Al compás de la viudez*

Dancing in my Nightgown is a truly enchanting, heartbreaking love story told with such honesty and humor that I ached for my beloved Steve Allen.

— JAYNE MEADOWS, Widow of Steve Allen (TV star)

I found *Dancing in my Nightgown* brave and touching.

— ROSEMARIE STACK
Widow of Robert Stack (TV star of *Unsolved Mysteries*)

The narrative is wonderfully nuanced, stretching the emotional spectrum from horizon to horizon. Betty Auchard's humanity shows brightly on each page.

— WALTER M. BORTZ, M.D., Author, *Dare To Be 100*

For those of us who have experienced an enormous loss, the stories in this book are palpable . . . providing comfort, compassion, hope, laughter at times, and peace of mind. This book is a must read!

— KAY ALLENBAUGH, Author, *Chocolate for a Woman's Soul* series

Betty Auchard clearly has a passion for storytelling. She is a gifted writer who evokes tears and humor from one moment to the next. *Dancing In My Nightgown* is a marvelous tale of a woman's journey from loss to wholeness.

— LINDA E. SAVAGE, PhD, Licensed Psychologist, Author,
Reclaiming Goddess Sexuality: The Power of the Feminine Way

Anyone who's lost a loved one will relate to the many wonderful moments in Betty Auchard's wise and funny book. These bittersweet reflections on widowhood will make you smile and make you cry. Best of all, Auchard helps us realize that we're never really alone in our grieving, and that it's okay to remember our loved ones' foibles as well as their shining qualities. These pages cheer the spirit and soothe the soul.

— Lolly Winston, Author, *Good Grief*

This charming and entrancing series of stories in the everyday life of a recent widow could serve as a guide to successful and fulfilling life after a long-term relationship for anyone, male, female . . . only the activities might be different.

— MARY FINN MAPLES, Ph.D., Professor, Counseling Educational Psychology,
University of Nevada–Reno

The HOME for the FRIENDLESS

Also by Betty Auchard

Dancing In My Nightgown: The Rhythms of Widowhood

Available in Spanish:

Bailando en mi camisón: Al compás de la viudez

The HOME for the FRIENDLESS

Finding hope, love, and family

Betty Auchard

LifeStories ◈ Las Vegas, Nevada

Edited by Sandi Corbitt-Sears
Copyedited by Jami Carpenter
Cover and layout by Sue Campbell
Author photo by Ryan Willis Photography

Second Printing 2011
Cataloging in Publication
Auchard, Betty.
Home for the friendless : finding hope, love, and family / Betty Auchard.
358 p. ; 23 cm, photos
ISBN: 1-935043-26-9
ISBN-13: 978-1-935043-26-3
In this memoir composed of a series of stories, the author tells of her dysfunctional
family as she grew from tot to teen in a poverty-stricken time in Iowa.
1. Family life—Iowa. I. Title
[B] dc22   2010   2010931235
e-book ISBN: 1-935043-28-5, ISBN 13: 978-1-935043-28-7
Audio book ISBN: 1-935043-29-3, ISBN 13: 978-1-935043-29-4

Life Stories

AN IMPRINT OF STEPHENS PRESS, LLC

Post Office Box 1600
Las Vegas, NV 89125-1600
www.LifeStoriesBooks.com

Printed in Hong Kong

This memoir is dedicated to:

Waneta Elizabeth Peal (Girl) ❧ *my mother*

Bassle Sylvester Peal (Butch) ❧ *my father*

Robert Irving Peal (Bobby) ❧ *my brother*

Patricia Ann Reffel (Patty) ❧ *my sister*

Contents

Acknowledgments 11

Introduction 13

PART 1: *The Early Years*

What's in a Name? 17

Where's Betty? 19

Pay Attention to Me. 20

Poetry in the Tavern. 21

Smile. 23

Show Me Yours and I'll Show You Mine 27

Betty to the Rescue. 29

Quite an Artist 32

Uncle Jiggs 34

Hattie Burke. 36

Little House on Young's Hill 39

Me Too Cool 43

I Remember Granny 45

Wet Weather Report 48

Sticky Fingers. 50

Curly Confidence 52

What about Grandma Blanche? 53

PART 2: *Life at the Home*
for the Friendless

Welcome to the Home for the Friendless 59

Getting Used to Life at the Home. 63

Sucking My Thumb 65

Wetting the Bed at the Home. 68

Being Brave. 70

Toothpaste Candy 72

Halloween and the End of the World. 74

Nose Rags 77

Tattling on Virginia. 79

Parties for Poor Kids 81

Happy Birthday, Bobby. 83

Stealing Stuff 86

The Ottumwa Home 89

History Lessons. 92

The "F" Word. 94

PART 3: *A Real Family*

A Real Home on 32nd Street 101

Improvements 102

The 32nd Street Museum 103

Things Change 104

Mom's Temper...105

Who's the Boss?..107

Outhouse Adventures 110

Tattling in the Teepee 114

Dishes and Switches...115

How to Break a Bone...118

Christmas on 32nd Street 119

Dying for a Dog...121

PART 4: *The War at Home*

War...129

Wartime in Winter 132

Eating Well in Tough Times..136

Black Market Grandmother 138

Recycling...140

Rations and Recipes...142

Doing Without 144

War Bonds and Patriots 146

Millie's Daughter and the USO 149

Letters from Soldiers 151

Victory Gardens 154

Getting Back to Normal..157

PART 5: *Growing Up*

Busted!...163

The Squirt Truck Run to Waterloo...165

Family Circus...170

Betty Grows Up 175

Junior High Blues...177

My Social Standing 179

Changing Keys 183

Back on Home Turf...189

The Altar Call 197

Passion for Music 198

First Love..200

PART 6: *The Denver Adventure*

Riding the Rails 207

Saying Goodbye..207

Welcome to Denver 212
Our New Home 215
Finding Hope at the Museum. 223
Summer on Champa Street 225
Kitchen Duty and Cockroaches. 231
Waiting for Dad 233
Letters from Home. 237
Breaking the Rules 240
Boxing in the Alley. 243
Dad Arrives 247

PART 7: *Starting Over*
Escape from Champa Street 255
Dad's Challenges 261
Ironing My Way into the Future 263
Fort Logan 266
Deeper in Debt 268
Longing to Belong 270
First Kiss 273
Obsessed with Angelina. 274
Payback 278
The Facts of Life 281
Out of the Pool!. 283
Blowing Down the Hill 285

PART 8: *Becoming Betty Peal*
Becoming Betty. 291
Not That Girl Anymore 295
Needing Money. 298
Mom Gets Religion 302
Damsy Moves In. 304
The Actress 308
Dancing Girl 310
Sweet Sixteen 313
Unsuitable Suitors 315
Auntie Marge to the Rescue 320
Betty Peal for Head Girl. 324
The Senior. 327

Afterword 335
Waneta and Butch 335
Don. 339

Epilogue 342
Betty's History Lessons 345

ACKNOWLEDGMENTS

MOST OF THESE STORIES WERE WRITTEN IN RESPONSE TO MEMories that floated to the surface and demanded to be captured. But they didn't come together until much later, after a decade of reflection and research.

The following people helped bring this book to life: Sandi Corbitt-Sears, my personal editor, friend, teacher, and writing partner, who spent more time with my stories than anyone besides me; Bruce McAllister, my mentor, coach, and consultant, whose encouragement and critiques pushed me even harder on this second book; Bob Peal, my brother, who knew the answers to everything I asked about our family history; Pat Reffel, my sister, who added her two cents whenever she could get a word in; Dodie Hively and Renee Ray, my daughters, and a competent critique team; and Don Elarton, my cousin, who read and reread my manuscript through numerous revisions.

Susan Letham's online writing classes started it all eleven years ago. I repeated her workshops because I loved learning about the craft. She couldn't get rid of me and suggested that I stop taking classes and start writing, which I did. Soon after that, Kay Allenbaugh accepted three stories about my childhood for publication in the *Chocolate for a Teen's Soul* anthologies. For the next several years, I relived my life in tales that I shared with anyone who could read.

It was in Sheila Dunec's memoir class four years ago in Los Gatos, California, that most of the stories in Part 2 of this book were written. By that time, I already knew that Stephens Press in Las Vegas was going to publish this book. For many years, Carolyn Hayes-Uber, my publisher, and her staff have been cherished colleagues, encouraging and supporting me in far too many ways to list here.

In addition to the people mentioned above, I was the grateful recipient of much help from the History Center in Cedar Rapids, Iowa. The enthusiasm of former project coordinator Beth Miller was a godsend. She personally sought out oldtimers who knew the answers to my many questions. Some of those knowledgeable folks were volunteers at the center who located photos and news clippings about people and places that no longer exist. Because they were natives of Cedar Rapids, they generously shared firsthand information on numerous topics.

I am also indebted to several dear friends for their support and efforts on my behalf. Al Adams and Gene and Genie Bernardini saw more substance in my writing than I knew existed. Marilyn Stark Drenkhahn, former child resident of The Home for the Friendless, filled in details I had long forgotten. Hubert Peal, my cousin who loves to tell Peal family tales, confirmed that they were all true. Linda Tucker was the first person outside my family to read a draft and give me helpful and enthusiastic feedback. And my best friend in high school, Joann Stratton Wanamaker, remembered more things than I had ever known.

Special thanks go to fellow members of the California Writers Club South Bay Branch who were brave enough to say, "Betty, I'd love to read one of your stories." I apologize for always sending three when you asked for one, but I loved hearing you gush. You egged me on, and that's just what I needed. I thank you all.

— Betty Auchard

INTRODUCTION

GOING TO BED AT 7:30 WAS CRAZY. IT WASN'T EVEN DARK. BUT that's the way they did things at the Home for the Friendless in Cedar Rapids, Iowa. The Home was an ancient brick building where my brother, sister, and I lived while our parents tried again to work out their problems. On our first night there, I bathed, brushed my teeth, put on nightclothes, and climbed into bed in the hot and stuffy dormitory.

Mrs. Stone, the monitor, shook her finger and said, "No more talking. Just stay quiet and go to sleep."

"But it's still light outside," whined one little girl.

"Shhh." As Mrs. Stone turned to leave, she stopped to add a warning. "If you get up during the night, don't drink any water or you'll wet the bed." Then she disappeared into her apartment near the bathroom sinks.

Even though I was there with other girls whose families had problems, I felt terribly alone. It was miserable being separated from Dad and Mama and relocated to a strange place. I had pretended it was normal so my little brother and sister wouldn't be scared. But that evening I couldn't comfort them because they were in their own dorms. I knew I wouldn't see them very often, and I already missed them so much I felt sick.

After flopping on top of the stiff sheets, I watched the last of the daylight spill over our beds from the windows. I felt abandoned. What were Mama and Dad doing while I was trying so hard to doze off? Were they arguing again or going to the movies? I got all twitchy, lying there thinking and waiting for cool air to arrive.

I could hear roller rink sounds from several blocks away. The organ was playing "Take Me out to the Ballgame," and I could hear hundreds of skate wheels humming on the rink floor. The mingling of steel wheels and music in the air hypnotized me. I began to imagine how different things would be if I were a magician. I would soar back to the past and live with Mama and Dad again so we three kids could be cozy under one blanket and go to sleep after dark like normal people. It was not normal for my brother and sister and me to sleep during the daytime, in three different beds, in rooms filled with kids we didn't know.

When the sun finally quit for the day, a kindhearted breeze wafted through the screens to cool my skin, and I finally drifted into slumber. I dreamed that I was flying with my brother under one arm and my sister under the other, and I was brave enough to fly wherever I wanted without asking permission.

It was fun zipping wherever I wanted to go, though something kept my flights from turning out right. It dawned on me that I had left Bobby and Patty behind, so I made a graceful U-turn back to the Home and into the boys' window. Bobby was too scared to join me because he had forgotten that I knew how to fly. I grabbed the back of his pajama top anyway and whooshed into the nursery to scoop up Patty, but she was sound asleep. I fluttered above her, calling her name softly so as not to wake the other little kids.

My plan was to float through my parents' window with Bobby and Patty and say, *Surprise!* But I didn't know where they lived or if they remembered who we were. Mama and Dad were always moving. Why couldn't they stay in one place for a while? It would make flying to them a whole lot easier.

Instead of gliding into my parents' house, I found myself trapped inside a huge room that was inside another room that was inside another room. I got so airsick that I had to abort the flight.

I awoke tangled in my sheets. It took a while for me to go to sleep again, and then once more I was flying. That time we three kids made it to the great outdoors and were surrounded by blue sky instead of wallpaper. I loved the sensation, so I floated for a long time, holding Patty by her middle finger and Bobby by his thumb and kicking as fast as I could to stay up ... until I saw telephone wires ahead. I dove under them and zoomed up, up, and away into wide open space only to find more telephone wires high above the earth.

I never did make it to freedom with my brother and sister that night, but since I didn't know where freedom was, I decided it was a whole lot easier just to wake up.

⋀

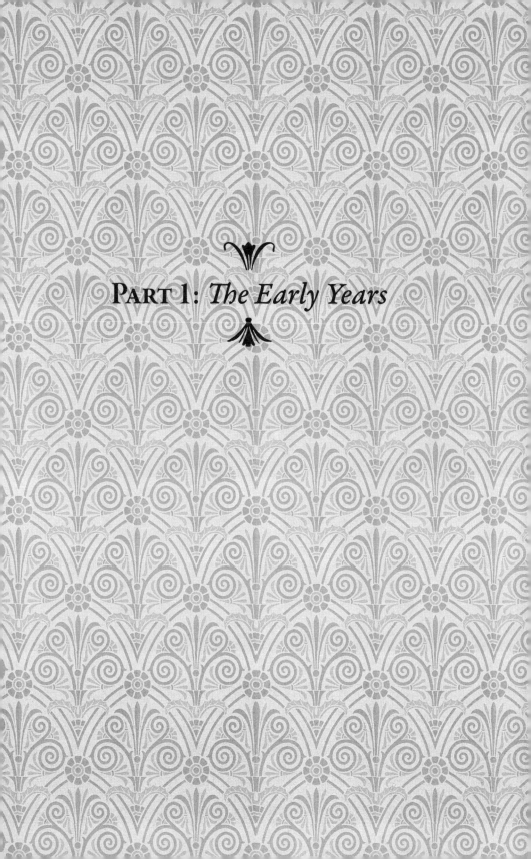

PART 1: *The Early Years*

The Peal kids 1936

What's in a Name?

DAD WAS BORN IN TENNESSEE WHERE IT WAS COMMON PRACtice for a man to call a woman "Girl," so that became my father's nickname for Mama. At other times, he referred to her as Nita. He used her real name, Waneta, only when he was mad.

Since my mother was born in Iowa instead of Tennessee, she never used the word "boy" to address Dad. He was Butch when she wasn't mad and Bassle when she was furious.

"Waneta, I don't know what in the Sam Hill to do about you!" (Dad always consulted Sam Hill when he had a problem.)

"Well, Bassle, here's what I think about that!"

When Mama and Dad used each other's proper names, it was a warning that pandemonium was about to begin. Witnessing those fights was nerve-racking because my mother's rage was usually accompanied by the sound of glass shattering as she hurled the nearest dishes to the floor. A few rounds later, they'd end up in each other's arms amidst the broken pottery, hugging and kissing as Nita and Butch. I was probably created during one of their make-up sessions.

When she was pregnant, my mother, who was barely five feet tall, gained sixty pounds. Dad was sure that meant a big, strapping son was in his near future, but 10 pounds 1 ounce of her extra weight was me. She was in labor for two days, and after all that work, my mother had just enough strength to consult with Dad about what to call their daughter. But my father was nowhere to be found.

He was eventually located at the neighborhood tavern where he'd spent the day waiting for the news that his "big boy" had been born. Finding out that he'd fathered a big girl instead disappointed him so much that he stayed at the bar and hoisted a few more drinks. Mama was too worn out to worry about him.

Without my father's help, she decided that I would be Pearl (in memory of her childhood friend) Elizabeth (her own middle name). Dad wasn't crazy about either one, so he called me Betty, and my mother went along with it.

I didn't learn about Pearl or Elizabeth until my first day of kindergarten. The teacher took attendance by reading what was printed on her enrollment sheet and seeing who raised a hand. "Did I miss anyone?" she asked when she reached the end of the list. Feeling terribly shy and nervous, I held up my hand.

"What is your name, dear?"

"Betty."

"Betty what?" I had no idea what she was talking about and didn't know how to reply.

"Speak up, dear. Is it Betty Smith?"

"No. Betty Peal."

She searched the class list for Peal and said, "Dear, you are listed as Elizabeth Peal, so that is who you will be." At first I thought it was a mistake, but since she was a grownup and a teacher, I knew she must be right. I was stunned. All that time I'd thought I was Betty. Finding out different in kindergarten was confusing. And not answering to Elizabeth got me in trouble for being a poor listener.

At home, I told Mama what had happened. She explained that my real name was Pearl Elizabeth Peal and that Betty was a nickname for Elizabeth. It would have been easier if she had told me before I started school. I guess she was too busy taking care of my little brother and sister.

I had no choice but to find a way to be Betty at home and Elizabeth at school. I felt like two completely different people. Hearing a teacher call me Elizabeth meant business and wasn't warm and fuzzy. The name was almost too heavy to carry.

I felt more like myself when my dad and five uncles dubbed me Betty Boop. By the sixth grade, my friends started calling me Lizzie, and I liked it even better than Betty Boop because it had zing.

I continued to be Lizzie until I grew up and became Betty again. But no one has ever called me Pearl, even when they were mad at me.

🔱

Where's Betty?

In school, I learned about Charles Lindbergh's historic flight, and our teacher asked if we knew anything else about the famous man and his family. My hand shot up because I'd heard my parents talk about the Lindbergh baby's kidnapping many times. Mom said the endless news updates about the shocking event had made them edgy. Parents all over the country, rich and poor, were immobilized with fear for their own children. I'd been the same age as the Lindbergh baby when he disappeared, which didn't help matters at all.

One Sunday morning, Dad realized it was unusually quiet in our apartment. He looked up from the latest bad news in the paper and asked, "Girl, where's Betty?"

"She's down for a nap."

"Ain't this kinda early for a nap?"

Mom mashed her cigarette into the ashtray and replied, "Yeah, it is. I think I'm wearing her out trying to potty train her."

Dad was casual about potty training. "Don't push it so hard," he advised. "She'll piss in the pot when she's good and ready."

"Easy for you to say, Butch," my mother would reply. "I'm the one scrubbing diapers on the washboard."

A few days later, it got too quiet again. When Dad asked, "Where's Betty?" Mom said, "I thought she was with you."

As they rummaged through our few small rooms, they blamed each other for my disappearance. "Waneta, you gotta keep yer eyes on her every minute!" Dad said as he looked under the bed.

"Butch, why is it always me . . . how about you helpin' out now and then?" Mom shot back as she looked behind the clothes in the closet.

It wasn't long before my parents were frantic with worry. They had peeked in the hamper, checked the bathtub, and opened every dresser drawer. No Betty Boop was to be found. My mother went from scared to panicked and my father from worry to fear. They rushed to enlist our neighbors in the search, praying that I had just wandered out the front door. After an hour of searching the neighborhood for a toddler running about, my mother said, "Butch, we've got to call the police!"

"Nita, just hold yer horses a goddamn minute. I don't see how in the Sam Hill she coulda walked out that front door. She's gotta be in the apartment." So back they went with a neighbor to help with the search.

It was the neighbor who found me behind the bathroom door. I was sitting on my tiny toilet chair, fast asleep, with my head flopped on my shoulder. It was the first time I'd ever used the potty by myself.

Dad was close to breaking down under the strain, but he never let on. Instead, he covered up his fear by joking. "Well, I guess she was finally good and ready."

🔻

Pay Attention to Me

DAD DIDN'T LIKE GOING TO CHURCH VERY MUCH, SO HE STAYED home while Mama and my grandmother Damsy took me to God's house every Sunday morning, Sunday evening, and sometimes during the week. I sang along with everyone even though I didn't know the tunes or the words, but I was too little to comprehend what all the praying and crying was about.

I amused myself by staring at everyone and trying to take money out of the offering basket as it passed by. But I felt left out of the communion snack of little white cookies and Kool-Aid that everyone got except me.

"Can I taste it?" I asked Mama.

"No."

"Does it taste good?"

"Hush."

I chattered endlessly, which caused Damsy to say, "Betty, shush and sit still." Other folks got to stand up and talk in church, and I didn't understand why I couldn't do the same.

One Sunday I had to go to the bathroom, but each time I started to tell Mama, Damsy would shush me again. My need to do number two was getting pretty serious. I patted my mother's arm and whispered, "I hafta go bom-bom."

"Shhh," she said. "Just wait."

I didn't know if I could wait or not and started wiggling.

"Sit still," Damsy hissed.

People were taking turns standing up and telling stories, then sitting down while someone else did the same. When no one else stood up, the preacher held his hand high and asked, "Anyone else out there want to share with the Lord today?"

All was quiet until, with great urgency, I pounded the pew and yelled, "I hafta go bom-bom!"

Most of the congregation laughed and several said, "Praise the Lord."

Damsy glared at me and said, "Shame on you, Betty."

I hid my face in my mother's lap because I was embarrassed. She grabbed my hand and led me to the bathroom real fast.

"Why did those people laugh at me?" I asked her.

"They laughed because they don't know what bom-bom means."

"Everybody knows what bom-bom means, Mama."

"No, Betty, they don't. It's our own family word for poop, but you can keep saying it anytime you need to go."

When Mama wasn't mad at somebody, she could be very, very nice.

I loved my mama.

Poetry in the Tavern

IN THE EARLY 1930s, AUNTIE MARGE AND UNCLE AL OWNED A TAVern called the Uptown Village Café. Booze was cheap and hamburgers, at fifteen cents each, were almost free. Uppity people called the Village a beer parlor; Auntie Marge said it was a family tavern.

"There's a big difference," she told me, "and people who come here know the difference." Auntie Marge always talked to me as if I understood every word she spoke, so I nodded in agreement no matter what she talked about.

My mother was the cook at the Village, and my father tended bar, so I practically grew up there. I was the luckiest girl in the world because I got to eat potato chips and drink soda pop whenever I wanted.

The bar ran along one wall, with booths along the other. A big ceiling fan turned lazily, not producing enough air to mess our hair or to cool us down in the summertime. Dad said, "Those damn fans are no use to man or beast and are just for atmosphere." I didn't understand what he meant, but being included in grownup conversations at the Uptown Village Café made me feel grown up, too.

Uncle Al's favorite spot in the tavern was at the far end of the bar near the kitchen where Mama cooked. From that position, he could keep an eye on the customers at all times. He considered it his job to make sure I could play safely in the tavern without any rowdy drinkers making a scene.

A large booth near the kitchen served many purposes. My family used it to do bookkeeping or have a beer with friends while I kept busy with my crayons and paper. The *Cedar Rapids Gazette* was there, too, and my favorite times happened when Dad was on a break. We would sit side by side in our cozy spot as he read the paper and I drew pictures in a Big Ben tablet.

When I was almost three, my uncle started showing me off to the patrons. He would place me on the bar with my legs hanging over the edge so that I could recite nursery rhymes to any customer who expressed the slightest interest. He would say, "Mr. Polochak, I invite you closer to meet Betty, my talented niece. She's Waneta's girl."

"Waneta, who's married to Butch?"

"Yes, Butch's little girl."

"His little girl? I thought he had a son."

"Yes, indeed, he had hoped for a son, but we all know how lucky he was to get Betty. Won't you join us, sir? The program is just about to begin, and tonight my niece will recite 'Mary Had a Little Lamb.'"

For a while, I was the main attraction at the Uptown Village Café, which turned me into Shirley Temple overnight. Every evening, the customers huddled around drinking and waiting for me to start, but I never began until Uncle Al had quieted the small audience.

Uncle Al always used grand gestures when introducing me. With a graceful motion in my direction, he said, "All right, Betty, you may begin."

When I couldn't remember all the words, I made up my own:

> *Mary had a little lamb and its fweece was white as snow*
> *and everywhere that Mary goed the lamb goed too.*
> *And the lamb goed to schoo wif her*
> *and it not posed to go to schoo*
> *so the kids laughed and laughed and laughed and laughed*
> *to see a lamb that goed to schoo.*

In appreciation for my efforts, the Village patrons dropped pennies in a beer mug. The click of coins against glass was so exciting that I would take a deep breath and stumble my way through another verse. I could never remember the last line that had something to do with wagging his tail behind him. I didn't understand what the words meant, even though Auntie Marge explained it over and over. "Betty, the lamb's tail is behind him and it's wagging." My confusion resulted in a slightly different version: *Leave dem alone to come back home and . . . uh . . . hind 'em tails. The end!*

The sound of applause was even more exciting than pennies clinking in a glass, and I could hardly wait to do it again.

One night after the applause ended, Dad said, "Nita, I'll tell ya for sure . . . performing's in her blood. She must've got it from your side of the family."

Dad didn't know how right he was. Someday people would pay me to tell my own stories to audiences so they could laugh, sigh, and sometimes cry, but always leave smiling.

Smile

AFTER MY BROTHER WAS BORN, DAD WAS VERY HAPPY THAT HE FI-nally had a boy, so he gazed at him all the time. Mama named our baby "Robert" after her brother, and Dad added "Irving" for Washington Irving, his favorite author. Even though Robert Irving Peal had two fancy names, we called him Bobby.

Dad talked to little Bobby like he was a grownup. He tickled his chin and said, "Do ya need a shave yet, Buddy?" or "How's the world treatin' ya, Robert Irving?" Talking to my baby brother was the same as pushing a happy button because his face lit up and his hands and feet wiggled. Dad said Bobby was born to smile. Even though Bobby got more attention than I got, I wasn't one bit jealous because I liked him as much as everyone else did.

On my third birthday, I was bursting with excitement because a professional photographer was coming to take pictures of my five-week-old brother and me. I could hardly wait. Bobby would look cute, as always, and I would finally be allowed to wear my beautiful, slippery smooth silk dress that Mama had been working on all week long. The photographs must have been very important because she had cut up her best garment to make a new one for me.

"You what?" asked Damsy when she learned about it.

"That's right. I want my daughter to look as pretty as possible for her first professional portrait."

"Waneta, you don't ruin a perfectly good piece of clothing for a few store-bought pictures."

Mama was not going to back down. "What good is a silk dress unless I go somewhere? I don't even go to church anymore because I'm too busy making baby food and washing diapers."

With no sewing machine, Mama stitched my new outfit by hand with a needle, thread, and thimble. Since it made me sad that Damsy had scolded my mother, I stopped thinking about it. I wanted to stay happy for our pictures.

After several days of hard work, Mama clipped the last thread, dropped the garment over my head, and stood back to see how it looked. She was delighted and, luckily, so was my grandmother.

I felt as pretty as girls in the movies. I wanted to keep it on, but Mama said, "It's too early to wear your new dress. You might get it dirty." I whined a lot, so she tried to explain. "Before that man gets here, I have to nurse the baby, change his diaper, and then trim your bangs. So sit still and be patient."

I was not one bit patient. I carried on something awful, but my mother wouldn't budge. "You sit there in your underwear, missy, until I'm ready," she said. "I don't want hairs to get all over your new dress when I trim your bangs."

Since my mother was so awfully busy and I was so fidgety, I decided to surprise her. I would cut my own hair. While she was concentrating on Bobby, I found what I needed in her sewing bag and got right to work.

I wasn't tall enough to see myself in the bathroom mirror, so I put the scissors against my forehead and started cutting blindly. It was easier than I expected, and slicing off the first clump made a sound that I liked. When a few hairs landed in my eyes, I blinked them away, squeezed my eyes shut, and kept cutting. Then hair went up my nose, landed on my tongue, and covered my arms and chest. Soon my face itched all over, so I quit.

I was proud of myself. My mama would be amazed to find out what a grownup girl I was, so into the kitchen I marched. I patted her on the hip to get her attention.

"Hold your horses, big sister," she said without looking at me. "I'm changing the baby's diaper."

"But lookie what I did for you."

She didn't answer, so I waited, wearing my proudest grin, until she finally looked down. Her eyes got real big and she stared at my forehead for a long time. Then she asked, "What the hell have you done?"

"I cut my bangs for you."

She was no longer looking at me, staring at the wall clock instead. In case she didn't understand my intentions, I explained. "I helped you, Mama."

I wanted her to say, "Thank you, honey bunch. What a big girl you are!" But she didn't say anything. She found the scissors, plopped me on the table, and spent precious time doing what I had already done for her. My happy feeling was gone. My mother wasn't proud of what I had done to help out, and I was sad and mad and confused.

When the photographer arrived, he set up his equipment and took pictures of my baby brother first because Bobby was already smiling. I just pouted. I didn't want my picture taken, and I didn't want to wear my new dress. But before I had a chance to whine, the photographer hoisted me on top of my grandmother's dark walnut library table where I sat with legs dangling over the edge. He urged me to sit up straighter and arranged my arms against my sides with the palms flat against the surface. I was so busy following his instructions that I forgot to be mad and soon felt a smile coming on.

Not quite satisfied with my position, the photographer crossed my ankles and announced, "Now that's a Shirley Temple pose."

Comparing me to Shirley Temple made me beam with pleasure. She was my age, and I'd grown up with her in the Rialto Theater. My parents started taking me to the movies when I was a few weeks old, and it became our weekly outing. I loved Shirley more than I loved the cartoons or Betty Boop or my only doll. Shirley's cheeks were plump, her dimples were deep, and her curls bounced when she danced. She sang spunky tunes and talked to grownups as though she was one of them. I was sure that Shirley Temple's mother wouldn't scold her if she cut her own hair.

While sitting as still as I could on the edge of the table, I pretended that I was Shirley Temple herself. The photographer must have noticed because from underneath the black thing that covered his head, he said, "Little Betty, you look just like a movie star." I was shy, but I couldn't help smiling at him. "Good girl!" he said as he snapped the picture.

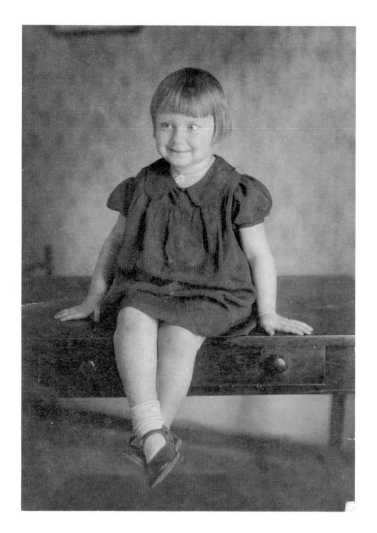

Betty's 1933 portrait

A few weeks later, the postman delivered the photos. Dad picked up the mail from the porch and opened the large envelope at the kitchen table. He grinned proudly when he looked at Bobby's picture and continued to smile as he studied my photos. Then he wrinkled his nose and said, "Betty's bangs are crooked."

"You just now noticed?" my mother asked. "They've been crooked for weeks!"

"Who the hell cut her hair?"

"She did . . . all by herself."

"Well, it looks like somethin' your mother might do."

"Keep that kind of talk to yourself, Butch."

Dad chuckled at his own ornery sense of humor, and Mama punched him playfully on the arm.

My parents spent a long time admiring our pictures. Finally, Dad said, "Them's sure a good-lookin' pair of kids."

My happy feeling was back.

Show Me Yours and I'll Show You Mine

MY FAVORITE COUSIN SHARED HIS STEELY MARBLES WITH ME WHENever I was extra special nice to him, so I was nice to him all the time. We had a lot in common. Sonny and I were four years old, and we both had baby brothers. Mama and Aunt Bernice got together once a week to sit around the kitchen table to gossip, drink coffee, and giggle while Sonny and I played and the babies drooled all over each other in the playpen. It was during a visit to my aunt's house that Sonny and I decided to play in the cellar.

Their cellar was different from the basement under Grandmother Peal's house, which had concrete walls and floors. My aunt's cellar had a floor and walls of dirt. It smelled like the deep hole that Dad dug when he had to bury a puppy that died. Even though it had been a sad experience, I'd loved the smell of the damp hole in the earth.

Under our bare feet were lots of little stones. We were tossing them to see if we could hit a nearby pail when my cousin said, "If you dare me to, I can pee right on top of that big rock over there."

"Uh uh," I replied. "You can't hit that."

"Can too," he replied, and he proved it to me. I didn't think it was such a big deal, but Sonny was so proud of his skill that he said, "Pick something else for me to hit."

"That thing," I said, pointing to a board farther away. He took careful aim and again hit his mark squarely on top. That time I was amazed. "Who taught you to do that?" I asked.

"No one. I learned it by myself."

"That's a pretty good trick."

"Come over here and I'll show you how I did it," he offered.

"Okay," I said.

I got up close to get a better look. My cousin's "pappy" looked pretty much the same as my little brother's. After Sonny performed his next trick, he asked, "Can you do that?"

"Sure I can," I boasted. "Just watch me hit that baby rock right there." I pointed to a nearby pebble, pulled down my flour-sack panties, and squatted over the target. I couldn't see where to aim, so he knelt down to guide me.

"Not that way. Move this way, over here. Yep, that's good. Now go!"

I let it go and everything but my target got wet. We thought it was so funny that we fell down on the dirt laughing and then took turns seeing what it looked like when pee came out of each other's pappies. That's what we were doing when my aunt opened the cellar door and yelled down the stairs, "What are you kids doin' down there?"

Sonny yelled back, "I'm watching Betty pee on some rocks."

"You're doing what?"

I wanted to get in on the credit. "Aunt Bernice, I'm showing Sonny how I pee."

My aunt flew down the cellar steps so fast I thought she would fall. She grabbed my cousin's arm and smacked his bare bottom all the way up to the kitchen where she continued to whale the daylights out of him. His howling was so loud it scared me silly.

I stood frozen with fear and confusion, thinking, *Why is she spanking him? Is she coming after me next?*

I didn't know what to do, so I just stood there with my pants around my ankles, hoping that Mama would rescue me. Then I heard my aunt and my mother yelling at each other. They sounded mad, so we must have done something wrong like messing up the dirt.

Finally, Mama came down the steps real fast and said in a quiet voice, "Pull up your panties, Betty. We're going home now." She got her purse, lifted Bobby from the playpen, told me to get my coloring book and crayons, and we left without saying goodbye.

Once we were in the car and headed for home, I asked, "Why did Sonny get spanked?" She didn't answer, so I patted her arm and tried again. "Mama, why was Aunt Bernice mad?"

My mother took a deep breath and said, "She was mad at me because I wouldn't give you a spanking, too."

"Why did she want us to get a spanking?"

Finally, she said, "Well, because Aunt Bernice thought you and Sonny were playing dirty."

"But he couldn't help getting dirty because it's dirty in Aunt Bernice's cellar." I wanted to show her that I had been more careful than my cousin. "I'm still clean. See?"

Mama smiled at me and said, "You sure are."

Betty to the Rescue

MY GRANDMOTHER DAMSY HAD A SIGN ON HER HOUSE IN CEDAR Rapids, Iowa, that read NOTARY PUBLIC. When she first read the sign to me, I thought she said "motor republic," which made sense to me because she was the only person in the family who had a car.

Even though my grandmother lived humbly, she had a lot of things that other people didn't have during the Depression. Mama said that our grandmother was an "entrepreneur merchant" because she dabbled in many commercial ventures, including super-low-rent housing. Damsy owned several shacks that she called houses. She rented them to poor people who didn't mind the inconvenience of going without electricity and plumbing as long as they had a roof over their heads. My family inhabited many of those one-room shelters.

When I was four and Bobby was a toddler, we were lucky enough to live in a "real" house with an indoor toilet and electric light switches on the wall. Our apartment included three rooms on the second floor of Damsy's shabby dwelling. It was a huge place, and as nice as it was to have the luxury of a toilet and electricity, it wasn't much fun because I had to be on my best behavior all the time. Mama said, "Betty, if you children are too noisy, Damsy will want us to move." So I was forced to grow up, learn to be quiet, and keep my baby brother occupied.

Being Damsy's family did not mean that our apartment was rent free. On the first of each month, my parents had to come up with $7.50, no matter what. Damsy wasn't just my grandmother. She was our landlord. Dad always referred to Damsy by her real name and said behind her back, "Landlord, hell. Allie is a slum lord."

Despite the restrictions, we were comfy in our three-room apartment. Bobby slept in a crib and I slept on a cot against the wall. In the opposite corner was a makeshift kitchen with a table, two mismatched chairs, an icebox, a two-burner stove on short legs that sat on a crate, and a second-hand sink with a curtain that concealed Damsy's do-it-yourself plumbing. A heating stove claimed the center of the room, and a bathroom and tiny bedroom were nearby.

Each room was lit by a bare light bulb with a pull chain that my mother decorated with a bow so our living quarters would appear more "middle class." My father wrinkled his nose at the decorations, saying, "What in the Sam Hill ya doin' that for, Girl? Bows at the end of pull chains are silly."

"Well, I like it, and it shows that I care how things look."

"Do whatcha want. Makes no difference to me."

If Mama happened to be in a good mood, she wouldn't let that kind of remark start an argument.

Dad created a cozy area near the kitchen for Bobby and me to play. It held a child-sized wooden table, two small chairs that someone had thrown away, and a divided apple crate nailed to the wall. The crate became a cupboard for my toy dishes. A curtain on a wire rod made it look pretty, and a matching tablecloth and tiny napkins dressed up the table. But the most fun part was taping my crayon drawings over the peeling wallpaper. I loved our private corner almost as much as I loved my little brother, so we ate lunch there every day.

During lunch one afternoon, my parents were having a minor argument at their table while sharing a cigarette and drinking coffee prepared from leftover grounds. Bobby and I were eating at ours when Mama said, "Betty, keep him happy so your father and I can talk."

But my brother wouldn't settle down and moseyed around with his peanut butter sandwich clutched in his hands, touching everything in sight. The windowsills were low to the floor, so he started tapping on the rusty screens. He babbled "dah dah dah," and left breadcrumbs squished into the tiny squares. I patted his chair seat and said, "Sit down with sister." Bobby just laughed, but he was so cute that I couldn't scold him. Then he pounded on the old screen harder with both hands, and his "dah dahs" and laughter grew more excited.

I took a few more bites of my lunch and a swig of milk before trying again to coax him to the chair. When I looked up, the screen and my brother were gone. In a matter-of-fact tone, I said, "Uh oh — Bobby fell out the window."

Mama spilled her coffee, Dad dropped his cigarette in midair, and they flew down the stairs so fast I couldn't catch up with them. When I reached the front porch, I saw my mother stretched out flat on her back and my father on his knees slapping her cheeks. He must have been mad at her for fainting.

I was glad that she had passed out so I could get to Bobby first. I stepped over my mother and dashed behind the house, eager to see what he looked like all flattened and squashed. When I reached him in our grandmother's weed-patch yard, he was struggling to his feet, bread and peanut butter still in his hand, but crusted with sand. He was bawling his lungs out. I thought he was mad because sand was stuck all over his sandwich, so I hugged him and dried his tears.

My curiosity about seeing Bobby flattened was replaced with the feeling that I had rescued him. I could hardly wait to show my parents that their son was still in one piece. When his bawling let up a bit, I led him to the front porch where my mother was trying to sit up, looking kind of pale. I handed him over with pride, announcing, "Heeere's your little boy."

Mama's ear-shattering scream scared all of us half to death, which caused Bobby to start bawling again.

The rest of the afternoon was not a bit peaceful. My mother was beside herself, struggling to comfort a whimpering toddler while my father secured the old screens by adding a bar across them. He pounded nails like he was mad at somebody. After the repair job was finished, he stomped down the steps, beat on Damsy's door, and presented her with a bill. They yelled at each other for a few minutes before she slammed the door. The ruckus made our mother cry again, wailing, "This is not working out, Butch. We've got to find another place to live."

Dad bounded back up the stairs two at a time yelling, "Girl, quit yer confounded bawlin' — you women are drivin' me crazy!"

The racket got Bobby crying again, too. The poor kid must've had a head-ache from all the noise. But it might have been from hitting the ground so hard.

I didn't cry at all. My brother's plunge from the second-story window had upset everyone in the house except me. I was so glad it happened that I couldn't wipe the smile off my face. After all, I was the big-shot hero who had rescued him. Although nobody gave me the credit I deserved, it was the best day of my life.

Quite an Artist

FROM THE TIME I COULD HOLD A PENCIL, I MADE MARKS ON PAPER that my proud parents called "cute scribbles." When the scribbles became shapes, I got lots of their attention.

"Butch, look at how coordinated she is."

"Damn, Girl, I think she just drew the sun."

It wasn't the sun at all. It was Mama's face. But that didn't discourage me. Next, I created a crooked oval covered with black spots, then added four straight lines sticking out at the bottom and one stuck onto the end. Auntie Marge, who had no children of her own, thought I was the most promising child in the world. She knew right away that I had drawn a dog.

Mama and Dad shared my scribbles with all our relatives and they started calling me the family artist. I felt important, and I liked showing them how easy it was to sketch things they recognized. Before I came along, my aunt Edith had been the family artist. She'd painted a big picture on a whole wall in her science classroom at Roosevelt High School. I hoped I could go to that school someday and paint a picture on the other wall so they would know we were related. I was sure Aunt Edith would love that because she always hugged me when she looked at my drawings, which was every time I saw her.

As a child, I was continually drawing pictures. People would say, "My goodness sakes alive, you are one talented little girl." That made me so happy that I tried to sell my art to folks in our neighborhood. They could decorate their walls with pride, saying, "You can buy one, too, because the artist lives right on our street."

So I put on my cleanest play dress, the one with a pocket to hold the nickels that would soon be mine. With unusual confidence, I knocked on each door. My neighbors admired my skill, but didn't want to spend five cents for a little kid's pencil drawing. I dropped the price to three cents; still no luck. By the time I strolled back home, Mama was anxious and asked, "Where were you? I was lookin' all over."

"I was selling my pictures to the neighbors, Mama."

"Betty, don't leave our yard," she ordered. "You might get kidnapped like the Lindbergh baby."

After that, I gave my drawings away for free to my doting family. Uncle Connie always studied each picture carefully. I knew he liked drawings because he had a lot of them on both arms. He would hold my artwork at a distance and then up close to study it. One day he said, "Explain to me how you drew this. Did you trace it from a magazine?"

"No, Uncle Connie. Pictures are in my head."

"They are?"

"Yes. I'm telling the truth."

"Well, well, well. I might let you draw on my arms someday."

"Will you pay me money to draw pictures on your arms?" I asked.

"You betcher booties I will."

I loved that kind of attention, especially when someone said something nice like, "Betty . . . you're quite an artist." But what I really wanted was for them to like my artwork so much that they would buy it.

After my uncle promised to pay me to draw pictures on his arms, I decided to practice on Bobby. The pen tickled his skin, so I had to keep washing off the wiggly lines that happened whenever Bobby squirmed. Finally, I got it right. The pretty lady I'd drawn on his arm did sit-ups when he bent his elbow.

I wouldn't let Bobby take a bath until Uncle Connie saw my work. When he said, "That's the best tattoo I've ever seen," I glowed with pride.

I asked him, "Why don't your tattoos wash away like Bobby's?"

"Because the artist used needles to push the ink under the skin," he replied.

Needles? Mama had lots of those in her sewing box . . .

He read my mind. "Slow down, Betty Boop. Someday people will pay you to draw, so forget about turning Bobby into a pincushion and stick to practicing on paper."

My brother was happy to hear that.

Uncle Jiggs

UNCLE JIGGS WAS THE OLDEST OF SIX BOYS IN MY DAD'S FAMILY. I liked his wife, Bernice, and their children were my favorite cousins, but whenever my uncle was around, I felt uneasy. He wasn't friendly and rarely spoke. His eyes were red and his nose ran. When he went to the bathroom, which was all the time, he couldn't even walk straight. When he talked, his words were hard to understand. "I neee a lil somethin' to wet m' lips," he'd say.

I heard Mama say more than once that Uncle Jiggs had a serious drinking problem. That really scared me because, apparently, I had the same problem. After supper, I wasn't allowed to have a drop of water even if I was dying of thirst. Sometimes I felt so desperate for something to drink that it made my eyes red and my nose runny just like his. To keep from drying up, I would sneak to the bathroom after bedtime and put my mouth right on the faucet to moisten my lips. My dad caught me and said, "Girl, I think Betty has a little problem. She drinks too much after supper." I wondered if my uncle wet his bed, too.

Every Monday, my mother would roll out the Maytag washing machine and the rinse tub and place them near the kitchen sink. Heaped on the bare floor would be mounds of dirty clothes where I'd sprawl while our dog Boots licked my face. Steam rising from the tubs blended with the gritty fragrance of Fels Naptha soap and the tantalizing scent of our usual washday meal (navy beans with bacon) to make the tiny house we'd rented on Oakland Road very cozy.

Laundry day always felt secure and comfy . . . except for the Monday that Uncle Jiggs dropped by for a visit. His nose was bright red and his smell reminded me of Auntie Marge's tavern. He was unusually chatty and didn't seem to notice that he was talking to himself. He babbled on and on, even though no one was listening. Now and then my mother said, "Uh, huh," but nothing more. That's how she was around her brother-in-law, courteous and quiet. I watched, listened, and tried to stay out of his way. That didn't last long.

Eventually, he turned his attention to me, asking silly questions like, "When ya gonna get married, Betty Boop?" Then he tickled me to make me laugh. I wasn't in the mood for laughing or talking, which prompted him to ask, "Hey, little niecie, hazja-cat-gotcher-tongue?" Boots pricked up her ears as though she sensed danger.

Suddenly, Uncle Jiggs scooped me up and hoisted me above his head, pressing me close to the ceiling. I wanted to say, "Please, put me down," but I was too shy. Apparently, so was my mother. She ignored me up there by the light bulb and concentrated on pushing overalls through the wringer.

His arms must have gotten tired because Uncle Jiggs began to lower me, an inch at a time, grinning as I neared the washing machine. I was suspended in midair, barely above the steaming, swishing surface. Then he dipped my bottom beneath the suds. I could feel the hot, wet clothes twitching back and forth. I was certain he intended to let me sink all the way into the water where the agitator and soap would scrub me to death.

My bulging eyes must have looked funny to him because he laughed so hard that he had a coughing fit. It forced him to set me down and continue his hacking in our bathroom. My mother focused her attention on the laundry as though nothing unusual was happening. I wasn't sure what to do next, so I just stood there with a dripping bottom.

When my uncle emerged from the bathroom, he left with no fare-thee-well or thank-you. I was relieved to see him go. Boots must have felt the same because she plunked herself down on a pile of laundry and sighed.

Once her brother-in-law was out of sight, my mother found dry clothes for me, but she said nothing about the incident. I finally got the courage to break the silence and said, "Mama, I don't like Uncle Jiggs."

I prepared myself for a scolding, but she only said, "He means no harm."

That night I overheard a conversation between my parents that made me wonder if she was wrong. "Butch, your brother was here today drunker 'n a skunk. He put Betty into the washing machine and scared her half to death."

"He put her where?"

After he heard the story, Dad said, "He drinks and drinks and doesn't know when to stop. Bernice told me that one night he ranted and raved about his bad luck in life and then went outside and chopped the heads off their baby rabbits."

"Oh, dear God!" Mama gasped.

After hearing how drinking too much affected Uncle Jiggs, I finally knew the other reason Mama never let me have water after supper.

Hattie Burke

WHEN MAMA WAS SICK OR WORKING OR HAD RUN AWAY FROM HOME again, Hattie Burke was our babysitter. She didn't talk much, but we knew that she liked us, and we felt the same about her. She was no relation, yet she watched over us as though she was our grandmother. She fed us, cleaned the house, and made sure we brushed our teeth once a day. She gave us "spit baths" before bedtime, saying, "You're not dirty enough to fill the tub."

Instead of using a washcloth, she got her hands all soapy and washed my hands with hers. Hattie's hard, gnarly skin felt good. When she washed my brother's ears, she used a soft rag instead of a washcloth. She said it did a better job of getting into all the nooks and crannies, and my brother's ears were always clean.

Hattie was poor, but she looked poorer than she was. She wore dark clothes, a black sweater, and a skirt that almost touched the floor. Her apron was always dirty and needed a bath more than we ever did. She was so tiny that she reminded me of an old child. I used to touch the top of her head and say, "I'm as tall as you!"

Her long, dark, wispy hair was pulled flat against her scalp and shaped into a tight ball in the back. From the front, it seemed she had no hair or that it was painted on her scalp. She had no teeth either, not even false ones, and when she talked, her words were hard to understand because her lips kind of flapped. Hattie was our gentle gnome. I felt safe with her because she never yelled or lost her temper.

Sometimes my brother and I played a game called "Who Am I?" One day when it was Bobby's turn, he pushed a pillow high under the back of his shirt and walked in front of me with short little steps, asking, "Sister, who am I, who am I?" He was so funny that I couldn't stop laughing. Mama put a stop to that. "Shame on you kids for making fun of Hattie's hunchback."

Then I felt embarrassed and was sorry for laughing at Bobby's pillow. It meant we were really laughing at her.

Our sweet, old babysitter lived in a small apartment on top of her son's garage because he didn't want her to live in the house. I didn't know why, but never questioned grownups for fear they would say, "That's none of your business." There were no stairs to climb because her son said, "There's no room for stairs." Instead, he built a very tall ladder with a railing and wide steps that his mother climbed to get inside her home. I was surprised that she didn't fall since she had to hunch over all the way up. Sometimes she carried a bag of groceries in one hand until her son built a pulley that made grocery day almost fun.

I envied our friend's home as much as I envied any kid who had a tree house. I imagined how cozy it must be and wanted to see inside Hattie's roof-top apartment. "You'll have to climb the ladder to get up there," she said. Since she made it look easy, I wasn't afraid to scramble ahead of her. Once we reached the roof, there was a little platform large enough to keep our feet flat instead of at an angle before we went through the door.

What a disappointment. Inside was a big, messy room with a couple of windows and rickety furniture along the edges. Her sleeping cot looked as though she had recently climbed out of it. A sink stood in one corner and a covered chamber pot in the other. A skinny cat was licking dishes on the table, and it rushed to hide when we started clearing a spot to sit down. Her home smelled odd, a mixture of leftover food and the kerosene she used for heating. It didn't smell bad; it smelled of Hattie. I wondered how she emptied her chamber pot. I didn't dare ask since it might be rude.

Hattie Burke was the only person I knew who was poorer than we were. Her humble place above the garage made me feel rich.

One evening Dad said, "Girl, I feel lucky. Let's get Hattie to stay with the kids so we can scoot on over to Bank Night." My mother hated Bank Night and went only because Dad bought lottery tickets every week. He kept hoping to win the big jackpot that had finally grown to five hundred dollars. Our babysitter had no phone in her rooftop apartment, so Dad called her son and got permission to give Hattie a ride to our house.

While my parents were getting dressed to leave, Mama's voice took on a familiar angry sound. When she got mad, even Boots stayed out of her way. Hattie was spooning corn chowder into our bowls when Dad joined in. As their argument grew louder, Hattie became so quiet that I thought she was mad at me. I snuck a peek at her face and saw tears in her eyes. I didn't know if it was my parents' angry words or her pitiful expression that caused my eyes to water. My brother and I ate silently while my parents' disagreement wound down. They'd reached the hugging stage by the time they left. Hattie looked as relieved as I felt.

Mom and Dad hadn't been gone very long when a strange thing happened. A car full of people came crawling up our long driveway making crunching sounds on the gravel. It moved so slowly that it gave me the creeps. Bob and I watched from the front window as the car stopped close to the house. Hattie looked nervous; she turned on the yard light, picked up the broom, and went outside. Boots followed her, so I knew she was protected.

A man greeted her and asked, "Ma'am, can my family say hello to Boots? She used to be our dog."

We sure didn't know those people, but Boots did. Her tail had started wagging and, before we knew what was happening, the car doors opened and everyone inside was taking turns petting her. All that time, Hattie stood nearby holding the broom like a rifle and watching the strangers as if she was the sheriff.

Our dog loved the attention because her tail was twirling in circles. Then, all of sudden, she was in their car and every door slammed shut. Hattie flew into action, smacking the hood with her broom as they backed away. Although bent and crooked, she chased the departing auto down the driveway with small, fast steps, yelling words I couldn't understand because of her toothless mouth. It sounded like, "Come back here, you sons of witches!"

When the strangers saw the crooked old woman advancing with a thrashing broom, they gunned the motor, racing backward down the driveway and onto Oakland Road. I was dumbfounded. I didn't know if our pet had jumped into the car because she wanted to or if they had tricked her with treats and rubbing behind her ears.

Hattie was so upset that she started to cry, and so did I. Bob just stood there looking confused.

It seemed like forever, but a couple of hours later my parents finally walked through the door. Dad said, "Well, we didn't win Bank Night, but the movie was dang good."

Mom took one look at Hattie's face and asked, "What happened?"

While telling the story, Hattie started to cry again. Mama glared at Dad and said, "So this is your lucky day, is it? I knew we should've stayed home tonight."

Dad ignored Mom's comment, but I could see that he was upset about what had happened. "For cryin' out loud," he said. "They told me they didn't want her anymore. If they changed their minds, they shoulda said so instead of kidnappin' her. Those people are low-down dirty thieves."

I guess Boots wanted to live with her other family again, but I missed her terribly. Our dear babysitter must have missed her, too, because she asked Dad to take her right home. I figured she wanted to crawl into her unmade bed and cry herself to sleep, because that's what I felt like doing, too.

After that night, Hattie still babysat us once in a while, though we never saw Boots again and we never heard from the sons of witches who took her away. For a long time whenever I heard the sound of a car crunching the gravel in our driveway, I hoped they were bringing our dog back home.

Little House on Young's Hill

The summer before I enrolled in kindergarten, our rent was raised. Dad was kind of down in the dumps when he announced, "Girl, we gotta move to a smaller place."

"You mean smaller than this house?" Mama said. "I don't think that's possible."

"It's possible," said Dad. "I've found a little house on Young's Hill."

So my parents packed our meager belongings into the back of a borrowed truck and drove to the south side of town where the houses were far apart. It was in the country, with no sidewalks where a kid could skate. Behind our house was a steep hill that looked perfect for sledding in the winter . . . if we stayed that long. We were always moving somewhere new, and sometimes it was exciting to be in a different place.

When my mother walked into our one-room dwelling, her mouth dropped open and her eyes got big. "Butch, is this a cabin or a shack?" she asked. Dad ignored the question and went about unloading the truck.

Mama was the boss of where things would go. She persuaded Dad, with the help of Uncle Cullen's fine carpentry skill and professional tools, to build a simple wall to separate the space into two rooms. Behind the divider were our parents' bed, a large dresser, and a three-gallon paint can that served as our nighttime toilet. The real toilet was in the backyard on the steep slope. In the front part of the house were a small wood-burning stove, sink, table, chairs, and icebox, along with a bed that Bobby and I shared.

At night our light came from kerosene lamps, but we usually went to bed early to save on lamp fuel. That's when I snuggled next to my two-year-old brother and told him stories about going to school. He loved hearing about "cool," as he called it, and I loved telling him all about it even though I didn't really know much about it myself. I was looking forward to kindergarten more than anything in the world.

Not long after we moved to Young's Hill, Bobby and I woke up whiny and red from scratching. Mama had a look at us and said, "Good grief! I believe you've caught your cousin's measles."

"Oh, no, Mama. They won't let me in school with the measles." My disappointment was terrible.

She tried to reassure me. "Don't worry yourself, Betty. By the time school starts, those prickly red spots will be gone." I hoped she was right.

To keep us happy while we were sick, Auntie Marge appeared at our door and said, "I hear there are two sick kids in this house." In a silly voice she called out, "Where are you hiding? Come out from under the covers."

We couldn't get up fast enough to see what Auntie Marge had brought. She never showed up empty-handed, and lots of times she emptied her purse so the coins that rested at the bottom would tumble out. I was sure Auntie Marge was related to the Christmas fairy because she brought gifts to us whenever she showed up.

Playing with our new toys helped take our minds off the itches we wanted so badly to scratch, and owning a handful of pennies, nickels, and dimes made me feel lucky to have such a rich aunt. On that visit, Bobby got a miniature dump truck that he could push around on top of the sheets, and

I got a set of paper dolls featuring the famous Dionne quintuplets who had just been born.

We recovered from the measles before the birth of our real baby that was supposed to happen in July. But our sister couldn't wait that long and arrived on May 24.

Aunt Edith took me to the hospital to see Patricia Ann. When we found my mother's room at Mercy Hospital, several of my aunts were paying her a visit. Mama was sitting up in bed holding a tiny bundle wrapped in pink flannel blankets.

"Come close, Betty, and see Patty, your sister," she said as she pulled the cloth away from a dark, wrinkled face. Aunt Edith lifted me up so I could have a better look at our baby and all I could do was gawk. She was strange looking, a newborn bird without feathers. I couldn't stop staring.

Aunt Edith's voice was all smiles as she asked, "Betty, what do you think of your sister?"

I didn't hesitate and told her the truth. "She looks like a monkey."

In unison, my three aunts sucked in their breath. "Shame on you, you naughty girl," they scolded. "That's not nice."

Mama laughed and said, "Well, you asked her."

The truth was not always what grownups wanted to hear. After that, I learned to weigh carefully whether an answer should be honest or a fib.

My parents didn't have the money to keep our Patty in the preemie ward for as long as she needed to be there, so my mother had a serious talk with Dr. Victoreen, who had helped when Bobby and I were born.

"Doctor, I know that I can keep my baby alive because I've always been a nurse at heart. I've kept birds breathing that were halfway out of eggs that had fallen from the nest."

"Well, I don't know, Waneta. It's a terrible risk."

Mama wouldn't give up. "I've practiced on pets all my life, and our daughter is about the size of the kittens and dogs I nursed back to health."

Dr. Victoreen couldn't resist my mother's strong desire to take care of her own infant, so with his instructions to guide her, she created a cozy nest for Patty. It was a cardboard box filled with soft blankets and two bricks that had been warmed on top of the woodstove and then wrapped in towels. My brother and I were allowed to peek at our sister, but only with a grownup's supervision.

Everything was going well until Bobby and I caught whooping cough. We coughed so hard and so often that we spent our days gagging or throwing up. Again I whined, "I'm not going to kindergarten, am I?" My mother was too preoccupied to put my worries to rest because Patty had also developed a fever that turned into whooping cough.

Mama became a full-time nurse to us three kids while Dad went to his job so that he could bring home some money each week. When Dad was home, he and our mother talked about things I didn't understand, and they didn't laugh very much. When I was feeling better, I tried to make my mother smile by showing her the Dionne quintuplet paper dolls all dressed in their paper clothes. I patted her hip over and over, repeating, "Mama, Mama, Mama. I want to show you something."

When I couldn't get her attention, I gave up and buried my face against her pudgy stomach instead. Through her cotton dress, her stomach was as soft as a pillow. I was so filled with affection for her that I had to do something. I tried pressing my face even harder into the soft bulge, but that wasn't enough. So I opened my mouth and bit her.

"Why did you do that?" she yelped.

I was shocked. I had not meant for the bite to hurt. I bit her because I loved her. My mother did not understand my explanation at all, but it was the truth.

She and Dad continued to have serious talks, and they never played cards anymore. I began to get used to it. Auntie Marge still dropped by now and then with coloring books and extra groceries, which helped our family a lot. Then, out of nowhere, she brought a new dress for me to wear to school.

After we three kids recovered from whooping cough, Dr. Victoreen came to our house to see how everything was going. He was very pleased with our progress and asked Bobby and me what we thought of our sister. Bobby didn't know what to say, so he picked his nose.

"Betty, what do you think of your new sister?"

"She's very pretty," I lied.

His eyebrows went up as though asking, "Really?" Maybe he was one of the grownups who let kids tell the truth. I had no idea how to tell that kind of grownup apart from the others until it was too late.

Dr. Victoreen then turned his full attention to my mother. "Waneta, I must admit that I felt certain your baby would die in that container. Anyone who could keep a premature infant with whooping cough alive in a cardboard box is a genius. You are, indeed, a miracle worker."

Mama finally smiled. I was so relieved. She was a good nurse and I wanted to tell her so, but I was too shy to say such an adult thing. So I just thought about it. I would have given her another love bite, but I was pretty sure she wouldn't understand it any more than I did.

Me Too Cool

I HAD JUST TURNED FIVE, WHICH MEANT THAT IN A FEW WEEKS I could attend kindergarten at Lincoln Elementary School at the top of Young's Hill. It was all I talked about. The night before school started, I couldn't sleep because I was so excited about wearing my new dress.

The next morning, Bobby thought we were both going to kindergarten. Mama said, "No, honey. Only Betty is going." Hearing that bad news made his eyes sad. His mouth turned down at the corners as he whimpered, "Me too cool."

Our neighbor, Vera Brogan, stayed with my brother so Mama could go along and teach me how to get to Lincoln Elementary. We left him stretching out of Vera's arms, grabbing the air and screaming over and over, "Me too cool!" I felt guilty about leaving him behind.

Mama pointed out landmarks for me to remember as we trudged to the end of our street and up a gravel road to the top of Young's Hill. When we reached it, she said, "Look around. Here's a long fence that leads to the neighborhood where the school is, so just watch for the fence." I tried hard to memorize everything she brought to my attention.

I don't remember what we did on my first day in kindergarten because all I could think about was finding my way home. When class was dismissed, the teacher led me out the door and pointed me in the right direction. It was very scary. I was afraid of getting lost.

Lincoln School, where Betty attended Kindergarten

Luckily, Mama's landmarks came back to me as I walked. All I had to do was get through the neighborhood, find the long fence, and go back down the gravel road that led to my house. I kept my eyes peeled for the fence, and when I saw the downhill slope, I stopped being scared because I was almost home. I was so happy that I decided to run down the road instead of walking.

Stretching my arms wide on my downward flight, I felt like a bird that had escaped its cage. But I couldn't put my brakes on and soon lost control on the gravel. When I fell, I landed hard on both knees and skidded. I couldn't breathe. I struggled for air, but nothing happened. Then all of a sudden air gushed into my lungs and I gasped in pain and shock. Both knees looked like red raspberries with their juice streaming down my legs.

I shuffled home, whimpering with each step. When I got there, I let out all the tears that I had saved up. Mama tried to calm me down, but all I could do was howl. The whole scene scared the wits out of Bobby, and he started crying almost as hard as I was.

When I saw how upset my brother was, I knew it was up to me to calm him down. I could only do that by pulling myself together and distracting him. It wasn't easy. I finally did what Mama had been telling me to do and took slow, deep breaths until I stopped crying. When Bobby and I were both feeling better, I got out my tablet and crayons. "Come to sister," I told him, "and I'll draw a picture of my school for you."

My little brother paid close attention to the likeness of Lincoln Elementary taking form right in front of his eyes. I drew the big entrance and the tall columns on each side. "This is my school," I said as I handed him the finished artwork. He was so happy that he clutched the paper to his chest all evening. That night, right before falling asleep, he murmured, "Me too cool."

By morning, the paper was wadded and wrinkled and wet with spit, but he would not let go of it, even while eating his oatmeal. I ate my own breakfast slowly, dreading the long walk to kindergarten with a big bandage on each knee. What if I fell on the gravel again? I didn't want to upset my brother, so I pretended to be as excited about the second day of school as I had been about the first.

It was a big, fat lie.

I Remember Granny

WITH COLD WEATHER APPROACHING AND LITTLE MONEY FOR FUEL, my parents decided that we couldn't stay in the little house on Young's Hill through the winter. So while Dad looked for a better house, Mom asked Damsy for help. Damsy was not a softhearted woman. She had grown tired of helping us whenever our parents had problems, which was most of the time. However, she agreed to let us stay if Mama helped with Granny, my bedridden great grandmother. So Mama, Bobby, my baby sister Patty, and I moved into the top floor apartment of Damsy's red brick house on 5th Street in Cedar Rapids, Iowa.

My mother's days were divided between her elderly grandmother and our baby, a sickly premature infant. Mama never had a chance to read a story or play with us and she was usually cranky. I was in charge of entertaining two-year-old Bobby, which was not a problem. I often hugged him so hard he cried. I adored him and planned to marry him when I grew up.

"You can't marry your brother," Mama snapped.

"I have to," I whimpered as I clutched him tightly. "I love him so much." Since there was no other boy I knew or loved, I decided I'd marry my brother behind my mother's back.

Bobby and I were sometimes allowed to play quietly in our great grandmother's room while she slept. She and our frail infant sister were not a part of our world. We didn't need them because we had our toys and each other.

One day as I played in her room alone, Granny spoke. It frightened me because I didn't know she could talk. I knew her only as a lump in the bed. I sat without moving, afraid to turn my head. I was staring at the wall when she spoke again.

"Hello, little mousy."

Was there a mouse in there, or did she think I was a mouse? I didn't know her, and I wasn't prepared for a conversation. I stared at the wallpaper for several more seconds, got slowly to my feet, and strolled out to find my mother.

She was giving the baby a bath, so I patted her thigh and whispered, "Mama!" When she didn't respond, I pounded on her hip and said, "Mama, Granny talked to me!"

"Stop pounding on me. What are you talking about?"

My answer tumbled out. "She thinks I'm a mouse. I'm too big to be a mouse — I'm five. Mama, I'm afraid of her!"

My mother barely acknowledged me, and I was frantic. Eventually, she could no longer ignore my fretting and gave me her attention. "She didn't mean to scare you, Betty. She calls all children "mousy." It means that you're a sweet little child. Now take your brother into Granny's room and play quietly." She emphasized the quiet part by holding a fingertip to her lips.

I found the courage to return to our play area, grateful that our great grandmother was asleep and, once again, just a lump in the bed. While my brother played, I was on the lookout for a mouse in case Mama was wrong.

A few days later, Damsy announced that we must get cleaned up and into our good clothes. A photographer would soon arrive to take pictures of all six of us. My mother cut Bobby's hair and trimmed my bangs and then helped me into my striped Shirley Temple dress with yarn balls hanging from the collar. We sat around without moving until the man arrived. I felt nervous, but excited, because I knew how pretty I must have looked.

Damsy, Granny, Mama, and the Peal Kids, 1935

When the photographer finally joined us, he set up a camera that stood on long legs and placed a black blanket on top of it. Damsy and Mama helped Granny out of bed and into a chair. That took a very long time, and it took even longer to prop her up straight. Damsy put a striped shawl around her mother's shoulders, and the camera man arranged us carefully.

Granny, in an upholstered chair, was the center of the composition. Mama stood behind her, cradling our sister, who could barely hold up her head. Patty's tiny neck tilted in one direction while Granny's leaned to the other.

Damsy, wearing the expression of a woman in charge, stood next to our mother, and my brother and I stood on either side of our great grandmother's knees.

When the photographer snapped the first picture, it took us by surprise. "Just kidding," he said. "I wanted to get your attention." He had it from then on. When he said, "Smile. Don't move," I was so nervous that I couldn't breathe, let alone smile. I had never been so close to such an elderly person. I could smell baby powder, but didn't know whether the fragrance came from Granny or from the baby.

A few weeks later, the photographs arrived. My brother was cute in his playsuit, our sister was a little doll, and I felt like a movie star in my Shirley Temple dress. Granny could have been a man with her hair cut so short and her large ears protruding. They were huge. She must have been cold because she was tugging at the edges of her striped shawl to draw it around her.

When my great grandmother died a few weeks later, Mama and Damsy cried a lot, but I was too young to be sad. The only change I noticed was that my mother seemed less busy and not one bit cranky. She even let me put a dish towel over my hair for a veil and helped make a bouquet of dandelions so Bobby and I could have a pretend wedding. Then we played house as noisily as we wanted in the room where we'd had to be quiet all the time.

Whenever I looked at the framed photograph of our family, I could almost hear the warm greeting that had scared me: "Hello, little mousy." I knew that I would never forget Granny.

Wet Weather Report

DAD FOUND A NEW JOB AT WHITING'S DAIRY, WHICH MEANT WE could move to a nice house on Center Point Road. It had a few more rooms, and the best part of all was the indoor toilet. Bobby and I were so excited that we pretended to go potty just so we could flush. "You kids stop flushing that thing!" my mother scolded. With an indoor toilet, our future was looking good.

Moving to a new place meant I had to change schools. Walking to Garfield Elementary took longer than walking to Lincoln, but it was an easy walk on sidewalks, with no gravel roads to fall down on and no confusing corners to turn. I couldn't get lost going to the new school. The only problem was that I usually had to go to the bathroom before I got home, so I often wet my pants.

My mother was frustrated. "Betty, why don't you go to the bathroom before leaving school?"

"I don't have to go then."

She sighed like all the air was coming out of her.

"What's wrong, Mama?"

"Every time something good happens, a snag comes with it."

"What's a snag?"

"It means that nothing is ever perfect."

"This house is perfect."

"Yes, it is, but it's too far away from school."

To solve the problem, my mother wrote a note to my teacher. Before pinning it on my blouse, she read it aloud:

Dear Mrs. Martin. Please tell Elizabeth to use the toilet before leaving school. She has a very small bladder and a long walk home.

I was worried that some smart kid in kindergarten who knew how to read might rip it off my blouse and tell everyone that I had a small bladder. And I didn't want Mrs. Martin to guess that I wet my pants every day after school.

I always tried really hard to hold it, but after walking several blocks, my urge to pee was too strong to ignore. The first time, there wasn't a good place to relieve myself, so the only thing I could do was squat down and pretend I was tying my shoe and just let it go. I was shocked at the big puddle on the sidewalk. From then on I pretended to tie my shoe on the grass — and never on the same lawn twice.

When I reached our house, my legs, socks, and shoes were usually soaked. Mama didn't ask; she just waited for me to tell her whether I was wet or dry. It was kind of like doing the weather report.

In the winter it was awful since there was a lot more stuff to get wet when wearing snow pants and boots. The worst part was that it sometimes froze, which made the inside of my thighs red and chapped. I always had a runny nose in the winter, too, and it froze on my upper lip. My lips were so dry and chapped from the cold that my bottom lip had a permanent split in the middle. I couldn't smile or laugh without causing it to bleed. My mother said, "Good Lord, Betty. You're a mess in the winter."

Each afternoon, my kindergarten class lined up at the door to wait for the dismissal bell to ring. After receiving the note, Mrs. Martin started asking right there in front of all my classmates, "Elizabeth, do you need to use the bathroom before you leave?" Everyone would look at me as though dying to know the answer, and each time I would shake my head with an expression that said, "What a silly question."

I wasn't lying. I never had to go to the bathroom until I was halfway home. Besides, none of the other kids had to use the toilet after school and I didn't want to be the only one. I really dreaded that long walk.

I wet my pants after school every day for the rest of the year. But before first grade started, I had it under control. Mama said it was because my bladder had finally grown up to match my body. I was so relieved. My teacher wouldn't have to ask that embarrassing question anymore, and my mother was happy again.

Our move to Center Point Road was finally perfect.

Sticky Fingers

I'D BEEN MAD AT MRS. CONFAIR EVER SINCE I TOOK MY LITTLE brother to school for show and tell and she told me to take him home. Three-year-old Bobby was the cutest thing I had to share, but my teacher didn't even let me introduce him. Instead, I had to help him back into snow pants, jacket, hat, and mittens. I had a terrible time fastening his galoshes because I couldn't see through my tears. As we trudged all the way to our house with me sniffling, Bobby whined, "Sister, I wanna go to school." Not me. I just wanted to run home and stay there forever.

Mama said, "Dry your eyes and get yourself back there. I had a hunch I shouldn't have let your brother go in the first place."

From that day on, I hated show and tell, especially when someone else hogged all the attention for bringing something stupid like the round metal doohickey that Arlene called a "compact." She said it was a gift from her aunt. Even though it was oddly interesting, I pretended not to care about it at all.

One of the smart-aleck boys asked, "Is that some kind of worn-out silver?"

"No," Miss Know-it-all said. "It's pewter."

She enunciated the word as if she expected us to be impressed, but we weren't. We had never heard of the stuff before, but Mrs. Confair had. "Well, I declare," she said. "I have never seen a pewter compact."

All of that fancy fussing over a little bit of nothing made me sick. Our teacher's reaction created so much interest that the kids gathered around oohing and ahing. I just sat with my arms folded across my chest and watched while Arlene got way more attention than she deserved.

When sharing time was over, she set the ugly thing on the corner of her desk so everyone could gawk at it all day. I wanted to grab it and throw it in the wastebasket where it belonged. Then another idea struck me as I was walking down the aisle to sharpen my pencil. No one was nearby, so I closed my hand over the compact and kept on walking. I dropped it into my sweater pocket just before reaching the pencil sharpener, pretending that nothing unusual had happened.

It wasn't long before the star of the show missed her auntie's gift. "Boys and girls — has anyone seen Arlene's pewter compact?" Mrs. Confair inquired. "She can't find it."

Nope, no one had seen it. When our teacher suggested that we all look for it, I helped search everywhere and asked questions as if I was Dick Tracy.

"Are you sure you didn't put it in your lunch bag?"

She checked to see if that's where it was. Nope, not there. I pretended to feel sorry for her, but I really felt like a movie star acting out a story. It was fun.

After school, I couldn't wait to show Mama what I had in my pocket. She studied it real close and then said, "Oh, my goodness gracious me. This is pewter. Where did it come from?"

Oh, no. Mama had heard of it, too.

"I found it on the side of the road," I lied, almost believing my story.

"Too bad," she said. "Someone will be very sad about losing that."

Suddenly, I didn't feel so good. The stolen object was a dreadful weight in my hand. It wasn't even pretty. I'd taken it because I was angry that I couldn't show my little brother, who was cute, and Arlene got to show something ugly. I was so jealous that I wanted her to be down in the dumps, not me.

What was I going to do with it? I had to think fast. Finally, I took Mama's big metal cooking spoon from the kitchen drawer, dug a shallow hole, and threw the compact into it. I pushed dirt on top until it was level with the ground and then stomped on it with both feet.

Once it had been buried, I figured I could forget all about the pilfered item. If I stopped thinking about it, I would probably forget where it was buried. And if I forgot where it was buried, maybe it would seem as if I hadn't stolen anything in the first place.

It didn't work . . . and feeling bad about stealing didn't stop me from doing it again two years later.

Curly Confidence

BOTH MAMA AND I WERE EXCITED WHEN AUNTIE MARGE SURPRISED us with a set of Kid Curlers. They were made from soft leather folded and sewn over flexible wires about six inches long. They reminded me of little snakes. After parting off a two-inch width of wet hair, Mama draped the strand over one of the contraptions and rolled it to the scalp. Both loose ends were then folded toward the middle like a pair of tiny brown arms that stayed put until everything dried. It was an easier, tidier method for Mama to use than the long, limp rags that she tied in knots. And my head didn't look raggedy anymore.

Even though Kid Curlers were nicer to look at, they weren't any easier to sleep on than the rag rolls. It was best to start the project early in the evening so I could practice tossing and turning before going to sleep.

During the night my hair seemed to shrink, which made my scalp very uncomfortable. By morning, my eyes were stretched so tight that I looked Chinese. After all the rolls were unwound, my eyes popped back to normal, but my head sprouted a garden of kinky springs. I didn't mind. The sensation of tight curls bouncing against each other felt so good that I found lots of reasons to move around. At school I sharpened my pencil repeatedly and hopped, skipped, and jumped my way across the room because I felt like Shirley Temple's twin sister.

Mrs. Campbell, my second grade teacher, was also the principal of Garfield school. She was very aware of me on "pretty hair" days. She smiled every time I raised my hand, and she commented on how nicely my curls bounced each time I moved my head. When it was my turn to write the answer on the blackboard, she said, "Elizabeth, I admire your peppy attitude."

I could tell that she liked me as much as I liked her and after report cards came out, I knew she also liked my Shirley Temple hairdo. When Mama read my report card from Mrs. Campbell, she looked happy.

"Did I get a good grade, Mama?" I asked.

She smiled and read from the card: *"Make curls for Elizabeth more often. It gives her confidence."*

I didn't know what "confidence" meant, but I knew it had to be good.

What about Grandma Blanche?

MY GRANDMOTHER DAMSY DRANK COFFEE AND SMOKED CIGA-rettes, but she was against liquor of any kind. After Grandpa Eastburn divorced Damsy, he married a very nice woman who didn't mind that Grandpa made his own beer. Damsy disliked Blanche, not because her ex-husband had married her, but because Blanche was the perfect housewife.

Grandma Blanche was strict but kind. When I touched her valuable little porcelain figurines, she gently warned, "Leave 'em be; they're precious. Let's get something else to play with." Then she'd pull out her stereoscopic viewer with pictures that looked so real that I could almost smell the flowers.

I liked visiting Grandma Blanche's house more than my other grand-mothers' houses because I felt more peaceful there. She never asked a lot of questions about Mama like Grandmother Peal did. And her house smelled clean, not like stale cigarettes or old coffee the way Damsy's did. Instead, it smelled of chocolate cake and Grandpa's sweet pipe tobacco. They were smells I could almost taste.

Having a step-grandmother was a puzzle to me. I knew that Grandpa and Damsy had gotten a divorce, but I couldn't figure out how Blanche fit into the family. One day I asked, "Mama, what about Grandma Blanche?"

"What do you mean?"

"How did she get to be my grandmother?"

"Well, she and your grandpa met at church, went out for a while, and then got married. Blanche brought her brother, Arthur, with her and Grandpa Eastburn brought B.O."

Arthur was mentally slow, but I liked him because he talked fast and giggled a lot. B.O. was the smelliest bulldog on earth. It surprised me that Grandma didn't have anything to say about a stinky dog in the house. Maybe since Grandpa didn't complain about Arthur's limitations, she decided not to complain about his dog.

Grandma Blanche was never idle. She was either working in the garden, cooking in the kitchen, or putting together a work of art on her sewing machine. She worked as if her hands were normal, but they weren't. Although her palms and thumbs were grownup in size, her fingers were smaller than mine. The teensy fingernails were as cute as a doll's, and I daydreamed of painting them with bright red polish. I asked Mama why Grandma's fingers never grew. Mama said it was a condition called Brachydactyly.

I thought Brachydactyly was the most beautiful word I'd ever heard. I couldn't stop saying it. "Brachy dac tilly, Brachy dac tilly, Brachy . . ."

"Stop that," Mama said. "Grandma Blanche will think you're making fun of her."

I stopped chanting the lovely word, but I continued to watch the way she did things because it was so different. Grandma held onto objects the way a bird might hold a bug in its beak. When she said with real affection, "You're such a sweetheart, Betty," she always pinched my cheek with her big thumb and tiny baby finger. I tried not to wince, but it hurt like heck.

Grandma Blanche created beautiful things with her special hands, sewing tiny pieces of fabric together to create bigger pieces that became quilts. It was magical.

"That's so pretty," I said one afternoon while she turned scraps into an especially beautiful design.

"I'm glad you like it. I'm making it for the church bazaar."

I sighed and said, "I wish I was the church bazaar."

My grandmother was so pleased that she dropped her hands in her lap and stopped rocking the treadle with her foot. She looked right into my eyes and smiled. "Betty, someday, when you're all grown up, I'll sew a quilt just for you."

I felt the corners of my mouth turn up into a big smile. My own quilt? I could hardly wait to grow up.

Years later, when I was about to get married, a large box arrived in the mail. Inside was the quilt my grandmother had promised to make just for me. It was meant for our bed, but I needed a pretty cover for our cheap old sofa. Over the years, my growing family lounged on the double wedding ring quilt until it became little more than a large, colorful rag. When it was time to throw it away, I thought about how much work it must have been for my step-grandmother to create that special gift with her funny little fingers.

I felt so guilty about wearing it out that I cried all the way to the trash bin. Then I remembered something that Grandma Blanche once said to me after Grandpa Eastburn died. "I've got things to do and crying takes up too much time."

So I wiped my eyes, went back inside, and got to work. I knew Grandma would approve because it's just what she would have done.

PART 2: *Life at the Home for the Friendless*

The caption on the photograph reads: HOME FOR THE FRIENDLESS.   CEDAR RAPIDS IOWA.

The Home in 1937

Welcome to the Home for
the Friendless

ONE DAY DURING THE WINTER OF 1937, WITH NO WARNING, Mama took my brother, sister, and me to live at the Home for the Friendless. All she said was, "This is a nice place. You'll like it here, and I'll visit you every week."

Whenever something went wrong between our parents, we three kids were used to staying at Grandmother Peal's house where our four aunts took care of us. When Mama was in control, I never questioned out loud why she did things. And maybe she was right; maybe we would like it there. But the sudden change made me so tense that my scalp hurt.

The Home for the Friendless was a dark brick three-story building that seemed as big as the Cedar Rapids Library. A lot of other children lived there, too, and they were outside playing when we arrived. I was eager to meet them, hoping they were as nice as our cousins.

The lady in charge appeared to be someone who might not crack a smile even if everyone else was laughing. Although I'd assumed she was a grump, once she started talking, her face brightened up right in front of us. "You can call me Mrs. Kurl, even though my hair is straight as a ruler," she said in a friendly voice. I could tell she was trying to drag a smile out of us. It didn't work on me.

Then she asked, "Would you children enjoy a tour of our facility?"

Facility? That sounded like a jail. I just wanted to go home, but Mama agreed to see every room and, naturally, we followed.

The Home reminded me of a rich family's house from olden times, but the musty smell was that of our church at night when we went back for meetings. There were no curtains at the windows, just shades that pulled down. The walls, floors, stairs, and handrails were all made of wood, so our voices echoed in the hallways.

When I saw where each of us would play, eat, take baths, and sleep, a hot, sweaty feeling broke out of my chest. Bobby, Patty, and I would not be eating, sleeping, or playing together.

I tried not to show my true feelings, but I could hardly squeeze back tears when Mama kissed us goodbye. "You three be brave now because this is a very nice place to be," she said.

We kids had moved more than anyone and sometimes it was kind of fun. However, going to the Home was the hardest move I'd ever made. It was just too strange living in the same building as my brother and sister and not being with them. Did it mean we were orphans?

I'd been in charge of my brother and sister when Mama wasn't around. Now the stranger in charge, the friendly Mrs. Kurl, had split us up. We were not used to sleeping in separate beds, and I wondered who would keep Patty warm if she couldn't sleep between Bobby and me.

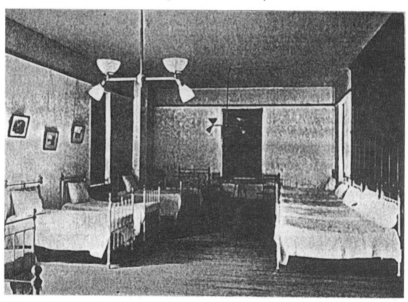

A dormitory in the Home for the Friendless when they had pillows

I lived in the girls' dorm on the third floor, ate with the girls in the basement dining room, and played on the huge, grassy area on the girls' side of the playground. My brother lived in the boys' dorm on the first floor, sat with the boys in the basement dining room, and played on the boys' side of the playground. My two-year-old sister's new home was the nursery. The younger kids never ate in the dining room, so I didn't even know what she had for breakfast each day. And she played in a special area under the huge elm trees away from the older girls. The towering fans of branches and leaves reminded me of a park.

I waved to Bobby and Patty whenever I could. I wanted to ask how they were doing, but I couldn't. I wanted to show them the tooth that had just come out of my mouth and especially the bloody hole it had left in my gum, but I couldn't. We could only be together on weekends when Mama, Damsy, or Grandmother Peal came to visit. By the time we finally got together, the empty hole in my gum was no longer repulsive enough to impress either one of them.

Bobby was happy at the Home because of the toys. When we first arrived, he couldn't stop playing with a red kiddy car that he drove by pedaling with his feet. He was as happy as a kid could be when he yelled to me across the hedge, "Sister, I like it here!" I wanted to squeeze him with a tight hug, but we'd been warned to stay in our assigned areas.

My brother claimed the red car as his own and wouldn't give it up. It was terrible watching the boys' monitor give him a harsh lecture about sharing toys. Whenever I looked over the peony hedge, he was still pedaling the kiddy car as fast as he could so no one else could play with it. The lecture on sharing had no effect, and I was afraid he might get a spanking.

I adored my brother and longed to play with him, but whenever I tried to get his attention, he was so busy playing with the other boys that he didn't seem to need me anymore. That's when sadness made me suck my thumb. Sucking my right thumb while fondling my left ear usually kept me from crying.

I saw my little sister more often because the nursery playground was on our side of the hedge. I wasn't allowed to play with her either. She never noticed me, so I thought she had forgotten who I was. From a private place behind the huge trunk of an enormous elm tree, I spied on her as much as I could. I pressed my body real close to the trunk so I would blend with the bark the way Chameleon did in comic books. The tree was closer to the forbidden area than I was supposed to be, but I loved watching Patty because she was so cute with her rosy cheeks and bright red hair. My uncles called her Carrot Top, which I never understood because I knew the top of a carrot was green. If the nursery monitor caught me right under her nose, she would shoo me away and scold, "Stay in your own area."

One frosty day when the air was so cold I could hardly talk, I noticed that my sister was crying. The woman in charge was busy with other children and wasn't aware of my baby sister's tears. I camouflaged myself against the tree trunk again and watched her up close. The woman had her hands so full with two screaming toddlers who had tumbled off the teeter-totter that she didn't hear my sister bawling.

My heart ached for Patty. She looked pitiful and cold. Her jacket was unzipped, her hat was on the ground, her mittens dangled from their strings, and her cheeks were as red as her hair. She was so close that I could see her nose running. I couldn't bear Patty's misery, so I marched straight over to the off-limits playground to hug her. The monitor, still controlling the screaming children, hadn't noticed me trespassing.

I wiped my sister's snotty nose with my mittens and pulled her cap over her messy hair. It wasn't easy getting her mittens onto her hands, so I started closing her jacket instead. Just then, she tilted her head down to watch what I was doing, and I caught her bottom lip in the zipper. When she screamed, I pulled back on the tab to set her lip free, and blood flowed down her chin.

When the monitor saw blood all over Patty's mouth, her eyes bulged as she rushed toward us. "What have you done to this little girl?"

I had no chance to explain before she thrust her finger in the direction behind me. "Get into your own area, and stay there. You are not uh-llowed on this playground!" As she punctuated the words, spit flew everywhere.

I refused to cry. I sneaked off to my place behind the tree trunk and thought about kidnapping Bobby and Patty. We would run away to Grandmother Peal's house. I couldn't remember which direction or which house, but I was pretty sure it was somewhere in that neighborhood. She would not be expecting us, but I could say, "Hello, Grandmother. How ya been? Would ya like some company?"

I knew I couldn't really run away, so I sucked my thumb instead and counted the days until the weekend.

🔱

Getting Used to Life at the Home

I MISSED BEING WITH MY BROTHER AND SISTER AFTER WE MOVED TO the Home for the Friendless, but I didn't have time to feel sorry for myself. I was too busy following the new rules. I wondered if the boys had to use baking soda as much as we girls did. If we ran out of toothpaste, we used soda instead. If we had an itchy mosquito bite that we'd scratched into a red lump, we mixed soda with a few drops of water and pressed the paste on top of the bite. It didn't stop the itch, but it gave us something to do so we could stop scratching.

One morning at breakfast, I saw a familiar-looking white powder in the bottom of my drinking glass. "Is this what I think it is?" I asked the girl next to me.

"Yep, it's soda," she confirmed.

Oh no, not again.

Then she leaned toward me and whispered a little rhyme:

Stir water in your glass
and please don't ask
why they tell each kid
to drink it down fast.

I had a pretty good idea how it tasted after brushing my teeth with it. However, brushing with it and drinking it were two different things. Mixed with water, soda was pretty hard to swallow. But the poem was right. The faster we gulped, the quicker it was over. It wasn't quick enough for one kid. She threw up right in front of us, which caused a brave girl to ask, "Why do we have to drink this stuff?"

"Why?" said a kitchen monitor like she was shocked that we didn't know. "Because it'll keep you kids from catching colds."

Baking soda in water wasn't all that we had to swallow at the Home. Sometimes cod liver oil was added to our orange juice. I almost threw up the first time I drank it. "You'll get used to it," said the helpful lunchroom monitor.

After breakfast, an older girl leaned close to my ear and said, "Hey, I don't want to scare you, but this nasty-tasting concoction is punishment for all the bad things we do."

"I'm not doing any bad things!" I replied.

"We don't have to know what bad things we're doing."

"But they know," someone else said.

I was so confused. "They know what?"

"They know everything we do, so don't think you've got any secrets because this stuff we swallow before breakfast is punishment for whatever we might be doing."

I had a feeling they were playing a trick on me so I would feel scared or guilty about something. Well, it worked. I felt guilty about wetting my bed and pulling the covers up to hide it. And when most of us caught colds that winter, I knew those big girls must be right because what we drank every day didn't keep us healthy.

At the Home for the Friendless, we were either a little kid or a big kid. And no one, big or little, ever walked to Polk School alone or came home alone. Everyone who was eleven or older was in charge of someone younger, and no one could leave school without his or her assigned kid.

No matter what age we were, each of us had to be a helper for someone younger because most of those young ones still needed bossing around. If we knew that someone in the dorm had wet her bed, we were supposed to jump right in and give her a hand. But if a girl wet the bed, she usually didn't tell anyone. Only when Mrs. Stone noticed a strong odor would she sniff out the guilty party and assign someone to help her rinse out the sheets in the bathtub. I had my own bedwetting problems, so I didn't like being in charge of more than I could handle.

Special occasions caused a lot of wet beds because we were allowed to eat popcorn and candy and drink soda pop late at night. After climbing out of bed the next morning, the bathtub was a very busy place as the bedwetters gathered there to rinse away the evidence.

One of those special late nights was our first New Year's Eve at the Home. A monitor rolled out a portable blackboard and placed it near a door that opened to the boys' playroom. She wrote on the blackboard in huge numbers: 1937. The closer it got to midnight, the more tired the little kids got. Some of them fell asleep on the bench lockers.

During the last half-hour before midnight, those who were still awake wrote the countdown on the blackboard.

Thirty minutes . . .

Twenty-five . . .

Twenty . . .

It was a big deal to write on a blackboard, so we shared the chalk and took turns erasing old numbers and making new ones. It was a rare privilege that made us feel like teachers. My turn would come at midnight because I had such good penmanship that Mrs. Stone had chosen me to erase 1937 and write the New Year, 1938.

At last, the final countdown arrived: *five, four, three, two, one . . .*

Erase fast. Write: *1938.* "Happy New Year!"

Whistles blew outside, horns honked, firecrackers crackled, and sleepy children on the bench lockers woke up confused, wondering where they were. The monitors hugged all of us, older kids hugged younger kids, and everyone kept saying "Happy New Year" to the air. Brave boys kissed older girls, so some of them kissed the boys back 'cause they were copycats. When the fun wore off and the outside noise faded, we finally settled down, trudged up the stairs, brushed our teeth, used the toilet, put on PJs, and went to bed, each of us praying that the sheets would be dry when we woke up.

My prayer for a dry bed was not answered that night.

Sucking My Thumb

WHEN BOBBY, PATTY, AND I FIRST MOVED TO THE HOME FOR THE Friendless, I was seven and still sucking my thumb. It was my favorite thing to do. And I had a favorite time to do it: in the evening when my left ear was cool. The perfect combination of my thumb and a cool left ear was all I needed to drift off to sleep on a hot summer night.

A lot of people felt I was too old to be sucking my thumb. Those folks didn't know how important it was to me. If I craved sweets, it could be dessert after supper. If I felt sad, it made those feelings go away.

Mama said that I probably started before I was born, and as strange as that sounded, I believed her. I was sure that when I was being assembled, God had said, "I'm almost finished inventing this little girl, but she needs one more gift before people meet her. I've got it! I'll give her the pleasure and comfort of sucking her thumb while she's growing up. And I'll give it to her right now before she is born so she can practice."

I figured that was what people meant when they said that God is love because I sure did love my bad habit. When people told Mama not to worry, that I would grow out of it, she replied, "Who's worried? Not me." I loved my mama.

I almost stopped using my gift after my baby brother was born. I was three years old, and I stared at him so much that I didn't have time for anything else. He was like a real live doll and I adored him. But the novelty of a baby in our house eventually wore off and my thumb found its way back to my mouth. That's when my grandmothers decided it was their job to take action.

While I was staying overnight with Grandma Blanche, she dressed me for bed. It didn't take long for me to find out what she was up to. My hands were trapped inside the long sleeves of my pajamas because she had sewn them shut. I pretended not to notice. Once the lights were out, I slipped my left hand up through the stretchy neck of my sleeper to find out if the ear on that side was cool.

Since it was not even slightly warm, my next job was to get my right hand out of the neck of my PJs as soon as possible. I had to go slow because moving around too much made my ears heat up, and there was nothing worse for thumb-sucking than an overheated ear. Two hands and a neck coming out of my collar made it pretty crowded, but that's how I fell asleep. Grandma Blanche told Mama that I looked like a strange creature with appendages growing out of its neck.

The next night she brushed Tabasco sauce all over my right thumb. After the lights were out, I felt a little panicked until I tasted the left one, which was certainly not my first choice. It was strange and unfamiliar, but better than Tabasco. When Grandma Blanche checked on me that night, she discovered that I had again adapted. I was becoming a challenge.

The next night she put hot sauce on both thumbs. After the light was off, I didn't swallow for a long time so a lot of spit would pile up in my mouth. I dribbled it all over my thumb of choice and let it soak for a while. Then I rubbed it off on the blanket, feeling pretty proud of myself. It took three spit-washings before the burning sting was gone. But it was worth anything I had to do to fall asleep in my own special way.

If there had been a fire in the house and we all had to grab something that meant a lot to us, I wouldn't have saved my Shirley Temple doll. I would have stuck my hands in my pockets and run real fast to keep my precious thumbs from getting burned up.

Next, it was Damsy's turn to break me down. In the drugstore, she found a black leather gizmo with silver snaps that fit over my hand as tight as new underwear. What my grandmother didn't know was that my gift now worked on both sides. Since she had bought only one of those doohickeys, I settled for the thumb that was not encased in leather.

There was just one problem. The black leather covering my right hand made it impossible to feel the ear on that side, so I had no idea if it was hot or cold. I was so desperate that I used my gift without caressing either ear. It wasn't a bit satisfying, but I didn't tell Damsy.

Grandmother Peal had too many things on her mind to join my other grandmothers on their mission. Her only comment was, "Betty, you're a big girl now and shouldn't be doing that anymore. Now stand up straight and pull your tummy in, and stop staring at your new patent leather shoes 'cause it makes you look vain."

When I started kindergarten, I liked the teacher, the books, the toys, and the kids, but I didn't feel at home because kindergarten wasn't a place where I could use my special gift from God. I didn't see anyone else using theirs so I gave it up during school hours. When school let out each day, I ran home as fast as I could and curled up on the bed I shared with Bobby to catch up on my thumb-sucking as though it was kindergarten homework.

Most of my family had given up trying to make me stop, but one of my aunts gave it one more try.

"Waneta, it's a shame that Betty is still a thumb-sucker."

"Why do you say that?"

"Her teeth are going to be crooked."

Brushing off the warning, Mama said, "Don't worry. She'll outgrow it."

My aunt just sighed and shook her head, and I got worried. Outgrow it? I sure hoped Mama was wrong.

After we moved to the Home, Damsy offered me a fifty-cent piece to give up my habit. Until she mentioned money, I hadn't even noticed that I had already forgotten all about my thumb. I didn't tell my grandmother.

I felt bad for fooling her, but the thought of the riches that would come my way kept me pretending that I still loved having my thumb in my mouth. The next time she came to visit us, I greeted her with the fake good news.

"Damsy, Damsy, you won't believe this; I don't suck my thumb anymore."

"Good girl. I've been saving this just for you," she said.

When the large, shiny coin landed in my palm, I didn't feel as good as I expected. It reminded me of the pewter compact I'd stolen and buried in the dirt. I felt so guilty that I told my grandmother the truth.

She didn't get mad; she just laughed. When I handed the money back to her, she surprised me by saying, "You keep it. I think you've earned it."

I couldn't believe my ears. "Thank you, Damsy. Oh, thank you, thank you."

Mama always told me that it pays to tell the truth. She was right. That day it paid me a whole fifty cents.

🌲

Wetting the Bed at the Home

THERE WERE STRICT ROUTINES REGARDING OUR BED LINENS. WHEN we were there, no kid had a pillow, and we slept between two flat sheets. Every Saturday we got a clean one. The used bottom sheet was stripped off the bed, the top sheet was moved to the bottom, and the clean one went on top. A dirty sheet was spread on the floor and the rest of them were piled onto it. After Mrs. Stone tied up the corners, she plopped the bundle inside the dumbwaiter to be sent to the basement. I wasn't the only kid who dreamed of hitching a ride inside that thing. It looked like a heap of fun.

Our weekly linen routine was one reason we kids were not allowed to drink water after 7:00 p.m. Those of us who were bedwetters sort of wrecked the sheet schedule. But summer nights in Iowa seemed even hotter than the days and by bedtime I was always so parched I thought I would die. I simply had to have a drink and broke the rules every night to get one.

I had to be very sneaky to get by with swallowing a sip after seven. I would lie in bed waiting for it to get dark while I daydreamed about being a movie star someday. When the girls in the dorm were snoring and our monitor seemed settled for the night, I crept into the bathroom, which was right outside her quarters. Our bathroom had three toilets, one tub, and three sinks, and the sinks were right by her door. That made sneaking a mouthful of moisture a dangerous activity. If I got caught, I would have to wash nose rags for a week.

As carefully as I could, I turned the cold water to a trickle and stretched up on my toes to reach the faucet with my mouth. I slurped silently until I was satisfied. The water was never cold, but it tasted heavenly.

Although I never got caught, sneaking a swallow after water curfew meant that I sometimes wet the bed. I never knew whether it had happened until morning. I felt so warm and comfy when I awoke that I couldn't tell damp from dry, so I was never quite sure. I didn't trust the comfort since I knew that warmth under the covers was a trick my brain sometimes played on me. The only way I could know for sure was to sneak my hand under my bottom, because I trusted my hands more than my brain.

But first I prayed, convinced that if I pleaded hard enough, God would magically make everything dry. Cautiously, I would inch a hand beneath my body to feel around with my fingertips and then with my palm. If the sheets were dry, I felt as happy as if I had just won first prize from Jesus. I bounced out of bed like a big shot, pulled up the blankets, smoothed the covers, got dressed, and lined up for breakfast. If I felt anything moist, I just lay there motionless, pondering my next move. When the spot beneath my butt was the only damp place, I could get by with just pulling the covers up over it. No one would ever know, and by nighttime the damp part would be a little smelly, but dry.

When both the top and bottom sheets were soaked, I was in trouble. I had no choice but to throw back the covers and rip off everything because that was just too much pee to hide. I had to follow the rules. I dragged the bedding to the tub, filled it with enough water to cover the fabric, and swished the soiled bedding around and around and back and forth as though my heart was really into doing a good job. I then drained the tub and wrung the fabric out by hand as best I could.

Soggy cloth was heavy, and I was small, so it was hard work. But I was a clever girl and twisted the sheets into coiled shapes that looked like I'd wrung them out with all my might. Then I left the sort of wrung-out sheets in the bottom of the tub. Someone else took them to the laundry room to be washed properly in a Maytag washer and rinsed well in tin tubs. The machine had a ringer that pressed out all the moisture for real.

The number of linens that hung on the clothesline during the week instead of waiting for washday was visible proof of how many kids at the Home still wet their beds. We belonged to the Clothesline Club, and membership in that group was humiliating.

Being Brave

ON A HOT, STILL SUMMER DAY, THE SKY EXPLODED IN A SEASONAL shower that included all the extras that come with a summer squall in Iowa. It was obvious that most of the kids who lived at the Home feared storms because the first sign of rain sent them running to the protection of the back porch. I always joined them, but I didn't understand why we dashed for shelter the minute raindrops fell from the sky, as though there was a penalty for getting wet.

Unlike the others, I loved a good thunderstorm. The loud explosions and flashes gave me goose bumps as rough as sandpaper. That afternoon the storm was wetter, louder, and brighter than usual, which I found thrilling. Once we'd reached the shelter of the porch, one of the big boys said, "Boy, it's a good thing we're not on the playground or we'd be dead by now."

"No, sir. We would not be dead," said one sassy little girl. "You think you know ever-thing."

"Well," replied the boy, "there are lightning bolts up there and they could strike us dead if we were still on the playground."

"Prove it, then, smarty pants," challenged sassy girl.

"I'm not stupid. You must think I am, but I'm not dumb enough to go out there and play with lightning."

Well, at almost eight years old, I was stupid enough to prove that I wouldn't die if I ran onto the playground with electricity flashing across the sky. I didn't even announce my plan, because I had no plan. I just felt a sudden urge to run out into that deluge. I was soaked the minute I left the porch. Everyone shouted, "Don't do it; stay here. You'll die!" I ignored them. I even sat down on the merry-go-round to prove how brave I was. Then I set it in slow motion by pushing the wet ground with my soaked feet. Although I was drenched, I pretended it was just another day. I could barely see, but I was not afraid. I even smiled and waved a greeting toward the building as I made lazy circles in the driving rain.

The dry kids on the porch were so scared by my foolishness that they screamed in horror. Their fear made one of the little ones cry because he didn't understand what the heck was going on. I didn't know either, but I was enjoying myself immensely.

Rain was pounding the ground so hard that it splashed mud onto my legs, and the scaredy cats were yelling so loud that I knew the noise would eventually draw the attention of our monitor, Mrs. B. I probably should have gotten back sooner, but I was relishing all the attention my bravado had created. I finally slipped off the merry-go-round and slogged through puddles on the grass as I slowly made my way back.

The rain stung my face and I could hardly see where I was going. Even so, I took my own sweet time as I passed by the inner tube swing and gave it a casual little push that left it in motion. Still squinting against the downpour, I sauntered to the protection of the overhang just before Mrs. B. came outside to see what the ruckus was all about.

"What's goin' on out here?" she asked, eyeglasses in hand.

Before anyone could tattle on me, I volunteered an explanation. "Ma'am, some of us were just scared of the storm — that's all."

"Then stop this racket and git yerselves indoors where ya belong."

"Yes, ma'am," we said in unison.

Mrs. B. was a sturdy woman who wore stiff butter-colored uniforms and a boy-bob haircut. She always smelled of Lifebuoy soap, and she never smiled. We paid attention when she planted her fists on her wide hips and scowled, as she did that day. "It's a good thing you youngsters came in outta the rain with lightnin' bolts flashin'. It's dangerous out there!"

Dangerous out there? She had my attention.

"You could be fried to a crisp if a bolt finds ya."

I tried to be casual, but I was riveted on every word of her lecture.

"In fact, the farther away you get from the playground equipment the better off we'll all be."

I was still brave enough to ask, "Is the merry-go-round . . . dangerous?"

"Is the merry-go-round dangerous?" she mimicked. "Yes, it's dangerous when it's all wet outside and lightnin' bolts are in the sky."

"Why?" I asked.

"Why? Because it's metal, that's why. Cast iron metal. It attracts lightnin' like a magnet. If one of those bolts hit that cast iron merry-go-round, there'd be nothin' left but a melted iron puddle."

I had never heard anything so scary in my life. That night I dreamed I was struck by lightning and melted into a puddle of Betty.

From that day on, when the other kids ran for safety during a storm, I went with them . . . and stayed there until the sun baked everything dry.

Toothpaste Candy

I MISSED SEEING MY PARENTS EVERY DAY. I ALSO MISSED SWEET treats, which were allowed at the Home only on very special occasions. Bobby, Patty, and I were used to getting a little sack of penny candy on Fridays when Dad paid the grocery bill. Just looking at all those goodies always made me drool. I would pretend to be a grownup as I sucked on sugary cigarettes and sipped from tiny wax bottles of make-believe soda pop. I didn't care that the colored water wasn't fizzy as long as it was sweet.

At the Home, I could only fantasize about those goodie bags. I dreamed that I found a mountain of Tootsie Rolls. I scooped up way more than my dress pocket could hold, so I pulled up the bottom of my skirt and turned it into a bag to hold oodles of the yummy chocolate pieces. My flour-sack panties were showing, but did I care? No sirree.

I could hardly wait for my eighth birthday. There would be cake with frosting, and I knew my wish would come true if I blew out all my candles without taking a breath. That year I was going to ask for a chocolate bar.

When the special day finally arrived, I couldn't wait for dinner to be over. I was so dizzy with excitement that it was impossible to sit still. At last, the candles on my cake were fired up and the kids in the dining room bellowed the birthday song at me in whatever pitch came to mind.

I had planned for a Hershey's bar to plop right into my lap where nobody else would see it. Then I thought about all the other kinds I could have. Should I ask for a Mars, a Clark Bar, or a Baby Ruth?

Demands to hurry up interrupted my thinking.

I squeezed my eyes shut extra tight and whispered, "I wish, I wish, I wish with all my might that a Clark Bar and a Baby Ruth will land in my lap."

Will I feel two thumps on my kneecaps? Will it hurt? Maybe I won't feel anything because they will come out of the air. I felt all jittery and nervous as I took a really deep breath and blew with all my might.

When I saw that I'd blown out all the candles, I couldn't stop smiling. I sneaked my hands under the table to feel around for my birthday presents. Nope, not there yet. I began to worry that maybe I was being greedy asking for two, but it was too late to change my mind. I peeked under the table to see if anything was there; my lap was still empty.

By the time a big slice of birthday cake was placed in front of me, I'd stopped checking my lap. I was so disappointed that I hardly tasted the frosting on my cake. If wishes didn't come true on your birthday, maybe they never came true at all. I felt like crying. Then I got mad. Who cared about magic anyway? Not me, that's for sure. It was better to daydream about real things like the treats Dad used to bring home in a sack.

But that didn't keep me from thinking about those candy bars. And the more I thought about them, the more I wanted something sweet to eat. One night as I put toothpaste onto my brush, I sang my favorite jingle:

You'll wonder where the yellow went when you brush your teeth with Pepsodent.

I was so in love with the taste of Pepsodent that I always sucked all the goodness out of my toothbrush before I rinsed it. I didn't want to waste any of that yummy taste because that was the flavor of breath mints. That night an idea popped into my head. Maybe I could make Pepsodent Lifesavers.

The next day I tore the cardboard backing off my drawing tablet and squeezed little circles of Pepsodent on top of it. They didn't look right, so I squeezed out chunks instead. Chunks were a lot easier. I decided to call them "Lifesaver Holes." I found a hidden spot on top of the radiator and left my cardboard tray there so they could bake. I peeked at the pieces a few times to see if anyone had tried to eat them while they were raw. Each time I touched the homemade candies, they were still soft, so I left them in the secret place overnight.

By morning they were warm and as hard as a real mint. The cardboard was kind of hot and curled up at the edges, and the treats came unstuck really easy. I tasted one of them and it was gooood. I was thrilled with my invention and shared it with my friend Virginia. She got so excited that her eyes bugged out. She thought it was even more wonderful than I did.

I tried to calm her down, saying, "Virginia, this is a big secret."

"I know that. You don't hafta tell me," she replied.

Virginia was not only a blabbermouth, but a big, fat liar because soon every girl in the dorm room wanted a taste of our toothpaste candy, and Virginia was getting all the credit for my invention.

"We could make more and sell them to all the kids," she said.

What a dumb idea that was. I reminded her that none of us kids had any money.

"Then we can sell them to the people who work here," she suggested.

"Virginia, we'll get in trouble with Mrs. Stone 'cause we might use up the whole tube."

"We'll just brush our teeth with water. Nobody will notice."

We baked a few more batches of Lifesaver Holes, and we still didn't have enough to sell because the kids kept eating them all. One of the stick-in-the-muds said, "You're gonna have fits and die if you eat toothpaste!"

Virginia corrected her. "It's not toothpaste. It's toothpaste candy."

"What's the difference?"

"There's a big difference. Toothpaste is soft and our candy is hard. And you may not know this, but Lifesavers are made out of Pepsodent." Virginia and I actually believed that.

In the end, we didn't stop making our toothpaste candy because we got tired of brushing our teeth with plain water. And we didn't stop because we got stomach cramps and diarrhea. We gave it up because it was a lot of work . . . and it would never measure up to the Baby Ruth bars I could taste in my sleep.

Halloween and the End of the World

ON HALLOWEEN WEEKEND, AFTER LISTENING TO A TERRIFYING AND soon-to-be-famous radio show starring Orson Welles, many of the staff members at the Home were anxious and fearful. In the middle of the broadcast, Mr. Welles had announced that aliens were invading our planet. He sounded so afraid that the staff believed it was really happening. Some of the kids were afraid, but at eight years of age, I wasn't. I didn't even ponder the safety of my little brother and sister in their dormitory rooms on the other side of the building.

I was curious, though. What if aliens did invade Cedar Rapids? Would they hurt us? Would the world be a big mess? However, none of that deep thinking kept me from sleeping soundly that night.

The next day at school it was hard to do our lessons because the only thing the kids could talk about was that radio show and Orson Welles, the man who wrote the script titled *The War of the Worlds*. The teacher even set aside our Palmer Method penmanship lesson so we could talk about what we had experienced. My third grade classroom at Polk Elementary School became a solid mass of arms in the air with hands wiggling, each kid begging to tell his or her story. I didn't dare say anything. What would they think if I said that I hadn't even been worried about my little brother and sister? I wished that I had been frightened so I would have something to say.

Arthur said, "I was scared to death, and I hid under the bed for a long time."

Violet said, "Not me. I knew it was a joke."

Phillip said, "It was not a joke, just a misunderstanding." Phillip was very grown up.

A boy whose father worked at the police station said someone phoned and asked, "What time is this going to happen?" A girl whose father was a fireman said a lady called the fire department and asked, "When it happens, shall I close my windows?" Another student said that when her mother checked on an elderly neighbor, the woman said, "I don't have time to talk right now! The end of the world is coming and I've got a lot to do!"

We all laughed about those stories, even the teacher. Then she told us another story, turning it into a lesson. "While I pull down the map, be ready to raise your hand if you know the answer to my question," she said. I was not good at geography so I didn't budge.

"There is a college in Brevard, North Carolina, where the entire student body panicked during last night's radio show. Who can tell me what the word panic means?"

Phillip's arm shot into the air. "It's the button my mother pushes when she loses her marbles."

"Phillip, explain for the class what you mean by pushing a button and losing her marbles."

"Well, when our new puppy went potty in my mother's lap, she screamed and tossed the pup to my dad. My dad said that she had lost her marbles and hit her panic button."

"So, Phillip, do you know what your dad meant by that?"

"I sure don't."

"Boys and girls, the word panic means being so frightened that you lose control and do things you wouldn't ordinarily do."

"You mean like my mom throwing our puppy in the air?" Phillip asked.

"That's right. Now, who would like to locate the state of North Carolina?"

Up jumped Bernard, Mr. Map himself, to point with pride at the state of North Carolina.

Our teacher said, "This is the location of the college where the students panicked during the broadcast." Then she read from a newspaper clipping:

Five students at Brevard College, North Carolina, fainted and panic gripped the campus for a half hour with many students fighting for telephones to ask their parents to come and get them.

If a pin had dropped in my classroom, we would've heard it because everyone was wide-eyed and speechless. We listened to every word as our teacher went on:

"A radio broadcast is usually heard by the whole country. So try to imagine how many other people were afraid last night and how many of them probably panicked."

Every kid nodded in agreement while she continued:

"When large groups of people become frightened by something they can't see, they sometimes do strange things to get away from the fear. It's called mass hysteria and it means that fear is sometimes contagious, like the measles."

That night after supper, all of the kids and staff at the Home gathered close to the big Zenith console to listen to the news. A lot of people were really mad about the show being broadcast, especially on Halloween. I felt sorry for Orson Welles because he probably had no idea what a ruckus he would cause. When a reporter asked Mr. Welles what he thought about the commotion, he said, "I apologize to the producers of the CBS Mercury

Theater for this getting out of control. The show was only a story and not real. That's why we announced that at the beginning."

"But, Mr. Welles, anyone who tuned in late didn't know that," the interviewer said. "The broadcast seemed so real that everyone was confused."

"I am so sorry. I don't think we will ever broadcast that program again."

While I was listening to the show, I had been a little bit confused, too, but I didn't think it was real. Maybe growing up with such hullabaloo in my family had taught me to take things in stride. When bad things happened in the adult world, like kidnapping and bank robberies, I felt certain the grownups would take care of it. After listening to *The War of the Worlds*, the nervous grownups at the Home must have caught fear from each other.

I was glad the world hadn't ended on Halloween. It would have wrecked our costume party, and I was really looking forward to stuffing my face with candy.

Nose Rags

An assignment I hated even more than washing my own sheets was nose rag duty. Nobody got out of it. If a girl was old enough to follow instructions, she had to take a turn, and at eight, I was old enough.

Mavis, one of the big girls, worked with two of us little girls to make a big pile of cloth squares for any kid who had to blow. We tore soft, worn-out bed sheets into twelve-inch pieces. They weren't hemmed, so loose threads sometimes got sniffed up a nostril to cause a sneeze tickle that almost blew our brains out. Some of the more creative girls pulled the threads away from each edge to make fluffy fringe. Mrs. Stone said, "Girls, that's not necessary. Get on with it."

"But fringe is fun," Mavis said, "and it makes the torn edges look nice."

"Fringe takes too much time. Children need to blow their noses, so you've got to make hankies faster."

After Mrs. Stone was gone, Mavis said, "I don't know about you kids, but I'm making fringe anyway, because a fake handkerchief should look nice."

Since she was older, we did whatever Mavis told us to do. Besides, adding fringe made a boring job fun.

We worked as fast as we could whenever Mrs. Stone stopped by to check up on us and a lot slower when she was gone. We finally put a finished pile into bins that tilted out from the wall. They looked like Grandma Blanche's flour container. One was labeled CLEAN and the other was labeled DIRTY. The clean bin was filled to the brim with rags that we could grab anytime the need occurred.

We blew into each piece more than once, wadding it into a ball after the first blow. When we felt a sneeze coming on, we would unfold it in a big, fat hurry and hunt like mad for a dry place. We did that over and over until there were no dry spots left and the rags had become deformed clumps. Then they were tossed into the dirty bin. While it was getting full, the clumps dried into crispy shapes that looked like my kindergarten art projects.

Used squares sometimes showed up where they weren't supposed to be. "Who dropped this on the floor?" the housekeeper would ask the air. "And who threw this into the wastebasket instead of putting it where it belongs?" We all did our best to look innocent and never admitted to breaking the nose rag rules.

The kids with the worst colds and the messiest rags would tease others by threatening, "You'd better be nice to me or I'll touch you with my icky hankie!"

A girl named Clarabelle was too lazy to go upstairs to get a fresh one. She had such a bad cold that she could hardly find a spot for blowing. "My goodness, Clarabelle," said Mrs. Stone. "Go throw that thing in the hamper."

"I'm scared to go up there alone," she said. What a helpless baby.

Mrs. Stone fell for it and said, "Betty, please take Clarabelle's dirty hankie and get her a clean one."

Some kids are smarter than adults will ever know. Barely clutching a corner of the disgusting thing with my fingertips, I tossed it into the proper place. After grabbing a fresh one, I ran back down the stairs. The clever whiner snatched it from my hand and pushed it against her face so fast you would've thought her snout was a magnet. She didn't even say, "Thank you," which proves that being smart has nothing to do with having good manners.

Used nose rags were germ traps that probably spread our colds to every kid who lived there. Drinking baking soda in water was never going to protect us from our own germ sharing. And since throwing the nose rags away was against the rules, we took turns doing the germ-sharing job of pre-washing those crusty balls with Fels Naptha soap. After they had been rinsed and squeezed, the damp cloths went into plastic pans and were sent to the basement by the dumbwaiter. There they were washed again, that time in hot, sudsy water in the Maytag. After a good rinsing in bleach water, they were squeezed through wringers that pressed out the liquid.

It was our job to attach the wet squares to clotheslines so they could dry in the sunshine. We pinched each bundle at the corner with wooden clothespins that looked like little men with no faces or arms. In summer the hankies dried fast. In winter they freeze-dried. Mrs. Stone said, "Freezing makes them whiter and it also kills germs." I believed her because she was a grownup, but I had a feeling it was clever encouragement to help us get the job done even when it was bitter cold outside.

We kids didn't care about germs or making cloth super white. But we understood when grownups told us, "You're learning to be responsible. Messes made by you have to be cleaned up by you." We just wished the messes didn't include nose rags.

Tattling on Virginia

I WAS EIGHT YEARS OLD WHEN I STARTED TATTLING. I DIDN'T PLAN to tattle. The opportunity just presented itself, and I jumped right in. It was a day when fresh snowfall had covered the grounds at the Home. Playing outside in the snow meant packing ourselves into cold-weather wraps and buckling our galoshes as fast as we could. We all wanted to be the first to break the pure white surface with our footprints.

But before we were allowed outside to play in the cold, we had to listen to Mrs. Stone's speech about the winter rules. "If you own a sled, please share it with those less fortunate. And if you own skates and your shoelaces are broken, do not be taking laces from someone else's skates to put into your own. And another thing . . . absolutely no snowball fights!"

With that final order, we were released to play in the winter wonderland. We didn't mind that the freezing weather made it hard to move our lips because we weren't planning to talk much. We built rows of fortress fences and an army of snowmen. Angel designs soon appeared on the surface everywhere you looked. We created them by free falling backwards to make a body print, then flapping our arms like crazy to make bigger wings than anyone else. Those of us who were lucky enough to own ice skates could show off our talent on the little kids' large circular wading pool that froze solid in the winter. I was one of the fortunate few since Auntie Marge had seen to it that Bobby had a sled and I had my very own skates. She labeled them with the words PEAL CHILDREN in bold, black letters.

After making my own angel, I helped the other girls roll a million round white missiles for ammunition in our war against the boys. We knew from experience that Mrs. Stone wouldn't check up on us, so we tried our best not to bash anyone's brains out. That battle warmed me up in a hurry, so I decided to take a break and try out my new equipment on the frozen wading pool. All personal belongings for out-of-doors play were stored in a basement room. I plodded awkwardly across the playground in the deep, white fluff and walked into the storeroom to find Virginia Shafer taking laces out of a pair of skates.

What was she thinking? She didn't even own any.

The rule-breaker was so busy unlacing that she didn't notice me. It made me mad that she was stealing laces, so I backed out real quiet and rushed upstairs, calling, "Mrs. Stone! Mrs. Stone!" The monitor interrupted her reading with an annoyed look and said, "Yes, what is it?"

I was breathless as I explained the crime I'd seen Virginia committing.

"Betty, Virginia doesn't own skates."

"I know, I know. That's why I'm telling you."

Our supervisor let out a little sigh and threw on her coat like she was mad at someone. I hoped it wasn't me. She huffed and puffed her way down the stairs and straight into the storage room just in time to see that I was tattling the truth. She caught the girl red-handed.

Mrs. Stone was really winded after her trip down the stairs. "Virginia (pant, pant), you heard what I said about the shoelaces and you (pant, pant) deliberately disobeyed."

When the girl let the half-laced skate slip to the floor, the lady in charge said, "Pick it up, missy. Lace it and put it back where it belongs. There will be no outdoor play for you today."

Since she'd have to stay inside, Virginia would miss out on our next secret snowball fight against the boys. It served her right. The big baby cried and cried. She just couldn't stop crying and, for a little while, I felt terrible for tattling . . . but I got over it real quick.

In fact, tattling became a job that I did better than anyone else. I reported Sophie for smoothing her sheets and covers after wetting the bed. I turned in Clara for throwing her nose rag away instead of putting it in the hamper. And when Maybelle changed the radio station without permission, she really got it because of me.

I was only trying to help everyone follow the rules, and no one ever thanked me.

Parties for Poor Kids

THERE WAS NO WAY I COULD BE LONESOME FOR PLAYMATES AT THE Home with children ranging from babies to young teenagers living there. We were like a family because we had so many things in common, such as parents who sometimes lived together and sometimes didn't. Some of the kids compared stories the way jailmates did in the movies. The difference was that prisoners talked about what banks they had robbed or who they'd beat up. At the Home, they whispered about the fights their parents had or why their moms ran away.

Not me. As long as I kept that kind of information to myself, I believed I was normal. So I didn't tell anyone that when my parents clashed, Mama would yell and cry and break dishes and then run away from home, leaving my aunts to take care of us at Grandmother's house.

Although I was embarrassed about my mother's temper tantrums, it didn't bother me at all that our family was poor. All of us at the Home were hard up. The county gave us free groceries like powdered milk, Cream of Wheat, and Wonder Bread. Sometimes people gave us clothes, shoes, and galoshes. I was thrilled when a cute hat with a matching coat came my way on Free Clothing Day. No child at the Home for the Friendless was poor on holidays. Because people felt sorry for us, we probably got more attention than any other kids in town.

Easter was especially fun because we gobbled all the candy we could eat. Candy of any kind made me smile so big that my cheeks hurt. The other kids must have been just as happy because on Easter Sunday, they all wore grins as big as mine. Our happiness was caused by a party that the nice ladies from the Cedar Rapids Women's Club threw for us under the elm trees. The women looked pretty in their silky dresses, hats, and gloves. I pretended the short lady was Mama and it made me not miss her as much.

Before the party started, colored eggs were hidden everywhere. Each of us received a beautiful basket with a bow on the handle before being set loose. Dozens of scrumptious treats peeked out of secret places all over the girls' side of the playground, and we ran around bumping into each other in our rush to grab more than anyone else. We all knew there was a special egg, a big hunk of chocolate wrapped in shiny yellow tinfoil. Everyone hoped to find that one . . . or to win the prize for finding the most stuff. The winner wasn't me because I ate all my treasures as soon as I found them. I just couldn't help myself.

Easter was fun, but the Fourth of July party was out of this world. A man, his wife, and their dog Pardner entertained us on the front lawn. The cowboy was more dressed up than Hopalong Cassidy, and his pooch wore a cowboy hat and a gun in a little holster while he performed flips in the air. When the cowboy pointed his finger like a gun and said, "Bang!" Pardner rolled onto his back and played dead. His legs stuck straight up in the air and his head rolled to the side as though it was all over for him. It made us laugh so hard that seeing the trick just once was not enough. We begged for it over and over, and each time that dog flopped on his side with his little legs pointing to heaven, we laughed until we rolled on the ground, hugging our sides. What a smart pooch. He could've been in the movies. Later, Pardner let us all pet him. He was the happiest little dog I'd ever seen in my life, but not as happy as I was that day.

Each of us was roped and "captured" by Mr. Cowboy while Mrs. Cowboy strummed a guitar and taught us the words to "Oh, Bury Me Not on the Lone Prairie." You could tell they loved doing it because the more we smiled, the more they sang.

After the show, we were treated to a weenie roast with cold soda pop and homemade ice cream. After dark, grownups shot off rockets, sparklers, and cherry bombs as we kids sat safely behind an imaginary line so no one would get his head blown off. It was exciting to stay outside way after dark, feeling scared and happy all at once. The fireflies were just as happy that night because they blinked their taillights faster than ever.

The last party that year was Christmas at the Elks' Club. I was sure their tree was the most sparkly tree in the whole world. It went clear to the ballroom ceiling, which was way up above the diamond chandeliers. We were each given a decorated stocking filled with an orange, a candy cane, and all kinds of penny candy like we received at the grocery store when Dad paid the bill. Then a real live Santa Claus showed up. He must have been invited to a million Christmas parties, so we were honored that he chose to attend ours. We knew he was not a fake because he let us pull on his beard . . . and because he knew all of our names.

We sat on the floor in front of him and when he called out each name, a different kid popped up for a present. When it was my turn, Santa acted like he had known me since the day I was born.

"Well, hello, Betty," he said. "Have you been practicing your violin?"

I was so amazed that my eyes bugged out and all I could do was shake my head yes. When it was my brother's turn, Santa said, "Hi, Bobby. Have you been sharing the kiddy car with the other boys?"

Bobby was so scared that he didn't know he was lying when he shook his head yes. He just did what everyone else did.

If our gift didn't appeal to us, we were allowed to trade with each other until we were satisfied. Mine was a bottle of green liquid labeled "Toilet Water." I had no idea what toilet water was, but an older girl said, "Dummy, you're supposed to put some of it on your skin each day."

"Why?" I asked.

"'Cause it'll make you smell good."

It didn't make sense to me that water from a toilet could smell good. It sounded so icky and looked so putrid that I traded the green liquid for a set of dominos. Even if we had not been given presents, holidays at the Home were so much fun that I forgot to be homesick for Mama and Dad.

Happy Birthday, Bobby

WHEN I WAS ALMOST NINE YEARS OLD, OUR MOTHER ANNOUNCED, "We're going to take you children out of the Home for the whole summer." My parents were getting along for a change, and they were so encouraged by their own progress that they decided to be a family again. I was speechless, excited, and scared. It sounded good, but it might not be.

My mother added, "We're going to be better parents." That made my heart beat faster, even though I wasn't sure what it meant. I had a feeling it meant they wouldn't fight so much, and maybe not at all. What a miracle that would be.

As soon as school was out for the summer, we packed all of our belongings into a cardboard box and joined our parents in their small rented house on Brown Avenue near the railroad tracks. Our humble, weather-beaten quarters included four rooms, an outdoor toilet, and a pump in the side yard for water. There wasn't a blade of grass in the yard, just dirt, rocks, and weeds. But grass was not important. Being a family again was.

During the summer of 1939, Bobby, Patty, and I played together every day instead of only on the weekends when someone came to visit. On sunny days, we were usually waist deep in water in the nearby slough at the Quaker Oats plant. There was no need for bathing suits because we swam with our clothes on and let them dry on our skin. It was a cooling-off experience that took the place of a bath. To protect our feet from broken bottles in the mud, we wore our shoes. Catching pinkeye several times that summer was just something we put up with in order to swim in the poor people's version of a public swimming pool.

Spending the summer with our parents meant we would celebrate Bobby's sixth birthday as a family. We three kids could barely stand the excitement that was stirring up inside of us like a milkshake.

Mama planned a nice birthday supper with the usual summer treats: fresh sweet corn (my favorite food of all time), vine-ripened tomatoes, cucumbers, and leaf lettuce. Bobby said, "I want root beer and hot dogs, too." So root beer, wieners, and buns were added to the grocery list. Dad always bought the groceries when he got off work because he was paid in cash and managed all the money by himself.

While he was at work, my mother baked a chocolate cake, Bobby's favorite, and covered it with powdered sugar frosting. I couldn't keep my fingers out of the bowl, and I couldn't wait for the party to begin. Although I was plenty happy about the special event, Bobby and Patty were practically vibrating with excitement.

After our father came home from the market, we kids dumped the contents of one sack onto the kitchen table and started shucking the corn. Our mother unloaded the other bag, then peered into the bottom and asked, "Butch, where are the candles?"

"What candles?"

"For the birthday cake. They were on the list."

"Didn't buy 'em."

"Why?"

"It's a waste of money."

My mother was so disappointed that her shoulders dropped two inches, but I could tell she didn't want to get mad on Bobby's birthday. A familiar dread crept over me as I watched a storm gathering in her face. I wondered what might be coming next and the wondering made me nervous.

During supper Mama was way too quiet. She stared at her plate while she ate. Every now and then she'd shake her head and murmur under her breath, "I can't believe you didn't buy candles."

Through clenched teeth, Dad finally said, "Nita, forget about it. We couldn't afford them."

"But you could afford a six-pack of beer?"

"We both drink beer and we sure as hell can't drink candles."

I knew my mother couldn't hold out much longer. Her temper was heating up. When she set the salt and pepper down with too much force, I tried to think good thoughts in case being positive might make a miracle happen.

By the time supper was over and the dishes cleared, my mother wasn't talking at all. Bobby didn't seem aware of her brooding quietness. He was so excited about his birthday and his presents that a smile was permanently stuck on his face.

The time finally came for dessert and singing "Happy Birthday." With no warm-hearted announcement whatever, Mama plunked the cake down in front of Bobby. Wooden matches were placed close together in the frosting to form the number six. As soon as she lit the first match, it spread to the rest of them and the top of the cake burst into flames. Dad jumped up so fast that his chair tipped over backwards. Bobby had no time to make a wish and neither of them could get close enough to the mini-bonfire to blow out the flames.

My father shouted, "Girl, what in the Sam Hill didja do that for?"

"Because you didn't buy candles!"

"Waneta, yer a crazy woman!"

"Yer a crazy man if you think a birthday cake doesn't need candles!"

Her fury now in full force, my mother grabbed the edge of the kitchen table, lifted it up like a toy, and tipped it over, dishes, root beer, birthday cake, and all. We kids jumped out of the way, and inside I got all quiet like I was hiding in a closet. Everything landed around me in an explosion of broken dishes, squashed cake, and matches sizzling in the icing. Mama smashed any dishes left whole while Dad cowered in the corner with his hands straight out in front of him like a policeman holding back a crowd. In a way he was, because at times like that our mother had the might of five madwomen. I was always afraid she might hurt one of us, not on purpose, but by accident.

That's the scene the police walked into after the neighbors called them. Even the two policemen were uneasy at the sight of our father hovering at a safe distance while a crazy woman continued to break anything she could set her hands on. Bobby, Patty, and I escaped to the front room where we huddled out of the direct line of fire. I wasn't scared anymore, just quietly upset. We kids had a lot of practice in staying calm when everything around us was falling apart.

It took a while, but the policemen got my mother calmed down. Then she couldn't stop crying. The officers talked to our parents for a long time and left only after they were sure that no one was going to be killed that night. Dad put Mama to bed and Bobby and I cleaned up the mess. Four-year-old Patty, looking bewildered and helpless, kept walking through the chocolate crumbs and broken glass.

Bobby still wanted cake.

"Bobby, it's all busted up," I told him.

"Not all of it," he said. "I see a big chunk in the dustpan."

"There's broken glass in it. Mama will bake you another one tomorrow."

"Okay," he replied quietly, "but I don't want any candles this time."

Stealing Stuff

IT WAS MY FIRST BOOK REPORT. MISS JOHNSON, OUR TEACHER AT Polk School, said, "Boys and girls, this assignment is a reader's version of show and tell. Today, we'll all go together to find something exciting to read. Then each of you will tell us about your story."

The class got so wound up about our trip down the hall you would have thought we'd never seen a library before. "Students," our teacher said, "you must be very quiet while we're there." I fell into place with the other fourth graders and filed down the school corridor.

A room full of shelves jam-packed with volumes of all kinds was one of the most exciting sights I'd ever seen. I would have stayed all day if they had let me because I loved the musty smell of old books. I judged all of them by their covers, most of which were dark green, deep blue, or faded black. Finally, I found a showy cover and fell in love with it on the spot. It was colorfully illustrated, and the artwork on the inside pages was breathtaking. The title was *All About American Indians*.

My passion for Indians began when my grandmother Damsy took us to a powwow in Tama, Iowa. Natives were chanting and dancing around the fire with not much on except their long headdresses. Layers of bird feathers swung like tails down their shiny brown backs. I was so thrilled that I said to Damsy, "I want to be an Indian."

"You can't," she said. "You have to be born an Indian."

I wanted it so badly that I prayed to God to turn me into an Indian princess while I was asleep. Each night I expected to wake up wearing feathers and a headband. I had to check out that book for my report. I was in heaven. It would be mine for a whole week.

I read the words over and over and looked at the pictures 'til my eyes burned. At the Home, I squeezed the volume into my locker next to my galoshes. I was so in love with it that I couldn't think about anything else. The thought of giving up such a treasure made me so sad that I got a stomach ache.

If I couldn't actually turn into an Indian, I could learn all about their ways so that a mighty warrior would marry me someday. That book contained everything I needed to know to reach my goal. I had to keep it.

The stamped label on the inside cover read Property Of The Polk School Library, but that didn't stop me. I scribbled over the Polk School part and carefully printed "Elizabeth Peal" above the scribbles.

Polk School

On the day of our reports, I took my treasure to school, gave my presentation, and showed the class the beautiful illustrations. The kids were all eyes and ears as they leaned forward with elbows on their desks. They loved the pictures as much as I did. I was so proud and confident that my report was way better than anyone else's that even my insides were smiling.

After everyone was finished and class had been dismissed, the teacher asked me to stay. A wave of goose bumps rushed over my skin because she was probably going to say, "What a good job you did. You weren't one bit shy today." Instead, she sat beside me and said, "Elizabeth, the librarian said you haven't returned the book you checked out last week. Is this it?" She didn't sound mad, but I knew I was in trouble.

With make-believe manners, I replied, "Oh, no, Miss Johnson. It wasn't this one. This used to be my aunt's, but she gave it to me because she knew how much I liked it."

She gently took it from my hands and opened it. In her nicest teacher voice, she asked, "This isn't really yours, is it? You scribbled over the school stamp and added your own name, didn't you, Elizabeth?"

I would probably get sent to the principal's office and everyone knew that Mrs. Tapper was hard on students who broke the rules. I was scared until I heard my teacher say, "Now you must erase your marks very carefully and take this back where it belongs."

I started to cry with shame and embarrassment. She put her arms around me and let me carry on like a baby until I stopped blubbering. When I came up for air she asked, "Why did you take this, Elizabeth?"

I could hardly talk for lack of oxygen, but I spilled out the honest-to-God truth. "I . . . I just love looking at the p-pictures because they're so (sniffle) b-beautiful, and I love Indians so much that I wa-wa-wanted to be one . . . waahhhhh."

I guess she understood because she told me I could renew *All About American Indians* any time I wanted so that I could keep it longer. Then she helped me erase the scribbles. It wasn't easy because I had pressed really hard with my pencil.

My teacher and I went together to check it out for another week. The librarian's glance lingered on the messy erased marks and she peered at me over the top of her glasses, but she didn't say a word. I knew what she was thinking. She stamped the new due date firmly on the card and reminded me that in seven days I had to return it.

Only seven days? Could I keep renewing it forever?

The Ottumwa Home

JUST BEFORE HALLOWEEN, MAMA DECIDED TO RELOCATE WITH US three kids. We never questioned the reason for anything our mother did; our job was to adapt. Most of the time, Bobby, Patty, and I adapted very well. So we packed up our belongings and the four of us moved to Ottumwa, Iowa, a town 109 miles south of Cedar Rapids. She had arranged everything ahead of time, finding a job and a place for us kids to stay. "This new place is like the Home for the Friendless, just smaller," she explained. "It's called the Ottumwa Home."

Our new home was built from the same dark brick as the Home in Cedar Rapids, except it was on a slight rise above the street instead of sitting on rolling, flat land. We had to go up a lot of cement steps to get to the large front porch. A lady named Mrs. Fields answered the door and invited us into the living room so we could get acquainted before Mama left.

Pretty soon, her husband joined us, and he was as friendly as his wife. I could tell they were trying to make us feel at home. I dreaded the thought that my mother would soon be leaving and we would have to get to know new kids all over again. Finally, it was time for us to say goodbye and go upstairs to see our rooms. I could feel tears tickling my eyes, but I forced them to stop so that Mama, Bobby, and Patty wouldn't see that I was starting to cry.

The next day we saw more of the Ottumwa Home. The dining room led straight to the backyard through two large French doors, but we weren't allowed to use them. After eating, we had to pass the staff table where Mrs. Fields sat at one end with her husband at the other. He didn't let any kid pass by without first stopping by his chair for a friendly chat.

The first time he stopped me, he asked if I was making friends. I was very shy and didn't enter into conversation with strangers easily. I simply answered, "Yes." Then he asked if I was happy there and I again said, "Yes." I didn't know if that was true or not, but I thought it was the right thing to say. Another day, he asked how I was doing and I answered, "Fine."

Mr. Fields always put his arm around me and just before I left his side, he'd give my behind a few friendly pats. After several days of butt-patting, he started putting his arm around my shoulder with his fingertips touching my left titty. It didn't feel right to me, and I didn't know what to do about it.

On the back lot there was a little guest house where the big girls played. I overheard them talking about "Fields," and it didn't sound as if they liked him very much. After a weenie roast one night, we got to play hide and seek after dark. There were lots and lots of trees to hide behind. One of the big girls said, "Watch out for Fields. He's playing, too." I thought it was strange that a grown man would want to play hide and seek with us kids. Something about the warning made me want to avoid him, so I hid real good.

The next day I tried to scoot around the kids who were talking to Mr. Fields in the dining room, but he caught me. "No, no . . . not so fast," he said. "I want to see how you're doing here." He patted my titty again and, as I was leaving, he gave my behind an extra pat.

When my mother came for a visit, I said, "Mama, I don't like Mr. Fields."

"Why?" she asked.

"Because he pats my titties."

"When?" My mother gave me her full attention.

"After we eat our meals and we want to go out to play, we hafta visit with him on the way out."

"Does he pat the other girls on their chests?"

I told her that I didn't know and then added, "When I'm starting to leave, he pats my butty, too."

"Hmm" is all she said, but I could tell she was thinking real hard.

A few days later, I went to the guest house to hang out with the other kids. I was surprised to see my mother sitting at the table with four of the teenagers. She was smoking a cigarette and having a serious conversation with them. I ran to her, squealing with excitement. "Mama, I didn't see you come in!"

"I didn't use the front door," she explained. "I cut across the back lot."

"Why?"

"Betty, I'm having a very important conversation. Don't tell anyone I'm here because this is a secret."

Then she told me to wait outside. I felt sort of left out and wondered if they were planning a party or something. I decided to stay near the door and listen carefully, but what I heard made no sense to me at all. One of the girls said, "I cleaned their apartment once a week and last week, right before I was finished, Fields put his hands on the wall and sort of trapped me at the front door. He asked me if I would like to have a baby. I said, 'No I would not.' Then I reached around behind my back and turned the doorknob. I got out and never went back. I told Mrs. Fields that I didn't want to clean the apartment anymore. She wasn't very happy, but she said she would get someone else to take my place."

I wondered why she didn't want to have a baby because it sounded nice to me. We didn't have any babies at the Ottumwa Home.

A few days later, Mama took us to a tiny apartment in Cedar Rapids that wasn't big enough for four people. She explained that we were going back to the Home for the Friendless in a few days. First she had to clean us up because all three of us had head lice. Damsy squeezed into the little place to help soak each of our heads with kerosene. It smelled awful and we had to keep our eyes shut tight for ten whole minutes so the stuff wouldn't make us go blind. After the lice were dead, we scrubbed our hair and eyelids and took a bath.

Later, my mother was reading the newspaper, looking at every page like she was hunting for something on sale. Finally, she said, "Aha! Here it is." She read an article aloud to Damsy, but I didn't really understand it. I heard Mr. Fields' name, so I asked, "Why is Mr. Fields' name in the paper, Mama?"

She explained that the Ottumwa Home had been closed and all of the children were being sent to other homes. "Mr. Fields was not a nice man," she said, "and he should not have been touching you the way he did. When I talked with the girls in the guest house that day, I found out that you weren't the only one he touched. I reported him to the authorities and they took away his license. That man won't ever get to have a children's home again."

A few days later, Mama took us back to the Home for the Friendless, where the kids didn't have lice and no one touched my titties except me (and that was only to see if they were growing).

History Lessons

ONE DAY A STUDENT WORKER FROM THE POLK ELEMENTARY SCHOOL office interrupted our fifth grade history lesson about Magellan to deliver an important announcement. Usually I didn't mind history lessons being interrupted; however, that time I was a little bit disappointed. I was caught up in the story about the first man to sail around the world because it sounded like such an adventure, and I wanted to hear the rest of it. The kid with the announcement had disrupted Magellan's trip at the most exciting part.

But Miss Marjorie Bywater, our pretty teacher, took announcements from the office seriously. She opened the note, read it to herself, got up from her seat at the desk, and said, "People, I need your undivided attention." She got it because we were all ears. "Any students in this room who live at the Home for the Friendless, please raise your hands."

The only people in our class who lived there were Virginia Shafer and me. We looked at each other with buggy eyes, not knowing if we were in trouble or if we were getting some kind of prize. We raised our hands slowly into the air as kids cranked their necks every which way to catch a glimpse of whoever lived at that infamous place. They never dreamed it would be Virginia and me because we'd never told anyone. People always changed once they knew where we lived as though they'd just found out that we came from a reform school.

"That's where you live?" the boy in front of me asked.

"Yeah."

"Why?"

"I dunno."

By that time every eye in the class was on us like they were seeing us for the first time. Virginia and I sat with our hands barely raised and held close to our heads. We must have looked like we weren't sure where we lived. Miss Bywater said, "Girls, you can put your hands down and, people, you can stop staring. Turn around in your seats, fold your hands, and listen to this announcement."

Miss Bywater cleared her throat gently and read in a sweet, clear voice, "We are announcing to every class in Polk School that the name of the Home for the Friendless has been changed. The official name will now be the Children's Home."

I liked it, though I didn't know why.

Our teacher handed the announcement back to the student messenger so he could carry the good news to the next classroom. The way he clicked his heels as he turned to leave made his job seem very important. I thought I might like to be an office messenger some day.

Once he was gone and the other kids had gotten tired of staring and whispering about the two girls from the Home, Miss Bywater returned to the exciting story of Magellan. She told us that Magellan was only one of the daring men we would learn about in the day's history lesson. There were also Vasco da Gama and Captain Cook, since you couldn't learn about one without learning about the other two guys. They explored new lands, and not through mountains and valleys with horses. Their discoveries were made from ships as they traveled the world by water.

By water? Maybe that's why our teacher, Miss Bywater, liked them so much, because she had something in common with them.

At the end of the day, our teacher, the prettiest one in Polk Elementary School, made Virginia and me feel special when she said to our class, "Ladies and gentlemen, today's lesson included Magellan, Vasco da Gama, Captain

Cook, and the Home for the Friendless, which will now go down in history as the Children's Home."

The "F" Word

WHAT A RELIEF. I WOKE UP TO DRY SHEETS, WHICH MEANT THAT MY excitement about the first day of summer vacation hadn't caused me to wet the bed again. Since good luck was on my side so early in the morning, I had a premonition that even more thrilling things might happen to me that day.

The fifty kids who lived at the Home and anyone who worked there would be celebrating with an end-of-school picnic in Daniels Park. When my family lived together, that's where we would tear down a steep slope of snow on our bobsleds each winter. In the summer we stretched out on blankets to watch the free movies projected on the side of a building. Dad insisted that God had created the hill in Daniels Park just for bobsledding and movie-watching.

I loved everything about the park. It was near Garfield Elementary School and when I'd been a student there, I cut through Daniels Park to reach whatever house we were living in at the time. It made the end of my school day special.

I even had a dream when I was little that Santa Claus saw me sledding in the park in the moonlight and landed his sleigh and reindeer on the snow beside me. He gave me a candy cane and asked if I would like a quick ride in the sky above our town. Even though my parents had said, "Never take candy or rides from a stranger," I felt safe with Santa Claus because everyone knew who he was.

Our end-of-school picnic in the park that year was a lot like the family reunions we used to have with aunts, uncles, cousins, and grandparents. We had a weenie roast with potato chips, burned-black marshmallows, and cupcakes. We got to grab bottles of root beer or orange, strawberry, or cream soda from ice-filled galvanized wash tubs. It was thrilling to have so many choices of pop . . . as long as we didn't mind dipping our hands into freezing water to find what was left.

A picnic also meant all kinds of running games like softball, volleyball, badminton, red rover, and tag. We always wore ourselves out having fun at a picnic of any kind.

I was sweaty from playing so hard and sat down on a bench to catch my breath before peeling the paper from a cupcake. I noticed a group of kids huddled near the wall of the pavilion as though they had discovered something incredible. I couldn't hear what they were saying because they were too far away, but I watched them for a while and could see that they were squeezing back giggles with their hands over their mouths. It had to be a secret or they would have yelled, "Hey, you guys. Look at this!"

I hurried to investigate because I didn't want to miss anything. Pushing my way into the middle of the secret cluster, I asked, "What is it?" Heads ducked down as they all shook with stifled laughter. Then I saw what had their attention. A word was carved in capital letters on the outside of the pavilion wall. I spelled it out loud. "EF . . . U . . . SEE . . . KAY."

"Don't spell so loud," one of the big kids hissed.

"Why?"

"Because someone might hear you."

I was confused. I pronounced it and said, "So what does it mean?"

Everyone was going crazy trying to shush me. Someone said, "Betty, be quiet. We'll get in trouble." I felt stupid and ignorant. I was the only one who didn't get it, so I whispered, "Is it a new swear word?"

No one was talking. The oldest girl in the group was thirteen, and she must have felt sorry for me because she finally said, "Betty, you're only ten, and that's not old enough to understand this stuff."

"What stuff?" I demanded.

"Can't tell 'til you're older."

"How much older do I hafta be?"

"Eleven . . . maybe twelve."

"I can't wait that long."

"You'll have to. You're just too young to know everything."

I didn't like being left out, and I wanted to know everything that minute. I was so down in the dumps that I threw my cupcake away.

I forgot about the letters and what they might mean when I found out that Mama was checking us three kids out for the weekend so we could spend some time in her new apartment. We would have to sleep on the floor, but we could choose our own radio shows and stay up really late. We would probably eat at the Made Rite hamburger stand and even see a movie. Best of all, Bobby, Patty, and I would be together instead of in our separate dormitories.

While my brother and sister played outside, I stayed inside and drew pictures in my typing tablet that had no blue lines to spoil my artwork. I loved to draw and was eager to show my mother's new friends down the hall that I was a child artist. While I sketched a lady with long hair and beautiful eyes and lips, my mother and I had a nice talk. When she asked me how things were going at the Home, I suddenly remembered the word that I was too young to understand. I blurted it out.

"Mama, what does EF . . . U . . . SEE . . . KAY mean?"

She just about fainted, then pulled herself together and asked, "Honey, why do you ask?"

I had no idea our conversation would change my life forever. I explained what had happened at the picnic, leaving nothing out. I told her that a thirteen-year-old said I would have to wait a few years before I understood. "The other kids know what it means," I complained.

She paused for a minute while she pondered what to do. Then she dived in. "Well . . . that's a naughty expression for something that is not naughty at all." I was sitting on the edge of the chair with my toes barely touching the floor. "Yes? Tell me more, Mama."

And she did. My mother said that a nicer term to use was "intercourse."

"What does intercourse mean?"

"Intercourse is how babies are created," she said.

I was thrilled because that was way better than I thought it was going to be. Those girls had been all wrong about me not being old enough to understand. I was in awe.

"Really?" I asked.

"Yes, really. It's when a husband plants a baby seed in his wife's body."

"He plants a seed? Where?"

In a matter-of-fact way, my mother said, "He puts his penis into his wife's vagina and plants the seed there."

I wasn't sure I'd heard right. Mama never lied, but that couldn't be the truth.

She proceeded to explain that sometimes the baby seed sprouted and sometimes it didn't. If a husband and wife were very eager to make a baby they had to plant a seed over and over again until it finally "took."

There was something else I had to understand. "Did you and Dad do that?"

"We sure did."

I found it hard to believe that's how Bobby, Patty, and I were made. When Mama asked if I had any more questions, I said, "Nope." I didn't want any more details.

When we returned to the Home that night, everyone seemed different. I couldn't look at their faces because I was sure they could tell what I was thinking. A part of me was tempted to rush up to the older girls and say, "I know what fuck means." But I couldn't bring myself to do that. Actually, I couldn't think about it anymore. I was ready to pretend that I hadn't learned anything about babies. If they started talking about it, I might learn more facts of life that I wasn't ready to know.

I decided that I wanted no part of having a baby seed planted in me. I figured I had two choices: (1) never grow up at all or (2) become a movie star and artist who had no time to get married. Making plans for my future helped me feel better and it seemed that my worries were over . . . until I overheard the thirteen-year-old say to her friend, "My period started."

I rushed in again and asked, "Your period? What's a period?"

Part 3: *A Real Family*

Waneta and Bassle Peal, 1941

A Real Home on 32nd Street

DURING OUR TWO YEARS AT THE HOME FOR THE FRIENDLESS, Bob, Patty, and I were growing up, though not together. That troubled Auntie Marge and Uncle Al. They never had children of their own and kind of adopted Mom, Dad, and us three kids. We were their favorite poor family. They decided it was time for us to be together again and put down some roots, so they came up with a grand plan to buy a nice house and rent it to us cheap.

My parents learned about the plan to reunite our family when they got together at my aunt and uncle's tavern. Even though they were living apart, Mom and Dad couldn't stay away from each other for very long.

Mom was excited, but Dad didn't like the idea at all. "I don't want any handouts," he said.

"Butch, it's not a handout. We would pay rent the way we always have. We'd just pay it to Marge and Al."

"I don't know, Girl. It doesn't feel right."

"Don't be so full of pride. This is our chance to start over."

Mom was so hopeful that she spilled the beans to us kids on her next visit. A week later Dad still hadn't made up his mind. I wanted to tell the other girls in the dorm that my brother, sister, and I were leaving the Home, but I couldn't. My spirits were in the dumps. If Dad didn't accept the offer, we might miss out on the best thing to happen in a long time.

When he finally gave in, I was giddy with relief and happiness. Not only would we be a family again, but we would finally get to live in a real home. I couldn't wait to pack my belongings. It was like getting ready for a vacation. The day before we moved I wondered if it was just a good dream. Would I wake up when all the fun was over?

I couldn't imagine what it would be like to live in one place for a long time. The thought of settling down put ideas in my head. I daydreamed about inviting girls for a slumber party. I had never done that before, but I had learned about it in the movies. Maybe I could have a birthday party and invite more people than just my family.

Moving to 32nd Street would be the beginning of the best time in my life. I just knew it.

Improvements

OUR NEW HOME WAS THE NICEST PLACE WE HAD EVER LIVED. IT WAS so big. There were two bedrooms and an indoor bathroom and a kitchen and a living room. And that wasn't all. The basement had a showerhead in the corner above a drain in the floor. We wouldn't have to haul the galvanized tub into the kitchen and heat water on the stove for baths anymore.

Although there was no curtain around our new shower, I seemed to be the only one bothered by it. Dad said, "A person outside would have to go to an awful lot of trouble if he wanted to see us buck naked." I was sure there were a lot of people who would go to that much trouble, but it didn't matter because our father was determined not to throw money away on a shower curtain we didn't need.

Besides, Dad had bigger plans for our new home. He was bursting with ideas for improvements. "If things go right for us, maybe we can buy this place and stop moving around so much," he said.

His first project was getting rid of the ramshackle garage that sat at the end of the gravel driveway. It was a dangerous, ugly mess and since we couldn't afford a car, we didn't need a garage. Uncle Cullen helped Dad tear it down. Once the boards were hauled away and the ground cleaned up and raked, the backyard suddenly got even larger. If empty space around a house made people happy, then we were a happy family. With arms spread wide open, Dad said, "Look at all this garden space. This means good eats for us." At last I would get to devour all the corn I wanted, just like a ravenous grasshopper clearing a field.

I was so happy that I had to run lickety-split from one end of our property to the other. Bobby and Patty joined me. Dad's grin spread clear to his sunburned ears as he watched us. Our father loved growing vegetables more than anyone I knew. He planted all kinds.

Because Dad liked vegetables, all of us liked vegetables, especially tomatoes. Bob, Patty, and I sneaked the salt shaker out of the house every day in the summer. We'd pick a big, ripe tomato and lick a spot to make the salt stick, then break the skin with our teeth to make the first bite easier. Hot tomato juice ran down our dirty arms and left clean pink streaks behind. We called that lighter line of skin on a dirty arm a "streak-of-clean."

Mom would yell at us from the back porch, "Do you kids have that salt shaker out there again?"

"Yes, we got it right here."

"Bring it back this minute."

"Yes, Mom, we will."

We'd gobble a few more bites of warm, vine-ripened tomato and then return the sticky salt shaker to the kitchen. But no matter where she hid it, we'd find it the next day.

The 32nd Street Museum

ONCE THE OLD GARAGE WAS GONE, THE ONLY BUILDING IN THE backyard was a junky old chicken shed with a corrugated metal roof. Whenever it rained, I dashed for the shed and sat on a box inside. It puzzled me that rain could make such a racket on a tin roof. I didn't know why, but the sound thrilled me.

One time it hailed and all three of us ran for the shed to listen to the sound. It was deafening. Hail on a metal roof was a spooky sound. Patty covered her ears and yelled, "I don't like this!" So we dashed back to the house and got pummeled on the way. Hail balls stung our skin and bounced off our heads. It was scary fun.

The shed was filled with old wooden apple crates. We poked around and found all kinds of treasures from nature. Dusty feathers were everywhere on the dirt floor, and they were mixed in with little white rocks. We had so much fun cleaning up the chicken shed that we decided to turn it into something special. We called it The 32nd Street Museum.

We put all kinds of good junk on display. To make the stuff look really important, we placed only one object at a time on top of each wooden box.

Bobby said, "That's wasting a lot of space. Let's put these pretty feathers and stones on there, too."

"No, Bobby. This is the way I've seen it done in museums. Important stuff has to be all by itself. Otherwise it doesn't look important."

Bobby asked, "When were you ever in a museum?"

"Dummy. I don't mean in real life. That's the way they do it in the movies. I learn a lot of important things at the movies."

My brother had no choice but to do as I said because I was the boss when Mom and Dad were at work.

We made little signs to put beside each special thing so people would know what it was. I wasn't sure what people we were planning for. We were more interested in preparing the museum than in worrying about attendance. We would get somebody to see our displays even if we had to promise cookies to get them there.

A rusty spike that I found in the dirt was an Indian Nail. I even displayed a feather from the baby bluejay that Bobby had accidentally stepped on when it was learning how to fly. Bobby printed the sign. It read: *Feather from a Dead Baby Blue Jay.* The little white rocks were displayed above a sign that said: *Petrified Chicken Poops.* Dried hollow stems from the tall weeds Dad had cut down were labeled: *Cigarette Peace Pipes.* We swore to visiting children that Indians sometimes used them instead of real pipes. Although we'd made it up, they believed us.

Things Change

DURING THE TWO YEARS THAT WE LIVED ON 32ND STREET, I GREW up a lot. I began calling my mother "Mom" instead of "Mama." I made new friends, and I learned to bake a one-egg cake. The recipe came from a cookbook that we bought from the *Cedar Rapids Gazette.* Whenever we paid our bill, we got another chapter for fifty cents. I used the cake chapter for my first attempt to bake something without my mother's help.

During those growing-up months, my hair got longer and I learned to braid it by myself. My drawings got better, too, because I spent a lot of time sketching things I saw or imagined.

But while I was going forward, Mom and Dad seemed to be going backward. I began to give up on them. Their fights happened more often, and they almost never ended with kissing and making up. Mom just left. But instead of going to Grandmother Peal's so our aunts could look after us, I started taking care of Bobby and Patty until our mother came back.

I was embarrassed about our problems and felt that whatever happened in our first real home should be kept a secret. Sometimes it leaked out, though not from me. I never knew for sure who it was. Maybe Dad got desperate when he had to go to work and Mom wasn't home. He probably broke down then and asked his sisters for help.

I was glad when my aunts showed up. It was too hard for me to manage by myself without Mom. Even though she was gone more and more, she was still the one who held our family together.

Mom's Temper

LOSING HER TEMPER WAS MOM'S HOBBY. WHEN SHE WAS NICE, SHE was very, very nice. When she was not, she was a raging maniac.

We kids had never been a target for her temper. But Patty was so full of "piss and vinegar" that she finally got it one day. Mom had just put the freshly washed chenille cover on our bed. Patty and I stretched out on it to look for pictures in the ceiling plaster, one of our favorite pastimes.

"There's a frog," said Patty.

"Where?" I asked.

"Right there by the ceiling light."

"Oh, yeah. It's right next to the map of Iowa."

When Mom saw us on the bed, she was not happy. "Girls, get off that clean spread right now," she ordered.

I jumped off in a hurry, but Patty didn't budge. Patty wasn't as smart as I thought she was.

"You heard me, young lady. Get off that bed."

"I don't have to." My gosh. Patty didn't value her own life.

Mom lunged forward, grabbed my sister's ankles, and pulled her off the bed. After Patty's head hit the floor with a crack, Mom pounded on her arms, legs, and back while my sister shrieked like a wildcat. It was as though our mother had temporarily lost her mind. I was in shock and screamed over and over for her to stop, which she finally did.

I didn't know why she lost her temper so easily. And I didn't understand why she ran away all the time. When Mom left, we never knew where she went. She might run to her friend Vera's house or to Auntie Marge and Uncle Al's tavern. Sometimes she called to say, "I'll be back in a few days." Sometimes she just appeared after several days or a whole week. Mom never explained or apologized.

Maybe the responsibility of being a wife, a mother, and a poor person at the same time was too much to bear. She had lots of health problems, too. Dad said frequently, "When we got married, I didn't know you were going to be sickly all the time." That's all the motivation Mom needed to stand up for herself and yell back, "Well, when we got married, I didn't know you were going to be such a jackass."

Even the most innocent topic of conversation could ignite a battle between my parents. That's when Mom either started breaking dishes or ran away. My parents bought dishes so often that we should have had enough for a lifetime; unfortunately, place settings didn't last very long at our house.

When we were younger, neighbors called the police when things got noisy. That always worried me because I thought our whole family was going to jail. But we didn't. The policeman usually had a heart-to-heart talk with our parents. Then he patted them on their backs, and said, "Now you folks get some help for your problems."

"We will," they promised as they waved goodbye.

Mom daydreamed of an easier life, which made her start a lot of sentences with "I wish."

Dad would usually respond with, "Waneta, if I had a nickel for every wish you had, I would be a rich man." Among other things, she wished that Dad would be more understanding and that he would spend less time at the tavern. But her wishes never came true.

Most of the women in Dad's family disapproved of my mother, so I stuck up for her, even when I was little. Aunt Lora was the most critical of the lot. She frequently reminded me of the role she played in my life. "I'm the one who practically raised you," she told me more than once. "I have a snapshot to prove it." And she did. In the old black and white photo, Dad's four sisters were watching a younger version of me trying to stay upright.

It looked as though I was trying to walk. Aunt Lora said, "You took your first steps to me."

After my brother and sister were born, my aunt's responsibilities increased. She was the oldest of four girls in Dad's family of ten siblings, and she never had a boyfriend. Since she was available, Dad asked for her help whenever Mom took off.

Dad's sisters were teenagers, but when I was little I thought they were grownup women. I spent a lot of time with them. They let me help in the kitchen by drying spoons with a clean white towel. One time, I kept touching my tongue to the dried spoons and Aunt Edith asked, "Why do you keep doing that?"

"I hafta see if the spoons got dry."

"Well, now they're wet, and I have to wash them again. Does your mother let you do that?" I just shrugged in response. I dried the spoons a second time and tried hard not to test them with my tongue.

Grandmother Peal asked questions about Mom, too. In fact, she asked the same questions every time we stayed at her house, and I never answered truthfully.

"Betty, does your mother smoke cigarettes?"

"No."

"Does she drink beer?"

"No."

"Does she ever leave you alone?"

"No."

Fibbing about Mom felt like the right thing to do. I had to protect her. It was my duty.

Who's the Boss?

WHILE WE LIVED ON 32ND STREET, MOM AND DAD WORKED AT AUNtie Marge and Uncle Al's Uptown Village Café. My aunt and uncle were Dad's bosses because he worked behind the bar. Since Mom was the only cook, she was the boss of the kitchen. In the summer, Bob, Patty, and I stayed home alone and Mom put me in charge, so I was the boss of them. Since I was babysitting, I felt I should get paid like everyone else. When

I asked Mom about it, she replied, "Betty, it's your responsibility to help out at home without getting money for it." I'd had a feeling she'd say that.

Before she and Dad left for work each day, my mother said, "You kids do as Betty says or you'll get a lickin' when we get home, ya hear?"

Eight-year-old Bob was easy to handle, but six-year-old Patty was what Mom called "a trial and a tribulation." Dad called her a "real pisser." Being in charge of a pisser was turning me into a mean person. I was born for better things than trying to tell my little sister what to do. I guess someone told her that redheads were supposed to be brats and she just went along with it. She could make me so mad that I sort of flipped my lid. At those times, I was awful. I squeezed her arm so hard that it should have fallen off. Her skin didn't bleed, but you could tell that it wanted to. Arm squeezes left funny little bruises behind, though it didn't make her any easier to boss around.

I wasn't always mean to my sister. When our parents were at work, we kids had a great time creating special hideaways and dens where we could spend time doing nothing. Doing nothing in a place that we'd built ourselves was the most fun we ever had.

If Patty liked the way things were going, she was a peach instead of a pisser. Patty the Peach said, "I am so happy in our hideaway. I wish we could live out here." I agreed. I felt peaceful in our handmade shelters and imagined they were real homes. Inside them I was a nice boss because everyone got along without fighting.

Our first creation was made with some of the wooden apple boxes we'd found in the shed. By stacking them on top of each other, we created a wall. Bob said, "Let's call it a fort."

I didn't care what we called our hangouts. I just had fun building them. There weren't enough boxes to surround ourselves like a real fort, but we didn't mind. We just camped out behind the wall and used the inside of the crates for storage of important things like popcorn and comic books. When my brother and sister stripped our bed and spread the blankets on the ground, the fort became a good place to live. How sweet it was to stretch out in my own hideaway with tree branches and sky above, a pillow under my head, and a comic book in my hands. It's one of the most heavenly memories I own.

As the boss, I sometimes had to interrupt my bliss to give orders. "You kids watch the clock so we can get this stuff back on our bed before Mom comes home." That was about the only time they cooperated and gave me no trouble at all.

When the apple crates started to fall apart, we made a new hangout in the field next door. That was the best camouflage of all because no one could tell we were there, especially if we whispered. I liked being invisible. That's when my world was perfect. If no one could see or hear me, I could do whatever I wanted and think all kinds of thoughts. It was a lot like running away without getting into trouble. The weeds and wild grasses were so tall they came above my waist. We pushed them down flat in a circle and created our first human nest. Kids came from down the street just to lie around in it. The nest was even cozier than our fort wall.

As more kids joined us with their own comic books, pillows, and blankets, we just pressed down more grass. Two or three nests were a lot easier to make than one fort, and they had a magical effect on us. When several kids were in different nests reading and trading comic books, I wondered if that was what heaven was like, because no one bickered.

The nests had to go when Dad cut down the weeds to make a garden. Later that summer when the garden had grown tall, we spread blankets in between rows of corn to create cornstalk hideaways. They were fun, but kind of itchy.

On rainy days, we took a break from building forts to play store in the basement. Every Sunday, the newspaper printed make-believe labels that kids could paste onto empty tin cans. On Wednesdays, they printed fake dollar bills. As we cut out food labels and play money week after week, our store shelves got better and better stocked. I was always the store owner. Patty didn't like that at all.

"Why do Bobby and I get the dumb jobs and you always get the best ones?"

"Because I'm the oldest and I'm the boss. Anyway, I don't see Bob complaining."

So Bob became the clerk and Patty was the customer in our pretend grocery store. Missing out on being the store owner made her a very bossy customer. "Okay," she said with her nose stuck in the air. "But if I'm going to be a customer, you've got to let me charge my groceries."

When Patty was being clever and a smart aleck at the same time, I never knew whether to smack her or be proud of her. Since there was no way to fire her from the job of being my sister, I decided to teach her a lesson.

"Patty, honey, climb inside that big old trunk in the basement."

"And why should I do that?" she asked.

"Because it's fun inside."

And it was fun. I knew because I'd tried it out myself. The trunk had a curved lid that made it seem like a cozy little house. I told my sister it was a good place to hide if bad guys broke in.

She had no idea I planned to pay her back for being mouthy. Once she was inside the steamer trunk, I closed the lid and sat on top of it while she screamed her head off. She screamed so long and hard that it scared me just a little bit. But being trapped inside the trunk made quite an impression on my sister. For a few hours she was a lot easier to boss around.

Before Mom came home, I asked, "Are you going to tattle on me?"

"Nope," she replied.

"How come?"

"Because Mama can be meaner than you."

Patty was a brat, but she was a smart brat, which meant I had to be even smarter. Being the Boss of Summer wasn't easy.

Outhouse Adventures

DURING THE HEAT AND HUMIDITY OF AN IOWA SUMMER, AUNT DEE gave birth to her seventh child at home. At the age of eleven, I knew only that babies were cute. I had no idea how much work they were or that a mother was worn out after her baby was born. Aunt Dee was no exception. She wasn't at all up to par, and she slept most of the time. Her husband, Uncle Connie, really needed help with their other kids. He had no hired man and too many farm chores that were not getting done.

So Grandmother (known as Josie Peal to her family), agreed to stay and help out for a week. She'd done it after each of her thirteen grandchildren came into the world. She was getting used to helping Uncle Connie and Aunt Dee because they had more kids than anyone in the family. A dog named Spike would show all of us just how far Josie would go to help her children.

Keeping track of all the grandkids and their mischief was not easy. And since cooking nonstop and staying ahead of the laundry was getting harder each year, looking after the needs of sickly Aunt Dee and the new baby just about wore her out. She knew she could get through it because she had done it before and wasn't about to allow herself to get discouraged. Each night after all of my cousins had been sent to bed and Aunt Dee and the new baby were down for a few hours, Grandmother had her nightly meditation. First, she read from the Bible. When that was finished, she knelt by her army cot with elbows on the blanket and prayed, "Lord, I love my grandchildren, but give me the strength and good humor to get through tomorrow without smacking one of these kids."

While Josie Peal, volunteer rescue worker for all of her grandchildren, was praying for courage in the country, her daughters, Laura, Edith, Sarah, and Naomi, stayed home to help our family. Mom had run away again, so my brother and sister and I were staying with them at Grandmother's house. While we were there, Aunt Edith called Grandmother to find out how she was doing on the farm.

She replied, "Well, it depends on what hour it is. This is no picnic."

That was a sure sign that help was needed. So Aunt Edith left my brother and sister with our three aunts and took me to the farm to play with my cousins while she helped with whatever had to be done. There would be vegetables to pick, corn to be shucked, laundry to be washed, and a baby to bathe.

I didn't care about any of that grownup stuff. I was beside myself with excitement because I could play on the farm with my cousins and eat fresh corn on the cob from Aunt Dee's garden.

It was a wonderful plan. But when we finally arrived at the farm, my grandmother didn't even have a chance to look relieved that help had arrived. My cousins slammed the screen door open, yelling, "Help! We gotta pull Spike outta the toilet!"

Her shoulders sagged. "Oh no . . . not again."

I was kind of confused. Who was Spike and what was going on? I had a feeling that my fun afternoon might not happen after all.

Grandmother yelled for us to stay put as she rushed into the yard. Aunt Edith and I obeyed and watched from a safe distance. Even though we felt guilty, we were glad that we'd been left out of whatever was going on outdoors. Soon my curiosity started driving me crazy. I just had to find out what was happening. So from the safety of the back porch, I watched my cousins dart this way and that like disorganized ants as they tried to follow our grandmother's orders. It was as much fun as watching a movie.

She hollered, "Clara, Dora, Hubert, Elma, Connie — come quick! Somebody pull the hose up close and somebody getcherself over here and give me yer ankles. The rest of you, grab holda my skirt and don't let go!"

My eight-year-old cousin Hubert saved the day. What a little hero. He volunteered to be lowered headfirst through the hole in the outhouse. It was the only way to rescue Spike. Grandmother grabbed Hubert's ankles, and three kids hung onto her long skirt to anchor the whole lot. We could hear him yell from down below, "I've got 'im!" It sounded like his voice was coming from a cave. I was in awe as I watched them pull my cousin and the family dog out of a pit full of summer-heated body waste.

Hubert was pretty yucky. He just stood there because he didn't know what to do next, but Spike knew exactly what to do. Once he found his legs on firm ground again, he shook his icky coat at high speed, projecting disgusting stuff everywhere.

I couldn't believe my eyes and yelled, "Oh, my gosh!" Spike was splattering the bushes, the cat, and every kid within range. Grandmother grabbed the smelly dog and helped hold him captive while my cousins hosed him off the best they could.

Although she was as stinky and repulsive as Spike, Josie Peal was still in charge. She yelled orders, which we all obeyed. My aunt and I helped hose off my cousins before they stripped naked. Then they put their filthy clothes in an old barrel filled with water. Next, they scrubbed their bodies with soap. Nobody cared one bit that they were all buck naked in the country air. It was way more fun than I thought it would be. After one last hosing off with cold spring water, they used up all the family towels. Doing the laundry added another hour to what was eventually referred to as Josie's Nightmare. I called it an adventure.

Hubert and Spike

After the kids got dressed, Hubert the Hero decided to play Indian with one of his sisters. She had stolen his lucky ring and wouldn't give it back. So he tied her to a tree and started laying out dry kindling to build a fire to sacrifice her to the gods. Luckily, Grandmother heard about his plan after the prisoner had unwillingly returned the loot. By that time, she was a nervous wreck even though she tried to hide it. I could tell she was near the end of her rope because she sighed a lot and said "good grief" more than usual.

When things had calmed down, she invited us for supper. Aunt Edith said, "We can't, Mother. I need to get back and help the girls with Bob and Patty."

I really wanted to stay since they were having all the freshly-picked corn on the cob they could eat. But I could tell that my aunt wanted to leave as much as I wanted to stay. I think washing all those stinky kids and clothes had made her lose her appetite.

Grandmother Peal later told us that her evening meditations that night took longer than usual. After reading extra chapters from the Bible to get God's attention, she prayed again for strength and wisdom and added a P.S.:

Lord, while I'm still sane, I want to thank you for sending help when I needed it. But I have another favor to ask. Please don't send any more babies to Connie and Dee. I'm too old for these outhouse adventures. Ay-men.

Tattling in the Teepee

AS MUCH FUN AS WE HAD IN THE DENS AND FORTS THAT WE KIDS built ourselves, the best of all places to play was the teepee Dad made with dried cornstalks from his garden. It was marvelous. Little kids we had never met walked down the street just to sit in our cornstalk teepee and ask, "Can we play Indians wif you guys?"

One crisp fall day, six of us crowded inside the structure with our legs crossed. Mom's clean towels hugged our shoulders like blankets, and chicken feathers were stuck in our hair. We were ready to play Indians. My nine-year-old brother announced in his fake Indian voice, "We smoke peace pipe now." Instead of a pipe, he held a dry, hollow stem between his fingers like a cigarette. In his other hand was a cigarette lighter that I knew he had swiped from a strictly off-limits place.

"Bob," I asked, "where did you get that?"

"From Dad's top dresser drawer."

"You're gonna get it."

"Uh uh."

The whole thing gave me a nervous feeling because I knew our father would not want Bob to start smoking at such a young age. As head Indian woman, it was my duty to report my brother to the chief (also known as Dad). So I let the blanket fall from my shoulders, uncrossed my legs, and stood up. "Me be right back. I . . . um . . . hafta make water inside house."

Bob said, "Sister squat behind bush like Indian woman." The neighbor kids fell all over each other, laughing their feathers off as though they'd heard a dirty joke for the first time. I ignored them, walking as fast as I could to reach my dad to make my report.

The minute I spotted him, I blurted out my news. "Dad! Dad! Bob has your lighter and is gonna smoke a stick in the teepee." I'd hoped to get a reaction, just not the one I got. Dad almost knocked me over getting out the back door. He ran across the field and dived headfirst into the teepee. When our father emerged seconds later, he held the cigarette lighter in one hand and Bob by his overall straps in the other. "You coulda been cremated!" he screamed.

Bob was so scared that he started crying in front of his new friends, and he cried even harder when Dad spanked him. Fearful they might be next, the rest of the Indians escaped back down the street to the white man's village. Dad was so upset that he dismantled the teepee immediately, explaining that all of us could have been burned alive. I shuddered at the thought.

Bob was a pitiful mess, and I felt so sorry for tattling that I was extra nice to him for a whole week. It didn't last. When he accidentally hammered his thumb while we were building our next fort and said, "Dammit," I had no choice but to report him again.

Dishes and Switches

MOM WAS IN THE KITCHEN SLAMMING THINGS AROUND WITH SUCH energy that we should have known she was mad. My eight-year-old brother and I were in the front room arguing about which radio show to turn on when Mom yelled, "I'm telling you kids for the last time! Turn off that radio and get in here and do the dishes . . . without fighting!"

We knew the rules but always tried to break them, especially the rule about getting our chores done before listening to our favorite programs. We got as caught up in those shows as we did the movies, and we knew the weekly schedule by heart.

Monday night was *Lux Radio Theater.* Tuesday was Fanny Brice as *Baby Snooks.* Wednesday was *Mr. District Attorney,* champion of the people and defender of the truth. On Thursday, we listened to *Lights Out.* On Friday, it was *The Shadow.* Saturday morning was *Let's Pretend,* with *I Love a Mystery* on Sunday night. We memorized the commercial ditties and sang them all the time. My favorite was *"Rinso white, Rinso bright. Happy little washday song."*

Bob and I especially loved the spooky programs, and we did whatever the announcer instructed in his deep, somber tone. When we heard him say, *"Turn . . . out . . . your . . . lights,"* my brother and I couldn't make the room dark fast enough. Patty, anticipating what was coming, curled up in a ball with her hands over her eyes, squeezing them shut. We laughed at her because Patty thought if her eyes were closed, she wouldn't hear the creepy organ music.

Listening to the radio was deliciously thrilling and way more fun than the movies because we could dream up our own frightening images. But none of that fun, scary stuff could happen until we got the supper dishes done. Washing dishes was our job every night, and every night we dawdled and argued and sang songs and argued some more. Mom seldom punished us. She just yelled, giving us "one last warning" at least five times before Bob and I finally listened and moved our wrangling to the kitchen sink.

"It's my turn to wash."

"You don't wash good."

"Do too."

"Do not."

Right on cue, Mom would yell, "Agree on something. I'm sick and tired of hearing this from you kids."

Grownups always seemed to be sick and tired. I couldn't wait to grow up so I could find out what sick and tired really felt like. When my mother got to the sick-and-tired point, Patty was smart enough to stay out of the direct line of fire. But Bob and I didn't stop even though we knew we were treading the thin line between getting a thrashing and tricking Mom into laughing and letting it go.

Sometimes we managed to get six-year-old Patty involved by thrusting a dish towel into her hands. She would dry the same spoon over and over until Bob suggested that she dry a fork now and then. She would whine, "I can't. They're too pointy." Patty usually got by with that excuse because it was too much trouble for me to keep her in line and fight with Bob at the same time.

Once in a while Mom changed her pattern. Instead of yelling at us, she would stroll into the kitchen without a word, casually open the cutlery drawer, and get out the sharpest knife we owned. She tested the sharpness of the blade against the surface of her fingernail and went straight out the back door to the apple tree.

Bob and I would get serious then, knowing what was coming next. Mom's calmness told us a human tornado was starting to form, so we became energetic about the dirty dishes, splashing, rinsing, and drying plates like we were trying to win a contest. We figured if we looked real busy, she might change her mind about cutting a switch. It was usually too late for that. She would glide into the kitchen and grab my arm, causing soapy suds to fly into the air, then whirl me around in front of her where she flipped the switch back and forth in the direction of my bare legs.

I hopped up and down like a frog doing a spastic dance to avoid contact with the thin, supple branch in my mother's hand. My goal was to make her laugh, which almost always worked. I'd keep up my crazy act and dance circles around Mom, who was still hanging onto my arm. I pleaded in a silly, teasing voice, "You don't really wanna whip me, Mama, do you? Don't whip me, Mama. I'll be good, I'll be good. I promise I'll be good." At eleven years old, I thought I was a pretty good actress.

Sometimes the dodging-the-switch act took longer than I expected before my mother broke down and started laughing at my silly antics. When she finally gave up and said, "Dammit!," I knew I had won. It made her mad when she broke down and laughed because she felt I really needed to be punished for not setting a better example for my brother and sister.

One time Mom said, "Dammit," but she didn't give up. As calmly as she had opened the kitchen drawer to get the knife, she unplugged the radio, took out a tube, and said quietly, "No radio shows until those dishes are done and put away even if it takes the rest of your lives." When her voice was soft and calm like that, we knew she meant business.

The night she removed the radio tube, Mom was so calm that I was afraid she would break the tube on purpose. I did not want to miss my favorite shows forever, so that evening I focused all my attention on doing what had to be done, and that was, obviously, the dishes.

🐦

How to Break a Bone

IN THE SIXTH GRADE, I TRIED TO BREAK A BONE. I DID IT BECAUSE I wanted someone to feel sorry for me. I wasn't trying to break a specific bone; any old bone would do just fine.

I was sure that flinging myself down the porch steps would do the trick. Yet every time I tried, I landed in a clumsy heap with all of my parts intact and no injury that required more than a band-aid. I was hoping for at least a sprained ankle. Throwing myself off the front porch was not easy and it hurt a whole lot, but all I had to show for my efforts were red scrapes on both knees and blue bruises on my butt.

I really wanted an injury that would show so that when people looked at it they would suck in their breath and say through clenched teeth, "Oh, gosh. That needs attention." It had to be something that would make me an invalid for a while so they would feel sorry for me the way they felt sorry for Arlene. She had always gotten more than her share of the limelight, but when her mother delivered her to school in a wheelchair with a bright white cast on her foot, you would have thought Arlene was a celebrity. She got more attention than anyone should get in a lifetime. It made me sick.

"Arlene — what happened?"

"Arlene, can I sign your cast?"

"Arlene, lean on me and I'll help you hobble to class." (That offer was made by the new boy at school who I'd hoped to marry some day.)

I hated Arlene. I'd hated her since she stole the limelight by bringing that ugly pewter compact to show and tell when we were in the first grade. Now she had a new bike, a cast, and the boy I loved. She probably got out of chores for six weeks because of her injury, too. I knew that if I had to wear a cast, Mom would do the same. She would stay home from work to take care of me, which meant that she would keep my brother and sister in line instead of expecting me to do it. Bob and Patty wouldn't dare sass Mom the way they sassed me.

But breaking a bone on purpose was not that easy. Even though I wanted a cast more than I wanted a bike (and I really wanted a bike), it looked like I wouldn't get either of them. Maybe, just maybe . . . if I was real nice to Arlene, she'd let me borrow hers since she couldn't ride with a cast on her leg. I might even fall off while learning and break a bone by accident.

Christmas on 32nd Street

Compared to those of other families, our Christmas was usually nothing to brag about. But there was always something under the tree for each person even if we'd made it ourselves. The best gifts I ever gave to my brother Bob and sister Patty were rolled-up notes tied with a ribbon. They were homemade gift certificates that said *20 minutes of free back tickles, no strings attached.* That was a very practical and appreciated gift. And it didn't cost a penny. I liked having my back tickled, too, so I wished someone had thought of that present for me.

All our gifts were practical, with no frills. Luxuries were called extras, and my family never bought extras. I tried not to hope for them, but I was secretly dying to own something extra. I turned down many corners of the pages in the big "wish book." The *Sears Roebuck* catalog was my favorite publication of all time. I could have given a great book report about that catalogue. All those pictures! I loved the lacy sweaters that girls my age wore on those pages. Dad said, "A kid could freeze to death in a sweater like that." I would have done dishes by myself for a month if I could have owned a lacy sweater, snow boots with fur around the cuffs, or a pair of pink angora socks.

Mom and Dad did the best they could for us; unfortunately, their wages did not allow for the fancy winter boots or silly rabbit hair socks that Dad said no one needed. In order to make his point, he said, "A poor girl wearing angora anklets shows bad taste." I have no idea where my dad got such notions. I think he made up a lot of stuff.

Thank God for Auntie Marge, our fairy godmother. She believed in owning all the unnecessary stuff a person could afford. Since we couldn't afford much, she was bound to show up near the holiday to make sure we got some of the things we wanted. Our auntie called one year and said, "Bassle, at Christmas all kids need to have extras. I'm coming to pick them up."

For a lady who had no kids of her own, our auntie was very smart. Right on time the week before Christmas, I heard my favorite sound: Auntie Marge's car wheels crunching on our gravel driveway. She climbed out of her dark green Buick wearing her fake fur coat and a hat that she said was stylish (I was glad she'd told me because I would've never known). What she had in mind that day was taking us three kids to buy presents for our parents. She gave each of us some money to stick in our pockets, and we drove to Kresge's dime store on First Avenue and Third Street. Patty was so up in the air that she couldn't stop wiggling in the back seat and saying, "Ohboyohboyohboy!" I was excited, too, but Patty was so annoying that I felt like punching her.

Kresge's was the only place in town where a person could find anything decent for under a dollar. Whenever I got money as a gift, Kresge's was where I spent it. On that visit, I bought lavender scented talcum powder for Mom and a hanky for Dad. Using multicolored thread, I sewed the letters D-A-D in the corner. I also wrote a note that said *Do not blow your nose on the embroidered letters. It will make your nose itchy and the letters full of snot.*

On Christmas Eve, after we three kids fell asleep, Uncle Cullen gave Dad a ride to the nearest lot to pick out a little tree. They knew that most of the lots closed before supper and one of them always left a sign that read ANY TREE FREE. MERRY CHRISTMAS. When Dad and Uncle Cullen returned with our free tree, my parents decorated it so quietly that we never knew what was happening.

On Christmas morning, we woke to a freezing house and squealed with delight at the sight of our most important gift of all: the tree. That glorious sight had magically appeared while we slept. There were lights in every hue, wrinkled tinsel, and packages placed carefully beneath it. Best of all was the fragrance of the forest right in our own house. No rich kid could have been happier than I was that morning.

Mom started the coffee and Dad disappeared to the basement to crank up the furnace. It was a special day and we all deserved heat. We kids dragged our blankets to the living room and enjoyed the magical beauty of the Christmas tree, the smell of coffee brewing, and carols playing on the radio. Once we felt heat wafting through the vents, Christmas morning became all that we ever hoped it could be.

As the warmth seeped through the kitchen and the living room, we threw off the blankets and started stripping paper from packages that had our names on them. What a happy mess! We shared our gifts, helped smooth and fold the wrapping paper for next year, and then wore ourselves out playing our new games: Bingo, Old Maid, and Authors. The pictures of the authors were interesting, and I was entranced by the fancy-sounding names like Robert Louis Stevenson and Henry Wadsworth Longfellow. When I asked, "Do you have the card *Little Women* by Louisa May Alcott?" I felt like a big shot.

While the family was occupied with other things, I stretched out on the floor under the tree, lying face up with my head close to the trunk and my nose nudging the lower branches. I closed my eyes and inhaled the perfume of pine. It smelled so good I could taste it. Then I gazed straight up the center through all the shiny stuff at my warped reflection in colored balls. I became something else: one of the branches, an ornament, a bug in a forest, a girl who believed in fairies. Music in the air, snow in the garden, and lying under our tree that had decorated itself transported me to my favorite place, the land of make-believe.

Mom said that I was too old for fantasy, so I never let her know what I was really doing with half my body sticking out from under pine branches. I was on the lookout for a Christmas elf.

Dying for a Dog

MY FATHER WAS STUBBORN. IF WE QUESTIONED HIS DECISIONS, HE might give a reason; he might not. He usually said, "That's just the way it is." But he wasn't always the tough guy he tried to be. Sometimes we three kids sensed that we could change his mind.

When Bob, Patty, and I were old enough to take care of a dog, Dad kept holding out no matter how nicely we asked. "We can't afford to feed any mutts," he said.

"I'll give it our table scraps," Patty offered.

"Nope, pets are nothin' but trouble."

Bob gave it a try. "We'll take care of it ourselves."

Dad wouldn't budge. "A male dog is gonna hump everything that doesn't move, and a female is gonna have pups we can't get rid of."

"I think somebody in town will fix a dog for free," I suggested.

Dad screwed up his nose in disgust. "That ain't natural. It makes 'em turn sluggish and fat, and then they ain't no use to nobody."

Because of Dad, ours was the only family in the large Peal clan that didn't own a dog. We had to be content with loving the nine dogs that belonged to our various aunts and uncles. One of those dogs was a half-breed collie that mated with another half-breed collie. Even with all that mixed blood, her pups looked like the real thing. Aunt Lora adopted the prettiest one and named her Tumpy. But she didn't get to choose Tumpy's boyfriend. Behind Aunt Lora's back, Tumpy hooked up with a tramp with no address. She had no idea what the pups would be like until after they were born. She was frantic. "Butch, the father is a bum. The little guys will be dimwitted and I'll have to put them to sleep."

"Oh for cryin' out loud, Lora. Dogs is dogs. In fact, I'll take one of 'em."

What? Out of nowhere, Dad ordered a dog like it was from a catalog? I thought I was dreaming, but I wasn't. He had finally changed his mind about our family owning one.

When birthing time was near, Tumpy started tearing newspapers with her teeth to make a nest. Aunt Lora helped her out and made a cozy bed out of old blankets in a private corner. She said that we three kids could watch the babies being born, but she warned us to stay quiet. My sister, who questioned everything, asked why.

"We don't want Tumpy getting nervous," our aunt explained.

When Patty asked why Tumpy would be nervous, Dad said, "That's just the way it is."

Patty had more questions. "Will the puppies come out of her mouth?"

"No," replied Aunt Lora.

"Where will they come out then?" I swear that sometimes I wanted to smack my little sister for asking embarrassing questions.

Aunt Lora acted like she didn't know what to say. It made me wonder if Grandmother Peal had ever told her where babies come from. Was I the only kid in the family who knew?

Finally, Aunt Lora said, "Just watch and you'll see where they come out."

When the time came, Tumpy grunted hard until a wet, dark bundle slid into view. Patty sat up straight and said, "She's doing a poop." Bob's hand flew to his mouth as he tried not to laugh. Then Tumpy started biting the shiny skin that covered the little bundle. Patty's voice went up a notch. "She's eating it!" My brother was having trouble holding back giggles.

"Don't worry," Aunt Lora told my sister. "New babies always come out in a little bag of skin and the mother takes it off. Tumpy is not eating her puppy."

We settled down to watch four more bundles slither into the world. Once Tumpy had licked her babies clean and they had dried off, we could see that they were small.

"Good," our father said. "I don't want a big dog. Big dogs mean big messes." Then he added, "I don't want no leg-humper either." So we chose a girl pup. I named her Curly because her tail coiled like a corkscrew. Curly came from all kinds of dogs. Dad had something to say about that, too. "No highbrow pets for me. Mutts are the best kind."

Curly wasn't a bit dim-witted, and she became a treasured member of our family. She was smart and lovable. Her one terrible habit was chasing anything that moved fast, like bicycles, cats, and birds. She would chase anything that was running. She even tried to bite the wheels of passing cars. More than once, she almost caused a wreck when a driver swerved to miss her. Once, a man skidded to a stop and backed up so fast I thought he wanted to run over us because he was mad at our dog. He shook his fist in the air, yelling, "I'm going to hit that damn dog if you don't keep it off the street!" I didn't know what to say, and he finally screeched away.

When I told Dad what had happened, he shook his head and said to Mom, "Girl, I don't know what in the Sam Hill we're gonna do about Curly."

Mom kept stirring the fried potatoes and replied, "Well, I don't know either."

I was sure that someday Curly's teeth were going to get stuck in a tire and she would get whirled to death under the wheels. One summer afternoon it actually happened. Our parents were at work and a neighbor named Millie called.

"Are you the family who owns the little dog that chases cars?"

"Yes," I said, "Her name is Curly."

"Oh, yes . . . Curly. Well . . . I'm awfully sorry to tell you this, dear, but Curly must have been hit by a car."

"Did she break her leg or something?"

"No, honey. I'm pretty sure that she's dead."

All of a sudden I couldn't talk right. My voice was shaky, but I managed to say, "Thank you, ma'am. I'll tell my dad when he gets home."

Thank goodness my sister wasn't a brat that day because I was so shocked I couldn't think straight. I wanted to cry, but I couldn't. I didn't even tell

Bob and Patty that our beloved Curly was dead. I spent the whole afternoon coming up with an easy way to tell my family something that only I knew. Finally, I got an idea. I would draw the story of Curly's life like they did in comic strips. When Mom and Dad reached the end of the page, they would discover the awful truth, and I wouldn't have to say it out loud.

Drawing pictures all afternoon about Curly's life and death helped me not to cry. I drew a few frames showing how she was related to our large family of dogs and a frame that showed us picking her out of the litter because of her funny tail. Another frame showed her chasing cars, followed by a frame of us scolding her. The next picture was supposed to be of Curly being hit by a car.

Suddenly, I didn't know how to draw a car. I didn't know what a dog looked like when it got hit by a car. Did Curly fly through the air? Did she die at that moment or did she lie in the snow at the side of the road, whimpering for me to help her? If I drew what I imagined might have happened, it meant that I was killing her again. It meant that she was really dead. I could see her in my head. I didn't know what to do. I pressed my face into folded arms and sobbed, gripping my pencil like it was a murder weapon.

The kitchen door clicked open and in walked Mom and Dad.

I was a muddle of blurred vision and uncertain words. I tried to say, "Curly is dead — she got hit by a car!" But the words didn't come out right.

Mom must have understood because she made a sound like letting air out of a tire. She didn't know what to say. Dad's shoulders sagged and his eyes were shiny when he said, "I'll go bring her back home."

We dug a deep hole by the wire fence in the backyard and buried our little dog under the climbing tree that Mom cut switches from when she was mad at us. It took a long time since the ground was frozen. We kids found some good stones and marked Curly's grave with them. On the smoothest stone, Patty printed CURLY with a black crayon. Since we had turned our old chicken coop into a natural history museum, my sister put the Curly rock on display along with other interesting junk that we and other kids in the neighborhood felt were important. Bob labeled the display with a flap of a cardboard box. It read: *Headstone of our dog who chased cars.* Of course every kid on our block knew which dog that was.

A few weeks later, a skinny little girl cat started hanging around our back door. She mewed and carried on until we gave her some of Curly's leftover dog food. In a weak moment, Dad, who missed Curly as much as we did, added a saucer of milk. In an even weaker moment, he said we could keep her. We named her Kitty Gay after a cat Mom had when she was a little girl. Kitty Gay pooped under the basement steps all the time, which made our whole house smell like a cat box.

Dad said, "I don't know what in the Sam Hill I was thinkin' when I said we could keep this damn cat. I hate cats."

He and Mom removed the basement stairs and raked through the dirt underneath. They sprinkled vinegar around the area, which made the house smell like pickles instead of poop. As soon as the steps were back in place, they found another home for Kitty Gay.

For a long time our family was without a pet. To satisfy our need for a creature of some kind, we made a homemade ant farm in a Mason jar. When we first scooped the ants out of the yard and put them into the jar of sand, they were hysterical. They tore around in sudden, jerky movements, bumping into each other as though they were saying, "Excuse me, excuse me!" while they looked for something familiar to call their own.

I hunched over the ants in the Mason jar for an hour watching them get used to their new place. Their confusion reminded me of how often we used to move and how upsetting it was. When no one was around, I spoke to the ants in a real soft voice and said, "I know how it is, but you'll get used to it real soon." I did it privately because I knew my family would think I was cuckoo talking to ants. But I think the ants actually heard me. It seemed they were having a meeting to let each other know that, like it or not, that glass jar was home. It made sense to me, and I really think that's what they were doing. I could see a routine starting to happen just as it did with our family each time we rearranged our lives.

Daily, we kids put teeny pinches of apple or finely crushed graham cracker crumbs into the jar. I had to supervise Patty because she was suffocating the ants with piles of crumbs, thinking she was being generous. In spite of that, the crumbs gradually disappeared from the surface and reappeared inside the tunnels. The ant farm was hypnotizing. Ants were sure easy to take care of. Even if they could chase cars, no one would care. And if the ants died, we wouldn't be sad.

One day while Patty was putting the lid back on the jar, she said, "I love our ants." Then I noticed several squashed bodies on her fingertips, and I actually felt bad. I supposed she loved them so much that she had tried to pet them. I went straight to my father, but this time not to tattle.

"Dad, our family needs something to pet."

He must have been thinking the same thing because he didn't brush me off this time. Instead, he said, "Yep, I agree. So whaddaya have in mind?"

Dad knew what I had in mind. He was dying for another dog as much as I was, so we agreed to start looking right away.

Part 4: *The War at Home*

WAR GARDENS

FOR VICTORY

GROW VITAMINS AT YOUR KITCHEN DOOR

War

Mom's thirty-second birthday was on Saturday, December 6, 1941. We never went hog wild over birthdays, but we did have a nice cake and a little family party. Damsy, Auntie Marge, and Uncle Al came, too. Although it was freezing cold outside, it was warm and inviting in our house. The afternoon was cheerful and, for a change, Dad was even courteous to Damsy. It was a miracle that eight people in my family were in good spirits at the same time. I was so filled with peace that I was nice to my sister all day long.

If Mom's birthday was a burst of sunshine and joy, the following day became the blackest I had ever known. All afternoon our parents talked in hushed tones on the telephone. I was used to sudden changes in Mom's moods, so I waited it out. I had no idea what was going on. *Are Mom and Dad having a quiet fight?* I wondered. *I guess we'll know if Mom gets her suitcase from under the bed.*

Finally, Dad pulled Bob, Patty, and me aside and said, "I need to tell you kids that a serious thing happened today."

Uh huh; here it comes, I thought.

"So tomorrow night we're all gonna sit down in the living room together . . . and listen to President Roosevelt talk on the radio."

What?

Bob asked, "How come we all have to listen?"

"Because it's important. Today a fleet of Japanese bombers attacked Pearl Harbor."

Eight-year-old Bob thought Pearl Harbor was a woman's name. "They bombed her? What did she do wrong?"

"Pearl Harbor is a United States naval base in Hawaii and the bombers sank our ships and killed a lot of the sailors. We might be going to war."

I was puzzled. "I thought we were already in a war."

"Not yet. Our country loaned ships and airplanes to other countries to help them out, and now we have to protect ourselves from Japan."

I was eleven and knew the news was probably more important than I realized, but I still didn't understand how it applied to us. I couldn't imagine that Japanese planes might actually drop bombs on 1615 32nd Street.

Two days after Mom's memorable birthday, our family and everyone else in the country gathered around radios to listen to President Roosevelt speak to the nation. We three kids sat cross-legged on the floor while Mom was swallowed up by the upholstered chair. Dad assumed his hunched-over radio listening position with his elbows on his legs while smoking a cigarette. Nobody had to tell us not to horse around during President Roosevelt's message. When Dad was that serious, we shut up.

Our parents always listened to the President's fireside chats, but that night his voice didn't rise and fall as usual. His words were heavy as though he was mad, though not yelling. Right off the bat he said that December 7th was "a day of infamy." I didn't understand what that meant, but it didn't sound good.

The things our president talked about were very clear to grownups, but not to us kids. When he said that a whole bunch of islands near the United States had been attacked, it started to worry me. I still didn't realize that President Roosevelt had declared war on Japan.

Our parents were so solemn that I felt nervous. Patty kept looking back and forth between Mom and Dad, and I knew that she sensed it, too. I could tell she wasn't sure about Mom's emotions. Mom might stay level-headed and calm, or she might not. That night she kept her head.

Over the next few days, people volunteered their homes so the air raid wardens could organize neighborhood meetings. They needed to explain the procedures for protecting ourselves from bombers. Mom and Dad said groups of volunteers were watching the skies at night from the rooftop of the Roosevelt Hotel and other tall buildings in our city. When Patty heard that, she said, "I'm scared!" I wasn't really frightened, but I could hardly believe it was happening.

Our warden said, "Folks, we'll soon be having blackouts and practice drills that will be announced by a factory whistle blowing after dark."

Everyone started talking at once, wanting to know what time, what day, and would the schedule be printed in the *Gazette.* The warden had a terrible time getting us to settle down and listen.

"So, people, when the factory whistle blows, that is your signal to turn off all your lights and cover the radio dial with a bath towel. If any light leaks outta your house, the warden for your block will spot it when he makes his rounds during a blackout."

During that serious explanation, Bob, Patty, and I were very quiet. We had no idea what to expect next. The warden spoke again. "Folks, let me tell ya that any light spotted from your house will result in a stiff fine no matter what financial problems you may have."

We barely had money for ourselves without paying a fine for accidentally pulling the towel off the lighted radio dial. So Mom and Dad were very strict about following the new rules.

During our first blackout drill, we kids huddled close and listened to our favorite scary programs: *Inner Sanctum* and *Lights Out.* Patty was edgy and whined pitifully. "Why do we hafta do all this stuff?"

Bob, the little general, explained. "Patty, if the Japs fly over Cedar Rapids looking for our house to bomb, they won't bomb us if they can't see us."

I'm not sure Patty understood, but hearing Bob's brave-boy explanation regarding blackout drill procedures made me more anxious than I wanted to be. Patty was so worried that she hid in the closet and wouldn't come out. My brother was being such a big shot that I rolled my eyes. I had a big-sister hunch he would soon be playing war.

It wasn't long before we saw newsreels at the Iowa Theater showing Pearl Harbor being bombed. The smoke boiling into the sky from the helpless ships in the harbor terrified me. Several days later, photographs of the destruction appeared in the *Cedar Rapids Gazette,* but the pictures in the paper didn't affect me as much as seeing the Movietone News. The deafening sounds and gruesome images on film were so shocking that I couldn't get them out of my head.

Whenever grownups congregated, they huddled in small groups, talked in hushed tones, and dabbed at their eyes with handkerchiefs. I was poor at geography and couldn't identify with Pearl Harbor as a real place even after my teacher had shown us the location on the pull-down map at school.

As the weeks and months passed, the reality of the war affected everyone. If we hadn't known where Pearl Harbor was before December 7, 1941, we soon found out.

From that point on, everything was about the war. There were war movies in abundance, ration stamps, savings stamps, war bonds, fund raisers, contests, the draft, and young men quitting college to enlist. They were so eager to defend our country that they couldn't wait for their draft numbers to come up.

A blue star in the window of someone's home meant that a boy from that house was a soldier. A gold star or a flag at half mast meant that a boy had died in battle. Mom could hardly stand to see any stars in windows and purposely didn't count them. But we kids did.

Patriotism was like oxygen that kept us alive. People of all ages helped the war effort by cutting both ends out of tin cans and stomping the cans flat for recycling. We all collected empty toothpaste tubes, which were made of metal, and saved bacon fat, newspapers, and rubber.

So much was rationed that we had to change our living habits. Common items such as butter, coffee, sugar, rubber tires, silk hose, and any item made of metal became precious. Buying a new washing machine was out of the question. Saving stuff became a way of life.

We were asked to cut back on what we used, share what we had, or do without. My family was poor, so doing without had been a way of life for us long before the war started. Rationing was probably harder for the Duster boys up the street because they were not used to doing without. They had things we didn't have such as a tent to play in, several bikes to ride, and all kinds of games. They were always getting something new to play with and we helped break it in. We also helped them eat all sorts of goodies and drink an endless supply of root beer.

Was all that going to end?

Wartime in Winter

DAD WOKE UP SHIVERING AND SAID, "GEE WHILLIKERS, IT'S COLD in here." Then he looked out the window. "Criminitly, Girl. Look at this."

During the night, the wind had howled so loud that it was hard to sleep. When we looked out the window that morning, snow had turned everything white. It was blinding. Tree branches drooped like tired arms that couldn't hold snow up that high any longer. And Dad was right. The house was too cold for indoors. We dressed as fast as we could and put on jackets and scarves. Bob put on his hat and mittens and announced, "It's so cold in here that I'm freezing. I'm going outside to play Eskimo."

"Play Eskimo? That's stupid," said Patty.

I thought it was a good idea since snow had drifted to the bottom of the windows. Mom turned on the radio in time to hear that folks were unable to drive anywhere and school was closed until snowplows could clear the roads. We were stranded in our own house.

"Hot dog!" Patty yelled.

Dad wasn't sure that deep snow was a reason to celebrate. "Where's Bob?" he asked. I told him that Bob was playing Eskimo outside.

"Well, we better keep an eye on him in case he starts digging tunnels in the drifts. We don't want him freezing to death out there." I knew he wasn't joking because there was no twinkle in his eyes.

Our house had never been without some kind of heat, but wartime fuel rationing and a horrible winter had made it harder to stay comfortable. Dad broke the bad news that we wouldn't be able to turn up the heat to get cozy that winter.

"How come?" asked Patty.

"We'll turn it up barely enough to keep the pipes from freezing. But we're only allowed a certain amount of fuel and we've almost used it up for this month." My curious sister asked what would happen if the pipes froze. Dad said, "If they freeze, they'll crack open. And when they thaw out again, water will leak all over the basement floor. Of course, if the floor freezes, you kids can ice skate in the basement instead of playing store."

Patty clapped her hands with excitement. "Oh, let's do it!" She never knew when Dad was joking.

When Bob came back in the house, he said, "It's too cold outside to play Eskimo. It's warmer in here." He and I decided it was fun being trapped in our own house and having to wear our winter wraps indoors. Mom told us it would keep our body warmth from leaking out.

Patty said, "My warm stuff already leaked out in the bathroom."

"Not all of it, so keep your wraps on."

"But it's too hard to color with my mittens on."

"Then take 'em off," said Bob.

"Then my fingers turn blue."

Bob was fed up. "Then go back to bed, ya big baby."

Later in the day we were trying to stay warm under a blanket while listening to the radio. Patty touched the top and asked, "Why isn't this thing as cold as we are?" We had no idea. We touched the radio, too, in case she had some trick in her mind. It was warm and felt so good that we kept our hands in place while listening to *Jack Armstrong, All American Boy.*

When the program was over, Bob broke down and complained about being cold. Dad said, "You kids need to move around instead of hiding out under a blanket. Go play tag in the basement."

Then Mom said, "I know what'll help. I'll make some hot cocoa."

She added water to thin down the milk because it was almost gone. The grocery store was only half a block away, but we couldn't bear to leave the house. Even watered down, hot chocolate had never tasted that good. Patty was in heaven. "Ohhh, I love this," she said as she cradled the cup.

By afternoon our house finally thawed out and Mom said, "Okay. It's time to make a plan before the next snowstorm hits. First of all, you kids need a bath."

Dad dragged the tin tub out of basement storage and Mom put the boiler on the stove. One at a time, we kids stripped. Although Patty was always the first to climb into four inches of hot water, that didn't stop her from complaining. "My legs are warm, but now goose bumps are crawling up my arms." When Mom knelt on the rag rug and pulled water up and over Patty with a saucepan, my sister closed her eyes and said, "Oooooh, this feels so good." It seemed that hot cocoa and a hot bath were all it took to put our feisty sister in a good mood.

Mom rinsed each of us before we climbed out of the tub. We didn't use much soap because it was too hard to rinse off. Dad was last, scrubbing himself clean in slightly used water that was deeper and warmer.

When baths were over, Mom made an announcement. "The time has come to stitch you girls into your long johns."

"Why doesn't Bobby have to wear long underwear?" Patty asked.

"Bob already wears long pants and knee socks, and you girls wear dresses."

I hated long johns. Mom always bought them too big so there would be room for growing, but they were all worn out before we ever grew into them. They never did fit snug against our legs until our mother came up with a solution for baggy underwear. After Patty and I bathed, dried off, and climbed into our long johns, Mom folded the extra fabric over and stitched it in place right against our legs. It made me a nervous wreck because I could feel the side of the needle glide along my flesh. Sometimes she sewed our skin by accident.

Long johns were only the first layer of our winter clothing, and we left them on until we bathed a week later. The second layer was a pair of long, brown ribbed stockings. It was hard to keep them straight and smooth over our bulky underwear. When the stockings were as high on our legs as we could coax them, they were held there by garters pinned to the bottom edge of our underpants, which had to be worn on top of our long johns. The garters were pulled tight, which sometimes caused the safety pin to pop open.

When the long john ordeal was over, Dad said, "Girl, we hafta do somethin' drastic or we're gonna run outta fuel."

"Either that or we'll freeze solid," she said.

"Okay. Here's what we're gonna do. And we all have to help."

We all pitched in and dragged both beds into the living room, followed by the two dressers. Next, we pulled the living room furniture into the two empty bedrooms. With the entire house rearranged, we closed the bedroom doors and prepared to live only in the kitchen and living room. All that furniture moving meant that we hadn't sat down for over an hour. When we finished, Patty's cheeks were rosy. "How come I feel so hot?" she asked.

"That's what happens when you move around a lot," Dad explained.

For the rest of that winter, we lived in two rooms except when Mom threw us out for getting rowdy, saying, "This is the last time I'm telling you kids to play in the basement." Running around the basement warmed us up during the day and snuggling like three puppies in a bed kept us warm at night.

Bob and I looked at our new living arrangement as an adventure, pretending that we were on a camping trip in a really big tent. When ice formed on the inside of the windows, we lifted off the chunks and put them into our mouths so they could melt to nothing. It was as much fun as sucking on chunks of ice in the summer. We called our winter treats "inside icicles." If a layer of skin froze and tore free from our lip, it was to be expected. A salty-tasting, bloody lip was part of icicle joy.

Patty could not adjust to the discomfort and whined, "I hate this. When are we gonna be warm again back in our own room?" Since nobody knew when that would be, we let her complain. She hadn't discovered yet that pretending made hard times a lot easier.

One morning nothing came out of the faucet and Dad said, "Dang! The pipes froze up."

He grabbed the blowtorch that was kept handy for that emergency. Then he ran the flame up and down the pipes in the basement until the cracked places where the metal had burst open started to leak. Next, he shut off the main valve and replaced the damaged sections.

Mom melted snow for the coffee pot and heated more in a pan so we could wash our faces. Washing up was so much work that it was easier to stay dirty. Anyway, in the winter we couldn't tell the difference between clean and dirty. Being cold made everything feel the same.

After the pipes were fixed, my parents left the kitchen faucets barely on so they would drip all the time. "Why are you doing that, Dad?" I asked.

"Water doesn't freeze as fast when it's moving as it does when it's sitting still. That's why I tell you kids to keep moving when you're outdoors and even in the house. You're mostly water, ya know."

"No, I didn't know that."

"Well, ya do now. If you don't keep moving, you'll freeze up just like these pipes."

That was a scary thing to hear.

Eating Well in Tough Times

DURING THE WAR, EVERYTHING WAS HARD TO COME BY: FUEL, MONey, clothing. For most people, food was scarce, too. Our family was used to making do, so we were better off than most. When money was tight, we came up with new food treats. Sandwiches made from catsup on Wonder Bread tasted pretty good. And inexpensive combinations such as eggs scrambled with calf brains had been family favorites even before the war.

I carried my lunch to school in a white tin tub with a wire handle and a label that read: *Fresh Calf Brains*. When Clarence Hickey said that reading it made him want to throw up, I said, "That's simple. Don't read it."

Liver was free for people who owned a cat. We didn't have a cat, but we pretended that we did. "Well, how nice," we'd say. "What cat doesn't love liver? I'd better take some as long as you're giving it away." Whenever Dad felt flush with money, he bought a pound of bacon. So liver, bacon, and onions were soon added to my list of favorite meals during hard times.

Real butter was in short supply, but you could buy a new substitute called oleomargarine. It came packaged as a white, lardy chunk with a little envelope of orange powder. Deciding who would mash it together with bare hands in a bowl always turned into an arguing match.

"It's my turn to mix the margarine," Patty said.

"Uh uh," Bob argued. "You did it last time because I was sick in bed."

"So? That means you missed your turn."

Mom usually had to settle those squabbles, and she seldom had much patience. I'm surprised that we kids didn't end up on the obituary page of the *Cedar Rapids Gazette*.

We didn't need oleomargarine for cornbread because Mom cooked it with bacon grease and sprinkled crisp bacon crumbs on top. Instead of cornflakes, we ate popped corn with milk and honey for breakfast or mixed margarine and syrup to make a creamy spread for pancakes. If we were out of grits, we'd sometimes eat hot oatmeal with margarine and salt and pepper for dinner.

Since sugar was a luxury during the war, we stopped baking cookies. I really missed that because I had just learned how to bake. My favorite part was measuring everything out ahead of time. I had my own apron, which meant I was a real cook. I loved rolling out balls of peanut butter cookie dough and then pressing grooves into them with a fork dipped in sugar. Sometimes I pressed them flat with the bottom of a drinking glass. I could hardly wait 'til the war was over so I could start baking again.

But we still had our share of goodies. Graham crackers spread with margarine became our new cookies. And clean, virgin snow mixed with a little bit of precious powdered sugar tasted as good as ice cream. Best of all was

Mom's personal invention. We thought she could've won a recipe contest with this concoction:

> *Recipe for Fake Strawberry Sundaes by Waneta Peal*
> *Powdered sugar, whatever amount you can afford*
> *1 cup of home-canned tomatoes cut into chunks, no juice*
> *Honey to dribble over everything*
> *About two quarts of clean, fresh snow*
> *Put in bowls and serve with a spoon. Enjoy and be grateful!*

With good things like that to eat, who could complain?

Black Market Grandmother

DAMSY ROARED INTO OUR GRAVEL DRIVEWAY SO FAST THAT I thought she wasn't going to stop. At the last minute, she slammed on her brakes so she wouldn't hit the fence. When she was mad, my grandmother behaved like Mom, and that sounded like mad driving. I stayed out of her way when she came into the kitchen because she was carrying on something awful.

"Waneta, I am so spittin' mad that I want to break something!"

"Have a cup of coffee and calm down," Mom said.

"Coffee? Those government people are probably drinkin' mine right now!"

What on earth was she talking about? I stayed out of sight, but I was dying for her to leave so I could ask Mom what had happened. Finally, my grandmother used up all of her steam and roared back down our driveway and off into the wild blue yonder. I came out of hiding and asked, "Mom, what's wrong with Damsy?"

"She had to pay a big fine."

"For reckless driving?"

"No, for hoarding coffee."

"How much did she have to pay?"

"A hundred dollars."

"Oh, my gosh."

We all knew that during the war we were supposed to manage our supplies carefully, but my grandmother was afraid of running out.

"Coffee is rationed, isn't it?" I asked.

"That's the point."

"So how did she get it?"

"She bought more than her share by illegal means."

"What does that mean?"

"She acquired it through the black market."

By that time Patty was listening. "I've heard of that place," she said. "A lot of folks shop there. Mama, is it only for Negroes?"

We kids didn't know very much about "coloreds" since we saw them only in movies. We'd seen a sign on a restaurant in our town that read: *White Trade Only*. I asked Dad what it meant and he said, "It means that Negroes can't eat in there." That didn't seem fair.

"Well, then, where are they supposed to eat?"

"In a restaurant that doesn't have that sign."

I'd never understood why the sign was up in the first place, but all of a sudden it made perfect sense to me. I wanted to sound smart, so I said, "Patty, if Negroes paint their grocery store black, then they don't need to put up a sign that says Colored Trade Only. White folks will understand."

Mom looked at us as though she had raised a couple of idiots. "No, no, no. That is not what the black market means." Then she explained it to us.

We found out that the black market wasn't even a building. It was law-breakers who knew how to obtain things that were rationed such as silk stockings, rubber tires, sugar, and coffee. Very secretly, they sold rationed things for a huge amount of money to selfish citizens who wanted more than their share.

Patty asked, "How do they find stuff if it's already rationed?"

Mom said, "Black 'marketeers' are the same as racketeers. They dig up rationed goods in all kinds of crooked ways and usually by stealing. It's against the law to shop with them."

So that's why my grandmother got in trouble with the government. I was still full of questions. "How did they know that she was hoarding?"

Mom knew it all. "A notary public client of hers was in the kitchen when Damsy was grinding coffee beans."

"Oh, yeah, that cranking thing she holds between her knees," Patty said.

"Yes, that thing. When she opened the cupboard to put her grinder away, the client saw all those packages stashed behind the oatmeal box, and she tattled."

I felt ashamed, not of my grandmother, but because I was a tattletale myself. I wondered if I could turn in someone's grandmother.

Mom went on. "She had to give up her stash and either go to jail for breaking the law or pay a stiff fine. She paid the fine."

Patty said, "Poor Damsy."

I was pretty sure it wouldn't be long before "poor Damsy" forgot about the fine and started hoarding again. She would just find a better hiding place.

Recycling

IT TOOK A WHILE BEFORE BOB, PATTY, AND I BECAME REAL HOME front soldiers. At first we did everything that was asked of us because we were supposed to. But when our school had a competition between the grades to see who could bring in the most recycling material, all of a sudden we really cared about trash. The class that won the competition would earn a field trip to the best ice cream place in town, the Dutch Mill Dairy Store. We three kids were ready to do our part.

"After we dump this corn in a pan, I get to flatten the can," Patty said as we helped Mom fix dinner.

Bob said, "No, sir. You've got two in your sack and I don't have any."

Every time we used the can opener, we went through the same thing.

Mom had showed us how to get the tin ready for the collection center by first rinsing it out really well. Then we removed the top and bottom of each container before taking it to the basement floor and stomping it flat. It was not easy, and while stomping that hard was a shock to the bottom of my foot, it was also kind of thrilling.

Keeping track of whose turn it was to take what to the collection center meant counting the number of items in each of our sacks. Patty didn't like fighting for every little piece of junk, and she was determined to do better than Bob or me. We didn't know it at the time, but our sister had come up with a plan to go way beyond the call of duty and help win the war all by herself. She went to the neighbors whose kids were all grown up and explained that she was trying to help her class win a recycling contest. They loaded her down with donated cans. She hid her treasures in private places like a crow hides shiny treasures in the holes of trees.

Bob and I argued about who got to take the empty toothpaste tube and the jar of bacon grease to class. We didn't even notice that Patty had stopped fighting for her turn. When we took our donations to school each day, Patty did the same, but she had very few items. Or so it seemed. She must have been hiding the extras in her lunch sack.

Once we'd turned in our collectables, we had no idea what happened to them. Our room mothers took boxes of precious junk to a collection center each week. I heard that someone had the job of separating toothpaste tubes from tires. From then on, what happened to everything was a mystery to me.

"Why do they want all this stuff?" I asked.

Dad loved answering questions like that. "Bacon fat is used to make glycerin for bombs."

"Really?"

"Yep, and toothpaste tubes are made of metal."

"Really?"

"Yep, and metal scraps of any kind are melted to make tanks and planes."

"Dad, it's hard to believe that tanks could be made out of toothpaste tubes."

"And old rubber tires are melted down to make new tires for jeeps, tanks, and what have you."

Whenever Dad said "what have you," it meant he was winding down. I guess whatever happened to the stuff that was collected must have been a mystery to him, too.

"The cloth that people recycle is used to make . . . all kinds of things."

Dad said "all kinds of things" when he didn't know the answer.

When the competition was over at the end of the semester, who would've ever dreamed that the little kids in first grade — Patty's class! — would beat us? And who would ever have imagined that our sister would earn a shiny blue ribbon for turning in the most cans? My family was in shock. When the principal asked how she got so many, she gave away her secret and then the whole school found out about it. She was practically famous, and she wouldn't let us forget it. I was so caught off guard that I didn't think to accuse her of pulling something fishy. She was so proud. Mom and Dad were proud. And after Bob and I pulled out of our shock, we were proud of her, too. She had been the runt for too long, and she deserved all that glory.

Patty's amazing accomplishment turned her into a pleasant little sister for a few weeks. But she must have missed her old bratty self because it didn't take long before Bob and I wanted to smack her every time we turned around. It was great while it lasted.

Rations and Recipes

DAD HAD REACHED THE BREAKING POINT. "JUMPIN' JEHOSAPHAT! IT might be easier to give up food and clothes altogether than to figure out this mess."

Every month, Dad was annoyed with how much time it took to figure out how to use the ration points assigned to our family. Sometimes I helped out by writing down the numbers he dictated. When he was mixed up, so was I. Then we had to start over.

I was feeling kind of sorry for myself when I said, "This is hard to learn."

Mom wasted no time feeling sorry for anybody. "That's fine and dandy, but we have no choice. What I want to hear as soon as possible is how many times we can buy meat next week. So start adding again."

We had to use meat rations carefully or we might use them up before the end of the month. Mom was pretty good at spreading out our allotment. "The points must come out even. I want nothing wasted. If we don't use them, we lose them."

The ration system was important, but it was a math test that never ended. Whenever we ran out of red meat coupons, we ate beans or cheese. We all tried very hard not to gripe in public because we knew our soldiers had even fewer things than we had. And some families received fewer points than ours. That confused me, so I asked the person in charge of our rationing.

"Mom, how come we get more points than the Duster family?"

Without looking up from her shopping list, she said, "We have more children. Now find that sugar card and let's try to bake something this month."

Luckily, we still had sugar points left. After I counted our coupons, I said, "We have a lot of blue coupons left, but only a couple of red ones."

"I knew I should have been more careful. Well, we'll be eating macaroni and cheese tonight."

"Oh, no. Not again. I'm getting tired of macaroni and cheese."

"Can't be helped. It takes the place of meat."

We had discovered that two boxes of Kraft Macaroni and Cheese used only one blue ration coupon. That was such a good deal that our family alone probably made the Kraft company rich.

Each coupon had an expiration date, and was as valuable as cash. They came in different colors for different items. Red coupons were only for butter, cooking oil, and meat. Blue coupons were used for practically everything else, such as dried beans, baby food, canned things, bottled items, frozen foods, and catsup. Everything my family needed was rationed.

A package came in the mail for Mom one day and she could hardly wait to open it.

"Girl, what the heck did you buy now?" Dad asked. "You know we can't afford extras."

"Butch, this is not an extra. Look at this." Mom unwrapped the package and held up the newest edition of the *Good Housekeeping Cookbook*.

"What didja do that for, Girl? You already own a cookbook."

"Not like this one. It includes a special recipe section for rationed foods to help them go farther." My mother won that argument.

After macaroni and cheese, cottage cheese became our other meat. Mom made a mixture that everyone loved. She dumped the cottage cheese in a bowl and added chopped green onions, hunks of cut-up tomatoes, chopped sweet green peppers, salt, and pepper. We called it "cottage salad." It was delectable.

Dad came up with a vegetable version of a bacon, lettuce, and tomato sandwich that was as yummy as our other food creations. He spread either mayonnaise or oleomargarine on slices of doughy white Wonder Bread, added a really thick pile of leaf lettuce from the garden, thinly sliced Bermuda onions or cucumbers, and a little bit of salt and pepper.

Our big onions were so sweet that Dad sprinkled salt on top and ate them from his hand. He said they were as good as apples. We ate better than most folks because we had such good vegetables from our garden. They were preserved in Mason jars and stored on shelves in our basement food room.

Mom created inspired soups out of whatever was in the refrigerator and cupboard. We called those concoctions "refrigerator soup." Our mother loved hearing praise for her made-up recipes. Raising a finger in the air to make a point, she often said, "The trick is not putting all our rations in one pot."

Doing Without

RATIONING WAS SO STRICT THAT IT SOMETIMES INTIMIDATED ME. Most of the time, I had no idea what the heck was going on. Grownups seemed to understand it, but I still had a lot to learn about conserving our resources.

One day I decided to go with Dad to buy groceries at the A & P Market because it was fun being with him alone. Once inside, something looked strange. "Dad, are they closing this store?"

"I don't think so. Where did ya' get that notion?"

"There's not much stuff on these shelves."

Dad did all the shopping so he was probably used to a partially-stocked grocery store. He looked around and said, "Oh, yeah . . . it's been this way for a long time."

"How come?"

"Practically everything we used to buy is now hard to come by."

"Why?"

"Things that were always at our fingertips are going to the soldiers and our allies."

"To our alleys?"

"No, allies. Our friends — the countries helping us win this war."

"Oh."

Even though I was eleven years old, the effects of war were hard to understand. Most of the time, I didn't even try. I took part in the things we were supposed to do because everyone else did.

"Dad, is every single thing hard to find now?"

"Probably, because we're sharing our food with other people. And any factory that made things for people now has to make things for the war."

"What kinda things, Dad?"

"Well, the Golden Bear Sportswear Company that made leather jackets now makes jackets for pilots. There's probably a hat and glove factory somewhere that now makes helmets and gloves for pilots."

"And uniforms, too?"

"Yep. Uniforms, shoes, underwear, you name it."

"You mean . . . there's not enough to go around?"

"You might say that. Or you might say there's not enough to fill up store shelves."

During wartime, if someone wanted a new car (which we never had in our lives), they had to put their name on a long waiting list even if they were rich. Clarence, who had made fun of Bob's overalls, complained something awful. "My dad has to wait six whole months to replace our old 1936 Chevy."

I wanted to say, "You poor thing." But he was a smart kid and would've known I didn't mean it. So I kept that comment to myself, but I was sure thinking it.

It was impossible to buy a new refrigerator. If a refrigerator was on the blink, the owners were lucky to find someone to fix it. If they had a well, they could manage without a refrigerator. We'd had a well when I was younger. Dad put milk, butter, and cottage cheese in a wooden box and lowered it into the well with a pulley. It used to scare me looking way down there. But that deep hole was nice and cool because it was close to the water. When we brought up the box, we sometimes found a frog or a baby snake cozied up against the cottage cheese. If a person wasn't lucky enough to have his own well, an old-fashioned ice box worked fine, except then you had to buy blocks of ice. So not having a refrigerator during the war was bad luck.

Keeping things cold wasn't the only challenge during the war. When Mom's last pair of silk stockings wore out, she figured she'd have to do without those, too, since silk was being used to make parachutes. Then she came home with a product called Liquid Hosiery.

The bottle of creamy brown lotion resembled a thick milkshake. I was as excited as Mom because Liquid Hosiery was an art project for legs. It was brand new on the market, and my mother was the first person in our neighborhood to try it. She read the directions out loud:

Legs must be clean, dry, and free of hair.

Pour small amount of contents into your palm.

Rub palms together to spread evenly onto both hands.

Spread mixture onto each leg, working quickly before liquid dries.

It was not a bit easy to apply that stuff evenly because it dried in record time. It took a lot of practice. At first her fake silk stockings ended up with streaks resembling runs and there was no seam down the back. Mom had a solution for that. "It's simple, Betty. You can draw a seam, and this leg makeup will fool everyone." She found her eyebrow pencil and sharpened it.

I couldn't wait to draw on skin, as Uncle Connie had predicted I'd do someday. I'd expected to make money drawing tattoos on arms, but my uncle would have been proud of the seams that I drew on the back of Mom's legs. It looked so real that I considered renting myself out to the neighborhood women who hadn't yet tried Liquid Hosiery. Or Mom and I could offer a class together since she was better at smoothing it on without streaking. Seam drawing was my specialty. But there was a hitch. When Mom was caught in the rain while wearing her unusual stockings, she had the runniest runs I'd ever seen in my life.

For years, Mom had taken her silk hosiery for granted. She usually adapted to going without, but the messy substitute bothered her a lot. "There's gotta be a better way to have your legs look good when you dress up."

Since nylons hadn't been invented yet, dressing up properly was one more thing Mom had to do without.

War Bonds and Patriots

MY PARENTS WEREN'T THE ONLY ONES WHO WERE WORRYING ABOUT money. Poor families everywhere shared the same fears. Then our president made a radio announcement. "We need every citizen to help pay for the war."

Dad was stunned. "For crying out loud. With what?"

His reaction had me so worried that I wrote a note to the president:

> *Dear President Roosevelt,*
>
> *Please excuse my dad from donating money to help our country. We hardly have enough for ourselves. I am sorry.*
>
> *Yours truly,*
>
> *Betty Peal*

I wanted to send it, but I didn't.

Finally, somebody thought of a good plan where all grownups and kids, rich and poor, could do their part by spending only ten cents at a time. Dad learned all about the Savings Stamps program and decided that we should take part.

He gathered Bob, Patty, Mom, and me around the kitchen table and said, "Okay, here's the way it works. Pay attention, Patty. You kids can pick up all this stuff at Tom Combs' grocery store. First, you use a little book to hold the stamps, which cost ten cents each."

That got Patty's attention. "You mean we lick 'em and stick 'em in the book?"

"That's right."

"Oh, yippee! That's gonna be fun."

"Hold your horses. I'm not through here."

Bob and I pretended to zip our lips shut, but not Patty. She gestured dramatically toward the small scar on her mouth and said, "Betty zipped my lip when I was a baby."

"Well, she didn't zip it tight enough," Bob said, pretending to close a giant zipper over her mouth, which never seemed to rest when someone else was talking.

Dad told us the booklets would each hold 187 stamps. "When one of those books is filled up, it's the same thing as saving $18.70. That's when you can trade it in for an actual savings bond."

Patty interrupted again. "Well, what's a savings bond anyway?"

"If we keep the savings bond in a safe place for ten years, we can trade it in for twenty-five dollars in cash."

I was not good at math, so once Dad started running figures by us, I lost track of what made all of that worth doing. Ten cents and 187 stamps and 10 years and 25 dollars were too many things to keep track of. He didn't realize that he'd lost me as soon as I heard numbers. I didn't want to hurt his feelings, so I kept my face looking real interested. My expression said it sounded like a good deal.

Bob had no problem keeping track. "Gosh, it's going to take a long time to fill that little book."

"That's true, but it's how you kids can become home front soldiers and learn about patriotism."

"What's patriotism?" Patty had been quiet way too long and couldn't hold it in any longer.

"Patriotism means being loyal and loving your country."

I'm patriotic, Dad, because I really love it here in the country," Patty said.

Bob rolled his eyes and pretended to choke himself.

I still couldn't grasp the purpose of bonds. "Mom, what kinds of things do they have to buy for a war?"

"Ask your father. He can explain that part better than I can."

So Dad jumped in again. "In order to protect us from any more attacks, we have to build ships, airplanes, guns, and ammunition. That takes a lot of money, so they need everybody's help. Even little kids."

"How can we help pay for an airplane? We can't even afford a car."

"Betty, they don't expect kids to pay for a whole airplane, just a piece of it."

"How are they gonna know which piece we want to pay for?" Bob asked.

We were asking way more questions than Dad had expected. "We can't choose anything. We buy stamps, fill up a book, and exchange it for a bond. A bond is the same thing as loaning the government money. When they have enough to get started, they'll decide what to build first."

"Okay." Bob seemed to get the picture. And I would do my part even if I still didn't understand how it would help.

To make investing in our defense more appealing, a bunch of movie stars and baseball players made personal appearances in our town. Their pictures were in the paper, their names were in the headlines, and they were on station WMT. There was even a parade downtown where the movie stars rode in convertibles, sitting on the backs of the seats so everyone could see them. They waved to us as though we were old friends and they were saying, "Hi there. So good to see you again." It made us feel that they actually knew us. Then they sat around tables in a huge tent and sold patriotism in exchange for autographed pictures of themselves.

I saw movies every week, and I'd never seen any of those people in movies before. Whoever they were, they did a good job. People were willing to pay for a bond if they could see a movie star up close. It was a fun way for everyone on the home front to support our country.

Dad said, "I don't believe they've overlooked anyone in this effort to raise money. Every living soul is becoming a patriot."

At eleven years of age, I was up and down with my patriotism. Several times my savings stamp book almost reached the full stage before I cashed it in. I never did get to the war bond stage, but I sure had fun buying stamps, licking them, sticking them in place, and then cashing them in for something I wanted more than a bond. My stamp books were my piggy banks.

Millie's Daughter and the USO

MY LITTLE SISTER WAS BUSY CUTTING OUT GLAMOROUS CLOTHES for her Jane Arden paper dolls when she said, "Millie's daughter works at the USO every night."

"You mean Flora?"

"Yeah, Flora."

"How do you know that?" I asked.

"Her mother told me so. Betty, is that one of those outdoor movies you watch in your car?"

I knew a lot about the USO and, with pride, volunteered an answer. "Patty, it is not an outdoor movie. It's a place for soldiers to have fun when they're away from home."

"Why is it fun there?"

"For all kinds of reasons. They show movies sometimes and they have piles of free magazines and books that soldiers can take with them. And they always have a private place set up for them to call home or write letters."

My little sister wrinkled her nose because she didn't think any of that sounded fun.

"It might not be fun for you, Patty, but if you were a soldier it would be."

"Why?"

"Soldiers are lonesome for their families, so it reminds them of home."

Patty thought about it for a few seconds. "Do the soldiers eat cake and cookies with cold milk?"

"Sure they do. And free beer and hamburgers and French fries and desserts of all kinds."

"Do you think Flora has to do dishes and serve food at the USO?"

"Yeah, maybe. But they also have dances every night."

"I think that's what she does because Millie says her daughter dresses up fit to kill before she leaves the house. Betty, what does 'fit to kill' mean?"

"It means that she dresses up to knock 'em dead."

"Knock who dead?"

"Those soldiers."

Patty flapped her hands as if shooing away flies. "I don't understand any of this. What makes you so smart, anyway?"

"The movies. I've learned all about the war at the Iowa Theater."

I loved movies more than I loved ice cream and, according to Hollywood, the USO was a good place to go if you were a soldier. I had a whole different impression after I heard Mom and our neighbor talking over coffee.

Millie said, "Waneta, my daughter met a nice soldier who is on leave for a couple of months. Almost every night they're together at the USO."

"Well, that's real nice, Millie."

"Yeah, it was nice. They were getting along so well that they even discussed marriage."

"How exciting."

"But he's changed his mind."

"What? When?"

"Only last night."

"Good heavens . . . what happened?"

Our neighbor filled Mom in on every detail. Naturally, I listened.

It seems that once the good-looking young private knew Flora better, he decided she was not what he was looking for. He had a "come-to-Jesus" talk with her. He said, "I'm sure this is going to be a surprise."

The word "surprise" made Flora's heart pound. She wondered if an engagement ring would appear out of nowhere.

He went on. "You've done things here that I don't approve of."

"Wh-what things?" Millie's daughter was so stunned that she barely managed to get it out. Her soldier continued.

"Things like smoking a cigarette."

"I was experimenting."

He ignored her protest. "And you drink beer."

"I love beer."

"I don't. But the activity I especially do not approve of is dancing. You dance with men."

"It's the USO," she said. "That's what we do here. We're showing the soldiers a good time."

"Yes, and I was having a good time talking over coffee until you cussed."

"What did I say?"

"You said, 'Damn, this coffee is hot.'"

"Yes, but . . .."

"I thought you ladies were supposed to have coffee with us and talk nice."

"Yes, but ...."

"I'm sorry; this is just not going to work for me."

Flora was heartbroken and confused, but the "boyfriend" wasn't finished. "I want a girl who hasn't done any of those things."

While Flora pondered whether to laugh or cry, tears started pouring without permission. The almost-boyfriend offered his handkerchief and waited for her to stop. Finally, she dried her eyes, folded the damp cloth with care, and handed it back. She raised her arms to give him a farewell hug, which he allowed, but his arms stayed stuck to his sides and his shoulders barely touched hers. Flora told her mother it was the worst hug she'd had in her life.

After hearing that sad story, I was sure confused. It sounded as though what they did at the USO was not very nice. Later, I asked about it. "Mom, I thought the USO was supposed to be such a good place. That soldier talked about cigarettes, beer, and dancing as though they were sinful. Are they really bad?"

Mom snorted. "Good riddance to bad rubbish. Millie's daughter is lucky she didn't settle for that guy. He couldn't protect our country from an invasion of ants."

What I hadn't learned in the movies, I was learning at home in my own kitchen. "Mom, what do those letters stand for anyway?"

"USO stands for the United Service Organization. It's like a family. That's why they call it a soldier's home away from home."

Thank goodness. That's what I'd thought it was all along.

Letters from Soldiers

THERE WERE FOUR THEATERS DOWNTOWN THAT WE KIDS ATTENDED because we could walk to them: the Iowa, the State, the Paramount, and the Rialto. Every week I went to one of them to see a film. I liked to read, but I liked to watch movies even more. I didn't feel bad about reading only the comic section of the newspaper. And I didn't even feel bad about listening only to spooky radio shows and my favorite soap opera called *Portia Faces*

Life. I loved those things more than anything I knew. Most kids my age felt the same way.

However, our sixth grade English teacher felt that kids needed to learn how to read the daily *Cedar Rapids Gazette*. So she made a list on the blackboard of topics that had something to do with the war. We each signed our name next to our favorite topic so no other kid could choose it. I picked "Letters from Soldiers," mostly because I was very good at writing notes to my girlfriends. It was the perfect way to find out if they could play after school or if they were grounded. I presented my report to the class.

Letters from Overseas
by Elizabeth Peal
Grade 6 Room 11
I love the movies. Two of my favorite things at the movies are the cartoons and the Movietone News. Why? Because the cartoons make me laugh and the Movietone News shows pictures about the war. I can tell that war is messy because all the scenery they show looks pretty much bombed to pieces.

Last Monday in the Cedar Rapids Gazette on page 7 at the bottom right column, I read an article about letter-writing during the war. They are not ordinary letters like you would send to your grandma. And they aren't always about anything interesting. The soldier might be telling you about what he's doing overseas. Letter-writing during the war is about national security. If you don't know what national security means, it means the different ways they keep us safe and sound. I never did find out who "they" were, but I suppose it's whoever is in charge of that kind of stuff.

Two of the things that keep soldiers from being lonesome are getting letters from home and visiting the USO. Someone else in this class is reporting on the USO, so I'm telling only about the letters. My fifth grade English class wrote letters to soldiers overseas. Before we mailed them, our teacher checked our spelling and if it wasn't perfect, we had to write the letter over. She didn't want us to look like dummies. After all, it was an English class. And our penmanship was just as important as our spelling.

The soldiers who wrote back were very nice. Some of them never wrote back at all and we never knew why. We tried not to think about it in case it might be sad news. Any student who received a letter from his soldier was asked to read it to the whole class. Writing to soldiers overseas was so much fun that I wanted to have a pen pal outside of Iowa for the rest of my life.

The End

After my report had been written and graded, I found out a whole lot more about letters during the war from our neighbor, Millie. Her daughter met a new soldier at the USO who was from Texas. That guy wasn't as fussy as the first soldier about what a girlfriend should and shouldn't do. He wrote to Millie's daughter all the time, not caring that she danced with other soldiers and cussed and drank now and then. Millie showed us some of his letters. "Wait till you see this," she said. She opened the envelope and showed us a message with black marks all over it.

"Did his pen leak or something?" I asked.

"No, Betty. Those parts have been censored."

Mom knew what she was talking about, but I sure did not. I asked what "censored" meant.

Millie said, "It means that they don't want anyone to see parts of this message because it might give a clue as to where the soldier is located."

"What's wrong with that?"

"Where soldiers are stationed is supposed to be a big secret."

"Why?"

"Because the enemy could sneak up on them while they're asleep."

"I see." But I didn't, not really.

Then Millie took out another envelope and said, "Now, have a look at this."

It was limp and full of holes. It was hard to hold flat, and it was also very hard to read. I figured the openings must have been made by specially-trained government people who learned to use tiny scissors to cut small, neat holes. Their job was to review every single word of a soldier's private correspondence while hunting for censored words. If they found one, they cut it out.

"Trying to figure out these messages is like solving a crossword puzzle," Millie said. I gave it a try.

Hi, Sweet Cheeks,

We've been camped by the (cut out) (cut out) (cut out) and enjoy eating the local (cut out). The unusual fruits and vegetables here are out of this

world. You would love it here because of the (cut out) and the (cut out).
Bye for now. I miss you.
   Your boyfriend, Raymond, writing from (cut out).
   Millie said that some military men were so chatty that their messages
home were little pieces of air held together by strips of paper. People started
calling those funny messages "confetti letters."
   I still didn't understand why it was so important to keep the soldiers' loca-
tions a secret, so Mom tried to make it clear. "Betty, if an innocent-looking
grandma next door was actually a spy, she could look over someone's shoulder and pass the location of the troops on to the enemy."
   It seemed impossible to me that a grandma would have a clue how to reach
the enemy. Where did the enemy live? Did the enemy have an address or
a phone number?
   "Betty, you've heard the saying a slip of the lip can sink a ship?"
   "Oh, yeah. So what does that mean?"
   "It means that people could accidently pass on the location of our troops
and it would no longer be a secret."
   I imagined a young wife saying, "Aha! Now I know where my husband
is stationed. He's in the little town in Austria where we stayed on our hon-
eymoon because we always said the food there was out of this world." If
she was smart, she wouldn't go blabbing that around. She would keep it to
herself in case the grandma next door really was a spy.
   Since Damsy had already gotten fined for her black market purchases, I
sure did hope she wasn't thinking of being a spy next. If that happened, my
family would have to move out of state, and I was sick to death of moving
anywhere new.

Victory Gardens

MISS JENSEN PASSED OUT AN ANNOUNCEMENT AND SAID, "STUDENTS,
take this important message home to your parents. It's a way that all of you
can help in the war effort."
   On the way home, I read it myself: *Your child can receive citizenship credit*
at school for planting a Victory Garden. This is a patriotic endeavor that will
support our troops.

I couldn't wait to show Dad. He would love the garden idea. Even though we kids knew all about gardens, growing our own would be more fun. That night, Dad sat at the kitchen table with the paper in his hands. "Okay, let's see what this is all about." He unfolded the announcement and smoothed it out to read silently until he reached the good part. "Okay, here we go. *Number one: create a plan for your garden. Number two . . . .*"

Patty was ready to start that minute. "I'm going to grow carrots since I'm called a carrot top because of my red hair."

"Now hold your horses, kiddo, until I finish reading this here paper."

She folded her hands in her lap. "Okay, but when can we start?"

He ignored her and continued reading. *"Plant things your family likes to eat."*

"I like peanuts. Can I plant peanuts?"

Dad was getting nowhere. "Sure, why not."

"Oh, goodie goodie gander. I get to grow peanuts!"

Bob grew impatient and said, "Sit down and shut up so we can find out what we're supposed to be doing."

Patty folded her hands in her lap again and said, "Okay."

Dad read silently to make sure my little sister would stay quiet. Finally, he looked up and said, "Kids, we know all this stuff already. So let's decide where you want your gardens and we'll buy seeds later."

Patty was raring to go and couldn't wait to start digging. Dad eventually took us to the nursery where he let us buy whatever seeds we wanted. It was so exciting that we wanted everything. Patty decided to add radishes to her peanut garden. Bob chose tomatoes and leaf lettuce, and I selected gourds.

Mom's eyebrows shot up. "Gourds? Why in the world are you planting gourds?"

"I'm not sure, Mom. Maybe it's the way they look. And when they're all dried up, they make good rattles."

"Betty, we can't eat gourds," she said. Dad explained to Mom that he had allowed us kids to pick out any seeds we wanted.

My gourd vines eventually took over the whole space at the side of the house and then traveled over the fence to wrap around the telephone pole. It was a glorious vine that grew over everything. We would never win the war with that harvest, but we sure had fun.

Our Victory Gardens were eventually graded by an attractive young teacher who zipped around the school district on a bicycle every two weeks to see how our gardens were progressing. Bob, only nine, had a crush on her. She wore farmerettes, cute knee-length overalls for girls. My brother knocked himself out making his garden better than Patty's and mine so he could impress her.

When the cute grader walked down the rows with a clipboard in her hands, Patty asked, "What're you writing about?"

"I'm looking to see if you have any weeds and if your garden looks healthy. You Peal children have done very well. And your gardens are much larger than those of most children."

Bob was dying to join the conversation and asked, "How big are other kids' gardens?"

"Well, size doesn't matter," she said. "Seeds can grow in a window box or a flower pot."

Bob couldn't believe it. "You mean that some kids have a Victory Garden in a flower pot?"

"Sure. As long as they're growing food or something that helps the war effort, they earn credit."

I was pretty sure my gourds wouldn't earn us any extra points.

Even though our sister was initially beside herself with excitement about the Victory Gardens, she gradually fell behind in taking care of her small plot, declaring, "I hate weeding!"

Bob barked back at her. "Traitor!"

Patty didn't understand what that meant, but she could tell he was mad at her. The night before grading day, not wanting his little sister to look bad in front of the cute blonde teacher in fake farm clothes, Bob helped Patty pull out all her weeds. When they were finished, he discovered there was nothing left in the radish row. She had eaten them as they grew, dirt and all.

In spite of Patty's eating-instead-of-weeding habit, Bob kept her from getting demerits that would have spoiled the Peal children's record. On Patty's final radish report, the grader wrote, "Somewhere between seven and fifteen radishes were harvested, but the student says it might have been thirty."

Our garden grades appeared on our regular school report cards under the title "Citizenship Points." Mom and Dad were proud of us, I was proud of us, and my sister took it in her stride. And Bob? He missed the pretty blonde teacher.

Getting Back to Normal

ALTHOUGH WE KIDS EVENTUALLY STARTED DOING THINGS WE'D done before our country went to war with Japan, the war was always in the background of our daily lives. Sometimes it even made its way into our neighborhood games.

Kids in the Neighborhood

When we weren't going to the movies, we kept busy weeding our Victory Gardens and playing with the kids who lived on our street. The Duster family (pronounced Dooster) lived in a large brick house next to the little grocery store on the corner. Mr. Duster was a businessman and also on Governor Hickenlooper's staff. He was so busy that he was rarely at home. Mrs. Duster was a nice lady with pure white hair. She was calm and quiet, very different from our mother.

Each of the Duster boys, Jimmy and Johnny, had a whole bedroom to himself. So did the family's helper, who sometimes stayed at the house overnight to help take care of the boys. She cooked and cleaned and told us to play in the basement, which was unlike any basement I had ever seen in my life. It was a regular house down there.

Jimmy was chubby and serious, with the prettiest eyes I'd ever seen on a boy. I enjoyed his company. His younger brother, Johnny, was a livewire who hung out with Bob all the time. The Duster boys rarely played at our house because the helper wanted them to stay close to home. A half block away was what I would call "close to home," but the arrangement was fine with my brother because the Dusters had better toys in their basement than any toy store. They also had a crank-up Victrola for playing old records. The singers had been famous a long time ago, but when I heard Enrico Caruso's high, shaky voice, I knew that I could sing better than he did.

Louise Shallenberger, the sixteen-year-old who lived next door, was the only teenager on the block. Way down the street was a younger kid named Albert who stayed home most of the time, but we managed to coax him into our cornstalk tepee with a few other kids on the street. That was the day we almost burned alive when my brother passed a "peace pipe" around. Albert said, "Playing at your house is dangerous, but I like it."

Across the street was the Potier family. Adolph was my age and Marie was the same age as Bob. She made fun of my brother for wearing overalls. Bob said, "That means she has a crush on me," as though he'd been around and really knew what he was talking about.

Instead of overalls, Adolph wore a tucked-in white shirt, slacks, nice black shoes, and a belt. If he had worn a tie, it would have seemed that he was going to church every day instead of school. Adolph was the most grownup boy I had ever known. We became good buddies even though he dressed so nicely that he looked odd. Since he liked the movies as much as I did, I liked him no matter what he wore. We both loved acting out our favorite scenes from movies, which resulted in shows we performed on our front porch.

One-Man Shows

One-man shows meant that Bob, Adolph, and I took turns being actors while the audience of younger kids sat on the ground at the bottom of the steps. We acted out something from a movie we had all seen. We didn't share the porch stage with Marie, Patty, and Albert because they were too young to have any good ideas and because we needed them for the audience. Their job was to guess the name of the actor we were imitating.

Bob always portrayed Red Skelton. He loved impersonating the "mean wittle kid" character and saying, "I dood it," when he got caught being naughty. Sometimes Bob became Lou Costello so he could stammer. I liked mimicking any role that starred Judy Garland or Shirley Temple.

"My neck hurts from looking up," Patty grumbled. It might have been better if the actors had been on the ground and the audience on the steps, but we actors were older and bossier, so the little kids had no choice. My sister was becoming a sassy little redheaded girl, and bossing her around got harder every day.

Playing War in the Garden

When we discovered that the gourds I was growing in our Victory Garden made perfect hand grenades, Bob and I invited our friends on the block to play war with us after supper.

Adolph and Marie said they didn't want to join us because it didn't appeal to them, but Johnny, Jimmy, and Albert were ready for battle. Albert usually played war by himself in his little foxhole at home, so he was thrilled to be invited to our war. He didn't have a helmet so he wore a coonskin cap. On his arm was an air raid band that belonged to his father.

We put the privates (Patty, Johnny, and Albert) in their own platoon and the captains (Bob, Jimmy, and me) in ours. We pretended that Adolph and his sister were a neutral country across the street. We three captains bivouacked in the midst of the tomato plants and the privates holed up near the cornstalks. When Bob and I got hungry during the battle, we picked a home-grown K ration and ate it. The troops on both sides took that as a signal that any of our family's vegetables were fair game, both as food and as weapons. I had a feeling Dad would be mad, though I wasn't worried enough to interrupt the war.

Battles involved getting close enough to lob pepper or tomato hand grenades at our opponents. I knew if Dad saw all the green tomatoes we threw at each other, he'd court-martial us, so everyone had to swear to pick up the ammunition after the war was over each night.

Both sides were pretty good at sneaking around to reposition themselves without being seen. During an early evening battle, I temporarily lost sight of the "enemy," so I popped up from the tomatoes to see where everyone was. That's when something hard and heavy smacked me in the middle of the forehead. I reeled backwards and stepped on Jimmy's fingers, and we yelled at the same time. Suddenly, using gourds as hand grenades didn't seem like such a good idea.

My head felt numb, and I thought it must be bleeding. All six of us went into the house for help because a bump was forming fast. Our parents had gone to the Uptown Village Café to enjoy a night out, and they'd hired Louise, the teenager next door, to babysit. She was so scared when she saw my injury that she didn't know what to do.

"It's not that bad," I said, making sure I sounded injured but brave. "We can take care of it ourselves with some ice cubes from the fridge."

Even though I had a war injury that made me feel cross-eyed, I loved all the attention. I didn't want our parents to come home too soon because the knot on my forehead wasn't yet gruesome. Pretty soon my eyes would be swollen. I could hardly wait. Finally, I had an injury that everyone could see!

PART 5: *Growing Up*

Inflation Bra
BY
Formfit

MORE WOMEN WEAR FORMFIT THAN ANY OTHER MAKE

Busted!

I PICKED UP THE TIGHTLY-FOLDED PAPER FROM MY SCHOOL DESK and wondered who had left it. I didn't know whether to be excited or nervous. It had to be from another sixth grader. Miss Jensen, our teacher, wouldn't fold paper into a little bundle that way. Maybe it was a secret message of some kind, like a love note from Bradley. Or it could be an apology from Clarence for making fun of my little brother for wearing overalls to school. But it probably wasn't.

Clarence's dad managed the dairy where my dad worked delivering milk at 5:00 every morning. One day Dad tripped on the way to someone's front porch. All the glass bottles fell out of the case and broke into a hundred pieces. Broken glass and milk were all over the ground, and Dad hurt his knees so bad that he had to get stitches. He stayed home for a week with his legs propped up with pillows. Clarence the Creep said, "Your dad fell on purpose to get out of work." That made me mad. If I'd been five instead of eleven, I would have bitten him. But I was too grown up for that kind of stuff. I just wanted to punch him in the face.

Clarence was never nice to me. He was stuck up and snotty and made fun of my homemade clothes and long braids. I promised myself that if the folded-up paper turned out to be a mean note from that rich kid, I would yell at him on the way home from school and use all the swear words I knew.

I slipped the paper into my pocket to read in private. Later, when no one was looking, I opened it up real carefully, smoothed the creases, and read:

Lizzie, if you can't afford to buy a bra, we'll pitch in money and buy one for you.

To hide my chest, I walked around with my arms crossed for the rest of the day.

When I got home, Mom read the message with no expression on her face at all. Without looking up, she asked, "Who wrote this?"

I studied the floor as if it was the most important thing in the world. "I don't know."

Mom tossed the paper aside like a piece of junk. Then she grabbed her purse. "Kids! Get in the car. We're goin' shoppin'."

We headed for Kresge's Dime Store. They didn't have a room where you could try on clothes. Mom knew our sizes by heart, but I don't think she knew what size my new titties were because they'd just started growing. I got nervous wondering how she would figure it out. I really dreaded it.

Once we got to the store, Mom waved my brother and sister away. "You kids go look at toys." While they ran up and down the aisles wanting everything they saw even though they knew we couldn't afford any of it, Mom pawed through the brassiere section for something that might fit me. Her method of sizing me up was to stretch each bra against the bumps on my chest and say "too small" or "too big." I just closed my eyes during the whole ordeal.

When Mom finally found one that might work, she fastened the hooks in back just to make sure. There I was in the dime store aisle, in front of everyone, wearing a white cotton brassiere over the top of my blouse. I wanted to die.

She purchased the garment for $1.69. When I discovered at home that the awful thing was a perfect fit, I said goodbye to my childhood forever.

I was different from other sixth grade girls. I dreaded growing up. I was probably the last girl in my class to wear a bra, and I should have been the first. I hid my developing chest with tight undershirts, but they didn't give enough support. When I played softball, I ran the bases with both arms pressed tight against my torso. If I was going to make a home run, I had to keep my new breasts from bouncing. And I couldn't jump rope without holding a hand over each of them.

My sixth grade photograph had been a real surprise. I'd worn my best secondhand sweater for picture day and braided my hair real nice. When the photos arrived, I was horrified. Staring back at me from the front row was a girl in long braids with the chest of a mother. That should have been a clue that it was time for me to wear a bra. Not until I got that note was it ever going to happen.

The day we bought my first brassiere was the day of our end-of-the-year school pageant. I would be dancing the Virginia reel with creepy Clarence as my partner. Auntie Marge had bought me a pink organdy dress and black patent leather shoes for the special occasion. I wasn't used to anything except hand-me-down clothes, so I was thrilled with her gift. But I dreaded any attention that new clothes might bring me. I was sure that everyone could tell I was wearing a gen-u-wine white cotton undergarment beneath all that fluff. Clarence would likely have something to say about that if he knew. I wanted to fake a sore throat and just skip the whole thing . . . but I didn't.

I took a long time dressing for the school program because my heart wasn't in it. After I slipped on the new brassiere, I couldn't help staring in the mirror at the shape of my bosom. I sort of liked the way I looked from the front, the back, and both sides. I hoped no one would catch me pretending to be a pinup girl. I wondered if that tight thing could help me become a movie star. Becoming an actress on the silver screen was my favorite fantasy. Suddenly, my future in a bra didn't seem so bad.

That night I danced with abandon and realized the Virginia reel was kind of fun. The only thing Clarence said to me was, "Lizzie, you look nice."

"I'm wearing a new dress!" I was quick to point out.

During recess the next day, I hopped and skipped with no discomfort and felt like a professional jump roper. While I ran the bases during softball, I flew to a home run with arms flung wide and breasts solidly in place. Growing up wasn't such a bad thing after all. In fact, I was ready to buy another brassiere — maybe pink satin with a little bit of lace around the edges.

The Squirt Truck Run to Waterloo

IN 1942, ALL THE STRONG YOUNG MEN LEFT THEIR JOB S AND WENT to war. That meant there were plenty of part-time openings for people like my dad. He was an older man of thirty-two and had a family to support, so he had to stay behind. I was sure glad of that because I didn't want him fighting, too. It was bad enough when Mom was on the warpath. And extra work meant our family had extra money to spend.

I asked my father, "Does this mean I could maybe buy an angora sweater?"

"Not a chance in hell." I'd had a feeling that's what he'd say.

The side money he earned was for delivering Squirt soda pop to Waterloo, Iowa, several times a month. Our family called those trips the Squirt truck runs. I was twelve years old and Squirt was my favorite drink in the world, so I couldn't believe that Dad's good luck was my good luck, too.

Squirt was bottled at the Dr. Pepper Bottling Company in downtown Cedar Rapids. Whenever their warehouse in Waterloo ran out of soda pop, Dad helped load the crates on Thursday after his real job at the Iowa Manufacturing Company. Then, after work on Friday, he delivered the load to Waterloo. Sometimes he invited a family member to ride with him.

When Uncle Cullen rode along, they detoured through the town of Center Point so they could visit their brother at the state hospital in Independence. Uncle Jiggs had a drinking problem and he turned himself in a couple of times to "dry out." My uncle was always glad to see two of his brothers since most of the family were so mad at him they didn't visit at all. Dad and Uncle Cullen didn't stay long because they wanted to get to Waterloo to unload and reload, eat supper, and get back home before midnight. By then they were usually tuckered out.

Without thinking about the hard work involved, the trips sounded like a fun, one-day vacation. I was thrilled when my father said, "Betty, how 'bout you going with me this week on the run to Waterloo?"

"Really, truly?" I asked.

"Yes siree."

"What's the Squirt truck run like?"

"That depends on the weather and which route I take."

I could tell how much he liked that job because he explained it like he was a tour guide. "Sometimes there's the distant rumble of thunder and flashes of lightning from the north, and that's always exciting."

Not to me it wasn't, but there was no stopping him once he got started.

"If I go through Vinton, I get there faster. But if I go through Center Point, I can enjoy the farms and fields, which is a sight for sore eyes."

My father was sure easy to please.

"Sometimes I have to pull over to let the engine cool off because it's so dang hot outside."

That "dang hot" part didn't appeal to me one bit, and I was getting less thrilled by the minute. Dad could tell I was about to turn him down. He leaned his head into me as though sharing a secret and added one more thing. "Betty Boop, we can stop any time we want and have all the Squirt we can drink for free." That's when he won me over.

"Okay, I'll go!" All I could drink for free was a dream come true.

I could hardly wait for him to get home from his real job the next Friday. I was not used to going places with my father, so I was pretty excited.

On the way to Waterloo, he and I talked about all kinds of things like the weather and wondering where the heck people were going. We waved at passing cars, hoping the people inside might wave back. Sometimes they did. It was really hot outside that day and riding inside the cab was like taking a bath in humid air. I was sticky all over and my blouse was so damp it stuck to the back of the seat. After an hour of that, I was powerfully thirsty and wondered when it would be time for our free drinks.

He must have read my mind because he finally pulled off the road and said, "It's time to quench our thirst." Thank goodness. He fetched four bottles from the back of the truck. With a quick flick of the wrist, he popped off the caps with an opener and handed me a hot bottle of soda pop. It did not go down well.

Dad was holding onto his own mouthful of hot liquid when he saw my pinched expression. He swallowed hard and said, "You'll get used to it." I wasn't sure I would.

The second hour of driving was kind of boring. What was I doing there anyway? The trip wasn't as much fun as I thought it would be.

Once we finally got to the Waterloo warehouse, the job of unloading was long and hard because I couldn't help lift the heavy cases. There was only one person at the warehouse to help, a lazy guy who said his job was to push the button that opened the electric warehouse door. Dad said under his breath, "What a waste of the human race." I sometimes had no idea what grownups meant, even when it sounded important.

After unloading the cargo and then reloading a huge number of empty bottles, it had gotten dark outside and was way past supper time. We were both sweaty and tired, and I hadn't even done anything. Before the long trip home, we ate a late meal in Corey's Cafe across the street from the Rath

Packing Company. We were starved and thirsty, and the first thing we ordered was an icy cold bottle of Squirt for me and a cold beer for my dad.

Looking kind of weary, he leaned both elbows on the counter and asked, "Didja have a good time today?"

"Yes, it was interesting." It was a lie, but I didn't want to hurt his feelings.

"Wouldja like to go again?"

"Bob should have a turn!"

My brother was only nine and wouldn't mind if the soda pop was hot.

The next week, Dad asked my brother to go with him on both nights. On Thursday, Bob got to watch the guys at the factory load the cases in Cedar Rapids for the Friday run. He saw how the beverage was manufactured, bottled, and cased in one continuous operation before being sent to the loading dock on roller conveyors with the help of gravity. Bob was awestruck and filled with appreciation after watching what pop had to go through before we ever drank it. The time between loading and waiting to leave the next day felt like a lifetime to him.

He was so excited on Friday that he stood by the roadside in front of our house watching for the big yellow truck to turn off Center Point Road and head down 32nd Street to pick him up. When Dad got there, he was glad my brother was ready so they could hit the road. By the time Bob climbed inside the cab, he was so wound up that he forgot to wave goodbye to Mom and me.

When they returned home late that night, Bob was fast asleep in the front seat. The next morning we couldn't shut him up. He was so full of chatter about all that he'd seen and done in half a day that you'd have thought he'd gone to the moon and back. Between father and son telling their stories, the Friday adventure never seemed to end.

Dad said, "Even though Waterloo is only seventy-five miles away, it took over two hours to get there." The new speed limit was thirty-five miles an hour because drivers had to take it easy on fuel and tires during wartime. But the funny old six-cylinder rig couldn't speed things up if it wanted to. He said, "With an enclosed van cargo body, that old Chevrolet is sturdy but stodgy. It might have been possible to go faster downhill with a tailwind if I had let it go, but I didn't."

During Dad's description of their first trip together, Bob butted in with comments like "that's right" . . . "oh yeah" . . . "it was fun!" My little brother must have watched every move our father made as he coaxed the vehicle up the hills. Bob made special sound effects to illustrate what he'd learned about driving.

"Dad shifted gears (scrrrunch) when we came to a town and had to drive real slow, like only fifteen miles an hour. When he pushed it to thirty-five, the truck was in pain (aaaaaaggghhh). He could keep it there until the next hill, and then he had to . . . uh . . . what did you call it, Dad?"

"Double clutch."

"Yeah, he had to double clutch (grrrrind) to the next gear to get to the top."

My little brother was so caught up in his adventure that he was sweating. "Wait 'til you hear this part," he continued. "At the top of the hill, he whooosshhhed down the other side so fast my hair was blowing off."

I said, "Gee, Bob, it was only thirty-five miles an hour."

"No, I think it was faster than that."

Dad agreed. "It was a lot faster than that."

Bob had memorized all the Burma-Shave rhymes he saw on the trip and insisted on reciting them several times. He thought they were hilarious.

IF YOU DON'T KNOW WHOSE SIGNS THESE ARE YOU CAN'T HAVE DRIVEN VERY FAR . . . BURMA-SHAVE

THIRTY DAYS HATH SEPTEMBER, APRIL, JUNE, AND THE SPEED OFFENDER . . . BURMA-SHAVE

Their first stop on the way to Waterloo was at Vinton to put water in the radiator and let it cool down. You had to take care of that old clunker as though it was a person. During those breaks there was enough time to have a cold drink, a cream soda for my father and a strawberry pop for my brother. I could tell they had way more fun than I had.

I knew that Bob would like Corey's Café in Waterloo because no fancy people were there. They were like our dad. It was open all day and all night because the men from Rath's Meat Packing Plant across the street worked all the time. The plant was never closed. During the war, that's the way a lot of factories operated, all day and all night.

It was at Corey's horseshoe lunch counter that Bob ate his first hot beef sandwich. We both agreed that Corey's Café smelled like the kitchen at Auntie Marge's Uptown Village Café, our home away from home.

Bob told us about the signs on Corey's wall. *Our silverware is not medicine so don't take it after meals.* I thought my little brother would die laughing, but he had another one for us. *Restroom, hell. I'm not tired. Where's the can?* Mom hushed him up real quick and warned him not to share that one again while Dad grinned from behind the *Cedar Rapids Gazette.*

After I gave up the trip to Waterloo on the first try, my little brother took most of the Squirt truck runs from then on. On the way home after dark there were not as many cars and it was cooler. Since Bob was only nine, he always fell asleep.

When I listened to my brother going on and on about every little thing he'd witnessed on those trips, I wondered what the heck I had missed. I couldn't understand why it was so thrilling for him. It was probably because he was a boy and more captivated with the manly things that fathers know about, like machinery, shifting gears, farming, and the weather. The only reason I'd gone was to get free soda pop.

Family Circus

MY GRANDMOTHER DAMSY SCREECHED TO A HALT IN FRONT OF OUR tiny house, slammed the door of her car, and marched straight into our front room. She was on another mission.

"Waneta, wash the kids' faces, and get everybody in the car."

"Mama, what's going on? I'm in the middle of the laundry."

"Well, leave it. There's a carnival outside of town for two days, and we don't want to miss it."

That's how my grandmother was. If she decided that we were going to do something, we did it in a hurry. So Mom went to the basement, unplugged the Maytag, and let the clothes sit in sudsy water. I begrudged going anywhere with my family, and any self-respecting twelve-year-old girl felt the same way. But, as usual, I sacrificed myself because the Family Circus was just too hard to resist.

In a few minutes, five of us piled into Damsy's '32 Chevy. Patty, the smallest, climbed onto the little shelf under the back window because she fit there perfectly. Bob and I sat in the rear seat, Damsy drove like a crazy woman, and Mom sat with shoulders sagging, resigned to another surprise outing with our grandmother. I hated to admit it, but Damsy's outings were never dull.

Upon arriving at the out-of-town carnival, we first armed ourselves with plenty of junk food, which was Damsy's treat. Then we strolled past all the sideshows, searching for one where children were allowed to buy a ticket if accompanied by an adult. Bob and I wanted to see the half-man-half-woman exhibit, but Mom said, "Not today, not ever." So we decided to see the woman whose unborn twin was still attached to her body.

My grandmother said, "Waneta, that's vile."

Mom said, "I think it could be very educational."

While Damsy watched Patty, Mom purchased three tickets and ushered my brother and me behind the red curtain. Inside was a small stage where people stood all around the edges. A man talked to the crowd about things that were pretty boring — something to do with the woman whose twin was still attached to her side. I couldn't wait to see that. I wondered if it was a boy or girl and what kind of clothes it wore.

From behind another red curtain, the woman finally whooshed out. She was dressed in a flowing black robe that hid everything except her head. The crowd hunkered around the stage, which caused Bob and me to stand on our tiptoes to have a closer look. The man who was doing all the talking asked the crowd to be very quiet while the woman pulled her robe open, but not very far. She probably wanted to keep the baby warm.

Bob stretched his neck as high as it could go and said very clearly for all to hear, "I can't see no twin baby." I was embarrassed, but the people laughed, so I thought it must have been funny. I couldn't see the twin either, though I was too mature to say so out loud. The lady turned very slowly and showed us a flap on her hip that looked like a piece of celluloid with fingers. Bob covered his eyes. "I don't like it!"

My mother said, "I don't either." She grabbed our hands and headed straight back through the red curtain. The announcer called after my fast departing mother. "Ma'am, wait! You haven't seen anything yet."

She whirled around on her heels. "Buster, I've seen all that I want to. The piece of plastic glued onto that dame's side is nothing but a fake, and you can stick that in your pipe and smoke it!"

We were out of there in a hurry in search of something truly educational. Damsy and Patty followed us everywhere we went while my sticky sister relished a pink mass of cotton candy. Mom passed up the bearded lady exhibit, the reptile man, and wolf boy. She chose, instead, the two-headed snake exhibit for free. The scaly thing was asleep while we were there, but it didn't look like a fake. Through the glass wall Mom inspected the two heads very carefully for any sign of a seam in case it was two snakes stitched together. She couldn't detect one and said with satisfaction, "Well, I think this weird thing is for real."

We soon left the side show exhibits and found the Giant Ferris Wheel, where Bob and I were allowed to ride in a seat together. The rest of the family stayed below. Whenever the Ferris Wheel stopped to let new people on, we were suspended in midair. It made my stomach tickle and my body sweaty all over, so my bratty brother rocked the seat to make me feel even worse. Each time we stopped a little higher in the sky to let another rider aboard, he rocked harder than the time before. It scared me to death. "Stop that, you snot, or I'll tell Mom."

My brother snickered. "She can't hear you." We were about ready to go around the highest point when we stopped for one more passenger. I couldn't see any part of the machinery without bending way over the front edge of the seat. I was frozen in space and couldn't speak. Bob watched my face pickle with fear and rocked the seat with all his might as he laughed out loud. I was panic-stricken but got brave enough to let go of the handle to wave at my mother a hundred miles below. "Mom! Make him staaahhp!"

I could barely see her wave a greeting back to me before scampering off to follow Patty. Then Damsy tilted her head way back, shaded her eyes with one hand, and also waved in a friendly manner. She dashed off to follow my mother and little sister. I thought I would faint, but Bob was so hysterical with laughter that he forgot to rock our seat. I was too frightened to raise my hand to smack him and he knew it.

That's when I remembered why I hated going places with my family. It always backfired on me. But I had no choice. When Damsy decided it was time to go for a ride, we piled into her car no matter where it might take us. She said we needed a change of scenery once in a while, though I seriously doubted her judgment.

I felt somewhat recovered from the frightening ride on the Giant Ferris Wheel when I discovered that our next destination was the Giant Barrel. It was lying on its side, open at both ends, and large enough for people to walk through. The barrel was turning slowly in a clockwise direction as people hopped their way to the opposite end. If they were lucky enough to remain upright after the trip to the other side, they jumped out onto a small deck and got a little prize. It looked like fun, so Damsy said, "Go ahead, try it. My treat."

I went in first, sidestepped easily, and made it through part way. Then I realized that the next section of the barrel was turning in a counterclock-wise direction. I hopped onto that part, switched feet, changed my rhythm, and made it to the last division of the barrel. That section was turning in a clockwise direction.

My body and brain were having trouble getting together, but, miracu-lously, I made it through to the other side, repressed a smile, and tried not to show how much I enjoyed it. I wondered how my little brother was doing. After I hopped out onto the deck, feeling triumphant, I discovered that Bob had never even started. His arms were hugging his body and I could tell that he was scared. I hated it when I felt sorry for him.

I saw my mother hand Bob's ticket to the man and assumed that she was getting a refund. I was wrong. She was preparing to step into the Giant Bar-rel herself. I was ashamed. Mothers didn't do things like that. She confident-ly hopped onto the first section of the barely-turning surface and danced her way through the clockwise part, then immediately lost her rhythm in the counterclockwise division. My hands flew to cover my mouth in fear of what might happen next. Was she going to lose her balance?

Yes, she was. My mother was actually falling down in public.

I covered my eyes and then peeked through my fingers. I couldn't believe what I was seeing. She rolled up the turning wall, slid back down, rolled back up the wall, and slid down again. Mom tried desperately to regain her footing, but each time she rolled up the wall, she slid down as the bar-rel continued to turn. She had no control over which way she flopped. I was mortified. My mother's dress was up to her armpits and her bloomers showed. People stopped what they were doing, alarmed to see a grown woman rolling around in the Giant Barrel.

She started yelling at the top of her lungs. "Stop this thing and let me outta here!" I couldn't breathe. I wanted a different mother, one who would have turned in the ticket for a refund.

I turned away and pretended that I didn't know who she was, but my brother was laughing his head off. The man who operated the machine eventually had to stop it so my mother could stand up, pull herself together, and stagger out of the big barrel. When she returned to where she had started, my brother was bending over and holding his sides from laughing. Mom said, "It's not funny, young man!" Bob thought it was hilarious and couldn't pull out of it. People gathered to make sure my mother was all right while I considered turning myself in for adoption.

She had barely caught her breath when Bob began to prance, clutching his crotch. "I've gotta go to the bathroom!"

It was growing dark and by that time my mother had to use a toilet, as well. But it was too late for Patty. She had already wet her pants. My grandmother threw up her hands and just looked at her eyebrows.

Mom said, "Follow me. We're gonna squat behind this tent. No one will see us in the dark. I've got paper napkins."

I was so revolted that I couldn't follow them, so Damsy, Patty, and I stayed behind near the lighted promenade and waited. Mom and my brother were gone for a very long time, and my grandmother was getting worried. "Maybe they got lost," I said. No sooner had I said it than out of the shadows came my mother. She was limping and Bob was holding her purse. Blood streamed from the shinbone of her left leg.

Damsy was alarmed. "Waneta, what happened to you?"

"I stumbled over a tent stake." Mom's voice was tight and she was visibly shaken.

There was a ragged wound on her shin and blood was dripping all over her shoe. I could tell that it hurt, and I wanted to cry. I had been embarrassed when she rolled up the wall of the Giant Barrel, but now I wanted to hug her and tell her that I was sorry. I looked after my sister while Damsy went to the root beer stand to get ice and paper towels to clean my mother's leg.

We helped Mom hobble to the car and Damsy took us all home. That time she drove carefully.

At our house, my grandmother spread Mercurochrome into the wound and bandaged it. She gave my mother two aspirin and said, "Waneta, go to bed."

I felt so sorry for my mom that I lay down beside her until my father came home later that night. I promised myself that first thing in the morning, I would work very hard to start liking her again.

Betty Grows Up

AFTER I'D LEARNED TO USE THE SEWING MACHINE AT THE AGE OF eleven, I made blankets and sheets for my dolls. When I needed filler for a tiny pillow, I raided Mom's box of sanitary pads for the cotton. In 1941, pads were made with stuffing that was wrapped with a coarsely woven net, very flimsy and easy to tear apart for a kid's nifty craft project.

But those pads weren't really my mother's; they were meant for me. Written on the box were the words FOR BETTY. My mother had purchased them in preparation for my fast-maturing body. I was so proud. "Betty, you're growing up now," she had said, and it made me excited about all the privileges that growing up might bring with it. "It's time to tell you about menstruation."

Okey-dokey, I thought. *I'm ready.*

She proceeded to demonstrate how those big bandage-like things would attach to my body when the time came.

"When will it happen?" I asked my mother ever so eagerly.

"Oh, next year. Maybe this year," she replied before filling me in on the details.

Her lecture about menstruation turned out to be more clinical and complicated than I'd expected, and I had trouble paying attention. When my period did start a year later, I barely remembered the details, and I was on my own because my mother was at work. I felt so sick that thinking clearly was not easy. I called Mom at her job at Auntie Marge's Uptown Village Café with what was beginning to feel like very bad news.

"Mama, my BP has started," I whimpered.

"BP? What BP?" she demanded.

"My blood period." Saying the words out loud caused tears to leak from my tightly squeezed eyes. I had a terrible stomach ache and sniveled, "Mama, please come home."

My mother was an efficient and practical woman. "Betty, the time has finally come to get the blue box from the closet." That's when I remembered that the odd-looking bandages I had used to stuff my doll's pillow were intended for my menstruation.

Mom could tell that I was anxious. "Honey, you'll be fine. I'll be home after work." After work? That was such a long time. I would have to stumble through it alone.

I found the blue box with my name on it, but I couldn't find the elastic belt with tabs and little safety pins. The pad on top was the one I had ripped open the year before for my craft project, and what remained was in a shapeless wad. I didn't remember how to use any of that stuff, though I tried. As I was pressing the loose netting and falling-out cotton onto the red crotch of my panties, Patty, my seven-year-old sister who followed me everywhere, got a glimpse of the blood. "Oh, Betty, what happened?" I told her that I had cut myself on some broken glass, which made no sense at all. Lucky for me, she bought it.

I felt so sick that I longed to crawl into bed and cry myself to sleep. What I really needed was my mother. When Mom finally got home, she was accompanied by a few concerned family members. My dad, Aunt Naomi, and Uncle Russ all peeked at me as I lay curled under the covers clutching my stomach. They used phrases like "all grown up" and "becoming a woman," but all I wanted to do was throw up, which I finally did because the cramps were so bad.

I survived the discomfort with a hot water bottle that Mom provided and a couple of aspirin thrown in for good luck. My second period was less nerve-wracking because I was better prepared. However, I was too shy to mark the calendar each month so I would know when to expect its arrival and too embarrassed to carry a sanitary pad in my purse. I didn't even own a purse.

I was soon introduced to the secret code between girlfriends in statements like, "I can't go swimming after school because Grandma is visiting."

"She is?" asked my little sister. "Where's her car?"

Patty didn't know the code yet. It was just a matter of time. Eventually, my little sister would learn the truth about becoming a woman: growing up was more complicated than we thought it would be.

Junior High Blues

I EXPECTED SEVENTH GRADE TO BE THE BEST EXPERIENCE OF MY LIFE. It wasn't. It was overwhelming. By the end of the first week at Franklin School, I wanted to stay in bed forever.

There were too many things to remember. I'm not talking about remembering the words of the Gettysburg address. I had to remember to do things Mom used to do for me before she got a full-time job. I had to set my own alarm clock and get up an hour earlier because the walk to school was longer. And if I didn't remember to pack my own lunch the night before, I went hungry.

Once I got to school, I always had to check my schedule of classes to see what started first and where it was located. Each class was in a different room and all the halls looked alike, so I got lost many times. I had to go to the bathroom too often because I was nervous, and I could never remember where the bathrooms were located. I couldn't find my locker or remember the combination, but I kept smiling, hoping that no one could tell how confused I was. I envied the way other kids zipped straight down a hallway and into a classroom with confidence. Before I entered, I had to check my piece of paper and the number on the door to see if they matched. It seemed that everyone but me knew what they were doing. If they'd known how much trouble I had remembering things, they would've called me a dummy.

I had five teachers instead of one, which meant five different homework assignments every night. I struggled daily to deal with the challenges of junior high while still babysitting my brother and sister after school each day.

"So, how's school going?" Mom asked after she came home from work.

"It's so hard. I can't keep up. I hate it!"

I was hoping she might feel sorry for me and lighten my jobs at home.

"Let's have a look at this," she said as she smoothed out the wrinkled paper that showed my schedule of classes. Help was on the way.

Suddenly she said, "For heaven's sake. I can't believe this!"

I took that to mean she agreed I had too much to do and would wake me up in the morning and fix my breakfast and pack my lunch.

"Your music teacher, Ruth Webster, used to date your dad when he was seventeen."

That got my attention.

"Mom, how did Dad and Miss Webster know each other?"

"They were in the same youth group at the Free Methodist Church."

That was at the same age and in the same place where Dad met Mom in the church orchestra. Did Dad dump my music teacher to marry my mother? My head was spinning. Was I proud of that information or worried? Should I ask Miss Webster if she remembered my dad? If she was mad at him for marrying Mom, would Miss Webster give me a bad grade? I pushed the subject behind my brain where I couldn't see it.

We'd gotten so distracted by Dad's long-ago romance with Miss Webster that Mom and I forgot to talk about my heavy workload. So I had two things to worry about instead of one.

I dragged my body out of bed each morning and took the long walk through my faded neighborhood and into the well-groomed area near Franklin School. It gave me plenty of time to get down in the dumps again before class started each day. I walked and wondered what new thing would happen to make me hate junior high even more than I already did. I would soon find out.

One morning in my first-period English class, the boy who sat next to me was stricken with a grand mal seizure, something I had never witnessed before. It scared me half to death. We students were shocked, thinking the boy was being attacked by invisible demons. But our teacher ever so calmly put down her book and stretched the poor boy out on the floor where he could vibrate without hurting himself. She clamped a pencil between his teeth and held his jaw tight while froth bubbled from his mouth. We clustered around, awestruck.

Still kneeling on the floor and without looking up, the teacher said, "Class . . . back to your seats and keep reading quietly." Easy for her to say. I just wanted to find the nearest bathroom, throw up, and run home.

Each day seemed endless. Days turned into weeks and weeks turned into the end of the semester and, all of a sudden, life at the new school was almost normal. I had forgotten my woes. But how could that be and when did it happen? I realized that sometime when I wasn't looking, a miracle had occurred. No wonder I believed in magic.

My Social Standing

Franklin School was in the northeast side of town, a part of Cedar Rapids that we called the silky sock district. We called it that because the neighborhoods were beautiful. The people who lived there had more money than my parents would earn in a lifetime. There were a few miles between our drab neighborhood and their well-to-do one, yet we all received our education in the same building: I was out of place at Franklin.

During the first semester, I had gotten acquainted with only a few of the upper-crust kids who were nice enough to be friendly. I made them laugh when I said, "I think I know your category."

"What?"

"Yeah, you're probably a medium."

When they realized that I had invented categories for all the students, they had just as much fun as I did putting people where they belonged. A boy asked, "Where do you fit in?"

"I'm in the smallest group here."

"Which is . . .?"

"The poor kids."

"Oh. Nice knowing you. Bye."

I didn't take it personally because I knew my place and stayed where I was put.

Middle-class kids were in the medium-sized group. The largest one at Franklin was filled to overflowing with rich kids. A "poor" friend pointed out that I had made a mistake. He said, "Lizzie, you left someone out."

"How come?"

"One of the seventh grade girls is richer than any of the rich kids."

"Really?"

"Yes, really."

Heavens to Betsy. That meant I had no classification for one girl. I had to find out who she was without talking to her because the well-to-do kids usually didn't even look at anyone beneath them. It was not going to be easy.

Eventually, I learned that the girl was Joan Killian. Her dad owned Killian's, a high-class department store in Cedar Rapids. Joan was pretty enough to be a pinup model, and I never saw her walking with anyone plain. Rich, pretty girls always hung out together.

From a distance, I admired her. When she opened her locker door, her fingers were as nimble as those of a piano player. It was like she was born with the locker combination in her fingerprints. She marched down the hall in her polished penny loafers with her long black curls flipping this way and that. If any girl would have angora socks that matched her angora sweater, it would be Joan Killian. Everything about her was a window display for her father's department store. She floated through the halls and nobody could touch her. As far as I was concerned, she was the same as a child movie star, but I hadn't invented that group yet. I wondered how it would feel to be Joan's friend. I would never know. We'd never been close enough to breathe the same air.

One day while I was waiting my turn in the bathroom, I couldn't believe what I was seeing. Joan Killian herself walked out of a stall to wash her hands. Then she looked in the mirror and patted her gorgeous curls. I watched every move she made, being careful that she didn't catch me staring at her. She did the same things the rest of us did, and all in the shared privacy of the common restroom. Before joining the ordinary kids in the halls, she looked herself over real well to make sure everything was the way she wanted it. Then she left.

It seemed unthinkable to me that a person of her position in life should have to do such personal things while we were looking. If teachers had their own bathrooms and we ordinary kids had ours, students like her should have a bathroom of their own. Since no such thing existed and since Joan Killian was using our bathroom, it meant that for that short time, I was in the same category as the richest girl in school.

Wow — it felt good.

Another student raised my social standing for a longer period of time than the department store princess. Mary Denton was a pretty, pink-faced seventh grader with a freckly nose and curly red hair. I was surprised when she invited me to her house. It wasn't common for an underprivileged girl like me to have a friend from the silky sock district. But we enjoyed a lot of the same things like drawing pictures and going to movies. She was nice enough to talk to me as though she didn't know about the categories.

Mary's father was a dentist and her mother stayed home to take care of the house and family. My father was a machinist at the Iowa Manufacturing Company, and my mother served beer and fifteen-cent hamburgers at the Uptown Village Café. You can bet your bootees I never told Mary that.

Mary's mother called mine to ask if I could walk home from school with her daughter to get this friendship thing started. On the way to her house, all I could do was walk and gawk. The clean homes in her neighborhood were in the middle of grass yards that had fluffy bushes and colorful flowers and trees of all kinds, not just elm trees. The whole neighborhood was a regular park.

When we got inside my new friend's house, the smell of chocolate cake meant that nobody smoked cigarettes. I had a pretty good feeling that we would have a snack real soon. What a treat! At my house when I came home hungry, I had a finger-full of peanut butter, a few soda crackers, and maybe some milk if any was left.

Mrs. Denton said, "How nice to meet you, Betty."

I felt so important.

"Mary has told us a lot about you."

Oh, my gosh.

"Are you ready for chocolate cake and a cold glass of milk?"

Absolutely! "Yes, thank you," I answered politely.

That perfect afternoon at the Denton's house was a good dream that I didn't want to end. But I had to wake up when it was time to go home. Her dad, Dr. Denton, drove the family Cadillac and Mary came along. We left the nicest area in town and eventually found our way to my world. It was not that far away. The neighborhood landscapes zipped by us like the scenes from a movie. Little homes started showing up on the streets. The grass wasn't as green and the yards were closer together. I couldn't help but notice how different things looked where I lived. Dr. Denton didn't seem to notice a thing. He just kept chatting with us about our day and asked me all kinds of questions. I could tell that he was getting to know me, and I loved all the attention.

"So, Betty, did you and Mary have a good time this afternoon?"

"Oh, yes, we did for sure."

"Which classes at school are your favorites?"

"I like my English class and music and especially art."

"Mary says you're a very good artist. Tell me about that."

My friend's father was the first grownup who had ever discussed things that interested me, and talking with him made me feel special. His daughter must have felt important every day of her life.

I dreaded reaching my own neighborhood because it was so humble. I was afraid I would lose my friend when she saw the house I lived in. I expected her to say, "You live . . . here?" But she didn't. She and her father acted as though it was no different from theirs. They said how nice it was to know me and asked if I would visit again sometime. They waited until I got to my front door and waved goodbye before leaving to go back where they came from.

Mary Denton was one of the nicest girls I ever met in the nine schools I attended. Our friendship made me feel that I was in the wrong world and that I belonged in hers. But that would never happen.

A few weeks after school let out for the summer, my life was interrupted by another move. I could hardly stand it when I had to say goodbye. I walked all the way to Mary's house so I could break the news gently, but my glum face must have given me away.

She asked, "Lizzie, what's wrong?"

"This is my last day in Cedar Rapids."

"What? How come?"

"We're moving again."

"Oh, no. I can't believe it. Where are you going?"

"Chicago, I think."

"I'm going to miss you so much. Will you write to me?"

"Yes, I will." My throat was cramping up as if I might cry.

"Well – is this goodbye?"

"Yeah, I guess so."

"Okay. Bye, Lizzie. Don't forget to write."

"I'll write."

As I started walking down the steps, she called out, "Lizzie, wait."

I stopped and turned as she came closer to give me a shy little hug and said, "You're the best friend I've ever had."

"You, too."

As I walked away, we waved until we couldn't see each other any longer.

Changing Keys

IN THE SUMMER OF 1943, OUR SECOND YEAR FOR VICTORY GARDENS, the earth was pushing up sweet peas so fast that it filled us with hope that we'd get high marks again. Dad said, "Gee whillikers, I woulda never thought you three kids were gonna turn into garden rats."

Our gardens were doing very well; unfortunately our parents were not. That summer the friction between them was growing as fast as the weeds in the tomato patch. It got so bad that my mother decided to transplant herself to Chicago where her favorite sister-in-law lived.

Aunt Sarah was the only one of Dad's four sisters bold enough to face her future outside the borders of our hometown. Whenever her name was mentioned, the rest of the Peal family sighed and looked at their eyebrows. Mom had a spirit that matched Aunt Sarah's, so when she joined her in the wicked city of Chicago, taking us three kids with her, it gave the family even more to talk about.

I viewed that turn of events as a real setback. We had a nice home, good neighbors, and the best vegetables we'd ever grown, and we were going to throw it all away because our parents couldn't get along. Mom tried to soften the uprooting by turning Chicago into a vacation spot.

"There's a real sand beach by Lake Michigan, just like in Hawaii, where people swim. And there's a train that runs on tracks high above the streets all over the city. I think you kids will love it there."

Bob and Patty were excited. Not me. Having to change schools again made me lose faith in my mother. But once she made up her mind, there was no stopping her, no matter who it affected.

She was aware of my dark mood because I didn't try to hide it. I wondered how long we'd be in Chicago before she decided to move again. "We're regular people, not gypsies," I wanted to tell her. I never spoke those thoughts out loud because she would've called me mouthy. I tried hard not to sulk because if I was okay, Bob and Patty would be okay. I was used to keeping unhappiness to myself, only this time it was harder than usual.

We took only what we could carry. Our bags and suitcases were filled with clothes and whatever each of us needed for entertainment. Patty took her doll. Bob packed a few brand new comic books, which he planned to read and then trade with the new friends he would make in the new place. I didn't plan to make new friends, so I packed my twelve-color set of Prang watercolors, a good brush, a few #2 pencils with new erasers, and a typing tablet for my artwork.

We stayed overnight in a hotel near the train station downtown so we could leave very early the next day. Dad didn't want us to leave in the first place, so he stayed with us in the hotel in order to say goodbye in the morning. My parents stopped arguing long enough for us to be together as a family that last night.

To take my mind off the move, Mom bought me the first housecoat I ever owned. It was a beautiful chenille robe, blue-green with snaps all the way down the front. I felt grownup and glamorous wearing it. I watched myself in the hotel mirror as I brushed my teeth, thinking that was probably the way movie star Betty Grable felt before bedtime. I took so long admiring myself that Dad finally rapped on the door, calling, "Step it up in there. We gotta get to bed."

My emotions were muddled, and I resented the fact that wearing my new housecoat made the dreaded move to a different state feel like an adventure.

As soon as we arrived in the city of Chicago, two hundred miles from home, we purchased tickets to board the "L," Chicago's above-the-street transportation system that would take us to our new neighborhood. I was scared riding so high off the ground and terrified that the L would fly off the tracks and land on people below.

My mother was cool as a cucumber. "Don't worry," she assured me. "The elevated train will never leave the tracks." I prayed she was right.

I was glad to get off the train even though we had to lug our belongings to the furnished apartment at 848 Waveland Avenue. What a surprise it was to see that our new home was right across the street from Lemoyne School where we kids would enroll. Bob would be in the fifth grade, Patty in third, and I would be in the eighth. Around the corner a few blocks away was the Cubs baseball stadium.

Before she searched the *Chicago Tribune* for a job, Mom got us registered for school. With that out of the way, she said, "Okay, since this is our summer vacation, let's have some fun."

I wanted so badly to stay mad at her, but it was wearing me out. In spite of myself, I actually started to have the fun that she wanted us to have. Aunt Sarah was often our sightseeing guide and escorted us all over the city on public transportation. It was no different from having two mothers who liked to play. We especially loved going to the movies. Sometimes we would leave one movie, get an ice cream cone, and go to the next movie. One theater had three balconies, and it was cheaper to buy tickets for the top level where the screen looked far away. "Good God!" Mom exclaimed, "We're almost in heaven up here. The air is even thin." With nobody sitting up there except us, she could smoke in comfort.

We still hadn't seen Lake Michigan with its real beach, so one day she loaded us onto public transportation again so we could swim in the lake and play in the sand. The water was so cold that we gasped in shock! We'd expected Lake Michigan to be as warm as the swimming pool in Marion Park back home. Even though the day was cloudy and the water was icy, we all got bad sunburns.

The full-time job that my mother found in the want ads was on the assembly line at Bendix Brake Company. That meant during the day, Bob, Patty, and I were on our own again. Bob found a friend his age. They hung out on his friend's balcony and traded comic books while Patty and I drew pictures, read, listened to radio shows, sang songs, and fought. Eventually, we discovered that we could walk to the movies a few blocks away. I saw *The Wizard of Oz* and *Snow White* at least seven times. For the small price of fifteen cents, I could be Dorothy or Snow White instead of Betty Peal, formerly of Cedar Rapids, Iowa. I practiced endlessly, singing "Over the Rainbow" and "Someday My Prince Will Come" while Mom was at work, and my singing and drawing skills got better each day.

We all settled into a routine that began to feel normal. It didn't last long. Mom started coming home late, bringing the scent of taverns with her.

That's when my worry knob got turned to the highest setting because the smell of alcohol meant trouble was brewing.

During that uneasy period, our grandmother Damsy visited us. We took her to Marshall Field's department store so she could ride the escalator. In the privacy of our family, I was relaxed with Damsy, but I was uncomfortable with her in public. Her deep, gravelly voice turned people's heads as they wondered whether she was a man or a woman. Damsy had no resemblance to any grandma I ever met, and it embarrassed me that she was so unusual. She rolled her own cigarettes, made sauerkraut, never baked cookies or bread, and didn't seem to care what she put on to go out in public.

Everywhere we went, Damsy and Mom lit up, clutching their cigarettes between two fingers and blowing smoke in the air. My mother never wore a girdle, so her chubby behind and stomach jiggled when she walked. She wore her nylons rolled to her ankles, a style worn by no mother I knew except mine. Being with Mom and Damsy in public made me aware of how different they were, and if I could have sat by myself in another booth without getting smacked, I would have done so.

That day in Marshall Field's was one of the most embarrassing days of my life. As Damsy was about to step off the escalator, her untied shoestring got caught in one of the slits on the step. She stumbled forward and hit the elegant Marshall Field's floor with a thud like a rolled-up rug. I ignored her stretched-out figure because I didn't want anyone to know we were related.

When strangers rushed to help Damsy back to her feet, I felt sorry for her and ashamed of myself. But I was so mad at the world that I didn't want my pity for her to show, so I walked away and pretended to be interested in the details of a sweater on a classy Marshall Field's mannequin.

While Damsy was visiting us in Chicago, Mom stuck close to home. Once my grandmother left, my mother returned to staying out late and listening to live music at whatever piano bar stayed open after hours.

She was a talented musician who learned to play the piano on her own when she was young. When Damsy realized that her youngest child was unusually skilled, she allowed her to have a private teacher. By that time my mother could make a piano talk. I heard grownups say that they had seen her push the piano bench aside at a party, remove one shoe, and play the ragtime melody with both hands and the bass part with her left foot. She also played the cornet and guitar and was a very good singer.

Waneta Elizabeth Peal wowed people with her ability to play anything by ear. She could change keys in the middle of a piece to accommodate the different ranges of the singers in the crowd, and she kept changing keys until the pitch suited everyone who wanted to sing along. When she played tunes with a strong beat, dancers boogied. If there was no room on the floor, they danced in place. People couldn't stand still when my mother was boss of the piano. She was a born entertainer.

On weekends, she sometimes took us kids with her to the "jams," as she called them. Long after the other children in Chicago were snug in bed, we fell asleep in a booth in the midst of singing, dancing, and piano playing. It took a long time to get comfortable in a tavern booth even with coats thrown over us and purses under our heads for pillows.

During the week, we kids stayed in the apartment alone, and I kept peace and order using any method that worked. Clearly, it was a job too big for me and Mom's presence was needed. If I woke in the morning and she was still gone, I was never afraid that something had happened to her. I was only afraid that the landlady would find out that our mother had been out all night. One morning my worst fear came true.

A knock on the door woke us. It was our landlady, wanting to talk with Mom. I automatically covered for her, saying, "She went to get milk for breakfast." Apparently, the landlady didn't buy that and called Aunt Sarah. Sarah found her favorite sister-in-law still listening to a guy at the piano bar. Even though she had been one of the performing stars that night, my mother was in hot water with everyone: Aunt Sarah, the landlady, us three kids, and, eventually, Dad.

It was then that he decided to pay us a visit. When Mom heard he was coming for the weekend, she was genuinely excited. She and Aunt Sarah huddled in our kitchen drinking coffee and chatting.

She said, "Sarah, it's so hard to live with your brother, but it's just as hard to live without him."

It seemed they were talking about owning a cat or a dog.

Aunt Sarah said, "Well, I'm sure that's true, but I still want to get married someday no matter how much heartache comes with it 'cause I've got a terrible case of the cold sheets."

I didn't really know what that meant, but the two women got as giggly as little kids.

On the day of Dad's arrival, Mom prettied herself so well that it seemed like a date instead of meeting our father at the depot. Dad must've had the same idea because he looked nicer than I had ever seen him. He was wearing a new jacket that zipped in the front and a man's dress hat instead of his striped engineer's cap with the AFL and CIO pins on the side. We hardly recognized him. It made me feel smoothed out to see Mom and Dad hugging and kissing again.

Our father brought gifts for all of us: freshly picked corn on the cob and vine-ripened tomatoes, cucumbers, and other fresh vegetables from our abandoned Victory Garden. As we gorged ourselves, Dad said through a mouthful of corn, "Boy oh boy oh boy . . . you kids would've gotten A's for sure." It was so good to be together again that I didn't care if our vegetables got graded or not. I just wanted to move back home, no matter how much heartache we all suffered.

I think Dad was almost glad that our mother had screwed up in Chicago. I couldn't hear all the words they said while talking at the kitchen table that night, though God knows I tried. I could tell that Dad was so lonesome he could hardly stand it.

"Girl," he asked, "when in the Sam Hill are you gonna come back home?"

She was quiet for a while, then said, "Butch, I just wish that I could . . ."

"Girl, you're never satisfied with the way things are, always wishin' for somethin' else."

I was certain that the quiet, serious conversation between my parents would erupt into one of their big fights . . . but it didn't.

The next morning we all rode the L to the train station to see Dad off. He was quiet all the way. We huddled close at the depot to say goodbye, but he didn't look at us. Then I saw why: his eyes were filled with tears. I had never seen my father cry, and it made my chest hurt so bad that I couldn't look at him anymore. In the Peal family, we weren't used to hugging or showing our feelings. So I squeezed my sadness back, holding it so tight inside as we waved goodbye that I thought my heart would burst.

Back on Home Turf

LIVING IN CHICAGO WORE ME DOWN. I SHUFFLED INSTEAD OF WALK-ing, like I didn't know where I was going. Then my parents' talks about getting together again made me smile all the time and walk with purpose.

We made plans to move back to Cedar Rapids and live close to our old schools. After Mom whisked us kids away to the windy city, Auntie Marge and Uncle Al had put our home on 32nd Street up for sale. It would soon belong to someone else, so Dad started looking for another place for us to live. "Boy, this isn't gonna be easy," he said. "There's not much out there."

The Marble Board House

Dad didn't give up looking and finally made progress by finding something temporary. "It ain't much, but we've got to take it so you kids can start school," he told us.

He was right. It wasn't much. The one-room structure was barely better than nothing at all. I didn't call that shack progress. It had probably been a storage shed for the big house in front of it. But it was low rent and the only thing available in a hurry.

Patty did some exploring and yelled from the side yard, "Lookie here! An outside toilet." There was no indoor plumbing, just a pump for water and a cute pot-belly stove in the middle of the room in case it got cold. I wondered if we would be there that long. It might be fun. I could pretend that I was playing house or camping in an abandoned cabin. Somehow, I would have to make it work for me, and pretending always worked.

The first thing that moved in was a new linoleum rug that curled up at the edges. Dad warned, "For the luvva Mike, don't trip over this thing. You'll either break the rug or your leg." It took several days for the new rug to get acquainted with the floor and stay flat. It took even less time for all of us to get used to humble living again. I still had hopes of us being an average family someday, though getting used to that place meant pushing those dreams to the back of my mind for a while.

It seemed that we were trying to get a fresh start, but only the future would tell. Dad was so happy to have us all back that he paid no attention to the fact that we lived in a shack where lawn mowers should be stored instead of people. Mom sensed that we kids were kind of down in the dumps about our new home and said, "I've got a surprise for all of us."

Oh no, what now?

"Just be patient and you'll find out what it is." And then she gave us our orders. "Patty, empty the towels out of that big box. Bob, get a knife and a pencil out of that shoebox on the floor. Betty, get that bottle of molasses on the shelf."

Whenever we needed something we couldn't afford to buy, Mom became an inventor. I could tell she was enjoying herself, and just seeing her happy made me feel less glum. We were off to a good start.

First, she cut two square sides out of the box while we huddled close to find out what she was up to. I was truly curious. Without using a ruler, she started making marks on one of the cardboard squares. She never hesitated. It was as though she had it all figured out in her head. Then it began to look familiar.

"You're drawing a marble board?" Bob asked.

Yes, yes — she was! The marble board was our favorite game. Some people called it Aggravation or Parcheesi. Mom just grinned and kept gluing the two pieces of cardboard together. Her "glue" was molasses smeared clear to the edges with her bare hands. Then she set it aside to dry, with canned goods placed all over the surface so it wouldn't warp. "Don't touch it," she said. "Don't even look at it."

By the next day it seemed dry enough to finish. On the marked dots, our mother punched holes through just the top layer of cardboard with a paring knife. Then she scraped the papery pulp out to make a little depression. That's where the marbles would rest. It took a long time, but she was completely dedicated to making that thing work. That night when we placed the homemade marble board on a card table, there was plenty of room around the edges for four people to throw dice. We spent our second night together as happy as any family could be, playing marbles just like old times.

We lived in the homey shack for several months. My side of the bed was against the wall where I could peek through a crack between the boards. It was my own private view of the world, and I loved it. I liked the primitive feeling of being an Indian in a tent or maybe even a thirteen-year-old cave dweller. Every night, I peeked at the moon with my left eye and went to sleep with crickets squawking close to my head.

Each morning when I walked from our shed-home to the richest school in town, I wondered what those kids at Franklin would think if they knew where I lived. Every night I prayed, "God, please don't let anybody from school come to visit."

The House with Chickens

Without a doubt, our marble board house was cozy, even though choosing to live there had been an emergency decision. Dad said, "We've got to find a place where I can stretch my legs and maybe even have a garden. Besides, if we're still here when snow comes, we'll freeze to death."

I knew he was right. Peeking through tiny openings to the outdoors was fun, but I never would have done that in the wintertime. I could've frozen my eyeball. It gave me the shivers just thinking about it. "Dad, do you think snow would actually come in through these cracks?" I asked.

"Sure as shootin'. The freezin' wind will blow right through them cracks, and whatever is on the other side will get its share of snow and ice." That would be my left eyeball. Yes, we had to move.

It made my heart happy when I heard my father announce, "I've found another house." Luckily, that place was in the same school district, though it was still in an old, run-down neighborhood. The owner lived on the second floor and we lived on the first. The outside surface was tired gray wood that needed a good hosing and a coat of paint. But we had running water again and an indoor toilet and a kitchen, and those things alone made me feel like celebrating.

As soon as grass started growing in the spring, Dad stood with both hands on his hips and stared at the big backyard. I could tell he was hatching a new idea. And he was. "By gum, I'm gonna forget about a garden and raise some chickens here."

Mom was not a bit interested in his new plan.

"But, Girl," he said, "I can't think of a better way for us to get meat real cheap."

"Butch, chickens are not meat. They're poultry."

"Well, they're meat to me."

I thought they were meat, too. I never appreciated how much interesting stuff Mom knew. All I knew was that I loved fried chicken almost as much as I loved corn on the cob. I could hardly wait to have as many drumsticks as I could stuff into my mouth. I was so excited that I went with Dad to the feed and grain store to buy baby chicks.

They were precious and made teeny little peeping sounds. I hadn't expected to fall in love with those things. While they were still tiny, Dad got busy building a chicken coop. We kept the babies in a large box in the living room where they peeped all night and drove Mom crazy. Their box became a toilet for chickens, which made our home smell kind of "barnyardy."

I started dreaming up names for them in alphabetical order. The first ones were Angel and Buckwheat, then Lucy, Ludicrous, Marilyn, and Paris. When they were old enough to be in the coop, the chickens ran to me when I tossed grain to them. I was sure it was because they knew their names.

As Dad and I looked them over, I said, "Aren't they pretty?"

"Yep, they sure are," he said. "And they're gonna look even prettier on a platter."

I had forgotten that we were raising our chickens to put some meat on the table.

When the chickens had gotten big, I watched through the window as Dad caught one and killed it for supper. I left the room gagging. That night we had a feast: mashed potatoes, sliced tomatoes and cucumbers from Uncle Cullen's garden, and a platter of golden brown fried chicken from our own back yard. I kept my eyelids at half mast during supper so I wouldn't see my family eating Lucy. But I couldn't help hearing Bob say with his mouth full, "Mmmmm, this is so crispy and good!" I think he did that on purpose. Dad's great idea of raising chickens instead of a garden didn't seem all that great anymore.

After that, whenever someone mentioned chicken for supper, all I could see was that headless body, unhinged and flopping all over the place and splattering blood everywhere. I could almost hear it screeching, "Where's my head, where's my head, where's my head!" Eventually, I was able to eat fried chicken again, but not chickens with names like Buckwheat or Paris.

Temporary Quarters

One day, Mom was in a real dither and couldn't stand still. I whispered to Bob, "What's wrong with Mom?" He had no idea. Mom lit up another cigarette and paced. I dreaded it when my mother started pacing. It meant a storm was coming, and I don't mean rain.

All of a sudden, she screwed her cigarette out in the tray and announced, "Kids, we've got to move again."

"Really? Where are we going?" Bob asked.

"We're not sure yet. We're staying at three different places until we find another house. It's only temporary."

"What does temporary mean?" Patty asked. I wanted to ask a question, too, but Mom didn't answer Patty and another question might take her over the edge. I didn't want that to happen again. I was afraid that someday Mom might fall off the edge and never come back.

She must have read my mind because she explained. "The landlady is selling this place. So each of you put your own things in a different box until I know who's going to stay where."

Even though I was used to moving, I was always unprepared. It was best just to do what we had to do without questioning. My hopefulness was going downhill fast.

However, I got lucky. I moved in with Aunt Edith. Patty and Mom stayed at Damsy's, and Bob and Dad were at Uncle Cullen's. When I arrived at Aunt Edith's, her smile was so big it made her face beam. She squeezed me tight and said, "I am so glad that I have you all to myself because we're going to have a great time. Did you bring any new drawings to show me?"

Aunt Edith was an artist, just as I was, and she also loved to cook and sew. From the time I was a little girl, she'd encouraged me to draw and to make doll clothes. "If you've never used a sewing machine I'll teach you how," she'd said.

I slept in the bedroom where my baby cousin slept. His four-year-old brother was in his own bedroom. While I lived there, it seemed that she and I were girlfriends instead of aunt and niece. With two little boys, she had no one to gussy up in curls and ribbons. So she gussied up me. She set my long hair on Pro Curlers a few times to show me how nice I would look without pigtails. I couldn't believe that just curling my hair could make me look so pretty. Together, Aunt Edith and I sewed, drew, fixed our hair, and polished our fingernails and toenails. I loved the attention.

Having me live with them gave my aunt and uncle a chance to go out on a date now and then because I was old enough to babysit. I changed my cousin's diapers and drew pictures for his big brother. He asked me to draw unusual things such as mashed potatoes, pork chops, and sliced tomatoes on a plate. No matter what he asked me to draw, I did it, so I was drawing all the time. He thought I was a magician. I was glad he never asked me to draw a motorcycle or a horse, because I had no idea how to draw those unless I looked at the real thing. My little cousin never knew that my magical drawing abilities were limited.

During my short stay with Aunt Edith's family, life was the way I'd always imagined it could be and hoped it would be. But, like everything else, it didn't last.

The Sad House

My parents had no luck finding a cheap place to rent on the prosperous side of town, so they made the decision to look on the west side where more middle-class people lived. It meant that we three kids would be changing schools for sure, which was nothing new. I couldn't even imagine going to the same school for a whole year. Maybe someday I would know.

Our new home was a two-story house next to the playground for an elementary school. My school was just down the street, and I was thrilled with it. I liked Roosevelt High School more than any school I had ever attended. It turned out to be a good move for me. My life soon included new friends at school and at the Olivet Presbyterian Church.

But life wasn't all rosy. While we lived there, Mom and Dad had an argument that almost ended in disaster. They were having a long discussion in lowered voices at the kitchen table. The kitchen was where bad things started and ended whenever my parents got quiet and serious. I was getting nervous and felt that trouble was just around the corner. And trouble was nearby, disguised in the form of an aunt and her two young children. Dad's brother and his wife were splitting up because of marital problems. My parents had decided to help out by inviting their sister-in-law and her two children to stay with us while the couple worked things out.

Bob and Patty jumped up and down with excitement. "One of them can sleep with me," said Bob.

"Well, if you get one I get the other," Patty shot back.

You would have thought they were buying a new toy. They looked forward to having our young cousins with us even if both kids were younger than five.

But eight people in our small house with no yard were three people too many. I had a lot of responsibility looking after my brother and sister as well as two little cousins. Gradually, tension between my parents and my aunt bubbled to the surface. From the tone of Mom's voice, I sensed she was jealous.

"Butch, your sister-in-law is quite a looker," Mom said.

Dad agreed. "Yep, you can say that again."

"She also dresses nice like she's going on a date."

"Yeah, I noticed that."

Mom worried about how aware Dad was of their very cute sister-in-law. My aunt tried to assure her that nothing was going on. "Waneta, you've got to be kidding if you think I'm sweet on Butch." But nothing my aunt said could change Mom's mind. Dad went around holding his cigarette between his thumb and forefinger and saying, "Oh, for crying out loud."

The tension that started in the kitchen eventually grew, and I knew what was coming next: a family fight. I said, "Hey kids. Let's all five of us go upstairs and use our new coloring books and read stories."

"Me first."

"I get to pick the story."

"Wait for me, you guys."

"I get the red crayon."

They just about trampled me to beat each other up the steps to our attic bedrooms. It was the easiest way to remove them from whatever was happening in the kitchen. I got them all involved in the fun, while I strained to hear what Mom, Dad, and my aunt were saying. Then something in their voices changed. It alarmed me. I crept back downstairs to eavesdrop and heard Mom screaming at Dad. Then I heard the bathroom door slam shut just as it did in the old days when neighbors had to call the police. Mom going into the bathroom in such a state of mind was an ominous warning.

A few minutes later, I heard Dad slam the bathroom door open and yell, "Girl, what in the hell have you done!?!"

The fear in his voice scared me into creeping closer to see what was happening. Dad was bringing Mom out of the bathroom with a large towel over her arm. My aunt grabbed her purse and a coat to throw over Mom's shoulders. Dad yelled upstairs, "Betty, stay with the kids 'til we get back!" He had no idea I was so close.

I stayed quiet and hidden until they drove away, knowing in my heart that my mother had tried to hurt herself. Then I went into the bathroom to see for myself. I wasn't surprised to see blood all over the sink and floor and Mom's medical scissors near the faucets. I couldn't move fast enough to turn on the water and wash it all away. I wiped the sink as quickly as I could with a wet washcloth in case one of the kids came down the steps to find out what was taking me so long. My hands shook and my heart pounded. I was afraid for Mom and afraid the little kids would come downstairs before I got the mess cleaned up.

Thank God they were so engrossed with crayons that they never knew what happened. When I finished wiping everything down, there wasn't a single red smear left anywhere and the washcloth was rinsed clean. I wrung it out and hung it on the edge of the tub, dried my hands, and went back upstairs to keep the little kids occupied.

I didn't feel right, and I couldn't think straight. I kept imagining my father returning with tears in his eyes to tell me that my mother was dead. I was afraid she was never coming home again. But I focused on staying calm and tried not to think about it by picking up a crayon and filling in a space in a coloring book.

My littlest cousin squealed and grabbed my hand. "You silly . . . you're coloring Snow White's hair green." I tried to laugh it off.

After a couple of hours, Dad, my aunt, and Mom returned. Mom had a large bandage on the crook of her right arm, but no explanation was offered. The three adults were sober, but not angry. It was as though nothing unusual had happened. There was never a word said about the event. I didn't know whether to be glad or puzzled.

Mom wore the bandage on her arm for a few weeks; most of the time a long-sleeved sweater hid it from view. Not long after that, my aunt and uncle got back together and life went on as though it was normal. But what was normal for us was not normal for any other family I knew.

Twenty-five years later, my mother sat in my kitchen as we chatted over coffee. She said, "Betty, there's something I should tell you that I've kept secret all these years." I had no idea what was coming. She continued with eyes lowered and hands in her lap. "A long time ago when you were in the eighth grade, I tried to take my own life."

"Was that when Aunt Kay and the twins lived with us?" I asked.

"Yes, it was, and all these years I've kept it from you three kids."

It was my turn to confess. "Mom, I've known about it ever since it happened."

Her head jerked up. "How could you?"

"I cleaned up the blood so the little kids wouldn't see it."

My mother was so shocked and saddened by that news that she pressed her palms to her face. In my whole life I never saw my mother cry, and that was the closest she ever came. Her sadness almost broke my heart . . . so I cried for both of us.

The Altar Call

I WAS THIRTEEN AND A VISITOR AT THE NAZARENE CHURCH WHEN a tap on my shoulder identified me as a sinner who needed to be saved. I already knew my soul was in serious danger because Delores Heimlich told me so when she found out my mother had not only been divorced, but smoked cigarettes.

Delores was a religious bully, always telling me that my parents were doing bad things. I didn't dare tell her that we also went to the theater on Sunday, which I thought was okay until Mom told me different. "Good Christians do not go to movies any day of the week, so we cannot be good Christians until we stop attending matinees." I knew then that I could never be the right kind of Christian because I couldn't possibly give up my weekend films.

I kept my non-Christian state a secret from Delores, hoping she would never discover that I was not only the daughter of a cigarette-smoking divorcee, but a movie-going sinner as well. I figured I'd been found out when a woman lightly tapped my shoulder and asked, "Would you like to come to the altar and pray through?" I didn't know what she meant, but I said, "Yeah, sure, thank you."

As I knelt at the rail with a bunch of other people, I kept wondering what they had done wrong and what was coming next. I soon found out. A man close to me began to sway back and forth, then suddenly lifted his arms to the ceiling and yelled, "Yes! Yes! Take me, Jesus. I'm yours!"

Maybe he just wanted to hurry things along and this was his way of wrapping it up. Or maybe he'd reached his breaking point. Whatever the reason, the altar helpers gathered around the screaming man and hugged him and kissed his head and patted his back as though he had just won Bank Night.

I got the feeling that I was expected to cry, pound my fists, and wring my hands until I felt clean again. For the life of me, I could not dredge up any tears or hysteria no matter how hard I tried. And I really did try. I thought hard about when our dog Curly got killed chasing cars and when Dad killed our chickens for dinner, but nothing could make me sad enough to cry so that I could pray myself clean.

Most of the people at the altar somehow managed to shed a few tears while calling upon God, but those of us who were there under false pretenses just wanted it to end. The piano played on and the people kept singing "Just as I Am without One Plea," and there I was at the railing with my head on my arms, waiting with a few other sinners. The Jesus helpers probably thought we were still praying through. I was praying, all right. I was praying that we could sit back down, even though it meant sitting next to the girl who had tricked me into spending Sunday night on my knees.

The minister finally let us return to our seats, after he patted our backs in encouragement and said, "That's okay. Maybe next time." The other folks thanked the pastor and promised to return, but I had no plans to join them. My plan was to dump Delores Heimlich as soon as her dad gave me a ride home.

Passion for Music

ONE CONSTANT THROUGH ALL OUR MOVES WAS AUNTIE MARGE. Sometimes she was the only stable thing in my life. When she was a kid, Auntie Marge had been almost as poor as we were. She hated it, mostly because poor kids couldn't afford music lessons. Music was my aunt's passion. She had always wanted to become a singer, so sweet Uncle Al, who gave my aunt anything she wanted, paid for her monthly voice lessons almost three hundred miles away in Minneapolis, Minnesota. It took most of the day to get there.

Auntie Marge paid no attention at all to my art abilities. She was interested only in my musical side. Since she never had children, she shared her enthusiasm for music with me. She knew how often I practiced singing the songs from *Snow White and the Seven Dwarfs* as well as the famous tunes of Shirley Temple. And she was aware that I enjoyed glee club at school and harmonizing with Bob and Patty in the kitchen when we were supposed to be doing dishes.

Auntie Marge wanted me to shine in music so badly that she gave me private voice instruction once a week. By the time I reached the fourth grade, she had already bought a violin so that I could take free lessons at Polk School. She was thrilled to see the grades I got in music appreciation.

"Betty, when you're old enough to get there by yourself, I'm going to buy you season concert tickets," she announced. She made good on that promise three years later when I lived in Englewood, Colorado. I caught the bus and transferred to a streetcar to hear concerts performed by the Denver Symphony Orchestra. With all that encouragement and support, my aunt was confident that developing my musical talents would transform me into a cultured kid. "Being cultured will be the ticket to your future," Auntie Marge told me.

Each day she grew more enthusiastic as it appeared that I was getting hooked on music. She added "new clothes for Betty" to her long list of refinement projects. Being gussied up disguised my poverty so that I didn't look like the poor girl that I was. Once I was properly attired, she could take me out in public to events that other refined people attended. We showed up for many of the recitals at the Cedar Rapids Women's Club. And she got two tickets for the Iowa Theater so I could see my first operetta, *The Student Prince*. I left the theater floating on feet that wouldn't touch the ground. That night I tossed and turned, wondering when I could be in a musical production. I longed to be on the stage, acting and singing like the performers I'd seen in the show.

As impressive as *The Student Prince* had been, the single event that would mark my life for the next two years was a student recital. It featured our town's youngest musicians, many of them my age.

The pianists were wonderful and the cellists superb, but I couldn't take my eyes off the boy who performed a violin concerto. My goodness, he was tall. And his hair was combed so nicely. He closed his eyes when he played and his face reflected the emotions in the music. I had never heard such compelling sounds from a violin, and I wished it might never end. But the music did end, and when he bowed, the audience gave him a standing ovation because they were knocked out of their seats.

Goose bumps tickled my flesh as I searched the program for that boy's name. Donald Johanos. I wanted to play my violin the way Donald did. Actually, I wanted him. Would he wait for me to get old enough to be wanted by a boy? Most likely I would never see him again. But I knew that I had found my true love. It made me want to practice even harder on my violin.

After the recital was over and Auntie Marge was driving me home, she asked, "Did you enjoy the recital, Betty?" "Oh, yes, I really did enjoy it. Thank you so much for taking me."

"You're welcome, honey. We'll do it again some time."

"Yes, I hope we can."

I closed my eyes in the dark car and prayed, *Dear God. Let me see that boy again.*

Auntie Marge's passion for music was changing my life, and not in the way she'd expected.

First Love

ON MY FIRST DAY AT ROOSEVELT I GOT LOST, AS USUAL. I COULDN'T find my locker or the bathroom, and I arrived late for orchestra. Everyone stared at me because I was new. My eyes scanned the string section for an empty seat, then stopped, frozen with surprise. There in the first chair was my true love, the boy violinist who had received a standing ovation when Auntie Marge took me to a student recital. Don Johanos even looked tall sitting down. His straight brown hair flew carelessly across his forehead as he laughed with other students. That's when I noticed his big, white teeth. I came out of my trance thinking, *Why didn't I braid my hair more carefully?*

I took the last seat in the string section, far away from the prized first chair that Don occupied. I floated through the rest of the day.

Life at Roosevelt revolved around my first love from then on. He was two grades ahead of me, so I made every effort to seem older than my long braids implied. He was a well-known leader on campus and attended every function at our school. So did I. He attended the Presbyterian Church, so I stopped visiting other churches and became a member. He sang bass in the church choir. I sang soprano.

I adored him. I attended every one of his recitals and scribbled a note about him every night in my diary. The pages were filled with profound thoughts about my eighth grade life:

Don said hi to me today.

Don smiled at me today.

Don said I was a good artist today.

Don said I was a good violinist today.

He was absent today — I miss him so much!

I became a fourteen-year-old stalker, doing everything in my power to capture his attention and earn his respect. I practiced endlessly on my violin to improve my performance. One day Don asked, "Lizzie, may I see your left hand?"

Callused fingertips were evidence that I had worked harder than the average student. He was so impressed that we compared calluses. What a thrill. Then he noticed the dry red patch under my left jaw from my chin rest, and he tilted his head so I could see his mark, as well. I had gazed at that red spot more than he would ever know, but that time I did it with his permission. I had never experienced such sweet intimacy.

One night I was invited to Don's home to listen to a new album with a group of his friends. We hovered near the record player on the floor with bowls of popcorn and bottles of iced Coca-Cola. Don sat closer to me than ever before as we enjoyed his latest collection of violin concertos. I was so atwitter to be sitting on the rug in the house where he actually lived that I could hardly chew my popcorn or swallow my Coke. I had to take deep breaths to keep from crying with happiness. Concertos always affected me that way, but Don's presence had a lot to do with it, too.

A few days later, I glanced out the window in my upstairs attic bedroom and noticed Don walking past our house. I had never seen anyone carry a violin case the way he did, under his left arm instead of by the handle. I concealed myself and peeked out to admire his stride. I soon realized he passed my house twice a week, always carrying his case in that manly fashion. It made my heart pound. I assumed he was attending his private lessons, so I seized the opportunity to impress him again.

On days that I didn't expect him to walk by, I practiced with such enthusiasm that my fingertips hurt and the red mark under my left jaw grew hot. On the days of his lessons, I waited for his approach and performed my "concert" as Don walked past. I hoped it sounded like practice. Sometimes, I demanded that my little sister peek out to see if he noticed. "Yes," she would hiss. "He looked up."

Don recognized the tones of my German-made violin broadcasting from the attic. He said, "Lizzie, you're getting good. Do you study privately now?"

I answered shyly, "Well — sort of." Of course I didn't study with anyone, but it wasn't a lie. When I practiced, I was alone in my attic bedroom.

Soon, however, my playing improved so much that Auntie Marge decided I should have private lessons. She arranged for them at Coe College with Professor Joseph Kitchen. Before my first meeting with the professor, I waited in the hall for the student before me to finish. It didn't take long to realize that student had to be Don, because no kid could make a violin cry the way he did. Fate had brought us together again.

Oh, how my fourteen-year-old soul ached for that sixteen-year-old boy. When I discovered he had a girlfriend, I knew Don Johanos saw me only as a young girl with pigtails and a violin. Still, I didn't give up hope that one day he'd see me as more than a friend.

In the winter of 1944, I overheard my parents discussing plans to move to Denver, Colorado. I looked it up on a map. Denver seemed so far away from Cedar Rapids, Iowa. I hoped it was a bad dream and I would soon wake up, but it wasn't. We prepared to move as soon as school was out the following June.

I dreaded the possibility that if we moved to another state I might never see my first love again. I worried that I might even forget about him. To plant him in my memory, I flung myself into his presence by attending every event that was planned for our church group. I didn't miss a thing. After one of those excursions, Don and another boy walked us girls home. It was freezing cold, and wide patches of ice lined the gutters of the brick streets. In order to avoid slipping as we crossed, we needed help from the two boys. They stood at each side of a girl and held her hands so she could leap over the treacherous icy spot without falling.

I longed to hold my true love's hand, but I chose to impress him with my athletic ability instead. I would leap like a gazelle over that ice and land squarely on both feet. My audience was nervous. Don, with a doubtful look, huddled amidst the others to witness my sail through the air. I backed up to gain momentum and sprung like a deer. Instead of clearing the ice, I crashed onto the glassy section with my left knee. The boys helped me up, then supported my arms while I limped home. It was humiliating. I'd made an impression on the boy I loved, but it wasn't the impression I'd intended to make.

I needed stitches, but my father didn't believe in them. "Stitches cost money," he grumbled. So Mom applied a bandage that pulled the gash together. I grimaced with pain and stared at the ugly wound, knowing that I might carry a scar forever. Forever? The word resonated like a harmonic in my head. That's when my real work began.

As the injury tried to heal, I picked the scab off carefully and daubed a little ink into the abrasion. I hoped to create a mark that would remind me of Don for the rest of my life. It took weeks before the wound finally closed. My mother was too busy packing for the big move to notice that my injury had left a very blue scar. I was thrilled.

The months passed, and departure day arrived. I dreaded waking up that morning, knowing I might never see my friends again. I didn't know how I could possibly exist without Don in my life. He was not only my first love, but my role model and my idol. For two years I had lived to impress him. My infatuation had made me a better violinist and kept me too busy to get into trouble.

As our family of five approached the train depot, I felt so sorrowful that I struggled to keep from crying. I was in bad shape, but my brother and sister were in jolly spirits. They viewed our move to another state as though it were a Sunday picnic. But they weren't in love. They just wanted to go someplace on a train.

I dragged myself to the station platform, my violin case bumping against me with every step and my eyes on the ground. My spirits lifted a little when my church buddies met me at the train to say goodbye. They each hugged me tight and said, "Please write" . . . even Don.

Then I cried.

PART 6: *The Denver Adventure*

Panoramic view of Denver and the Rockies, about 1940

Riding the Rails

Saying Goodbye

I T WAS TORTURE GETTING ON THE TRAIN THAT WOULD TAKE ME away from home. Moving to Denver and leaving my friends felt like the end of the world. I forced myself up the steps and into the passenger car. My vision was blurry as I wiped tears away so Bob wouldn't call me a whiney-assed baby.

Our family claimed only four seats because Dad had to stay behind for a few months. I scrambled to our window to wave to my friends on the station platform. Then I stashed my violin and suitcase overhead and settled into the seat to pull myself together.

All kinds of people climbed aboard, and I wondered if they were leaving their best friends behind, too. Despite feeling sorry for myself, I began to notice the details of my surroundings. The train car was old and worn out like some of the places my family had lived. And it smelled of cigarettes like Damsy's house.

Through the haze of smoke hanging in midair, I watched a little boy run up and down the aisle, excited about his first train ride. I hoped watching the wild kid would take my mind off memories of Iowa. But after the boy's cranky mother grabbed his shirttail and yanked him into his seat, I had nothing to distract me from the worst day of my life.

On Our Way

"All aboard!"

Hearing the conductor's announcement snapped me out of my daydreaming and inspired Bob, Patty, and the wild boy to yell, "Yippee! Hot dog!" I had to admit that the all-aboard call gave me tingles that I tried not to show because excitement and sadness didn't blend.

I could tell that Mom was really tired because her forehead was shiny and she sighed a lot. She pulled her crochet bag close to her hip and gave it a little pat, but didn't open it. I had a feeling my mother felt as lost as I did.

The whistle blasted long hoots as our train, the City of Denver, began the two-day trip from Cedar Rapids, Iowa, to Denver, Colorado. The screech of wheels on metal went clear through me, causing goose bumps to explode on my left leg. That only happened when I felt unexpectedly thrilled about something.

Mom sighed louder and said, "We're finally on our way." Was she glad or not glad? I couldn't tell. After a few minutes, she relaxed and pulled a crochet project from her bag. She was making doilies for our new apartment.

Bob had just opened his Captain Marvel comic book when the landscape rushing by suddenly became cows rushing by. Patty tapped against the glass with her forefinger. "Three . . . four . . . five . . . oh, my gosh . . . six, seven, eight."

"What the heck are you doing?" I asked.

"I'm counting cows . . . nine, ten, eleven . . .uh . . . twelve, thirteen."

It was nerve-wracking, like listening to a crowd singing "99 Bottles of Beer on the Wall." But counting kept my ten-year-old sister happy.

Bob said, "Count to yourself. I'm trying to read." So she did. When we flew by trees and buildings at an ever-increasing speed, Patty stopped counting and began waving.

"What're you wavin' at?" Bob asked.

"Everything."

"Why?"

"I'm waving goodbye to everything."

I understood what she meant. If I hadn't been almost fifteen years old, I would have waved goodbye to everything, too.

My mother was tired of me acting glum all the time and wanted to know what was going on. "Why are you still down in the mouth about moving?"

I couldn't tell her that my heart was breaking about leaving Don Johanos.

"Betty, you've got to snap out of it and move on."

I also couldn't tell her that I didn't want to snap out of it. Staying sad served a purpose. If I started feeling happy, I might forget my friends. After all, I had purposely turned my scab into a scar so I would never forget Don. I didn't make that scar for nothing.

Patty continued to wave, which was almost as annoying as her counting. Bob gave up trying to read Captain Marvel and annoyed me instead.

"Whatcha doin' that for?" he asked.

"Doing what?"

"Writing letters already."

"I miss my friends."

"Ya just saw them a little while ago."

"Keep your opinions to yourself."

Mom sensed that our bickering was becoming a contest and said, "That's enough." That caused Patty to snicker behind her hands, so Mom said, "You, too!"

No one else would have understood our mother's code language, but we knew well that we'd better not start something in public. Our mother wouldn't hesitate to whack us on a leg or arm, no matter who was watching. But she never slapped us in the face.

Once the train reached open countryside with nothing to see but flat ground, Bob said, "I wanna go exploring."

Patty said, "Me, too."

"Not you, Patty. Bob, mind your Ps and Qs, ya hear?"

We didn't know what Ps and Qs were, but we knew that minding them meant we should pay attention to what we were doing. It also meant that my brother had permission to explore as long as he stayed out of trouble.

He'd been gone for about twenty minutes when he came back all excited. "Hey, you guys, the men's lounge looks just like the boys' locker room at school!" He had made friends with the conductor and told us the lounge was where the conductor hung out when he wasn't roaming the cars. The train was a regular hotel on wheels.

Eating and Sleeping on a Train

That afternoon we got to stop in a small-town depot store for a twenty-minute shopping spree. Mom gave us a warning before she relaxed with a cigarette. "Stick together and don't dilly-dally." She allowed each of us ten cents for an ice cream cone or a brand new comic book. We sweet-talked her into both. She worried that with twenty cents to spend and too many choices to make, one of us would get left behind. She told us a million times to listen for the first warning whistle, stop whatever we were doing, and get on the train.

When the whistle shrieked, we did just as she'd said and hustled back to our seats so fast that we got there first. We had no idea that she was frantically looking around the little store and yelling our names. When she came aboard to see if we were there, she wasn't sure whether to scold us or praise us for a job well done.

We got comfy with our cones and new comics, which were actually old. They had no covers so we'd gotten three for the price of one. I still liked comics, but I was happiest when I had a brand new typing tablet with plain white paper, a sharp new pencil with soft lead, and a good eraser. Those were my favorite things. I spent most of the trip drawing pictures or writing more letters to my friends.

Patty soon started getting so twitchy that Mom said, "Sit still or go to the toilet."

"I don't have to she-she."

"Then what's wrong with you?"

"I'm hungry."

"Me, too," Bob added.

I wanted us to eat in the dining car, but Mom said, "Not a chance in hell."

With that, she reached under the seat for a sack and produced cold fried chicken that she had wrapped in waxed paper and stored in a boot-sized shoebox. Her hot coffee was in a thermos, and our cold milk was in another. We shared one cup for milk and one soup spoon for her apple pie that we ate right out of the tin.

Our dining experience had been carried aboard in a double-layered brown paper grocery bag so nothing would break through. It tasted delicious, though I was embarrassed that we had packed our own food when most families were leaving for the train restaurant. I wanted to see what it was like, but Mom said we couldn't afford such a luxury.

Nighttime on the train was no picnic either. It was hard to sleep because we couldn't stretch out in the seats. I shifted constantly, trying to get comfortable. My mother reclined the back of her chair, and she and Patty went to sleep in no time at all. Patty's head hung so low to one side that her neck looked broken, and Mom's snoring sounded like a truck shifting gears. I was glad most of the people in our car were asleep. Bob's eyes were closed, but his mouth hung open. Feeling motherly, I wiped slobber from his chin.

Finally, I curled my legs under and hunkered down for the night. I dreamed of the homey touch Mom's doilies would make in our furnished apartment in Denver.

Troop Train Delays

"Please set watches back one hour for Mountain Time!"

Sleepy passengers were jolted awake by the announcement. We were passing through McCook, Nebraska, where it had rained all night. Mom and I did as we were told and reset our watches. Mine was a prized Mickey Mouse timepiece, a gift from Damsy for my eleventh birthday. The simple act of setting Mickey's hands to Mountain Time made me feel strangely mature even though my watch was designed for little kids. I was resetting my watch for the future.

During the trip, there were many unexpected delays when we were sidetracked to allow troop trains to pass. Sometimes we sat for hours. To keep us from getting impatient, the conductor explained.

"Folks, listen up. In case you don't know what's goin' on in the world, it is my duty to enlighten you. Today, June 6, 1945, is the one-year anniversary of D-Day, which was the beginning of the end of the war in Europe. A month ago, on May 8th, Germany surrendered, so now our boys are starting to come home on these troop trains ya see whizzin' by. Can ya tell how drunk they are with happiness?

Come to think of it, those jolly soldiers did seem kinda drunk to me, but with more than just happiness. And I should know because I'd seen my share of tipsy people in my life.

He went on. "There are only so many railroad tracks to go around, and the soldiers have priority. That's why we get sidetracked for so long." Then he paused dramatically before saying, "Let's give these boys a great big hand."

Everybody in our car suddenly felt patriotic. We cheered and clapped and waved at the soldiers and threw a million kisses and smiles that were a mile wide. The soldiers returned the favor by laughing and yelling as they waved like they knew each one of us personally. They were traveling back home. We were moving toward our new home.

Even though I hadn't expected happy soldiers to lift my spirits, the sadness began to float away as I joined in the cheering and clapping. But I kept my newfound excitement a secret because I wasn't quite ready to let it show.

Welcome to Denver

I HAD DAYDREAMED MY WAY ACROSS THE COUNTRY WHILE TRYING to picture our new life in Denver. Finally, after a two-day journey that had stretched into three, we slowed to a grinding halt at the Denver Rio Grande and Western Railroad station. I felt that I'd been in a cocoon and could now unfold and say hello to the world.

It was an impressive depot with a huge indoor space and hordes of hustling people. Suddenly, I wanted to join them.

Bob and Patty each carried two things. I carried three: my violin, a sack that held my tablet and pencils, and the grocery bag with empty containers from our meals on the train. We struggled to stay together as we made our way to the women's lounge.

Bob said, "I'm not goin' in the girls' toilet!"

Mom was too tired to argue. "You can go to the men's room by yourself, then, but don't talk to any strangers, ya hear?"

Bob promised, but I thought everyone we saw looked strange, so how could he tell the difference? Excitement and leftover homesickness were making me feel dizzy, and the ladies' room didn't help any. It was packed with weary, half-naked mothers giving themselves sponge baths, washing their children's faces, or bathing babies in the basins. We needed to join them and wash away three days of grime. After claiming the first empty spot, three of us squeezed together over one sink and declared it our own private territory.

There was barely room to push our luggage under the counter and no place near the faucet for a washcloth, towel, and toothbrushes. But we didn't dare leave our spot until we were finished for fear another traveler would grab it. Mom, Patty, and I stood so close that we spit on each other while brushing our teeth. Patty looked like a mad dog with her mouth hanging open and Pepsodent foam running down her chin.

"Don't swallow that toothpaste," Mom said. "Cup your hands to collect water, then slurp it up and rinse."

Denver's Union Station

Cleaning up for breakfast took a long time, and Bob was waiting for us when we finally emerged. "Bob, did you wash your hands and brush your teeth?" Mom asked.

"I washed my hands, but you had all the toothbrushes."

Mom decided it wasn't worth opening the bags again to find my brother's toothbrush.

"But, Mom, his breath is terrible," I said.

"Then don't sit next to him because I'm not digging around in that bag for one little toothbrush." The subject of Bob's bad breath was over, so we each claimed our assigned bags and took our hungry selves in search of the diner.

We found it, but it was packed, with no empty booth in sight. Mom was clearly in charge. She didn't ask people at the counter to please scoot over and fill empty places to make room for us. She ordered them to move, and her tone meant business.

We plunked our luggage down close to our legs and perched atop four red plastic seats on high swivel stools. We remained perched for a long time. Waitresses dashed back and forth in front of us, but no one paid attention.

My family had become invisible. Finally, after my rowdy red-headed sister started clutching her throat and gasping as though having a fit, a poker-faced waitress glanced our way.

"Whadaya want?"

Mom recited our order like a pro since she'd been a waitress herself at Auntie Marge's Café. Blank Face repeated the order as she wrote: "Pancakes, milk, coffee, orange juice, got it." We really wanted bacon, eggs, and fried potatoes, but had to budget our cash. After eating mostly snacks on the train, we were so hungry we could've eaten napkins.

We sat forever and still no pancakes came our way. Patty got bored and started spinning around on her swivel stool. She almost knocked an old man down with her feet.

Our mother was in no mood to put up with foolishness. "Stop that or you know what'll happen." The warning didn't hamper Patty's stool spinning a bit. She was used to playing deaf. Something bad was bound to happen. Either Patty would hit someone else with her legs or she would get smacked with no warning.

No sooner did I think it than it happened. Patty received a whack on her legs that brought her twirling to an abrupt halt. She then entered her dramatic pouting stage, which we all ignored.

Waiting and hunger were getting to all of us. Bob pretended he was starving. He grabbed his stomach, leaned to one side, and moaned. "Aaaaahhh . . . I'm dying."

Mom finally waved a white handkerchief to get the attention of a waitress. "Ma'am, we've been waiting one half-hour for our order."

The woman snapped her chin sharply in our direction and shouted, "I've got two hands, lady . . . two hands!"

Our mother kept her composure, which was a true miracle, while we watched our waitress go crazy in front of everyone. Suddenly, I lost my appetite. We sat in stunned silence while other customers chewed and swallowed as though nothing unusual had happened. Eventually, the rude waitress slung plates of food in front of us with the dexterity of a discus thrower. Bob's plate almost flew past him onto the floor. We ate without saying a word.

That experience was not a friendly welcome to our new city. We were disheartened, but we rarely admitted such things out loud. Instead, we pretended it had never happened. I felt sick to my stomach.

So far I did not like Denver one bit.

Our New Home

OUR ARRIVAL IN DENVER WAS NOT QUITE WHAT WE HAD HOPED for. Instead of nice people saying, "Hello, there; welcome to our city," we got bawled out by a very grumpy waitress. I was sure she was the president of the Mean Waitress Club. Whatever she was, she left her mark on me. I was still recovering when Mom hauled us into the Union Station foyer to plan our next move.

"What are we doing now?" Patty asked.

"We're going to sit down someplace so I can have a cigarette and look at the map."

"At the map? Are we lost?"

In a voice as flat as a robot's, she said, "No . . . we're not lost."

"Then why do we need a map?" Patty was either curious or being a smarty pants.

Bob said, "We're looking for a place to dump you."

"Why me?"

"Dummy, she's looking for our new address."

"Do we have to walk there?"

Our mother had barely been holding herself together and exploded. "Patty!" Then she started counting. "One one-thousand, two one-thousand, three one-thousand." After taking a deep, slow breath, she continued. "I don't know yet. I'll find out in a minute."

Was Mom taking a class on how to stay calm? She was doing pretty well. I appeared to be unruffled, but I felt fuzzy and out of focus.

Bob yelled to us from the other side of the foyer. "I found an empty bench. I'll save it!"

The bench looked like it had been stolen from the Baptist church back home. It was long enough to hold all four of us and our junk. We hogged the whole space with our parcels stacked between us so they wouldn't get lost. Then we three kids watched the world go by while our mother pored over the Denver street map in her left hand, with a cigarette in the other. The hurly-burly reminded me of Chicago. It was noisy and everything moved too fast. I would never catch up.

Nobody had time to look at our faces because they all seemed to be late for appointments. I envied their sense of direction. They didn't need a map while we had no idea where we were going. I looked for something familiar to put me at ease, but everything was too new and different.

I jumped when Mom said "oh hell" under her breath and stood up. "You kids stay put. Don't move. I've got to talk to someone at that information counter." I watched her approach the counter and drop her cigarette hand to her side to keep the smoke away from the lady who worked there.

When she returned to our bench, she said, "The bus won't take us far enough, and our address is too far to walk with all these bags."

Patty started wringing her hands. "Oh, no, Mama. What are we going to do?"

"I hate spending the money, but we'll have to take a taxi." We claimed our bundles and trudged outside. "I hope these guys are honest," Mom said as she scanned the cabbies with her inner wisdom periscope to determine who would pass the test. She found a likely prospect and approached him. "Sir, you look honest. How much do you charge to go to Champa Street?"

After he stopped laughing, the honest-looking guy asked, "Ma'am, where on Champa?"

When she gave him the address, the cabbie said, "Heck, lady, that's only a few miles from here. Let's see — ya got three people and seven parcels. Five dollars will get you to Champa Street."

"Five dollars? Oh, my God. That doesn't sound honest to me."

"Lady, that's a bargain. The only other way to get there is to walk or drive your own car."

Mom could hardly bear to part with five dollars for a taxi ride, but she had no choice. She snapped open her purse and started rummaging noisily through the contents. I loved pocketbook sounds. It was a silly thing to pop into my head, but in that moment of tension, purse rummaging gave me comfort.

Finally, she came up with a five to hand over to the driver once we reached our destination. You would've thought she was being held up by a robber.

I didn't care what it cost. I just wanted to go. Moving so often created a terrible clash of emotions. After zigzagging between excitement and sadness for days, I was a jumbled-up mess.

The driver crammed our odd luggage into the trunk while we piled into the cab to head for Champa Street. On the way to our new address, I kept thinking about the rude waitress at the Union Station diner. It was a hard memory to shake, so I tried not to think about her anymore except to tell myself that I would never treat people the way she had treated us. I finally decided to stop thinking at all, relax against the seat, and enjoy the ride.

Bob must have felt crowded because he nudged me and said, "Hey, you're taking up too much room."

"Hey, and your breath stinks."

He responded with another nudge. Ordinarily, I would have punched him back to find out who would give up first, but I wasn't in the mood.

It wasn't even close to being an argument, but our mother had her psychic buttons turned too high. She jerked her head in our direction and said, "Don't start something, you two, or you know what'll happen." Yes, we knew what would happen if we didn't shut up. Mom would embarrass us in front of the driver by reaching behind the seat to whack our knees or whatever her wild swing landed on. So I distracted myself by concentrating on the vacant lots and lack of scenery.

Bob made trivial news reports now and then such as, "Wow, those buildings are tall." They weren't a bit tall. It was his way of letting everyone know he was behaving.

Then the cabbie asked, "Ma'am, where are you folks from anyway?"

Patty answered for her. "We're from Cedar Rapids, Iowa, and we're moving here."

"You're moving here?"

"Yes, we're moving to Champa Street."

"To Champa Street?"

"Yes, we are."

"I thought maybe you were visiting someone."

Patty said, "No, we're gonna live here."

"Good luck."

Mom said, "Thank you. That's very nice."

I wondered whether the driver was wishing us well or warning us. Maybe I was paranoid. Denver wasn't bringing out the best in me. I was eager to get settled so I could resume my usual activities: drawing, listening to spooky radio shows, and practicing my violin. I knew I could adjust my attitude once we put down some roots. That's what Dad said every time we moved: "We've got to put down some roots."

I always thought that meant we had to plant a garden as soon as possible. Well, after Dad arrived, this would be a good spot for a garden because there wasn't any grass. There was nothing but lots of dirt, vacant lots, and cement.

Mom turned and stared hard at me. "Betty, you've been awfully quiet. What's going on with you?"

"I'm fine. There's so much to see here that I'm taking it all in."

That wasn't the truth and she knew it, because there wasn't that much to take in.

We turned a corner onto a street lined with tall, leafy trees. The old two-story homes had probably housed rich people long ago when the houses were grand and welcoming. Bob said, "Wow, those trees are tall."

Yeah, they were tall all right. But I was thinking, *Bob, take your eyes off the treetops. Don't you notice how shabby these buildings are? Mother Nature keeps the trees alive, but the houses are dying. The people who live here don't give a hoot or holler about their homes.*

Kids were playing in dirt yards. Car parts and tires were piled where shrubs could have been growing. Those neighborhoods were nothing like the ones in my daydreams. I was glad my mother didn't look at my face because she might've read my thoughts again. I wondered what she was thinking. Was she as downhearted as I was but putting on a contented act?

Eventually, our driver slowed down to peer at house numbers to find the right address. I wanted to send a magic thought-message to his brain: *Don't slow down here. You're making a mistake.*

People were huddled on porches, talking to each other in tight groups as though it was a day off work. Several police cars sat in the streets. The cab driver pulled to the curb in front of one of the houses, put on his parking brake, and said, "Well . . . this is it."

We had stopped in front of a two-story house with tall, round pillars that stretched from the porch to the second story roof. It resembled Scarlet O'Hara's home in *Gone with the Wind* after the Yankee soldiers had wrecked it. My mother's doilies wouldn't be much help there.

My mother was confused, too. "Sir, this can't be right. Are you sure you've got the correct address?"

"Ma'am, you told me to drive you to 1041 Champa Street." He jabbed his thumb toward the decrepit house. "And this here house is 1041 on Champa. Ya see the numbers up there on the pillar?" Yes, we saw the numbers on the pillar, but we were still in disbelief.

"Sir, you wait right here. I want to see if this is where we're supposed to be."

Our cabbie let his breath out real slow and looked at his watch like he couldn't wait to get off work. I was glad he had parked near the front door, because I could hear everything. I crossed my fingers and held my breath, hoping it was the wrong house.

Mom went to the front door and knocked. Three dusty kids ran up close to find out who she was. She knocked several more times and waited. Finally, the door opened to reveal a skinny woman with a cigarette dangling from her lips. A naked toddler clutched the hem of her housecoat while she squinted against the smoke drifting close to her face.

She removed the cigarette and, with the same hand, picked something from her tongue. "Well, hello there. We've been expecting you folks."

My heart fell. I had to pretend the scene was not real life, but a movie, and I was the star. Whenever I pretended things were different from real life, my mother said I was practicing denial. I had no idea if that was the same as practicing the violin or memorizing Bible verses.

She explained to the lady that there were only four of us, but that Dad would join us at the end of August. Then she waved us into the house. We kids piled out of the taxi in slow motion. It took a while to gather our belongings. The dusty children gawked at us with curiosity. I reminded myself that my family and I were the actors, and they were our audience.

Once we were on the porch, Mom returned to the cab and begrudgingly handed a five dollar bill to the driver. He must have expected a tip because he kept his hand out, but she ignored it. As far as she was concerned, he didn't even have a hand. I knew she blamed him for bringing us to that pitiful place, and I blamed him, too. I had to blame someone, and I would never set eyes on him again.

Hauling stuff upstairs was slow going, but it gave me a chance to look at things up close. I studied the pattern on the wall because the artist in me was interested. It was unusual. Bob noticed it, too. He said, "Wow, look at these nifty designs." They were mottled shades of gray with a hint of rust blended in as an accent. I'd never seen anything like it and wondered how the paint had been applied. I was the camera moving in for a close-up when I recoiled. "Bob, don't touch it!"

"Why not?"

His hand was already exploring the surface when I said, "These are human handprints."

He cringed and shook his hands to fling away the germs he had just adopted. I didn't know whether to throw up or laugh. Bob did not think it was funny.

Our second-floor apartment was located very close to the top of the stairs, the perfect location if we needed to escape. Our landlady, with her unclothed child in tow, opened the door and introduced us to our front room. She grinned with pride and said, "You'll be happy to know that this here unit is completely furnished."

It had to be a joke. There was a bed in the living room, an end table, a lamp, and a wooden rocker. I expected someone to say, "You folks are in a movie, so remember that this is not real." But it was real. The furniture was what Dad would call piss poor. We were poor, but we'd never been piss poor.

While checking out the apartment, I trailed behind Mom and the landlady on someone else's legs. I couldn't feel mine. The landlady proudly pointed out the details of our furnishings in the living room. She gave a short speech about each item, so I pretended she was leading a tour through the White House. "This is a good, strong metal bed." The striped mattress was "good, sturdy material." Gesturing toward the small round table with a lamp on top, she said, "A good setup for readin' and writin'.

I tried to see humor in the situation and imagined I was an understudy tour guide. "And here we have a mission-style rocker like the one that Granddad sat in by the big window in his house. He always faced the outside, ignoring anyone in the living room no matter how far they had come to see him. To our left we have a soiled pull-down shade that covers the window that overlooks a grass-free lawn."

It felt so good to make fun of the place that I was glad no one could read my thoughts. But I was never sure about my mother's secret powers. She may have been a bit off-center, but she was obviously remarkable. She had unexplored potential, and maybe she blew up so easily because all that talent was getting crowded inside of her. I had no idea how she was going to handle the incredible disappointment of our new home, though sometimes she was at her best in an emergency.

Mom was speechless as we took it all in. The landlady continued her tour in the tiny kitchen. She stepped aside and gestured as if she was on camera. "You'll notice that everything in this kitchen matches."

That caught Patty's attention. "What did she say about kitchen matches?"

I told her to shush and she said, "We're not allowed to use matches."

I told her to shush again or she would get it.

"Get what? Matches?"

Bob couldn't stand it anymore. "Patty, shut up!"

Mom ignored us, which meant she would give us heck as soon as we were alone. But maybe not. She might have been in shock, and that worried me. Then I turned my attention to what the landlady had said. The ugly green table was surrounded by four homely green folding chairs, and the hand-painted green refrigerator was the most repulsive thing I'd ever seen. It could have been in a circus side show all by itself. The only thing that didn't match was the small gas stove that used to be white. It was now prematurely gray and would have looked at home in the city dump. The décor of the apartment amused me. I hoped the feeling would last.

A screen door opened from the kitchen onto a platform with a shaky railing and steep narrow steps that led to the dirt yard near the alley. The view of the backyard from our second-story porch matched the unattractiveness of the kitchen.

Bob and Patty kept themselves busy by standing on the platform watching tough kids punch each other in the alley. Would those kids ever play hide-and-seek with my brother and sister? I imagined the scene. *Hide-and-seek? What kinda sissy game is that?* Bob and Patty would get beaten up if they even mentioned our favorite game here. I'd have to come up with action and dialogue for Bob and Patty to practice in case they got in a tight spot.

Since my mother hadn't said a word during our home tour, I assumed she was as down in the mouth as I was. I tried to act unruffled for my brother and sister by keeping my mouth shut, which meant they would do the same.

Mom finally broke her silence. "Ma'am, where is our bathroom?"

"Hey, you're the lucky ones who're the closest to the john." She led us out to the hall, pointed to a door, and said, "It's right here outside your apartment." Mom pushed the door open and all four of us stared at the community bathroom. If that toilet could talk, it would have said, *Thank God. Help has arrived. I thought you'd never get here.*

The bathroom was so awful I didn't know whether to laugh or cry. I tried hard to do neither for fear of getting hysterical.

But our mother was still in the real world and asked, "Who cleans this?"

"Oh, the families sometimes take turns."

"But who is in charge of the cleaning schedule?"

"Well . . . they sorta work it out among themselves."

The bathroom was long and narrow with cracked, dark linoleum that once had pattern and color. There was a grimy bathtub on legs, a dirty wash basin, a soiled tubular towel on a wooden dowel, and yellowed lace curtains that hung to the floor. The windowsill was about knee-high to whoever was sitting on the toilet. While sitting there, you'd be able to see the whole world outside and the whole world could see you. I tried to make a joke for Bob and Patty. "Look, we can wave at the folks outside while we're going pee."

That broke the ice for a few seconds until we learned that we would share the bathroom with three other families on the second floor. That meant at least twelve to fifteen people would be using "our" bathroom. I made a vow to drink water only when I was dying of thirst so I wouldn't have to go she-she very often.

Mom and the landlady returned to the kitchen table to discuss the details of our rental while Bob and Patty stared out the window at those tough-looking kids beating each other up for fun. They were wearing boxing gloves, which made it appear to be an orderly fight.

The whole dismal dwelling was such a shock that I was overwhelmed with what was now turning into grief. I went to the living room so I could sit alone in the rocker that reminded me of Granddad. Then I knew why he sat facing the window all the time, away from the rest of the family. He must have been as depressed as I felt. I tried to look casual as I studied the unusual dirt yard below, the abandoned car over there, and that pile of old tires. But I was really praying, *Dear God, don't let my family come in here until I pull myself together, and please, please do not let me cry.*

It didn't work. My eyes stung and I couldn't stop the tears, so I leaked them out as quietly as possible. Crying with no sound made my throat ache. I felt strangled. I wiped the wetness away as fast as I could so my family wouldn't notice. I was as low as earthworms could ever go.

After cigarette-lady closed the door behind her, we were alone, surrounded by nervous silence. No one knew what to say. Even Patty could feel the tension and had the good sense not to try any smart stuff. I was relieved when Mom finally spoke. With a knowing smile and using an honest-to-God cheery voice, she said, "Well, kids — it's for damn sure we're not staying in this dump any longer than we have to."

Oh, happy day! Our mother had come through the home tour with flying colors. My low spirits lifted at least two inches, and Bob and Patty looked like they had just been let out of reform school.

Finding Hope at the Museum

AFTER THE DISAPPOINTING TOUR OF OUR NEW APARTMENT, I DIDN'T know how to stop feeling gloomy in those ugly rooms. We didn't unpack one single thing. Instead, we left the building and inquired about the streetcar schedule. We soon climbed aboard and grabbed seats by the window, off to see the nicer sights of Denver. I seriously doubted any such thing existed, but for the first time since we'd arrived in the city, I was hopeful.

Bob said, "I hope Mom knows where we're going."

Patty said, "I hope it's to the movies."

I didn't care what our destination was as long as I could clear my head. I knew it wouldn't be easy to change my attitude. Even though I was fourteen, I still wanted a childhood fairy to wave her magic wand in front of my face and say, "Ta-da! Doncha just love it here?"

I stopped moping when I noticed that the scenery had changed. Where did that grass come from? And those nice old houses — where did they keep their tires and old cars? The trees formed a beautiful canopy over the street. Where were we heading on that magical street car?

If I had been ten years old instead of fourteen, I would have said the fairies were on vacation and had sent a streetcar to take their place. I still believed in the kind of magic that happened when I sensed things I had never noticed before. Hearing the brakes squawk as we slowed and the bell clang each time the driver picked up speed was exciting. Everything we lumbered past was easy on the eyes, so the city suddenly looked different. The air even smelled good. A ride on an enchanted streetcar was changing my mind about Denver, and my mother's new behavior helped a lot, too.

We still didn't know our destination until we stopped at the city park. Then my mother told us we were headed to the Museum of Natural History because we all needed a culture break, and it was free.

When we reached the entrance, she gave us instructions for museum visiting. "Okay, kids, act refined."

"What does refined mean, Mom?" Patty asked.

"It means not noisy or wild or rowdy. You can't play tag in here."

"You mean like church?"

"Yes, a little bit like church, but with no collection plates, no praying, and no preaching."

"Yippee!"

"Don't do anything in here to make me mad or I'll forget where we are."

"I have to go to the toilet."

"Fine, we'll do that first." And off we went for a potty break in a spotless bathroom with a clean toilet.

It was so good to be there that I forgot we had just moved from another state. While viewing stuffed coyotes and wild turkeys in dusty, life-sized dioramas behind walls of glass, I knew I was getting over the awful relocation blues. The museum was interesting, even though some of the displays needed to be freshened up a bit. Maybe our mother could get a part-time job there, giving the stuffed animals and fake plants a spit shine.

All of a sudden I cared about things. Ascending from hell to heaven within an hour was as good as winning bingo.

Bob waved me over to where he was looking at something. "Look at this. Isn't it nifty?" It really was nifty, a miniature version of the Rocky Mountain area with diminutive trees and lakes. I was a giant looking down at the small world and wondered if that's the way God felt. Then I remembered what I heard at church one Sunday. The preacher said that wherever a rock, tree, mountain, or lake existed, the Creator was there.

I couldn't take my eyes off the tiny trees and mountains that looked so real. I imagined itsy bitsy people hiking on microscopic trails. It was easy to imagine that God could be a miniature boss of the world at the same time that he was the boss of our large world. Maybe he was everywhere.

I felt guilty that I prayed only when desperate for favors, so I talked to Him inside my head right there in the museum. *Hey, God, wherever you are right now, I am so sorry for always asking for help and then not saying thank you. About an hour ago, I asked you not to let me cry in front of my family. And even though I did cry, they didn't see me. I sure do thank you for that. Now I need another favor. Please, oh please, help me not to be so sad about moving here. And help me to like this place just a little, because despising it is making me feel sick. Thanks a lot. Bye.*

I was worn out from all that had happened so far. But I had enough energy to decide right then and there to get used to our new home. It was so simple. All I had to do was stop hating it. What a relief that was.

When we returned to our dismal dwelling, we unpacked all we had brought, knowing that the rest of our belongings would arrive later. We each chose a dresser drawer and put our own towel and washcloth in with our underwear. Then we made the rooms as livable as possible. Patty said, "I get to put the new doilies around." Then she arranged them on every flat surface. The effect was cluttered, but it prettied things up.

I plugged in our small white radio that somebody had crammed into a suitcase, and we listened to music while making a list. We needed to buy lots of supplies in order to clean up the joint, as Mom put it.

The summer of 1945 was going to be different from any other summer in my life, and I couldn't wait for Dad to join us before school started. School? I had almost forgotten about it. Then I started thinking, "If our new neighborhood is this bad, what on earth will the school be like?"

Summer on Champa Street

MOM AND I WERE SITTING ON THE PORCH STEPS WATCHING BOB AND Patty argue about who could bounce a ball the highest when our landlady joined us and lit a cigarette. She stared at the house on the other side of the street for a few minutes, then said, "I wonder if they figured out who did it."

"Who did what? What happened?" Mom asked.

"Someone murdered the old lady who lived in that house." The landlady pointed across the street.

"When?"

"The day before you got here."

Mom almost choked. "Kids, you're staying in the apartment for the rest of the summer."

I sucked in my breath when I realized the awful coincidence. We were on our way to that neighborhood at the same time the murder was happening. I wished our guardian angel could have flown into our train car and said, *Uh uh, folks. Don't go there. Go somewhere else, but don't go there.* I got the chills just thinking about it.

It scared the living daylights out of all of us, so Bob, Patty, and I stayed inside with no argument. Could things get any worse? I wondered if my mother felt the way I did, but she wasn't showing any kind of misery, so I assumed calamity was in her blood. After sentencing us to an indoor life for the summer, she went about her business, so I did the same. But the harder I worked at not being sad, the more desperate I felt. I finally decided I'd either have to get used to our new home or put myself up for adoption.

It hardly mattered where we spent our time, indoors with my family or outdoors with strangers. Champa Street in Denver was just a mean place to live. How could I possibly learn to like it there? Everything was grimy, ragged, faded, or smelly. Staying in the apartment for the whole summer meant we three kids were cellmates in a prison for homesick children.

The community bathroom on our second floor was the worst part of our captivity. The first day Mom cleaned it, we heard her shout, "Oh, my God!" A few minutes later, she rushed into our apartment to get a chair so she could reach the curtain rod to dismantle it.

"What's wrong?" I asked.

My mother lowered her voice and said behind her hand, "Someone used the bottom of the curtain for toilet paper."

She pulled on her rubber gloves, took down the curtain, and threw the disgusting mess into a trash bin by the alley. Soon the landlady was knocking on every door asking, "Does anyone know what happened to the curtain in the bathroom?"

When it was our turn to answer the question, Mom said, "I have no idea what happened to that crappy curtain."

Since there were no housekeeping rules about the bathroom, and the other families didn't seem to care, my mother bought cleaning supplies and attacked everything in sight with Lysol and a scrub brush. Even though the floor was supposedly germ-free when she was through with it, we didn't want to set bare feet on the old linoleum because it was covered with cracks and raggedy holes. We even paid attention to our mother's warning to cover the seat with toilet paper before doing our business.

I was so tired of rules and warnings that I didn't know if my attitude toward our new home could change. If I actually accepted that place, it meant that I was dumping my high standards.

Every trip to the bathroom meant toting things in and remembering to tote them back. We each took our own towel, washcloth, soap, rug, and toilet paper. Whatever we left behind disappeared before we could rush in and say, "Don't take that towel. It's mine." Reading a comic book in the bathroom was out of the question, and it was one of Bob's favorite things to do. He told us that he tried it only once because someone banged on the door and yelled, "Hey, are ya dead in there?"

I was so ashamed of where we lived that I used my imagination to describe the place in a letter to Don and other friends at home. I wrote:

> *Dear friends, the house where we live is a grand old place with tall columns on the porch. It is so large that it has been converted to family apartments. Ours is furnished.*

I didn't lie about our apartment on Champa Street in Denver, though I didn't exactly tell the truth. My imaginative letters sometimes made me feel that everything was not so bad.

I avoided our neighbors like I might catch something if I got too close. Mom agreed that we had nothing in common with those folks, but she was civil to everyone and said, "Betty, this is not the place to make enemies."

"I'm not making enemies with these people."

"Well, you're not making friends with them either."

I didn't tell her that I had no intention of making friends with anyone at that place.

Bob and Patty missed playing hide-and-seek outdoors at night, but even during the daytime the neighborhood kids were too tough to play with. There were no bushes to hide behind anyway.

I really missed bushes. Just thinking about them made me homesick for the lilacs back home. Our lilacs were supposed to be bushes, but they had minds of their own and grew into trees. I knew down deep that I was acting like a snotty lilac bush who didn't think she belonged there. I was becoming an elegant elm tree from Cedar Rapids that looked down on everything below.

On Champa Street, I could look in any direction and see no grass or flowers growing anywhere. I yearned for grassy slopes and peonies separating yards from each other. My hometown neighborhoods had been pretty, while Champa Street was so ugly it gave me a headache. My mother said I had an attitude problem, and I guess I did. But I couldn't bear to change it.

Mom made our living quarters as decent as she could without spending money, but we had to escape now and then. She said, "I know there are interesting things to see in Denver, so let's find them." Our ventures always included movies. We kids had grown up on movies and we weren't about to change that habit. Sometimes we caught a streetcar that carried us clear across the city just to see the latest show.

When we did stay home, we each had our favorite radio programs. Bob and Patty liked *The Lone Ranger, Captain Midnight, Jack Armstrong,* and *Terry and the Pirates.* I preferred *Pepper Young's Family, Our Gal Sunday, Ma Perkins,* and *Backstage Wife.* On Saturday mornings, none of us ever missed *Let's Pretend, Grand Central Station,* or *Point Sublime.*

What broke up my movie and radio routine was my interest in a skinny cat that hung around the back stairs. I named her Buttercup. We fed the kitty milk and little bits of cut-up food in case she wasn't used to chewing on chunks. Petting the cat made me feel normal again, the way I felt on 32nd Street before Curly got hit by a car. Bob and Patty grew so fond of Buttercup that I think she had the same effect on them that she had on me. We started pretending that she was ours, even though we never let her into the apartment. No pets were allowed for fear they would make a mess.

What a joke. No animal could make a mess as bad as the ones my mother cleaned up in our community bathroom.

To break the monotony of living an indoor life, Mom sometimes gave us a few dollars to go to the corner store to buy food for one of our "junk suppers." They were a tradition in our family before the term "junk food" became popular. Junk suppers were never purchased by an adult. We kids bought whatever we wanted to eat, and we took as long as we wanted to decide what to buy. A typical junk supper would include fresh bologna, doughy white bread, kosher pickles, American cheese, potato salad, soda pop, and Twinkies. I was in heaven when I had a Twinkie in my hand that I didn't have to share with anyone. For dessert we bought chocolate-covered peanuts and Hershey's bars. Sometimes we shared our junk supper money with Buttercup by including a can of tuna for her. Mom said, "Making food decisions on your own will teach you kids the value of money." I think she just needed a break from grocery shopping.

During a junk-supper shopping spree, my brother and I saw something unexpected. It was so incredible that we had to escape to the dog food section to giggle away our shock. An obese woman lumbered toward us. She took up the whole aisle, but Bob and I tried not to look at her. The neck of her dress was so big and sloppy that it hung off her shoulders. Her breasts were huge, and it was obvious that she was not wearing a brassiere. Without turning our heads, we peeked at her from the corners of our eyes because she was a curiosity. I felt certain that if the woman bent over to reach something on the bottom shelf, her breasts would fall out.

And that's exactly what happened.

Bob and I were immobilized. I didn't know that breasts could be that gargantuan and hang down that far, like two baby whales.

The lady acted as if it happened all the time. She scooped them up and pushed them inside her dress where they belonged. That's when my brother and I escaped to the dog food aisle to stifle our hysteria. Holding back pent-up giggles put me in pain, gasping for air.

When we told Patty about the bare-breasted lady, she said, "Uh uh. That did not happen."

"Patty, it happened," Bob said.

"You're makin' that up."

Bob was exasperated that Patty thought we were lying, but I think she made herself believe we were lying so she wouldn't feel jealous.

A few days later, something else broke the monotony of our summer. We started hearing a woman down the hall moaning and crying. Sometimes she screamed. It was the scariest sound I had ever heard outside a movie theater. During a courteous conversation with a neighbor, Mom discovered that Moaning Woman lived with her adult children and she was dying from an incurable disease. At night we didn't hear her cry because they gave her a double shot of morphine. The poor woman lived in her bed, and someone always had to be nearby.

Mom had been a licensed practical nurse in Cedar Rapids and she knew how to care for dying people. I don't know how she did it, but she occasionally helped that family out so the daughter could have a break. I usually thought our mother was just plain nuts, but that was not one of those times. When she became a caregiver for someone she barely knew, my mother turned into Florence Nightingale.

I could not bear the crying and moaning. The sound made me sad and lonely, and I missed my friends back home more than ever. Mom had no idea how miserable I was, and I didn't intend to tell her. We couldn't change the way things were so my job was to adjust.

Whenever the sounds of moaning and crying floated down the hall, I vanished into my own world where I could be alone. I turned the radio dial to classical music and painted watercolor pictures in my typing tablet. When I was busy creating enchanting fairies and glamorous women on paper, I could forget about the real people at the end of the hall.

I didn't spend all of my time drawing and painting. During kitchen duty, my brother, sister, and I practiced singing three-part harmony. It slowed our progress with the dishes, but it didn't matter since we had nothing else to do. Bob and Patty enjoyed singing as much as I did, and making up music and teaching them how to harmonize got my mind off our imprisonment.

Sometimes I turned into Hitler in the kitchen, inventing major and minor musical chords that shifted from one to the other. I forced Bob and Patty to memorize each note. I added special effects to make the chords fancy, and we sounded great because we blended well. Mom was so impressed that she added a fourth part that turned us into a quartet. I looked forward to performing for Dad when he joined us. I knew he would naturally add bass notes to my chords, which would make us sound magnificent.

The summer was half over when I heard something on the radio that changed everything. A bowed, elderly man had gone into the local police station, removed his hat, and said, *"I'm the person you're looking for."*

The officers on duty thought it was a joke until the white-haired fellow started to cry and said, *"I'm not making this up. I just wanted to scare her and didn't mean to shoot her. I'm sorry."*

"Why were you trying to scare her?" they asked.

"She was leaving me for a younger man."

The officer being interviewed on the radio said, *"The old guy started crying again. He was so full of grief that he was drowning in his own tears."*

I was glad I was alone in the apartment when I heard the broadcast because it was so pitiful it made me cry. I was about to drown in my own tears, but I didn't know why I was crying. It was confusing. It was a good thing that the killer had been found, though it was sad that he was an unfortunate old man.

When Mom heard the startling news, she said, "Well, I guess you kids are on parole and can go outside to play now. Just don't leave the yard."

With the "murder" solved, I wasn't scared anymore. I didn't even feel so mad at everybody all the time. Mom noticed the difference in my attitude, but she wouldn't let me get by with blaming it on the murder. She said that I'd had a come-to-Jesus meeting with my mind. That's what my family said whenever someone came to their senses.

Whatever had caused the change, I was finally free to conjure up new images, like a house of our own with a private bathroom and plants growing around the borders of a grass lawn. I was afraid to hope for it in case it never came true. Instead, I just pictured it in my head.

Kitchen Duty and Cockroaches

WHENEVER MOM WAS AWAY FROM THE APARTMENT, I WAS IN CHARGE, and my brother and sister were supposed to cooperate. It was a plan that didn't work. We argued a lot, and the system usually broke down in the kitchen.

"Patty, stop fooling around. You're supposed to be drying the dishes. And where's Bob, anyway?"

"He's in the bathroom . . . as usual."

During kitchen duty, Bob always had to use the bathroom, which meant my sister and I were left to finish the job. I decided to put an end to that. The next time he pulled that trick on us, I would be ready to pounce.

I pounced two days later. My brother and sister were in the living room when I yelled, "Bob, Patty, come get a dish towel 'cause the drainer is getting full!"

My brother must have been holding his pee for that very moment. "Okay, just gimmee a chance to go to the toilet."

"Nope," I said. "You can wait 'til we're finished with the dishes."

"But, Betty, I really have to go bad!" he insisted as he wiggled dramatically.

"You're lying. Stop that phony prancing."

"Betty, if you don't let me go, I'll wet my pants."

"You can just hold it."

"I can't hold it."

"You can."

Bob reluctantly headed to the kitchen and picked up a dish towel. In the middle of drying the first plate, he stopped pushing the towel around and appeared to be concentrating. There was a devilish look in his eye.

"What are you doing?" I asked.

A wicked grin spread over his face as a wet spot spread over the crotch of his pants. I was shocked and furious.

"You brat! You did that on purpose!"

My bratty brother smiled sweetly. "I told you I might wet my pants if you didn't let me go to the toilet. Now I have to go change."

"Not so fast. You stay right here and finish the dishes."

"You're kidding."

"I'm not."

"Mom's gonna be mad at you."

"She's gonna be mad at you for making more laundry."

Bob had never been a problem before, but after we moved to Champa Street, he joined Patty in making things difficult for me. Whenever my sister got too annoying, I still squeezed her arm and pressed my fingernails into her skin until she gave in. Even though it was wretched, it was the only way I could keep her under control. Arm-squeezing didn't work with my brother since he was bigger and tougher than my sister. So I had to be sneakier to control him. I was sure I would never make a good mother.

We didn't fight *every* time we cleaned the kitchen after dinner. Sometimes we practiced singing our three-part chords until the dishes dried themselves. And sometimes we hurried through our chores so we could listen to one of our favorite programs on the little white radio.

Listening to the radio in the evening came with a bonus. During the day, the cockroaches napped inside of it. But when the radio tubes started heating up, the cockroaches woke up and poked their antennae through the louvered cover. They seemed to be feeling the air to see if the coast was clear.

It wasn't.

With a pair of scissors in his hand, Bob kept his eyes glued to the radio, waiting to see the "feelers." I told him they were called "antennae," expecting my brother to be impressed, but he just said, "You think you know everything" and went on calling them by the wrong name.

Cockroach-feeler-snipping was a fine art, and Bob got very good at it because he practiced almost every night. Patty and I tried our best to match our brother's skill, but we couldn't beat him.

When it was completely dark outside, we played a different cockroach game. We turned off all the lights and waited quietly. When enough time had gone by for the cockroaches to start exploring, we flipped on the switch and watched them scurry for cover in zigzag patterns across the counters. The sudden light confused them.

Whenever Mom was away, those stupid cockroaches became our favorite form of entertainment. It was a lot of fun, but I sure didn't tell my friends back home about it. They would have known for sure that we lived in a dump.

Waiting for Dad

WHILE OUR MOTHER WAS FIXING OATMEAL FOR BREAKFAST, PATTY asked the same old question. "When is Dad gonna get here?"

"I've told you more than once that your father's job in Denver doesn't start 'til August."

My sister usually dropped it there, but that morning she wanted to know more. "Why can't he come before his job starts?"

"Without a job, we'd have no money."

"But August is a long time from now."

"Please don't start whining again. Help your sister and brother with the bed."

We were getting used to Mom's calm behavior. She hadn't blown her stack in a long time. We had fallen into a daily pattern that gave us a sense of order. We three kids would lie around under the covers until we heard kitchen sounds. Then we would drag ourselves out of bed and work together to smooth the sheets, spreading the blanket on top.

After breakfast we moved back onto the bed, where we stayed most of the day. We listened to our favorite radio shows, read comic books, played Chinese checkers, and argued over nothing. When I wasn't there with Bob and Patty, I claimed the small table with the lamp as my own space. I wrote letters, drew, and painted pictures with my watercolors.

My mother spent mornings at the kitchen table with her cigarette, a cup of coffee, and the *Denver Post*. She had a pretty good view of the kids playing in the alley below and did whatever she could to protect us from their influence. As far as she was concerned, fighting for fun was a dumb activity. When she fought with Dad, it was about something important.

In the afternoon, Mom cleaned our apartment and the community bathroom. She didn't bother to recruit neighbors to help because it was obvious her standards for cleanliness were higher than theirs. After dinner, she sat in the wooden rocker and listened to the radio while she finished crocheting doilies. Our apartment looked like a doily factory, but too many doilies were better than none. They added a touch of refinement that transformed our living quarters from drab to almost acceptable.

I had toned down my resentment a lot and my softer attitude almost resembled acceptance. But something important was missing from our new life in Denver. It was Dad. I really missed him. Once he arrived, Dad would surely have some ideas about finding somewhere else to live. All five of us couldn't live there after he arrived. It wasn't even as private as the one-room house on 11th Avenue back home. The future was on hold until Dad joined us.

To take our minds off the empty space in our lives, we sometimes left the apartment to play tourist. There was always something going on in the Denver City Park and it was easy to get there. In addition to the Museum of Natural History, we went to the Lakeside Amusement Park and rented rowboats. Most of our outings involved going to the movies. Transportation costs, movie tickets, and eating out were sucking money right out of Mom's purse. It was supposed to last until Dad joined us, and that was still two months away.

She said, "Kids, I've got to get a job."

I knew things were getting tight, so her announcement didn't surprise me. Bob and Patty groaned in unison.

"I have to, kids. We're running out of cash."

They just kept groaning.

"While I'm at work, Betty will be in charge."

Bob stopped groaning and glared at me. My sister stomped her feet and said, "I'm running away."

Our mother was good at many things. She could have been a housekeeper for a rich family. And she would have wowed people as a piano player in a restaurant or a lounge. But she took a job as a lowly waitress in a diner because she knew she would get lots of tips. When the manager discovered that she was an experienced restaurant worker, he promoted her to boss of the kitchen. "I could've gotten more money as a waitress," Mom grumbled. But I could tell she was pleased to be the boss of something, even if it was just the kitchen at a diner.

While Mom was gone, we listened to the radio, read comic books over and over, and played Old Maid. I painted with my watercolors more than ever before, and I continued to write to my friends often. Because I had nothing but time on my hands, I sometimes wrote three letters to their one.

We looked forward to Mom's homecoming after work when she entertained us with tales about her day. It was my favorite time because it felt cozy and close. As soon as she arrived, off came the sensible waitress-type shoes. Then she poured a cup of coffee and gathered her ashtray and cigarettes. That was our signal to cluster around the green table in the kitchen. My sister would give the cue. "Okay. What happened today?"

One night Mom grinned and said, "You kids are going to love this. I had quite an entertaining ride this morning!" She paused to take a drag on her cigarette and a sip of coffee, keeping us in suspense.

"A man and woman who sat next to me on the streetcar argued 'til they ended up in a fight."

Patty asked, "Was it a talking fight or a hitting fight?" She had seen both kinds with our parents, so it was natural to ask.

"Well . . . it was sort of a hitting fight because she finally whacked him in the chest with her purse and hit him on the head with a rolled-up newspaper."

"Did the man cry?"

"No, but the woman yelled all kinds of swear words at him and got off at the next stop."

"Did he follow her?" My sister sounded like a roving reporter.

"Nope." He yelled, 'Good riddance!'"

"Good what?"

Bob couldn't stand the interruptions any longer. "Good riddance means he was glad to get rid . . . of . . . her."

"You don't hafta yell, smarty pants."

Mom stopped what was about to become an argument. "Settle down, kids, and listen to what happened tonight."

Bob and Patty moved apart so they wouldn't be tempted to poke each other, and our mother resumed her tale.

"When I came home tonight, the streetcar was completely filled and the only place to sit was by a snoring drunk taking up the whole seat."

It was Bob's turn to ask silly questions. "Did you pretend you didn't notice and sit down on him?"

"No, but I had to push his legs over so I could sit on a little spot. Half of my behind was hanging over the edge."

We got the giggles because Mom needed more than a little *spot* for her backside.

"When I got off, the guy was still asleep. Golly, I wonder what'll happen if they don't notice he's there."

"He'll probably stay overnight," Patty said.

"I expect he might."

"I hope he doesn't wet his bed."

"I expect he might."

As the latest tall tale from the Mile High City came to an end, we all busted out laughing. I was sure that Denver must be the oddest place in the world because I had never seen so many unusual folks before. People there made my wacky family look normal.

When Mom was transferred to a later shift, we kids stayed up 'til the wee hours of the morning listening to the radio because the apartment was cooler after the sun went down. On an especially hot evening, a commotion in the hallway got our attention. I stuck my head out the door, saw a lot of people milling around, and asked, "What's going on?"

"Someone died," a neighbor answered.

Just then, some men came out of the apartment down the hall carrying a stretcher. The body under the white sheet didn't take up much space, and I knew it must be Moaning Lady. Even though I had never met her, I felt I knew the poor woman because I often heard her crying. Sometimes her cries were high and wailing. Other times they were soft and low as though she was running out of gas. Our mother said that was when her morphine kicked in.

Later, a hound-dog kind of howling floated our way, and it was almost too heartbreaking to bear. Was the ghost of Moaning Lady roaming the hall? But it wasn't a ghost. It was the dead woman's daughter, crying her eyes out.

Staying up late and sleeping late usually kept us away from the scary world outside until Mom came home. But that night, the scary world had come closer. In a hushed voice, I said, "I want Dad to take us away from here."

Bob whispered, "Me, too."

Letters from Home

I WROTE SO MANY LETTERS TO MY FRIENDS BACK HOME THAT I RE-ceived a lot in return. My flood of mail caused Patty to feel sad and lonely because her friends, who had promised to write, didn't.

I tried not to announce the arrival of each correspondence, but it wasn't easy staying calm when the postman dropped mail in our box. I lived for letters from my girlfriends. One day a letter arrived from a boy, Bill Pfeiffer. He was the best buddy of my first love, Don Johanos. I was eager to open it to see what Bill had to say, but as I read, my excitement became panic. Bill wrote:

Dear Lizzie,

It was so nice to hear from you and to read about your lovely new home in Denver. I'm so glad that you like it there and that your family is happy. I might be able to attend a church youth conference in Denver this summer and I would love to drop by for a visit.

Your friend,

Bill

Bill could never see where we really lived. I had used my imagination when writing to my friends, describing the house where we lived as if it were Tara, the plantation home in *Gone with the Wind*. It was easier to live in such an ugly place if I pretended it was nice. But I never dreamed anyone from home would ever see the house the way it really was.

So I wrote back to Bill and threw myself on his mercy, begging him not to look us up. I confessed that I had pretended it was nice because it was so terrible. I told him everything bad about Champa, even about the killing across the street. I mailed my confession to Bill — and he never wrote back. I was both relieved and sad.

The May before we moved to Denver, Patty had celebrated her tenth birthday in Cedar Rapids. Mom planned a party that only Auntie Marge attended because Uncle Al and Dad had to work. Mom had given her a small black book with a black tassel and ribbon on the left side of the cover. It was my sister's first autograph book and she was like a kid with a new toy.

"Ohhhh, Mama, thank you, thank you, thank you. I love it! I'm going to keep it for the rest of my life."

"Get all your friends to sign it and put their addresses in there so you can write to them after we move," Mom had suggested.

Patty was so proud of that book. She carried it around under her arm so that she would look important. Auntie Marge, Mom, Bob, and I were the first ones to sign it, and my little sister could hardly wait to take it to school so all her friends could do the same.

Her very best friend, Patti Wall, was the fifth person to sign the autograph book. She wrote: *I am very sad you are leaving so pleese rite and this here is my adres.* After we moved to Denver, Patty must have read her autograph book a thousand times. She was touched by the mass of sentimental notes, all written just for her.

The first letter Patty sent after we moved to Denver was to Patti Wall, and she made sure to include our new address on Champa Street. Patty was a nervous wreck waiting to hear from her best friend. Bob said, "It takes at least a week to get mail to Cedar Rapids and another week for a letter to come back to you." We urged her to be patient.

But every day Patty asked, "Did the mail come yet? Where's my letter? Oh, no, Betty got another one. I want one, too." She talked of nothing else, and Bob and I were starting to feel sorry for our sister.

"That girl should have written by now because it's been three weeks," I said to Bob. He agreed. That's when we cooked up an idea to make our sister happy. I found Patti Wall's address in the autograph book and Bob found Mom's stationery. I wrote the note, disguised my handwriting, and threw in a few misspelled words.

Dear Patty,

How are you doing. I am fine and I miss you a lot. I hope you like where you are living and I will bet it is very nice. Please rite back as soon as you can because I have some new statinery."

Your best frend

Patti Wall

We knew when our sister saw a letter with her name on it she would no longer be sad and disappointed. But we forgot about the stamp. I told Bob I could draw the stamp and he said, "What a great idea."

I drew privately all afternoon, and it was the best darned drawing I had ever rendered in my life. I swear it could have passed for the real thing. We folded the paper, stuck it in the envelope, licked it shut, and dropped it in the mail slot for our apartment. Then we waited for the real mail to come.

Bob announced, "Hey, looky here, Patty. A letter for you!"

My sister was beside herself with excitement as she ripped it open and read the message aloud so many times that I thought I would die. Bob had to leave the room giggling when she read it for the gazillionth time. Our sister carried the precious paper inside her autograph book, taking it out several times a day to study the words before tucking it back inside the envelope.

But something clued her in that it wasn't really from Patti Wall. Maybe it was the hand-drawn stamp. I said, "Sometimes the post office runs out of stamps and they allow artists to draw them in."

"But the writing is too grown up," she said.

"We've been gone a whole month and she probably has grown up some since we left."

Patty wasn't buying any of it. "What about the wavy lines on the envelope?" she asked.

"What wavy lines?"

"There are supposed to be wavy lines on an envelope when you mail it. Where are they?"

The jig was up. Bob and I confessed that we had written the letter and drawn the stamp so she wouldn't feel left out. By then our sister was more than just sad; she was heartbroken. No matter how much we explained that we just wanted her to be happy, Patty couldn't stop crying.

"I can't wait (sniffle) to grow up (choke) and get even with you guys," she sobbed. "In fact, I can't wait to tell Mom. Waaaahhh."

And did she ever.

Bob and I got scolded so hard it hurt, and no manner of explanation could excuse us for what we had done. Although we insisted we'd done it to make our sister feel less sad, I think the real truth was that we wanted to see if we could get away with it.

Well, we failed.

Breaking the Rules

I WAS THE BOSS OF BOB AND PATTY, BUT MOM LAID DOWN THE RULES for all three of us and we were expected to stick to them. When she left for work each day, she said the same thing. "Stay inside now, ya hear?"

"Yeah, we hear," we answered.

But the rule about staying indoors was very hard to follow. The apartment was hot, and the little fan didn't help unless you sat smack dab in front of it. Mom didn't get home 'til late each night, so I figured she'd never find out if we stayed inside or outside unless one of us tattled. I finally brought up the subject.

"Let's go outside and cool off."

I thought my brother and sister would squeal with delight, but Patty said, "Mmm . . . I don't think we should do that. Mom will be mad if she finds out."

"She doesn't have to find out. We stay in this apartment all day long, and I can't stand it anymore. I need some air and a change of scenery. Besides, Buttercup probably misses us."

Bob seemed uncertain and waited to see which of his sisters would win. I told Patty there was nothing to worry about if we sat outside on the top step for just ten minutes. She was a worrywart and not easy to convince. "Okay, then," she finally said. "But I hope there aren't any dangerous kids out there that we have to talk to. One of them might decide to beat us up."

"Patty, don't be such a scaredy cat. We'll be just fine."

I was sure we'd be safe sitting only a few steps from our kitchen door. I didn't know at the time that it would be the beginning of a true adventure.

That evening the three of us sat close to each other on the top step and just soaked up the ugly view. We were prisoners making a jail break. The truth is we enjoyed the risk of doing what we wanted instead of what our mother wanted. It was thrilling. The only story she would hear was that we needed some fresh air. It was the truth. And our timing was good since no hooligans were around to scare Patty.

Before then we had never paid attention to what time the Mexicans got together in the alley, but it seemed that their socializing started between supper and dark. When we saw the boys and girls gathering, we slipped back inside the apartment before they noticed we were there. We always looked forward to the field trips on our second story porch.

Late one afternoon when dusk had softened the light, we decided to do it differently. We would wait indoors until after the alley kids had congregated and then sneak out to the top step to observe them more closely. We were curious about what kept them together and how they had so much fun. Again, my sister was filled with dread. "What if they see us up here?" she said.

"Let 'em see us."

After watching and listening to them every evening, I was feeling less afraid. Maybe I had misjudged them. Sometimes they played rough games and sometimes they sat in a tight circle and talked very softly, then laughed very loudly. They ranged in age, but most of them were young teenagers like me. I looked younger than fifteen because I still wore my hair in long braids.

Bob said, "I know what they're doing."

"What are they doing?" asked Patty.

"They're telling dirty jokes."

"How can you tell?"

"It's hard to explain, but that's what they're doing."

Patty didn't believe him. "Bob, you think you're so smart." Maybe she was wrong. Maybe my brother did know about dirty jokes.

One night, Bob, Patty, and I agreed to move closer, which meant halfway down the steps. We were dying to find out what they were saying and what made them laugh so hard in case it was dirty jokes. It wasn't easy because they spoke in English and Spanish at the same time.

We must have become obvious because we soon had a visitor. Approaching us was a young, bald, barefoot Mexican kid about nine or ten. He wore striped overalls without a shirt. As he got closer, I could tell that he wasn't naturally bald; his head was shaved. He walked right up to the bottom step, looked up at us, and said, "Hi."

"Hi," I replied.

"Why you guys sitting up there?"

"The view is better up here."

The boy coaxed us to the bottom of the stairs so he could visit. Patty was getting nervous and said, "Oh, no," under her breath.

"It's okay," I said. "Stay calm. We're just going to talk with this little kid."

We moved cautiously to the bottom step, which was closer than I wanted to be, though I couldn't explain why. The boy was talkative and chatted about all kinds of things. He seemed grateful to have an audience and the more attentive we were, the more he talked. He changed subjects so fast that I couldn't keep up. In the process, he told us more than I cared to know about the others.

He pointed to two handsome teenagers and said, "Delores and Jose are the bosses. They do things that husbands and wives do to make a baby."

Did Bob and Patty hear what I heard? Did they understand? Worse yet, were they going to ask me to explain?

But they weren't paying attention to the boy. I was riveted. I got brave enough to ask, "How do you know so much?"

"I watch them through a crack in that garage over there, but they can't see me."

"Maybe you shouldn't watch them. They might get mad and box your head off."

He laughed and said, "If they beat me up, I will tell on them and Delores' madre will get mad and cut off Delores' hair so she won't look so good."

"Why would she do that?"

"Because she don't want Delores making no baby before she is married."

I asked him how he was so sure what Delores' mother might do, and his answer was simple: "Because Delores' madre is my tía."

"Your what?"

"Delores' madre is my tía, my aunt."

That child was so full of surprises that I was spellbound. I said, "You're an interesting boy."

"I'm no boy. My name is Maria."

I was speechless, but I managed to say, "Ya coulda fooled me. So why is your head shaved?"

"I have lice."

I remembered having lice when Bob, Patty, and I left the Ottumwa Home. Damsy and Mom had washed our hair with kerosene to kill the nits, but there was never any talk of shaving our heads. I tried not to cringe in front of Maria, but I did sneak a peek at the smooth tan skin on her noggin. I saw no sign of nits . . . thank the Lord!

From then on, we watched the backyard boxing matches on the bottom step whenever our mother was at work. The three of us swore an oath that she would never find out we were breaking the rules.

Boxing in the Alley

AFTER SUPPER EACH NIGHT, WE FINISHED THE DISHES SO FAST THAT when we put them away they were only half dry. The reason for our speedy job was that we'd become boxing fans. Bob, Patty, and I had the best seats in the house even though we were technically outside the house.

One evening was as hot as an oven, which drove the entire neighborhood outdoors. That meant more kids than usual had been enticed to the alley to try their hand in the ring. After round three, which lasted sixty seconds, a girl broke away from the group and swaggered toward us.

Patty, whose lips barely moved as if she was practicing ventriloquism, whispered, "Oh, no. She's coming over here."

"Sit still and smile," I said.

It was Delores, the girl who Maria had spied upon. She seemed to glow. Was it her sunny, brown skin and the long, black hair that hung like a little cape over her shoulders? Or was it her sultry, dark eyes? She was definitely not ugly.

She started talking before she reached us. "Hey, you with the braids . . . ya wanna box?"

"Oh, no, thank you." It was the polite thing to say.

"Chicken!" She glared at me. I could see I'd insulted her by turning down the invitation.

The rest of the gang joined in, chanting, "Chicken, chicken," as they cackled and flapped their arms like wings. They weren't in the mood to let it go, and I didn't want to be rude, especially to kids who hung around our apartment building. But I was afraid to box in the alley with any of those girls. I had responsibilities. They could hurt me. Then who would take care of my brother and sister while Mom was at work?

"I don't know how."

"Hey, we will teach you. It's so easy. You hit the other person real hard and she falls down." Then they laughed their heads off.

I would probably take a beating, but something told me that being pummeled would be better than being the Chicken of Champa Street. Besides, they might decide to beat me up anyway if I refused. With fear in my heart and a squeaky voice, I said, "Okay."

My brother's mouth snapped open, and my sister gasped. "Mom's gonna be mad!" She was so scared that she flew back up the steps and hid in the apartment. My brother, eyes bugging, stayed on our ringside seat on the bottom step while the beautiful, but scary, Delores took my hand and led me to the alley.

I was sure that she had grabbed my hand not so much as a friendly gesture but to keep me from getting away. She and the other girls rummaged through a pile of old, mismatched boxing gloves and found a pair for me, the victim. It was decided that I would fight Delores, the female leader of the group and Jose's babe, with whom he did grownup things.

We stood facing each other, she with confidence and I with a great deal of phony-baloney fearlessness. A couple of handsome Mexican boys laced her gloves while two grinning girls laced mine way too tight. I didn't say a word, deciding that tight was all right.

Jose, the most handsome boy I had ever seen, was the overseer of the alley activities. His presence made me mute as panic spread through my body. I knew that I would probably be smashed around, but getting hurt seemed better than living a coward's life in that neighborhood. Yes, indeedy, I was doing the right thing by accepting their invitation. But I should have gone to the toilet first because if I got punched in the stomach, I would probably wet my pants. Then what would they call me? Pee Pants?

A kitchen timer was set for one minute. Jose said, "Go!" and Delores punched me in the face.

I assumed that meant the fight had started, so I boxed . . . at least that's what I thought I was doing. I swung my arms wildly, hoping to hit something. My brother told me later that I looked funny. I didn't feel funny. I felt like a windmill flailing at the air. I was so busy warding off blows that I had no chance to land a single punch on my opponent's beautiful chin. What a beating I was taking. I heard Patty screech, "Oh, no!" from the steps, and I knew that she had left her hiding place in the apartment to sit with Bob.

My cheeks and forehead were getting pounded and it was shattering my courage, but I willed myself not to cry even though my face hurt a lot. Kids were yelling for Delores, and nobody was yelling for me. Were Bob and Patty too scared to cheer me on? I was dizzy and afraid of wetting my pants and considered pretending to be knocked out, but they would see through my act.

Delores was relentless. I tried to keep up with her, but I wanted to scream, "When does this minute end?"

Then I heard someone say, "Take it easy on her." That was Jose, the gang leader. But his girlfriend was either hard of hearing or she was trying to kill me.

"Okay, that's enough!" Jose again.

He was stopping the fight. He was rescuing me.

In my pitiful condition, I was so grateful that I instantly got a crush on him for being so kind. The girls in the gang moved in to unlace our gloves while Jose patted me on the back and said, "You are a good kid."

Since Jose was obviously their leader, no one would disagree with him. Even Delores, whose hair was not a bit ruffled, joined my fan club. I could hardly stand up, but each boy and girl pounded my back and shoulders and said, "You sure are a good kid."

To avoid appearing wimpy, I smiled and said, "Thank you, thank you." I strolled to our bottom step to sit down by my brother and sister, trying desperately to look casual as if I was thinking, *This is no big deal.* But boxing in the alley was a big deal. I was shaken and dizzy, my body was sweaty, and my skin stung. At least it was over. What a relief. I pulled myself together, knowing I had passed a test, and acted as though nothing was more important than watching the rest of the fights.

Patty whispered, "Did it hurt? Are you gonna cry? Mom will be so mad when she finds out you had a fight with these kids."

"It was not a fight."

"Was too."

"It was a boxing match."

"Same thing."

I wanted to punch my sister, but instead I shushed her and said, "Let's just sit here for a while and watch. We'll talk about it later."

I began to feel the nervous dreads sneaking up because I knew how mad Mom would be. When it started to get dark and the kids in the alley had forgotten about me, I said to Bob and Patty, "Act real casual, but let's go upstairs now."

I turned on the light to use the bathroom and the cockroaches scurried for cover. The mirror over the sink showed red and swollen cheeks. My eyes ached, but my urge to cry had passed.

I would have to explain my dinged-up face to Mom when she came home. Patty couldn't stop saying, "Mom is sure gonna be mad at you," and she was probably right.

Usually, we stayed up late to hear the stories Mom told about the people who had crossed her path during the day. But that night was different because we were telling the story. We explained the whole thing to her, leaving nothing out. Mom was speechless as she listened to every word. She looked frozen in place, with an unlit cigarette hanging from her lips. When we finished, she tore the cigarette from her mouth. Instead of lighting it, she threw it aside and lit into me.

"Betty, I just knew this could happen. You don't listen. I said not to leave this apartment!"

"Mom, it was so hot in here."

"Then you turn on the fan and prop the kitchen door open, but never go into that alley again when I am at work."

She didn't have to tell us. We'd figured that out for ourselves.

Dad Arrives

Near the end of July, Dad finally joined us in Denver. We were so excited to see him that we could hardly stand it. When he stepped off the train at the Union Station depot wearing his best Sunday suit and hat and carrying his suitcase, I didn't recognize him. He looked like a man coming home from a business trip.

My father never hugged or kissed us; he just stood back, looked us over real good, and said, "You guys are a sight for sore eyes." That's when I knew how much he'd really missed us.

Getting from the train station to our neighborhood meant taking the streetcar and then walking a few more blocks to our house, so we kids took turns carrying his suitcase. I felt stronger than usual because I was filled with happy energy from having our family together again.

When Dad finally saw where we lived, his eyebrows went up. "Ain't much to look at, that's fer damn sure." That was a good sign that he didn't like it, which gave me hope that we wouldn't be living on Champa Street much longer.

At dinner that night, he told us about his new job at the machine shop for the Rio Grande Western Railroad. "My letter from the shop foreman says that my shift is from 4:00 p.m. to midnight."

When my father figured out how far he'd have to walk from the bus stop to home, he seemed nervous. He said he didn't mind the exercise, but it kind of spooked him to go through such a rough neighborhood at midnight. Mom had walked through the same area late at night and it didn't seem to bother her. I had a feeling my mother's "don't mess with me" attitude scared off any tough guys.

Sunday night we sat around the kitchen table entertaining our father with tales of our wild summer adventures in the alley, thinking he would laugh out loud. But he was not amused. He worried about living on Champa Street, but he wasn't sure we would be allowed to move since he was still a government employee and the Housing Authority had to approve it. "We'll have to stay put if we don't get permission to relocate."

I wanted to plug my ears and not listen. Was he giving up before we even started? With all my heart I wanted to move away from there. I couldn't give up my dream of a nice house with nice kids and friendly parents who mowed their lawns and planted flowers. Dad could not give up that easily. I felt certain that in another week he would see what living on Champa was really like. Then he wouldn't ask permission to move; he would demand it.

While I tried not to worry, my father got acquainted with the neighbors on our floor because he was a friendly guy. He and Bob were heading outside when they met the father of the "Crummy" family in the hallway. That was the name we'd given them because they always appeared to need baths and a change of clothes. The Crummies had three sons, one who was my brother's age. The older boys were eighteen and twenty.

"Nice to meetcha," my father said. "I'm Butch Peal. You must be Mr. Crummy."

"The last name is Berger. I'm Dave Berger."

Dad shot a puzzled look at Bob as though saying, *What the hell?* My brother later told me he thought "Booger" was an even better name for that family than Crummy.

Mr. Berger invited Dad in for a shot of whiskey, and Bob went in, too. The two men talked and drank while the eighteen-year-old boy lounged on the living-room bed. The twenty-year-old came home and plopped down beside his brother. He stretched as though he was getting ready for a nap and then lowered his hand and touched his younger brother in a private place.

I was shocked when my brother told me that part. "He touched him where?" I asked.

"On his crotch, dummy."

"Weren't you embarrassed?"

"Heck, yes. I was so embarrassed that I turned my head to look at somethin' else and my eyes landed on a portrait of Jesus whose eyes were lookin' right through me. Their father told them to cut it out, but they ignored him."

Bob then told me that when Mrs. Booger saw them on the bed, she got mad and said, "Getcher selves off that bed with yer shoes on." She didn't say a thing about what they were doing on the bed.

My father polished off his drink real fast. Once he and my brother were back in the hall, Dad said, "I don't want you hangin' around that apartment anymore."

Dad said to Mom, "Girl, I'm never goin' back there again 'cause those folks give me the willies!"

Things were looking so bad that I was thrilled.

My brother still hung out with Mike, the youngest boy. One day Mrs. Crummy-Booger sent Mike to the same corner market where Mom let us kids buy junk suppers once a week. She gave Mike a short list and some cash, and Mike asked my brother to go with him. As they walked home with the groceries, Mike lit up a cigarette. Bob was shocked to see a twelve-year-old smoking and asked, "Where did you get that?"

"I stole it from my mother. I do it all the time so I won't have to steal cigs from the store."

Three tough-acting Mexican boys about the same age as my brother and his friend approached them. The shortest one stepped close to the boys, blocking their way, and said, "Hey! What're you guys doin' in our neighborhood?"

My brother was so petrified that he couldn't answer. The three toughs started pushing the boys around. Then one of them saw a homemade metal ring on Mike's finger. "Gimmee that ring and yer cigarettes, too," he demanded.

Bob and Mike didn't budge, so the tough kid said, "Okay, then, gimmee some money for cigarettes."

My brother's fear was turning to anger and he yelled, "I don't have any money!" That earned him a punch in the face. He was startled, but it made him madder.

One of the tough kids said, "Leave 'em alone. We gotta go 'cause we're late."

After the three bullies left, my brother and the neighbor boy pulled themselves together and continued home with the grocery bags still intact. Bob decided not to tell Mom what happened, but he told our father every detail.

Dad was full of questions. "Why dincha hit the kid back?"

"It was three against two."

"So?"

"Mike stood there and took it, and I figured I should do that, too."

My father wouldn't let up. "I still think you shoulda stuck up for yerselves."

"Dad, we had to take Mrs. Booger's groceries home."

"Mrs. who?"

"Mrs. Booger, Mike's mother."

"It's Berger. You kids gotta get people's names right, especially in this neighborhood."

Thank God our father was finding out that the Champa neighborhood was not a safe place to raise us kids. He finally agreed that we had to move.

The Housing Authority inspector in charge of our family came to our apartment to find out why we wanted to relocate. I crossed my fingers and prayed really hard so my message for help would reach God. Without approval, we were stuck on Champa Street indefinitely. It was supper time when he arrived, and Dad was already at work on the night shift. Mom had set the table with fresh produce and it looked so nice that the inspector stopped to admire it. "What a beautiful table you've set, Mrs. Peal."

Anyone who admired a beautiful table and fresh vegetables had to be a good guy. That was my clue that God had received my message.

"You're welcome to join us," Mom said. He declined, explaining that he had one more family to visit before heading home to his own wife and kids.

"I don't want to hold up your dinner, so this will not take long at all. I need to see every part of your apartment and then discuss a few things. Let's start with the bedrooms. How many do you have?"

Mom showed him the one bedroom she and Dad shared and then the double bed in the living room where Bob, Patty, and I slept. The inspector said nothing but wrote a lot on his tablet. Next he surveyed the kitchen. Mom told him about the cockroaches and bedbugs, and he wrote down a lot more. He then looked out the back door to the alley below and out the windows to the dirt yard filled with abandoned car parts. That was the only time I'd been thrilled with how trashy everything looked.

Finally, he asked to see the bathroom, which Mom had cleaned up real well just for that occasion. She led him out the door and into the hall and said, "This is the only bathroom, and we share it with three other families on this floor."

The inspector snapped shut his tablet. "This is not going to be a problem. You folks need to move into another place, and I'll take care of it immediately."

Thank you, God. Thank you, God. Thank you, thank you, thank you, God!

I was ready to burst out crying with joy, but I didn't show it. Mom kept her composure, too, as though it was an everyday thing. After the inspector left, she turned to us and said, "Maybe after we move your father can get off this ungodly night shift."

What Mom didn't know was that my father had confided to Bob that he liked working nights. "It pays five cents an hour more, but don't tell yer mother." My brother did the math and figured that two dollars a week of unaccounted-for dollars must have been Dad's beer money.

At that moment, I didn't care what shift he worked. We were actually going to leave Champa Street, and nothing could make me happier.

Mom, Bob, Patty, and I celebrated the good news with our Iowa supper: pork chops, vine-ripened tomatoes, fresh green cucumbers, and sweet onions in sugar and vinegar. In the middle of the table sat a platter of golden corn on the cob and a big bowl of salted leaf lettuce that we ate with our fingers.

Food never tasted better.

Part 7: *Starting Over*

The Peals first winter at Sunset Ridge, 1946

Escape from Champa Street

WHEN DAD SHARED THE NEWS AT WORK THAT WE'D BE MOVING, he said, "I hope to God we can find something decent that doesn't cost an arm and a leg because we're already half broke."

His friend Hank said, "Butch, I know of a place outside of Fort Logan, but you have to get on a waiting list."

"A waiting list for what?"

"To move in."

"Why, for God's sake?"

"I'm not sure. Maybe a lot of government employees are moving there. You'd better call."

It was good advice. We contacted our inspector, who found that the community was called Sunset Ridge, a housing project with several two- and three-bedroom apartments. My parents couldn't believe our good luck and moved fast to put our names on a list for a three-bedroom unit.

Three bedrooms? What a luxury. My parents felt that Bob, at twelve years of age, was too old to be sharing a bedroom with his sisters. My brother was delirious about having more privacy, and Patty and I were just as happy to have more space to call our own.

When the inspector called back, he had good and bad news. "There's an apartment available at Sunset Ridge, but it has only two bedrooms."

"But all is not lost," he said. "I advise you folks to move in and wait for a larger unit."

"How long do you think that will take?" Dad asked.

"It might be four months."

"Hold on a minute. Let me see what the family thinks." He put his hand over the mouthpiece and gave us the news.

I don't know who groaned the loudest, Bob, our parents, Patty, or me. But we all agreed that any amount of waiting would be better than staying on Champa Street, and four months didn't seem all that long. He took his hand off the mouthpiece. "Sir, are you still there?"

"Yep, still here. What's your decision?"

"We'll take it."

What a simple little sentence that was . . . we'll take it. The words made my stomach do flip-flops. Was I going to laugh or cry? Bob's face lit up like a light, Mom beamed a wide smile, and Patty squeezed my arm so tight it hurt. Our father wrapped up the details, said goodbye, and hung up. Then he punched the air with his fist and said, "Hallelujah!"

Mom gave our landlady two weeks' notice even though we planned to leave right away. We were inmates busting out of jail, throwing our stuff into boxes and paper bags. After Bob grabbed his comic books and Patty rescued her black autograph book, they stayed out of the way. My parents were packing so fast that I was sure my personal treasures would be mixed up with cleaning supplies and clothes. So I found a large paper grocery bag to protect my letters, stationery, paints, pens, tablet of unlined paper, and all of my watercolors and drawings.

Mom nestled pots, pans, and dishes into a box with no room left over for the frying pan. Dad packed faster than any of us, squeezing dishes on top of underwear. "Girl, there's room in here for the skillet."

"Butch, be careful how you're packing. I don't want anything broken."

"Ha, that's funny coming from you, the dish-breaking queen."

"Don't be a smart mouth, Butch. You're packing too fast."

"Girl, if I break a dish, I'll buy another one. I want outta here. I've been bitten by bedbugs for the last time!"

I was beside myself with joy that my father not only hated living there as much as I did, but that he and Mom were joking about her habit of breaking dishes whenever she got mad. Things were looking up.

After everything we owned had been stuffed into whatever we could carry, we said goodbye to the landlady and the Crummies, not because we would miss them, but because my family still practiced courtesy. There was nothing we could possibly miss there except Buttercup.

Dad said, "Girl, don't break your neck cleaning up this dump."

"Well, at least I need to sweep the floor."

"Okay, then. Give it a lick and a promise and let's hit the road."

Hank, who had told us about Sunset Ridge in the first place, was helping us move because he had a truck. We kids climbed into the truck bed with the suitcases and boxes. When Mom lingered to see if we'd left anything behind, Dad yelled, "Hurry up! We want to be settled before dark."

"Okay, I found what I was looking for." She snatched up Buttercup and climbed into the cab next to the men.

Dad said, "We could catch holy hell for kidnapping someone's cat."

"So call me a thief. Buttercup belongs with us."

"Nita, you know how I feel about cats."

Mom cradled Buttercup in her lap and stroked her fur. "Yeah, but this cat is different."

"Different how?"

"I think she's pregnant."

"God almighty, Girl, what are you thinking?"

"Shut up." She meant it in an affectionate manner.

Then she turned to holler through the window of the cab. "Hang onto stuff back there so nothing blows away . . . and stay seated!"

And away we went without looking back at Champa Street.

Riding in the truck with my braids flapping in the breeze was so thrilling that my grin spread from one ear to the other. Bob and Patty had smiles glued to their faces while their hair whipped about as though desperate to break loose.

We must have looked odd with hair in the air and arms clutching boxes to keep them inside the truck. But the truth was the stuff we were hanging onto kept us from bouncing out. I had to squeeze my eyes shut because the wind made them water. Maybe they were tears of happiness. I was so elated I couldn't tell the difference. I memorized my good feelings so I wouldn't forget them.

When we slowed down through Englewood, we had a chance to look it over. The downtown was nice and not nearly as big as downtown Cedar Rapids. It had a homey feeling that I liked. I imagined myself walking down the street with a new friend or buying school supplies in the corner drugstore. I felt at home there.

Hank found Oxford Avenue and turned west, driving through a residential neighborhood before crossing a busy highway. He traveled a few miles past open fields with nothing blocking the landscape but a few trees. Questions raced through my head. Why are we going so far? Are we lost? How will we get to school living way out there? Then I noticed the impressive view of a distant mountain range.

Patty, sensing the change in speed, finally opened her eyes and looked around. "Oh, my gosh . . . look at those mountains . . . they're moving."

We watched them for a few seconds, and I realized Patty was right. The mountains seemed to be moving toward us. They were welcoming us to Sunset Ridge, wherever it was.

After several miles, we finally reached Hooker Street and turned into the driveway of the building with a sign that said OFFICE. Mom and Dad left Buttercup in the cab with Hank and went inside to introduce themselves to the manager. My brother and sister were quiet as we studied the neighborhood of our next home.

I broke the silence. "What do you think?"

Bob said, "It's nice."

Patty said, "I like the grass."

A narrow road wound up a graceful hill and curved into a big U shape. Along the large curve was a row of white two-story apartments with four units to each building. In the open space in the middle of the grounds were a few single-family units, several duplexes, and a playground. The modest buildings were plain, fresh, and clean. Everything was surrounded by lush grass and young trees. It was the greenest sight I'd seen since leaving Iowa.

I said, "Hey, you guys, this is really nice." But the thoughts in my head were more personal. *We're going to be happy here.* My family didn't say personal things out loud, but I wondered what was going through my parents' heads. I couldn't ask them because it would be considered disrespectful. Children were supposed to be seen and not heard.

They took so long that I was afraid there was a problem. I prayed that nothing would happen that might break my happy bubble. I watched them through the windows and saw that everyone was smiling as our parents talked with the person in charge. Finally, he handed them a piece of paper and the keys to our apartment.

We were quiet but excited as the truck crawled up the slight hill to one of the two-story buildings at the top. We parked in front of the middle unit and sat for a few minutes to stare before Dad climbed out. He turned the key in our new front door, and we all went inside. The clean smell of fresh paint greeted us. We headed in different directions to check things out. On the first floor were a small furnace room, a kitchen, and a living room. Upstairs I found two bedrooms and a bathroom to call our own — with no cracked linoleum. What a relief. We wanted to go outside to explore some more, but Dad said, "We can explore later. We need to unload the truck so Hank can go home."

It didn't take long to pull all of our stuff out of the truck, and Mom had a plan. "Don't set anything down in the house. Go straight to the backyard and put every single parcel on the grass."

Patty asked, "Why do we have to do that?"

Our mother lowered her voice almost to a whisper. "Patty, we have to inspect the boxes outdoors in case we see cockroaches. If we find any, we'll spray them dead on the spot." She didn't want vermin hitching a free ride with our belongings.

From our backyard, I could see across all the yards that were close to our unit. They ran together with no fences anywhere. Most included a garden or a clothesline. Aside from the house on 32nd Street, it was the nicest house my family ever had. The sight of that clean, bright neighborhood made me limp with relief. The contrast with Champa Street was almost too good to be real.

I was overwhelmed with an unfamiliar feeling that I assumed was bliss, but maybe it was just something I ate. My stomach hurt and nausea was just around the corner. Adjusting to frequent moves was nothing new to me. Maybe we'd jumped too high on the social ladder. I felt nervous, wondering if the kids who lived at Sunset Ridge were watching us from their upstairs windows. Once they saw that we didn't own furniture, they might feel the same about us that I felt about the Crummy family. With that sudden attack of worries, I didn't know whether to cry or throw up.

I ran upstairs to use the toilet for the first time and discovered why I felt so off balance. My monthly period had started. I had no idea where I'd packed my pads, though I was almost relieved that there was a good reason for my strange mood. I gazed at the bathroom in wonder. We had our very own private and super-clean toilet and sink. There was also a gleaming white bathtub with no dirty rings left by other people. No one would be knocking on the door but my own family. I could even read comic books in there if Bob decided to share his.

Being alone in the bathroom gave me the time I needed to pull myself together. My emotions were messing me up. I thought about all the friends I would meet, which just reminded me of the friends I'd left behind in Iowa. So I gave up deep breathing and just sat on the toilet and cried.

My mother yelled up the stairs, "Betty, what in the ever lovin' world is taking so long?"

"Mom, my BP started."

"Well, take care of your needs and hustle back down here. We need your help."

Sometimes, my mother was heartless. I wanted her to feel pity for me, but she had too much on her mind for that. I made an emergency pad for protection by folding many layers of toilet paper and holding the makeshift package in place with my panties. I dried my eyes, washed my face with cold water, and ran downstairs to help the family.

After all the boxes had reached the backyard, we inspected each item before placing it in a clean container that would go inside the house. During our scrutiny, we spotted a couple of cockroaches. Mom moved as fast as a sharpshooter to squirt them up close with bug spray, and they died a foaming, spastic death.

Bob was so impressed that he yelled, "Wow! This is better than cutting off their feelers with scissors. I want my turn at spraying cockroaches." I hoped desperately that no nice kids were watching or listening from upstairs bedroom windows.

On the first night, we all slept on the floor with pillows and blankets. The next day, Dad returned to Denver by bus to order three cheap beds and mattresses on a payment plan at the Montgomery Ward store. We had started over many times, but never with one stick of new furniture. As a special treat, he added a floor model console Zenith radio to our bill. We called those household items our family's Christmas presents, although it was still summer.

I finally had a dream come true. We were getting a fresh start and, with a small miracle, this time we would be successful.

Dad's Challenges

Dad's job at the machine shop in Denver was very far away after we moved, so he paid a visit to the manager's office to find out where the bus stop was located. He was gone so long that Mom said, "He hasn't changed. He's probably shooting the bull or having a beer with the manager." Mom's critical tone put me on guard because I didn't know where it might lead. I didn't want to start our new life with a family argument.

Dad returned home with two things: the directions to work and a discouraged look on his face that worried me. I longed to have things happen with no snags for a change. My parents were magnets for snags.

Mom asked, "What's wrong, Butch?"

My dad tossed the papers on the kitchen table like he was throwing them in the garbage. "Criminitly! I hafta get up at dawn, catch a bus, then a streetcar, and still walk three blocks."

I rarely saw him upset, but I'd become an expert at sniffing out trouble when it was brewing. I'd had years of practice, and I was as accurate as a barometer. I didn't trust my happy feelings because they often turned sour. I might have said our father was having a pisserinctum, a term he invented that meant having a "shit fit." But a pisserinctum was usually light-hearted, and his mood looked like serious exasperation that could turn into anger. I kept quiet because it was not the time to ask questions or try to make my parents laugh. In truth, whenever a problem threatened to mess up any progress we'd made, I held my breath and my tongue at the same time.

The directions covered the whole page, not because the manager wrote big but because the instructions were complicated. The ink lines on the hand-drawn map matched the frown lines on my father's forehead. He studied the paper and finally came up with a condensed version. "Okay, Girl, listen to this. I walk down the road out here in front of the office for a few blocks and take the Hampden Avenue bus to Englewood where I transfer to a #3 streetcar and ride all the way to the north side of the city and walk a few blocks to the shop."

"Whew," Mom said. "I didn't quite catch all of that. It's a good thing the manager helped out. You could've been late."

"Yeah, I guess so."

Dad soon grew sick of spending over an hour on public transportation every day. "Hell's bells. I need to find something closer to home," he told Mom.

Would Dad's frustration be another snag in my "dreams-coming-true" plan? Since I wasn't sure what it meant for our family, I stayed calm and waited it out.

By then I understood the process that would either set us in motion or hold us back. In order to leave the railroad, our father still had to have permission from the government because the war wasn't over. The only way that would happen was to find other employment in an approved war effort industry. Poor Dad. He searched for something closer to home, but he became so discouraged and worried that he was down in the dumps all the time.

"Girl, you may have to start looking for work," he told Mom.

She said, "I was hoping to stay home."

"Don't count on it. It might take me a long time to find another job closer by, and I don't think I can make that trip every day once winter gets here."

I was feeling the nervous dreads again. We kids were not used to seeing him this way, and when he was down, Mom was down. And when my mother wasn't happy, all of us would suffer. My hope for family happiness might not last the night. Feeling so worried caused me to turn prayerful. I had another talk with God.

Please, please, oh please, God, let there be a job that is closer to home so my family can stay happy. I would sure appreciate it if this could happen before my parents have a big fight since they seem to have trouble staying calm during times like this. God, I promise to be nicer to Patty if you could just help us out again. And I am so sorry that I forgot to thank you for this nice place to live. That's it for now. Please answer soon. Amen.

God must've liked me a lot, because Dad found a machinist position with a little company that had made fishing reels before the war. In 1941, they converted to a war-related product. The ride to the new job at Sark-man Barker was still long and tedious, but not half as bad as the one to the machine shop in Denver. I was so relieved when I heard the news that I slept like a dead person that night.

To save money, Dad bought a used bicycle and rode it whenever the weather was nice. His workplace was several miles away at the bottom of a big hill. The bike ride on the way to work wasn't half bad, but the trip home was a whole different story. He had to walk and push his bike up steep Oxford Avenue and, whether he liked it or not, he had to accept it.

Dad's physique became trim and his cheeks turned rosy from the sun. It might have been my imagination, but it seemed that he and Mom got along better once he had a trim, tanned body. Could parents get a crush on each other after years of fighting? I found that hard to believe until I heard Mom say, "Butch, I've gotta keep my eyes on you because you're turning into a hubba-hubba man."

Our father had caught bike fever. He was so excited about it that he said, "Girl, I think this whole family should start ridin' bikes."

"Butch, you know damn well we can't afford bikes for all of us."

"I'll build 'em."

Mom couldn't believe her ears. "Build bikes out of what?"

"I'll buy old bikes and use the parts."

"That will take forever. The kids will be married, buried, and gone before you build four bikes."

"No sirree. I'll get 'em made before Betty turns sixteen."

Mom just sighed and looked at the ceiling.

Ironing My Way into the Future

ON AUGUST 15, 1945, DAD WAS AT WORK, MOM AND PATTY WERE getting groceries, and Bob was with his friend on the playground. I loved being by myself in the house with only a few responsibilities. It felt like being grown up and on my own. And to make my mood better, in only seventy-two hours I would celebrate my fifteenth birthday. I could hardly believe that I was almost that old. My whole family had been in good spirits for weeks, and I was in an unusually contented, peaceful mood. Everything in my life was hunky dory.

I mentally reviewed my simple task list. First, I would finish ironing Mr. Fender's white shirts because he was my best customer and I wanted to keep him happy. While doing that, I would occasionally check on my brother. Nothing could be easier.

I loved earning some money to call my own. Mom had become the laundry lady in the neighborhood, and I was her assistant. She'd had a job at the Modern Laundry in Cedar Rapids and taught me how to perfectly press a man's starched garment. There were five steps to follow, some short and sweet and others more complicated. I didn't mind, and how many girls my age could say they excelled at ironing? It gave me a sense of confidence. I could always earn my own money because there would always be wrinkled clothes.

Mom had previously starched and dried Mr. Fender's shirts, so I sprinkled them with water from an empty coke bottle fitted with a tin stopper that had tiny holes punched in the lid. Once they were evenly dampened, I folded and rolled them into a sausage shape, then wrapped the bundle in a damp dish towel to soak for a few hours.

If I was in the right frame of mind, ironing became an art project. On that day, my mind was in the right frame because everything was falling into place. I was so immersed in my mission that nothing else mattered, and I forgot to check on Bob. All I could think about was making pressed clothes so picture perfect that I could raise my price to fifteen cents a garment. I had already saved $2.60 in a jelly jar labeled "Grape Flavored IRONING." I had purposely printed over the word "jelly" because the result was so odd it made me smile.

After two hours of soaking, the shirts had reached the optimum stage of dampness. I completed step one, which involved pressing both sides of the stiff collar with the hottest setting. It was flawless, with no crinkles anywhere.

After that was done, I started on the back yoke, which had to be folded flat to allow the collar to stand straight up and out of the way. It was as though the collar was bragging to the rest of the shirt that it always finished first.

As I continued to work, faraway noise trickled through the windows and into my ears. I didn't pay close attention because I was concentrating on smoothing the yoke with my hands so the iron could glide over it in one long, continuous movement. The distant sounds became slightly noticeable, and I subconsciously wondered what they were. I listened more carefully, and they grew distinct. Were those car horns or factory whistles? Or was it a tornado warning like I'd seen in the movies? It was impossible to ignore.

Suddenly my gut sent my brain a message: *The war has ended!*

Right in the middle of an important step, I turned on the radio. Every station was broadcasting news of the Japanese surrender that marked the end of four years of battle. It was hard to believe. I knew I was not going to finish my work, so I set the hot iron on the asbestos pad and ran out the front door to see what was happening.

Neighbors were gathering in clusters on the grass, hugging and yelling across their lawns to each other. It felt like a dream. A man dashed out of his house clutching as many beers as he could hold and passed them around 'til they were gone.

Thoughts collided with each other in my mind. *Have Mom and Patty heard about it in the grocery store? Did Dad hear about it at his job? Oh, gosh — where's Bob?*

Since I was the only member of my family at home, I was left to mark the historic event by myself. If I'd been old enough to drink beer, I would have run across the street and joined the grownups. I think they would've said, "Here, have one," even if they knew I wasn't quite fifteen.

Knowing that the war had ended was an unexpected birthday gift. First we had gotten a new home and now we were getting a new future. My life was looking better by the minute. That time, I did not forget to be grateful. I said out loud, "Thank you, God."

I was sure that getting good news when I was already feeling happy was a sign of things to come. Our lives were going to be great. I wanted to share my euphoria with someone, so I went looking for my brother. I found him on the teeter totters with his friend. He was confused.

"Betty, what's going on?" he asked as soon as he saw me.

"The war is over."

Bob just looked at me, then at his buddy. "What are we supposed to do now?"

The other boy noticed people celebrating in the neighborhood and said, "I think we're supposed to yell and drink beer."

I knew what I needed to do. I dashed for our building to check on the job I'd abandoned so suddenly. I didn't want to celebrate the historic event by setting our apartment on fire.

The radio was still proclaiming the unbelievably good news. Mr. Fender's white shirt had already dried out too much to finish, so I refilled the sprinkler bottle with fresh water and started the process from scratch. As I waited again for the cloth to return to the perfect stage of dampness, it occurred to me that wars happened all the time and in places I'd never heard of. But those wars never interrupted my ironing.

Fort Logan

NOT MANY PEOPLE HAVE AN HISTORIC MILITARY BASE RIGHT NEXT door, but Fort Logan was just a stone's throw from our front yard in Sunset Ridge. The Army had settled there about sixty years earlier, so we were surrounded by men in uniform. Since World War II had ended, soon there would be no more brave soldiers, no uniforms or marching drills, and no German prisoners held under guard.

Our military neighbors were very accommodating, so we spent almost as much time on the base as at home. And who wouldn't? They let us use their movie theater, their store (which they called a PX), their bowling alley, and their church. The church welcomed everyone, even if they didn't believe in God. If a stranger wanted to sit for a spell and enjoy the peace and quiet, it was okay with them.

Bob probably liked Fort Logan more than any of us. He worked at the post bowling alley on weekends as a pinsetter, earning as much as six dollars a weekend, which he blew at the PX. The soldiers asked him if he had any sisters they could date. When my brother and I argued, he'd sometimes threaten to tell those soldiers about me. But I was certain he wouldn't do it 'cause Dad would mop the floor with him.

Besides, my brother was too busy hauling stuff home from the fort's dump to make good on silly threats. He and his buddy ignored the big sign at the entrance to the dump that said NO TRESPASSING and used it as their own personal store. He told me the Army threw away all sorts of things like old footballs and volleyballs, mess kits, canteens, cartridge belts, back packs, first aid pouches, and clothing.

"You boys will get in trouble with the Army," I warned.

"No, we won't. We go when no one is around to see us."

"Someday someone will see you there and they'll put you guys in the brig."

"They don't have a brig anymore. That was in the olden days."

I was pretty sure Bob was wrong because I'd seen German Prisoners of War, called POWs, on the base. But they didn't seem like jailbirds. Except for the prisoner jackets they wore, they resembled ordinary people, so it was hard to think of them as dangerous. They were always under guard by soldiers with guns, but most of the guards didn't mind that we interacted with the enemy. So Bob and I became acquainted with the Germans without speaking their language.

The POWs were friendly and roamed freely, sweeping grass off the walks and painting the barracks. Sometimes they just leaned against their rakes, shooting the breeze with each other in their own language. Since the war was over, they were just waiting to be shipped back to their own country.

One of the young prisoners winked whenever he saw me and said, "Gooten morgan." I just nodded my head and said, "Hi there." I enjoyed the attention, but my mother said, "Don't get emotionally involved." How could I? Everyone knew you couldn't get involved with the opposite sex unless you spoke their language. At least that's what I believed then. Besides, they would all be leaving soon to go back to Germany.

In the meantime, I had regular babysitting jobs on the base, and I took in ironing for many of the officers' wives. Mom had gotten a regular job cleaning their quarters. The homes were beautiful two-story buildings with wraparound porches, and each housed two families. The wives of officers could afford to hire people to keep their elegant homes clean, and when word spread that my mother was very good, all the wives wanted to be her clients. I worked with her to help out and earn some cash of my own. I thought it was a real a waste of someone's hard-earned money to have us dusting and mopping rooms that weren't dirty, but it was fun to see how high-ranking soldiers lived.

In one of the houses there was an old poster framed for display on the living room wall. It was yellowed with age and read: *Shooting Buffalo from the Barracks Windows is Prohibited*. It reminded me of Dad's warning to my brother: *Don't you go shooting your new BB gun at nothin' but the target in the pasture.*

In the same room was a shiny cabinet with two doors that latched in the middle. I was dying to find out what was inside, so I opened the doors and saw a radio on the left and a round fifteen-inch opening on the right.

"What in the world is this thing?" I asked my mother.

"Isn't that a curiosity?"

"Sure is."

"The woman who hired me said some day that round opening will hold a television."

"A tella-what?"

"It's an invention that will allow you to see a radio broadcast while you're listening to it."

I was curious about the new contraption. "Do you mean movies could come straight to this cabinet as though they were radio programs?"

Mom shrugged and said, "I guess so."

"But what if television never gets invented?"

"Well, I guess they'll have a beautiful cabinet with a little radio on one side and a big hole in the other."

I considered that peculiar piece of furniture another waste of money. But what did I know? A few years later my own children would be watching *Pinky Lee, Ding Dong School,* and *Buffalo Bob* on our own black Bakelite television set.

Deeper in Debt

WHEN MERLE TRAVIS WROTE "SIXTEEN TONS" AND SANG "ANOTHER day older and deeper in debt," everyone in our house understood. My father said that getting deeper in debt was becoming the family hobby. He came home from work one day, plunked his lunch pail on the kitchen table, and announced, "Well, I'm no longer a government employee."

"What? You've been fired?" Mom asked.

"Nope. I got laid off."

"Butch, we have a loan to pay off."

"I know. I know."

"What happened?

"When the war ended, it took a while, but Mr. Sarkman's government contract ended, too. He's gonna build fishin' reels again and he doesn't need a machinist for those."

"What are you going to do?"

"I'm gonna find me another job."

Dad wasn't alone. A lot of fathers were looking for work after the war. But our father was lucky. He found a position in the machine shop for the Colorado Building Supply Company (COBUSCO).

Even though a weekly paycheck was coming our way again, lack of cash was still a problem. Monthly payments on our new furnishings meant there was nothing for extras, including nice clothes. I had been sewing since I was eleven years old, so I started making my own. In order to buy patterns and fabric, I took in more ironing and started babysitting.

There were two things at the top of our wish list that were not extras because we really needed them: transportation for Dad and a washing machine for Mom. After the weather had turned wintry, he came home from work on his bicycle, set his lunch bucket on the table as usual, and rubbed his hands together to warm them up. His lips were so stiff he could barely speak, but he had something important to say.

"Uh foze m' ass off t' day. Fore it snows uh need a car."

Bob piped up. "Can we buy a new one?"

"Can't talk." He sipped hot coffee until his lips warmed up enough to answer my brother's question. Then he said, "Bob, mark my words. Our name will not be on any year-long waiting lists for two reasons: I need a car soon, and we can't afford anything new."

If Dad bought what he needed, it meant Mom could buy what she needed. And that meant we would be spending money we didn't have. But it didn't worry our mother. "Where's the newspaper?" she asked. "I need to look at the want ads." She scoured each listing, putting a check mark by some of them. When she said, "Bingo!," we knew she'd found a good deal.

"Butch, listen to this: *Englewood family moving. Eight yr old Maytag, automatic wringer release. Includes double rinse tubs. Best offer.* We can't pass this up."

Dad's friend and his truck came to our rescue again. After paying eight dollars for the appliances, the men hauled them home. Owning a washing machine made us popular in the neighborhood. Mom charged the women twenty-five cents a load to use our laundry equipment. When she wasn't home, I took her place. She said, "Betty, it's your job to be sure the women don't overload the washer just to save a quarter."

I hated that job. I didn't feel comfortable saying, "Mrs. Levine, can't you tell that the agitator is barely agitating? I think you're cramming too many overalls into the washer." It put me in the terrible position of being a boss to the neighborhood mothers. So I pretended not to notice when the agitator struggled and the machine shook.

Soon after the washer was purchased, Dad found a 1936 Chevy in good running condition, but it was more than he planned to spend. He said, "Girl, I don't know how we're gonna pay for this."

"Butch, that's easy. We'll just add to our loan and pay it off by the month. It's the only way we can get ahead."

"Yeah, sure. The only way we can get ahead is to borrow money from the bank."

Mom laughed even though Dad was not making a joke. He was thinking about the Merle Travis "deeper in debt" song.

Longing to Belong

FINDING MY OWN GROUP OF FRIENDS AT ENGLEWOOD HIGH SCHOOL was not easy because I was rather quiet and easily overlooked. I didn't have much in common with most of the kids at school because they went to the dances and were nuts about popular music and modern singers. I could hear them in the halls singing the words to the songs I heard on the radio. The only popular tunes that stuck to my brain were "Dream When You're Feelin' Blue," and "My Dreams are Gettin' Better All the Time." I liked those because I was a dreamer.

Mom asked how school was going, and I said, "It's going pretty well, but I haven't met any friends yet who don't dance and who don't listen to Frank Sinatra."

"They're around, I'm sure. Just be patient."

"Mom, I don't get it. Why does anyone swoon over Frank Sinatra's slurpy voice?"

"For the same reason you swoon over 'Rachmaninoff's Concerto in D Minor.'"

It was true. I felt enlightened when I heard classical music. And I always got goose bumps when listening to Debussy's "Claire de Lune" on the piano. I was sometimes so moved by music that I cried. "Boogie Woogie Blues" never made me feel that way. I guess I was a wee bit prejudiced.

In spite of my difference from other students, I yearned to become part of the "in" crowd. But I didn't seem designed for cliques.

When Mom said I would find my own kind if I gave it enough time, I didn't believe her. But she was right. It started with the student who was assigned to third chair in the violin section of the orchestra. I was assigned to second position. Joann Stratton introduced herself and said, "I hope you don't mind if I challenge for your spot."

"Okay." I didn't know what else to say.

"You see, it's like this. I'm taking private lessons now, and I want to find out if I've improved enough to move up."

"I understand." I was terrified of losing.

To defend your placement was a very important process. We had to play for the rest of the orchestra members from behind a folding screen. They voted on who played best. If they voted for Joann, it meant that she would move up and I would move down. I was unprepared to defend my position. Back home, Auntie Marge had paid for private lessons. But I was on my own in Colorado, and I was getting rusty. When I told Mom about the competition, she asked, "Why don't you play variations on the theme of 'Blue Bells of Scotland' like you did for your recital?"

"Oh, no, Mom. That's too hard."

"So what are you going to play?"

"Hungarian Rhapsody."

"The whole thing?"

"No, just the first part because it's so showy."

On the day of the challenge, Joann played a more difficult selection than mine. But when it was my turn to play, I hammed it up so much that you expected gypsies to come dancing into the room. Thanks to my theatrics, I got to keep my place. In spite of her defeat, Joann and I soon formed a close friendship. We talked and laughed about many things, including classical music and how much we each dreamed of having a boyfriend.

Another person who drifted our way was the first chair in the cello section. She also played piano for the orchestra, choir, glee club, and small ensembles. I was in most of those ensembles, so we ran into each other a lot. Her name was Joanne Oberg. I named them "piano Joanne" and "violin Joann." Piano Joanne was tall and lanky and had the longest fingers I had ever seen. I loved watching her hands dance over the keys. They reminded me of high-speed windup toys.

Then along came Priscilla Greene, who enrolled in school after it had started. In addition to being a soloist, she joined the soprano section of the choir, glee club, and girls' trio. Priscilla and I respected each other right off the bat. Her father was a professor at Denver University, which didn't surprise me a bit because she was the smartest person I had ever known. Our friends agreed that her presence made the rest of us appear to be more intelligent than we were. Priscilla's beautiful voice was so high and clear that I knew if I ever got married, she would sing at my wedding.

The last person to join our group was Claire Holberg. After Joann introduced her at lunch one day, Claire became our token non-musical member. She was almost as smart as Priscilla. Her father owned the local greenhouse so her family was not poor, and she had a knack for choosing clothes that I wanted to borrow. Claire was so spunky and down-to-earth that she fit right in.

Outside of the small world that included my four friends, I didn't fit in at all. Other students referred to me as "that girl with long braids." There was no one else on our campus who wore braids, which made me feel a little out of place. Whenever I took part in a school program with the music department, I had to dress up. But I owned no dressy clothes and the only way I could make my hair fit the occasion was to wrap my braids in a circle on top of my head. It was a hair crown, and the kids thought I was Amish.

I should have been satisfied to have four people who liked me, but it wasn't enough. I longed to belong to a large group that always sat together at football games. I didn't know who they were, but they seemed to be in a special clique of some kind.

I thought about it a lot and sometimes felt a little sorry for myself. One day, Patty overheard me sigh and say to myself, "I wish I could join a clique."

My sister had the answer to my problem. "That's easy," she said. "Just go to the school office and sign up."

If only it had been that easy.

First Kiss

ANGELINA CORDONA LIVED IN AN APARTMENT IN THE BUILDING next to ours. She and I became friends soon after my family moved to Sunset Ridge, and we started to spend a lot of time together. I'd never met her big brother, but I soon developed a crush on his Navy picture. He was the most striking sailor I'd ever gazed upon. With thick, black hair; dark eyes; a wide, cocky grin; and big, white teeth, Frankie Cordona was a Pepsodent commercial in uniform. When he came home on leave, Angie said, "Stay overnight at our house and I'll introduce you." I couldn't wait to pack my toothbrush and best pajamas.

Her handsome brother was out on a date when Angie and I got ready for bed. We slept on the folded-out davenport with our heads facing the front hall. If I could stay awake long enough, I would know when he returned. Angie started snoring right away, while I lay there afraid of how I would look asleep with my mouth open and spit trickling down my chin. I dreaded the possibility that Frankie might see me that way. So I practiced different sleeping positions that might look attractive, ending up with my long braids across my shoulders and one hand draped casually on my chest. The other hand rested palm up outside the covers. Eventually, one hand went numb and I had to clench my fist over and over to get the blood circulating. I was really tired of holding that pretty pose, but I didn't want to fall asleep before Frankie saw me. I wanted to be staged for his return.

Eventually, the front door creaked open and the light flipped on. It had to be Frankie at last. He shut the front door so quietly that I was sure he had a lot of practice sneaking in late. I could tell that he was creeping toward us on his tiptoes. Then his faint footsteps stopped abruptly. I imagined his surprise at seeing his sister and me asleep in the living room. I kept my hands still and my eyes closed, hoping I looked like Sleeping Beauty herself. I was lying still, but I was out of breath. I could sense that he was right by my head because the air around my cheek seemed warmer. He must have knelt down to have a closer look. Should I pretend to snore softly? I couldn't take the chance of it coming out as a snort.

While I was trying to breathe normally, I felt his hands ever so gently slip under the covers and cup both my breasts and give them a few squeezes. I had to pretend that I felt nothing. It was almost impossible. I lay stiff as a fork not knowing what to do. Then he bent closer and planted a long, deliciously soft kiss on my lips.

I had never been kissed by a boy. But this guy was not a boy. He was a nineteen-year-old sailor who tasted of aftershave mixed with beer. I barely breathed, but did not budge, and waited for whatever came next. When he stood up, his knees cracked and I exhaled tiny amounts of air at a time. He turned out the light, then padded upstairs to his own bed. I coasted to sleep right before sunup.

At home that morning, I wrote in my diary: *Frankie Cordona kissed me and felt my breasts last night.*

A few weeks later, I discovered my mother sitting on the edge of my bed reading my private thoughts. She didn't raise her head when she said, "Betty, I am so disappointed in you."

I knew she had just seen the "Frankie felt my breasts" part, so I explained what had actually happened. I don't think Mom believed me, but it didn't matter. Later that day I took my much-loved journal and pushed it deep into the garbage can where it belonged, with potato peels, eggshells, and the dog's poop.

I never kept a diary again. Who needed to write things down in a book that other people might read? My first kiss was permanently written in my memory.

Obsessed with Angelina

ANGELINA CORDONA AND I HAD ONLY ONE THING IN COMMON: WE were girls. I didn't need her as a friend. I had four terrific girlfriends, and we had everything in common. We didn't smoke, drink, neck with boys, or get bad grades. We were all conservative and well-liked by our teachers. Nobody in our group was trendy or modern. We weren't the type who would faint at a Frank Sinatra concert because we never listened to him in the first place.

Angelina was different. She was worldly, confident, and attention-grabbing. For some reason that I could not explain, I went out of my way to impress the seventeen-year-old girl next door. I would jaywalk just to say hi to her, which puzzled Mom.

Angie was everything that I secretly wanted to be. She was older, taller, more outspoken, and much prettier. She had sun-kissed skin, eyes black as midnight, and long, dark hair. I was short and pale, with blue eyes and mouse-colored braids. I wasn't hard to look at, just plain.

She said, "Betty, you would sure look better if you had some color on your face."

"But my cheeks are always rosy."

"That's not enough. You need to start wearing lipstick."

I was sure she must be right because she knew all about looking good. So in the privacy of our bathroom, I tried Mom's tube of "Raving Red." Oh, my gosh. Intense red lips and pigtails did not blend. I needed my own color, so I went shopping for a shade that was closer to bland. I found what I wanted at Myers Drug Store. It was a ten-cent tube of tinted lip balm that looked and felt like lipstick. Wearing it didn't change the way I looked, but I felt and acted different. I thought if Angie and I were buddies, more good stuff would rub off on me.

Angie knew the words to every song on the 1946 Hit Parade. I could hum the melody to any popular tune, but I never remembered the words or the titles. I was filled with heroine worship when she sang "Baby, It's Cold Outside" all the way through while snapping her fingers and wiggling her hips. "Golly, how do you remember all those words?" I asked.

She raised her eyebrows, shocked that I couldn't sing "Baby, It's Cold Outside." "How do I remember? I could sing that song in my sleep because I have all of his albums."

"Whose albums?"

"Johnny Mercer's, of course."

Of course.

I'd heard his name before, but that didn't help me remember who he was or the words to his songs. If I had owned a record player, I would have played classical music all day long. When I listened to music on the radio, I tuned in to the Saturday morning opera and listened to songs in Italian, for heaven's sake. When I shared that with Angie, she said, "Interesting, but why would you listen to opera?"

I didn't know why, so I tried again to squeeze a compliment out of her. "I can sing 'Ave Maria' in Latin."

"In Latin? Who would understand that?"

I had failed miserably at impressing my new friend, yet I was determined to keep trying. It was the same as hoping to earn a high grade from a really tough teacher. I was good at many things and I didn't need her to prove it, but I kept trying anyway. I wanted her to know that I was an artist, so I left my drawings lying here and there and everywhere. Finally, she noticed and asked, "Who drew this?"

"I drew it."

"Really? You did this?" I think she was disappointed to find out I was an artist. "Prove it. Draw a picture of me."

She sat very still while I drew a portrait that was a darn good likeness. I showed it to her, bursting with pride. Her only comment was, "My mouth is too big."

When she talked of becoming a model, I decided to help her reach that goal. I purchased some black and white film and, with my little Brownie camera loaded and ready to go, I became a fashion photographer. I took all kinds of elaborately posed photos of Angie in different skirts and sweaters. In the first picture, she was kissing a face that we'd drawn on a balloon. In another photo, she struck a sassy pose while wearing her best pleated skirt, saddle oxfords, and pink angora sweater.

The pictures were cute. But she studied all the photos and said, "They're so small."

"Yeah, that's the size you get with a Brownie camera."

I wanted her to appreciate me for the things I did well, but I was beginning to wonder why I knocked myself out for her approval. Mom thought I was crazy, but she didn't interfere with the good work I was trying to do for my new friend.

For my next attempt to impress Angelina, I managed an audition for her with a local dance band made up of Englewood High School graduates. If she was discovered at a school dance, she would be obliged to throw a thank-you my way. I could picture her at the microphone saying, "I could not have done this if it hadn't been for Betty Peal. I owe it all to her."

I had imagined a display of gratitude, but I was surprised when she showed genuine excitement about the audition. She started bouncing around and singing her favorite tunes from Jonny Mercer's album. I hummed along and invented some dance steps because I was pretty excited myself.

When audition day arrived, my friend was a lot less perky and a little distracted. I had a feeling she was getting cold feet when she started worrying out loud. "I hope these guys in the band know what they're doing."

"Don't worry, They know what they're doing."

"They'd better not play too loud 'cause I have a soft voice."

She did not have a soft voice. I'd heard her belting out songs on my behalf for weeks on end. What was going on with her?

Thanks to her out-of-the-blue piss-ant attitude, the audition was a flop. In fact, I was embarrassed, not for her, but for me. Angie's voice was as soft as Kleenex. There was no flashy finger-snapping or hip-wiggling. She didn't seem all that worldly and experienced with a microphone in her hand.

After she stomped off the stage like some temperamental movie star, I thanked the band for trying. I should have learned my lesson, but I felt bad and tried to lift her spirits. However, getting her spirits lifted was not what she had on her mind. She was just plain mad and ready to blame everyone but herself. "Those guys couldn't even stay with me."

That wasn't true, and I felt I could've done way better than she did. I could sing. I had rhythm. And I wasn't a quitter. I was beginning to think that I had more going for me than I had realized.

Because I wasn't a quitter, I wasn't ready to give up on her. I gave it one more shot. Since Angie seemed to know everything, it was a mystery why she had dropped out of school at sixteen. Most kids who dropped out seemed grubby and hopeless. My friend was a dreamer and the most attractive quitter I had ever seen. I was sure that she would learn to love homework if I helped her with it. I was genuinely excited about my crazy plan.

After a week of hinting and nagging, I finally convinced Angie to register for classes. "Oh, what the heck. Why not?" she said. But moods changed overnight with her. While riding the bus the first day of classes, her silence suggested that it was another doomed adventure. She was too calm. There was no eagerness, no nervousness, nothing.

When she registered at the office, she was rudely indifferent like she hadn't been taught good manners. In my head, I said a couple of very bad words that I would never say out loud. It was obvious that Angie did not feel at home when she was at school. I wondered if she felt at home anywhere except inside her own house, dreaming about things she would probably never do.

On the third day of my quest for her intellectual enlightenment, she slithered up to me in the hall, looked over her shoulder, and squinted. "Hey, Betty, you're really into this school stuff, aren't you?"

"Well, yeah. I guess I am."

"Not me. I'll see you at home."

And off she went without signing out or dropping out or anything. Just straight out the door like a really slow arrow. As I watched her leave, I finally understood that she and I were too different to be close friends. I decided then and there to stop helping Angie develop her talents and start polishing my own.

Payback

PATTY AND I STILL SHARED A DOUBLE BED AFTER WE MOVED TO SUN-set Ridge. I didn't mind. With my sister so close to me, she was easier to scare. My favorite time to do that was, naturally, at night. We sat cross-legged in our nightgowns on top of the bed, and I lured her into a casual conversation loaded with lies that sounded true.

"Hey, Patty, have you met the new kids up the street?"

"There are new kids up the street?"

Actually, there were no new children on our block, but I kept her attention by staring into her face and saying, "Yeah, sure . . . five in the family."

"Really? Have you seen them?"

I plunged into a description of each nonexistent child. "Well, let's see . . . the oldest boy is sort of pudgy and quiet, and the girl your age has red hair like yours, and she . . . ."

Without blinking, my gaze shifted past my sister's face to the space behind her head. Then I made my eyes bulge with fake fear. She screamed, clawing the air and trying to escape from whatever horror I'd seen behind her.

I exploded with hysterics, and my sister, knowing she'd been "had" again, punched me hard on the arm and yelled, "I'm telling Mom!" She never learned her lesson and was so gullible that she trusted me each time I tricked her.

She was such an easy mark that I eventually became bored and invented a scarier version of the prank that took place in the dark. Once the lights were out, I yakked on and on about whatever popped into my mind, such as telling her that dogs catch more mice than cats.

"Really?" she said. "I didn't know that."

Once more Patty became the innocent victim of my prank. At the most interesting part of whatever chit chat I was making up, I stopped mid-sentence. The result was a deep, dead silence . . . in the dark. She clutched my arm with both hands.

"You're staring at something, aren't you? What are you staring at?"

Not a peep from me.

"Your eyes are bulging, aren't they?"

I didn't say a word.

"Stop it! I'm telling!"

And she always did, but it was always worth it.

Scaring my sister was so easy and so much fun that I shared the story with one of the neighbor girls. She tested it on her younger brother and reported that staring-and-scaring him was worth the bawling out from her mother. She kept the prank alive by passing it on to her girlfriends at the Ridge.

Gossip about our nighttime activity spread until it finally reached Mom. She pulled me into the kitchen. With arms crossed over her chest, she asked, "This prank that everyone's talking about — is it yours?"

I was proud to admit that it was, indeed, my own invention. Mom took a slow, deep drag on her cigarette, exhaled, and said, "Well, there are certainly better things to do with your time than scaring the hell out of little kids."

My mother was so wrong.

❖

But that winter, my bad deeds came back to haunt me. Dad hated to spend money to keep the apartment toasty at night, so he always turned the furnace way down. One night when I scooched closer to Patty to stay warm, my old nightgown split down the middle. The frail flannel didn't even make a tiny tearing sound; it just popped open. With a ripped-open nightie, no matter which way I turned, my front side felt wafts of cold air. The only way out of the situation was to go downstairs and use the electric sewing machine to stitch it shut. For once, I didn't care about making a straight seam. I just wanted to close the gap and crawl back under the covers.

I padded barefoot down the stairs, happy to see that moonlight was shining through the window so I didn't have to turn on the lamp. Since no one outside could see in, I could raise my nightgown past my waist and run the machine while standing up. Even more of my body was exposed to the chilly air, which caused me to shiver as I tried hard to concentrate.

Stitching the first six inches without sitting down was as easy as pie. But when the seam grew longer and closer to my front body parts, sewing in that uncomfortable position became dangerous. I took a deep breath and exhaled to stay steady, then shifted my body and continued stitching my torn nightgown together. By balancing on one bare foot and pressing the pedal with the other, I stitched forward a few inches at a time.

Then I heard a creaking sound in the dark that scared me. When I jumped, the needle nailed my finger. I screamed and released my foot from the pedal, almost losing my balance. But having a finger attached to the needle kept me upright.

I heard Dad's feet hit the floor with a thud as he threw himself out of bed and stumbled down the steps to rescue me from some unknown horror in the living room. At the bottom of the stairs, Dad snapped on the lights to find me with my nightie wadded around my waist, bare backside exposed, in a close encounter with the Singer sewing machine. It was Dad's turn to yell.
"What the hell . . . ?"
"Dad, I sewed my finger," I whimpered.

My father peered closely and saw that my left forefinger had truly been impaled by the needle. He knew just what to do. I looked away as he placed his hands on either side of the finger that was held captive and slid it down and off the dull point. When I was brave enough to look, I saw that I'd been released, but was still attached to the Singer by a double strand of light blue J. & P. Coats All Purpose Mercerized thread. It was a horrible sight.

Dad cut the two threads, and his rough working hands ever so gently prepared to pull them up and out of my flesh. I focused on the back of his head so I wouldn't see the operation, but I sure could feel it. I squealed through tightly-shut lips. Finally released, I pulled my nightgown down to cover my nakedness. Then I started bawling.

"Betty . . . what in the Sam Hill were you doing?" Dad asked.

I stopped crying long enough to explain the torn garment and my attempts to fix it in a hurry. With his mouth hanging open, Dad listened in disbelief. Because my finger hadn't bled even one drop, he squeezed it so that any germs that had snuck in would squirt out. He finished the job with a sloppy splash of alcohol before heading to bed, shaking his head all the way.

I was mortified. But since I hadn't finished closing the ripped front of my nightie, tender body parts were still exposed to cold air. In Mom's round tin button box that had once held a fruitcake, I found four safety pins and used them to close the rest of the opening. Then I climbed back under the covers next to my sister. She was still snoring, completely unaware that I'd just gotten the scare of my life . . . from a sewing machine.

If that wasn't payback enough, my finger really started to hurt. And it throbbed all night long.

The Facts of Life

Mom was very upset with Dad because he kept putting off his father-son talk with Bob about human reproduction.

"Butch, it's the father's duty to tell the boys and the mother's duty to tell the girls."

"Bob can learn the way I learned," he replied.

"And how did you learn, Butch?"

"By sowing my wild oats."

She got tired of nagging and stomped out, saying, "Fine. I'll tell 'im myself."

"Don't leave anything out!" Dad yelled.

Of course that made her even angrier. She decided that if she was responsible for our sex education, it would be more efficient to enlighten all three of us at the same time.

"But I've already heard this talk. Remember?" I said.

"A little review never hurt anyone."

So Mom took Patty, Bob, and me to her bedroom where each of us perched on a corner of the chenille spread and waited for sex class to begin.

She kept the information short and to the point by explaining that babies are made in the woman's stomach when the father plants the seed. Bob was wide-eyed. "How does the seed know how to get in there?"

She explained that a man and a woman join their bodies together when they're in bed at night, and the seed gets planted during that time.

Bob continued to ask embarrassing questions while I sat and listened. Patty was too bewildered to know what to ask. Finally, she came up with a question. "Can I go out and play now?"

Our mother felt that we'd learned enough for the first sex education class, so we were dismissed. I was relieved that she'd kept it a lot simpler than when she explained the facts of life to me.

While we were in the bedroom learning about reproduction, our new dog Ginger escaped from the house. That morning, Dad had said, "You guys have to keep her on a leash when she's outside 'cause she's in heat." We didn't want her to have puppies yet, but we kept forgetting to close the doors.

By the time we realized she'd gotten outside again, male mutts were rushing her from all directions. We waved our hands furiously and yelled, "Shoo, scram, beat it. Get outta here!" Four of them refused to leave and almost got in a fight about which one would join his body with Ginger first. She wanted all of them, but a shaggy mixed breed claimed her as his own right there on our front lawn. They were mating with such enthusiasm that Patty stared wide-eyed. "Betty, what are they doing?"

I saw it as an opportunity to back up the story about reproduction and explained the situation in the know-it-all tone of an older, wiser sister. "That dog is planting his seed in her right now so she can have puppies."

My sister was wide-eyed with wonder. "You mean that Ginger will have puppies right now?"

"No ... not right now. I don't know how long it takes. Maybe as long as it took your radishes to grow in the Victory Garden. But we'll ask Mom."

"Did a boy cat plant seeds in Buttercup?"

"Yes, but he planted them while she was still living on Champa Street. They had to grow inside of her first and she had her kittens after we moved here."

"Did she run away from us because she wanted that boy cat to give her more kittens?"

Bob, who had been focused on the action on the lawn, asked a question of his own. "Patty, why don't you run away?" Patty stuck her tongue out at him.

By then, Ginger and her boyfriend seemed to be stuck together, hopping about awkwardly like confused Siamese twins. My sister was so excited that she jumped up and down, shouting, "Ride 'em, cowboy!"

Just then Dad came out of our house to see what all the yelping was about. He grabbed my sister's arm and said, "Get in the house, young lady."

"Dad, guess what?" she said. "That dog is planting puppy seeds in Ginger so she can have babies."

"Yeah, yeah, yeah. I know all about that," was all Dad had to say.

I had just learned why Patty got such good grades in school. She caught on real quick.

Out of the Pool!

MY BROTHER WAS BESIDE HIMSELF WITH EXCITEMENT WHEN HIS Cub Scout troop scheduled a field trip to the YMCA in Denver. After he came home, Mom was full of questions. "Did you have a good time? How many boys went? Who were they?" Bob was not as excited as we expected he would be. When he told us about the field trip, we understood why.

He said the twenty scouts in his troop had really looked forward to swimming. They laughed and joked on the bus and sang all the silly songs they could remember. They could hardly wait to get out of their clothes and into their swim trunks to jump in the pool for an afternoon of wild fun. They lined up outside the bus while the leader turned a list of names in to the office. Then they tore into the locker room to undress for the water. Bob had brand new swim trunks for the occasion because he had never owned a pair.

"I really wanted to wear my new trunks," he told us.

"Did they fit right?" Mom asked.

"I don't know."

"What do you mean, you don't know?"

"I never put 'em on."

"What? Why not?"

"My shirt was off and my pants were down when a man wearing a YMCA T-shirt came into the locker room and told us to stop what we were doing and listen. Some of us were naked, but we did as we were told and just stood there."

"What did the man want?"

"He asked which one of us was Henry Yakimura."

My mother snorted in disbelief. "A name like Yakimura and he couldn't tell?"

She was unusually attentive, and I was dying to find out what it was all about.

Bob continued. "The man asked Henry to wait in the office until the rest of us finished swimming."

"Then what happened?"

"Henry put his suit and towel back into his bag and did as he was told. I asked one of the other kids why Henry couldn't swim with us and he said it was probably because he was a Jap."

Mom said, "He is not a Jap. He's Japanese."

I was confused. I knew that the soldiers who attacked Pearl Harbor had been our enemies. But the war was over. And how could a twelve-year-old Cub Scout be our enemy anyway?

Bob said, "When our troop leader came into the locker room, he counted nineteen heads and realized one guy was missing."

I was on the edge of my seat as I remembered that many Japanese families had been put into camps during the war. But I never heard much about it because it happened so far away from us. Was it to protect us from them or to protect them from us? I couldn't remember. While I was temporarily distracted by my thoughts, my brother kept talking because he was so wound up that there was no stopping him.

"When our troop leader heard the story, he was so mad that he stomped out of the locker room and back to the office. We heard him yell, 'Which guy in here is afraid of a little Japanese kid?'

"We dressed in a hurry and snuck closer so we could hear the argument. T-shirt man was telling our troop leader that Japanese people were not allowed to swim at the Y. I didn't know what was coming next because our leader was having a fit."

I was dead silent, and all Mom could say was, "Oh, my."

I didn't understand why that man would kick a little kid out of the pool. He had nothing to do with our enemies. Maybe the Y guy just hated him because he was Japanese. But Henry was also American, so I was pretty confused. Bob went on with his story.

"By that time we were all squashed near the office door so we wouldn't miss a thing. We thought Mr. Bradley was gonna hit that man. His hands were on his hips and his jaw was stickin' out and his face was real close to the Y guy's nose. Then, all of a sudden, he straightened up tall and his voice was so calm it was kinda scary. He said, 'If that boy can't swim . . . no one swims.'"

"Then what happened?" I asked.

"We climbed on the bus and left."

Poor Henry. I felt terrible, and I could tell that Mom felt bad, too. I wondered if she would get the YMCA T-shirt man fired the way she'd gotten Mr. and Mrs. Fields fired from the Ottumwa Home. It seemed like a good idea to me.

After Bob had finished his story, he was quiet for several minutes. He seemed far away and thoughtful. Finally, he said, "I'm glad we all had to leave."

"Why is that?" Mom asked.

"I would've felt guilty having fun in the water when Henry was stuck in the office."

I was so proud of my brother that I almost hugged him. But I didn't.

Blowing Down the Hill

As soon as the three-bedroom apartment we were waiting for became available, we packed up again and moved just half a block away.

Since the move was all downhill, we carried what we could lift and got Dad's truck-driving friend to help us again. Patty and I were delighted to have a room to ourselves. Our brother was just as happy to have a bedroom of his own, but Bob was so full of himself that I felt like smacking him.

The day of the big move started sunny and bright, but the sun soon disappeared behind dark clouds, makingeverything feel gloomy and weird. Dad took a worried look at the sky and said, "I don't know for sure, but I have a bad feeling that the weather is turning against us." I wondered if we might not get to move that day. But he added, "If we don't dilly-dally, we might get done before this storm hits."

So we decided not to dilly-dally. All six of us trekked up and down the hill countless times, our arms overflowing with whatever we could hold onto. Bob and I got tired of the small stuff and decided to cart something more impressive, such as kitchen chairs. On our first kitchen chair run, the blustery wind blew Bob's hair across his eyes, which made it hard for him to walk straight. With braids whipping my cheeks, I wasn't walking so straight either. We were contestants in a race against Mother Nature, and we really wanted to win.

As we hustled back up the hill for two more chairs, the weather turned cold. Halfway to our new apartment, the sky grew darker than daylight should ever be and the gusts turned into an icy squall. We fought desperately to keep the chairs from being torn from our hands as they defied gravity.

Puffing and panting, my brother and I hurled ourselves and our two wild chairs across the threshold of our new home. Scary scenes from the movie *Hurricane* were running through my mind.

With no fanfare or drama, Dad said, "We've got to stay put 'til this storm blows over." That's what Jon Hall said to Dorothy Lamour in the last scene as he strapped her to a palm tree so she wouldn't blow away.

It was the first bad storm we'd experienced since moving to Colorado. Dad, Bob, and I went upstairs to the room Patty and I would share. With no trees or buildings on the east side of Sunset Ridge, we had a spectacular view of the sky as far as we could see. What we saw in the distance rendered us speechless.

Along the horizon was a straight black edge with seven tornados hanging down from it. We were hypnotized. Some of the wispy tails grew shorter while others became longer. They were twister snakes playing a game. As we watched, the snakes disappeared into the clouds, the sun came out, and the storm ended as suddenly as it had begun.

That night we heard an announcement on the radio:

This morning, several tornadoes caused extensive damage to buildings on the Lowry Air Force Base thirty miles east of Denver. The same storm system caused even more destruction in rural areas of western Kansas. Many Colorado residents witnessed this event from afar.

"Yes, we saw that!" Bob said to the radio.

"You betcher booties we saw it," Dad added.

"If we were closer to those tornados, could we get blown away like Dorothy in *The Wizard of Oz?*"

"You betcher booties we could."

It was obvious my brother and I had been raised at the movies. But in the Peal family matinee that day, we had been blown down the hill into our new home instead of away to the Land of Oz.

PART 8: *Becoming Betty Peal*

Betty, before . . .

Becoming Betty

WHEN I ENTERED THE TENTH GRADE, I DIDN'T KNOW ANYONE because I was quiet and not very social. But kids knew who I was because of my outdated appearance. They referred to me as "that girl with long braids."

I often imagined myself twisting pin curls each night instead of making braids every morning. But the thought of changing my hair was scary. I'd had braids since I was eleven and cutting them off would be almost the same as lopping off my ears. I thought about it so much that I was torn, and it drove me crazy. Finally, I got sick of going back and forth and said, "To heck with it. I'm going to do it!" But first I had to get permission from my parents.

Dad said, "If you do this, you'll look like everyone else."

"Yeah, Dad, that's my goal."

"Well, why the Sam Hill would you want to do that?"

"I'm tired of being old-fashioned."

"I don't like the idea of you gettin' all modern 'cause who knows where that'll lead."

That was Dad's way of saying no, and it took a lot of debate to persuade him that I would still be the same girl. Finally, begrudgingly, he agreed.

Mom said, "If you're determined to do this, I'm going along to supervise the job."

We made an appointment for two days later to give Mom time to take before and after photos. In one picture, my long braids were showing. In the other, my loose hair cascaded down my back. I was Alice in Wonderland herself.

I couldn't quit grinning. Patty was puzzled. "Why are you so happy about this?"

"Cutting my hair feels like an adventure because I don't know what will happen."

When the big day arrived, Mom and I went to the shop where the deed would take place. The beautician held each long, plaited strand so lovingly that you would've thought she'd just opened the Bible.

"Oh, my . . . I've never cut hair this long," she sighed.

Her reaction made me nervous. Would she botch the job?

She asked, "Are you sure you want these beautiful things cut off?"

"Oh, yes, ma'am. I'm very sure."

"Why?"

"I'm going to be modern."

She sighed again. "Well . . . okay . . . how short?"

"Before you start cutting, there's something you need to know. I want to keep my braids after you remove them."

"Really? Why?"

That question made me unsure of my decision. I turned to Mom, who was sitting in the background just watching the show. She had no idea what we were talking about, but when our eyes met, she smiled. I smiled back and took a deep breath. "I'm not sure why," I replied. "I just don't want them tossed in the trash."

"Okay, dear. Show me where to cut."

That was scary. I hadn't thought much about how short it should be. I imagined how it would look by placing my fingers at three different levels. Finally, I made a wild guess, pointed, and said, "Cut right here."

She wrapped string below the "right here" place and tied a strong knot so my plaits wouldn't fall apart after the cutting started. When she hacked through the thick bundles and dropped two braids into my lap, my head felt so light it could have floated off my neck. What replaced the weight was excitement.

She said, "Okay, that's the first step."

I could feel the pulse beat in my neck, and I was so jumpy that I got the hiccups. The stylist gave me a drink of water and suggested I hold my breath. I couldn't take my eyes off my reflection, so she turned me away from the mirror.

The next hour was a life-altering experience. The beautician was busy snipping, shaping, and coaxing my hair into the right length for my face. I felt myself changing. Next came a fragrant shampoo and conditioner with head massage, towel drying, pin curling, electric drying, brushing, combing, and shaping. After a touch here and a pat there, my transformation was complete. The stylist whirled me around to face the mirror again and asked, "Well, whaddaya think?"

I just stared.

Mom asked, "Do you like it?"

I liked it so much that I was speechless. I shook my head "yes" and finally said, "Oh yeah, yeah, I really, really, really love it a whole lot. In fact, a whole, whole lot."

I knew we were supposed to pay and leave, but I couldn't stop staring at the girl in the mirror. It was hard to believe that was really me. Since there were mirrors everywhere, I studied all angles, soaking up the new me. After paying our bill, I left as an honest-to-God teenager instead of looking like a girl who had just gotten off a wagon train.

On the way home, Mom and I stopped at Englewood Dry Goods and outfitted me in a pleated skirt, sloppy joe sweater, penny loafers, and a new pair of white bobby socks. I was ready to be admired at school the next day. I couldn't wait. I was so dizzy with joy I could've fainted.

I said, "Mom, I'm so excited I can't think straight. I'm going to sleep sitting up tonight so I won't muss up my curls."

"You can't do that. You'll be worn out for school."

"But my hair has to stay nice."

"You'll have to learn how to set it."

"Oh, yeah, I forgot about that."

From then on, it would be up to me to maintain the image I had adopted. Before going to bed, Mom showed me how to twist a strand into a pin curl, a ritual I would perform every night. It took us an hour, and when I was done my head had turned into a helmet of bobby pins. Sleep did not come easily, for a girl must learn how to position her head on thirty-seven cookie-shaped coils.

Betty, after.

The next morning, I woke up weary but ready to meet the world. I took all thirty-seven bobby pins out of the "curly-cues," and the result of that many coils being released from captivity was nothing short of spectacular.

"Mom, look!"

"Good heavens. Get the brush." My mother brushed and brushed and brushed to calm the curls back down onto my head where they belonged. I still had to put on my new clothes, eat a bowl of cereal, and brush my teeth. I finally tamed my tresses and added a touch of color to my lips to heighten the effect of my self-improvement project. By the time I was fed, dressed, brushed, and combed, I was a different person. But I had almost primped myself into missing the bus. On the way to school, I thought, *Looking good sure takes a lot of time.* But I felt fantastic and couldn't wait for people at school to witness my miraculous transformation.

After the elaborate prepping, my grand entrance at school was a letdown. Instead of widespread admiration, I got flat expressions of non-recognition. Most of the students didn't know who I was or where I had come from. But, of course, they'd never known who I was in the first place. Only my four girlfriends recognized me, and they were impressed and full of compliments.

Since I was new to most of the student population, I used that to my advantage and decided to change my name along with my image. I asked my friends to call me Betty instead of Elizabeth or Lizzie, and I planned to ask my teachers to do the same.

It was my good luck that the Drama Club was having a picture taken that day for the 1946 yearbook called "The Pirate Log." Was I ready for that? You betcher booties I was. I sat upright, perky, and curly as if to say, "I'm Betty, the cutest girl in the front row." Even though the photo was black and white, it recorded the glow on my face for posterity.

Later that memorable day, a boy stopped me in the hall and said, "Hi there. I've never seen you before. Are you new?"

I smiled and said, "Yeah, I sure am."

Not That Girl Anymore

AFTER MY BRAIDS WERE CUT OFF, I FELT SO SPECIAL THAT I ACTED special. Confidence infused my being. I became one of the gang, and I joined so many clubs that my grades slipped.

Dad groaned and said, "I knew this would happen."

Mom was mad at me most of the time because I didn't come straight home, staying late for activities instead. My after-school involvement list was a mile long. I sang second soprano in the girls' trio, and we practiced every day for the state music festival competition in Longmont. The Drama Club was writing a short version of *Taming of the Shrew* with our advisor's help. She had chosen me to play the famous shrew, Katherine. There were posters to make for the Pep Club rally, and I was the best artist in the club. The orchestra was having a fundraiser to buy instruments for kids who were poorer than I had ever been. And I had to finish my part of the library report for my English group project on *The Ancient Mariner*, which I didn't understand at all. But none of that stuff was drudgery. In fact, I loved every single bit of it, but Mom resented having to share me with Englewood High School.

I was happy and proud that I was a good student and respected by so many kids and teachers. And I was beginning to resent all that my mother expected of me at home. Dad never said boo, letting her do all the talking when it involved teaching us kids how to behave and what our responsibilities were. But I wasn't a little kid anymore. I felt different, very different. It was hard to stay true to my mother and be true to myself at the same time.

My jobs at home were suffering. One neighbor said, "Mrs. Peal, Betty's ironing is no longer perfect." Another woman was frantic when she realized that not only were her husband's shirts un-ironed after a whole week of waiting, but they were still damp and rolled up in a towel. I was horrified when I realized I had completely forgotten about Mr. Fender's shirts. I unrolled them to discover what appeared to be a science lab experiment. It not only reeked, but was badly mildewed. Mom bailed me out and labored to get the black spots out of four white shirts. Mr. Fender smelled like bleach for a week, and Mom grew more impatient. "When is this gallivanting around going to stop?" she asked more than once. She and I argued a lot since I was no longer afraid to disagree with her.

"I'm not gallivanting anywhere. After play practice we all go to Myers' Drug Store and have cherry cokes while we're waiting for the bus."

"Well, there's an awful lot of late bus catching, if you ask me."

"It can't be helped."

"Oh, yes, it can be helped."

"But it's important that I be involved at school."

"It's more important to carry your own weight here at home."

"But other girls take part in lots of activities. Why can't I?"

"Because I need your help here."

"My friends' mothers don't care if they stay after class."

"I'm not the mother of your friends."

"It's not fair."

"It's not fair to us either."

"So what do you expect me to do?"

"Betty, don't raise your voice to me!"

"I can't help it. What do you want me to do?"

"Drop out of some activities!"

With tears squirting from my eyes, I stomped up the stairs to my room, pounding my head with my fist over and over and saying under my breath, *I hate her I hate her I hate her.* I wanted to say it out loud, but I didn't want Mom to hear. So I pushed my face deep into the pillow where I struggled to cry and breathe and say, *I hate her,* all at the same time.

I was a mess. My mother and I no longer agreed on my choices, and it was obvious that we were becoming adversaries. Things had changed. I stopped playing follow the leader, and standing up to her became my newest hobby. But big arguments always gave me a headache that lasted for days.

We argued about more than school. Mom had warned me not to shave my legs. "Once you start, you'll be buying razors for the rest of your life, so don't ever start."

I had replied, "Don't worry, Mom. I won't." But that was before my haircut. I had no idea I would ever want to shave hair off my body. But my mother's hairy legs looked so unrefined that I changed my mind. I shaved in private, not even telling Patty, and I made sure to hide it from my parents.

Eventually, they learned that I had been doing the awful thing behind their backs. Dad said, "Whenever I put a new blade in my razor, it gets dull in a few days." My mother moseyed over to check out my legs. When she slid the palm of her hand over my shins, the smooth, silky skin revealed my secret. At that moment, I became responsible for buying my own razor and blades.

Dad never groaned out loud again about the changes that had come over me, but he had been right. Short, curly hair; shaved legs; and lipstick meant that Lizzie was gone forever. I had become a free spirit called Betty.

A few weeks after my transformation, Mr. Brooks, our psychology teacher, said to the class, "How we look has a lot to do with how we act, and anyone who knows Betty Peal will understand. Many of you thought she was a new student, but she's been here since classes started in September. She just changed her appearance. Betty Peal was the young lady with long braids."

My classmates were stunned. They couldn't believe it and asked, "Betty, is this a joke? Were you really that girl who wore braids to her butt?"

"Yep," I replied. "But I'm not that girl anymore."

Needing Money

AFTER MY MAKEOVER, I WAS NO LONGER SHY, AND I TALKED TO STUdents I didn't even know.

"Well, hi there. Aren't you Ralph, the guy in my art class?"

I wanted to meet everyone, even the boys I used to admire from a safe distance. The more confident I got, the more other students noticed that I existed. It was a miraculous transformation. Even when I didn't know for sure what I was doing or why I was doing it, my self-confidence pushed me forward.

The kids in my activities were class leaders who showed up at every function. I was becoming one of them, but slowly. Life at school was a whole lot more interesting and fun than life at home, and it was pulling me away from my family. I felt guilty, but not a lot, especially when my social group began to include the girls in cliques who dressed well.

"Hello, Betty. Do you want to eat lunch with us today?"

"Sure. Where are you going to sit, on the front steps or on the grass by the gym?"

If I was going to eat lunch with the Sub Debs, I wanted to dress the way they did so it appeared that I belonged. Before attending EHS, I had never hung out with girls who looked good all the time. They walked with confidence, their pleated skirts swinging back and forth, so I did my best to copy them. It felt as good as it had in third grade when my peppy stride made my curls bounce. Even if I couldn't afford to dress the way they did, I longed to look more modern than my homemade wardrobe implied. So I started buying skirts and sweaters with my ironing money. But I also wanted the shoes that went with them, like penny loafers and saddle oxfords. The answer to my dilemma was simple: I needed more money.

To pay for my club dues and the clothes I wanted to own, I took on more babysitting jobs at twenty cents an hour, but only if they fit my schedule. I continued to iron starched and dampened shirts for the neighbors. But I never allowed things to mildew again because it was made very clear that the next time it happened, I would use my own money to replace the ruined shirts.

I knew I didn't earn enough to replace shirts. I wasn't even sure how I would pay for the uniforms I needed for two of the organizations I had joined. Mom wasn't very happy about it when she found out. "Why in the ever-loving world did you join two clubs that require uniforms?"

But, in the end, she came to my rescue by paying for the ill-fitting blue Pep Club uniform that we had to wear every Friday. She also paid for the unflattering salmon-colored Sub Deb outfit that I wore every Thursday.

"What in the world do Sub Debs do, anyway?" she asked.

I had to ponder that for a minute because I wasn't sure. "I think we're a service organization." Naturally, she asked what services we supplied, and I said, "Whatever needs doing at school."

In spite of the fact that my mother thought pep clubs and sub deb clubs were a waste of time, she bailed me out. I could tell that she resented it terribly. My parents both worked hard and we needed every penny just to live on. So if any more money was coming my way, I would have to earn it myself. Making money became my new goal.

Betty and girlfriends lunching at school.

Then, out of nowhere, my friends and I heard about a real job in the outside world. The Red Seal Potato Chip factory on South Broadway in Denver was hiring girls at forty cents an hour. Lordy, that was a fortune! Two of us decided to apply. Not only did we get the jobs, but they wanted us to recruit a few more girls. So my girlfriends and I became assembly line workers after classes each day.

To get to work on time, we had to leave the building immediately after dismissal, dash for the streetcar at the bottom of the hill, and ride to Denver to punch in by 3:30. We got off at 8:00 p.m., smelling of grease and tasting like salt. On most nights, I still had homework to finish and pin curls to set. If there was a football game, I missed it, and I stopped attending after-school activities. Earning my own money became more important than anything, and my mother was thrilled.

Working on an assembly line was a growing-up experience with no resemblance to babysitting or ironing shirts while listening to the radio. We couldn't gab on the job or laugh while working. That was hard because we all looked goofy in hairnets and wanted to make fun of each other. But acting casual on the job meant that production slowed, and we risked being fired unless we looked as though getting potato chips inside the bags was our sole purpose for living. Whenever the boss approached our station, one of us would whisper, "Look busy."

The women who worked there were coarse and rough-talking, so we were surprised that they were also quite friendly and helpful. Our boss, Bruce, turned out to be a nice man, and he checked on us frequently because he knew that getting comfortable with the tasks we performed took time. The hardest job of all was learning to run the machine that filled the bags. Operating a foot lever while holding an empty bag as it filled took as much coordination as I imagined learning to drive a car might take. For a week, I bagged potato chips in my sleep and woke up worn out.

Each night we went to work promising not to indulge in the salty goodies and crossed our hearts, hoping to die if we tasted even a crumb. Once we put one crispy chip in our mouths, we couldn't stop, and we were all getting grease-fueled pimples.

Despite the pimples, grease, and salty lips, I liked earning more money than I'd ever earned before. But the more I earned, the more my mother wanted me to help with expenses. I was disappointed when I learned that I had to pay my own dental bill. I had planned to buy an angora sweater that I put on layaway at the Mode-O-Day shop. When I protested, my mother said, "There are no funds for even one of your cavities." I was truly discouraged. The harder I worked to save money, the less I ended up with.

To cut costs, I once asked the dentist to drill a tooth without Novocain, but I never did that again. It was a huge filling and getting through the ordeal made me a little bit out of my mind. I resented sharing my hard-earned cash with the dentist, but I resented even more that I was expected to pay for our Fourth of July fireworks. That time I refused, and Mom said I was selfish for not thinking of the rest of the family. Bob and Patty were bitterly disappointed when they found out we would have no firecrackers that year. Seeing them so down-in-the-mouth filled me with such remorse that I felt as guilty as a shoplifter. When Patty said, "Betty, you're a poop head," I didn't know whether to be mad at her or sad for her.

My career as a potato chip bag filler ended soon after I heard an announcement over the PA system at school: *Next month will be tryouts for the junior play. If you've always wanted to act, here's your chance.*

With a heavy heart, I told my drama teacher that I would not be able to participate because I had a job. Miss Hudson was sincerely disappointed. Sadness settled over my spirit when I thought about not trying out for the play. I could hardly tolerate knowing that someone else would get a good part. The more I thought about it, the more I wanted to audition. So with no discussion except with myself, I quit the factory job.

My mother grew more and more irritated as I again immersed myself in activities away from home. She showed her disapproval by saying often, "Betty, I wish I could count on you" or "I could sure use your help at home."

I couldn't help it. Before enrolling at Englewood, I had never been in one school long enough to feel connected to it. That time I had bonded, and it was the right place to be. I was the happiest I'd been since moving away from Cedar Rapids.

But the more involved I was away from home, the more upset Mom grew. I think if I had dropped out of school and gotten a full-time job, she would have been delighted. Of course, I had no intention of changing the direction

I was heading. When I continued putting my own needs first, my mother and I became full-time adversaries.

Mom Gets Religion

MY MOTHER WAS A CREATIVE WOMAN WHO PLAYED TRUMPET, BANJO, and piano. But she was also volatile, and I dreaded her mood swings more than I dreaded pimples. When Mom was angry, she lost her senses and couldn't see or hear. At least that's what she said. In spite of her temper, my mother had firm values and disapproved of much that Dad allowed. Dad had firm values, too, but he wasn't a bit pretentious.

He said, "Girl, I'm preparin' these kids for the real world."

She said, "I'm protecting them from the real world."

It was one of the many things about which they argued.

Even though Mom was the bossy parent, we knew that Dad was the head of the family. Our mother would take a switch to our legs if she thought we deserved it, but Dad never raised a hand to us. He was quiet and usually stayed in the background, though sometimes he gave us bits of advice that he thought might come in handy some day. He'd say, "Don't ever try to beat up anyone bigger than you. Just get the hell outta there."

He also told slightly off-color jokes at the dinner table and allowed us to sip his wine and sneak a puff on his cigarette if it was sitting in the ashtray. All of that went against Mom's notion of what was right or wrong, and she squabbled with Dad all the time.

"Butch, don't tell those stupid dirty jokes at the dinner table!"

"Why not, for God's sake?"

"Because it's not couth!"

"What the hell does that mean?"

"It means uncivilized."

Dad just laughed and said, "They're gonna hear clean dirty jokes from me before some snot-nosed kid tells 'em real dirty jokes!"

"At least don't look the other way when they sip your wine and try out your cigarettes!"

"Why not, for God's sake?"

"Because it's not good for them!"

"They're gonna try it someday, and they may as well try it here at home."

Dad felt he was doing his duty as a father, so my mother was not going to change him no matter how long they argued. But if she couldn't change his influence on Bob and Patty, maybe she could place them in a sterile environment that would make them less vulnerable to his smoking, drinking, and cussing. She started looking into church schools and found one for Patty nearby. Bob was enrolled in a private school in Winfield, Kansas. Dad went along with it only because he knew what life would be like if he opposed Mom's wishes.

Our mother might not have taken that step if she hadn't heard Reverend Walter Meier on the Sunday morning *Lutheran Hour*. When his radio show was about to begin, Mom would say, "Be ready to shut your program off as soon as my sermon starts."

She was ecstatic when she discovered there was a Missouri Synod Lutheran congregation right under our noses in Englewood. Her devoutness affected all of us except Dad, who believed in God but not in going to church.

He loved saying, "You'll never catch me dead in church!" I caught the joke and it always made me laugh. But a place to worship was the most important thing on my mother's mind in those days. We were not allowed to vote on whether or not we wanted to become members. She simply enrolled herself and us three kids in the weekly catechism classes. When I saw the religion book we had to study each week, I protested.

"This means more homework for all of us."

"Your religious education is just as important as school," she replied.

So, after weeks of throwing ourselves into reading and memorizing for our Saturday morning classes, we graduated to being baptized and confirmed. It was like buying insurance for going to heaven when we died, but only if we kept the faith. I didn't know it at the time, but we had just signed up for a very strict doctrine that did not believe in having fun.

My brother hadn't been in Kansas very long when his letters showed how homesick he was. Mom was worried sick and said, "Butch, maybe this was a mistake. What should we do?"

"Hell's bells, Girl. You shoulda left well enough alone."

That's all my parents talked about for weeks . . . what to do about Bob. I was so mad at my brother that I wrote a letter to bawl him out.

Bob,

You big baby. Mom and Dad can't afford to send you away to school and here you are whining and they're thinking of laying out even more money to bring you back. GROW UP. If you're homesick, don't tell them about it. Keep it to yourself until you get over it. And don't tell Mom I wrote this letter or you'll be sorry.

    Betty

Our parents had already set things in motion to bring my brother home by the time his next letter arrived.

Dear Mom and Dad,

I really like it here. I've met some new friends and I want to stay.

    Bob

I privately patted myself on the back and decided to get some credit for my efforts. "Mom, the little baby changed his mind because of me. I bawled him out and told him to grow up and stop whining."

I was shocked when she said, "You did what? You had no right to stick your nose where it did not belong."

From then on, when I stuck my nose in someone's business, I kept it to myself.

🔻

Damsy Moves In

AFTER WE MOVED AWAY FROM IOWA, I HAD NOT MISSED MY GRAND-mother at all. I assumed she was relieved that our family didn't need her help anymore, so I was surprised when Mom said, "Having no one to rescue is making Damsy pretty blue. She misses us." It showed me a softer side of our grandmother that I had never seen before. Learning that she missed us made me curious. When Mom called her on the phone, I eavesdropped.

"Mama, sitting around the house all day is not helping. You need to get out and see your friends . . . What? They're all dead? They can't be. What about Hattie Burke? . . . Oh, really? That's too bad. I'm so sorry to hear that."

Dad sensed something was up and mouthed the word "no," but Mom waved him off. He got closer and shook his head "no" again, making sure she understood. Dad knew very well that Damsy was going to be invited for a visit, and he did not want that to happen. When the phone conversation ended, we discovered the plan was worse than he imagined.

"Butch, we've got to let her live with us for a while."

"Criminitly, Girl. You must be outta your mind."

"She's really down in the dumps."

"She's really nuts, that's what she is."

Mom didn't get mad at Dad for saying that because she knew he was right. But it didn't change her mind about inviting her mother to stay with us.

After hearing about our grandmother's state of mind, I had compassion for her, too. Not Dad. Even though Damsy had given us a place to live whenever my parents split up, he dreaded the thought of sharing the same house with her. Still, Mom wouldn't let up.

"Butch, with Bob away at school, Mama can use his bedroom."

"Criminitly," Dad muttered.

"We owe her, Butch."

"Girl, I'm caught between a rock and a hard spot. But, okay. We'll give it a try."

The plan to move Damsy to Sunset Ridge was set into motion. Mom seemed excited about the decision, so she must have missed her mother a little bit, too. I joined in her excitement and daydreamed about setting my grandmother's straggly gray hair in pin curls so she would look nicer than she usually looked. My grandmother was a bohemian gypsy type who didn't bake cookies or sew clothing. She rolled her own cigarettes and always acted grumpy and unfriendly. I couldn't change the way she acted, but I wanted her to look more like other grandmothers I knew, and I intended to help her out. Maybe I'd have better luck with her than I had with my friend Angie.

Damsy had only been with us at Sunset Ridge for twenty-four hours when we realized our mistake. We must have been suffering from amnesia. We had forgotten how unpleasant she could be. She didn't like anything and complained about everything.

Patty tried to be helpful and asked, "Would you like Wheaties or Puffed Wheat for breakfast?"

"Neither," she grumbled in the gravelly voice that was rougher than I remembered.

Patty said, "Okay," and put the boxes back in the cupboard.

Mom asked, "How about some bacon and eggs, Mama?"

"Coffee. Black coffee. That's all I want for breakfast. And hand me my cigarettes."

I didn't know why she was difficult and grouchy, but I hated being around her when she was like that. She was especially irritable the day I decided to put my hairdressing plan in motion. The rough edges of the bobby pins kept snagging her hair, so she finally shoved my hand away and yelled, "Stop! I can't take any more!" Then she tore out all the bobby pins and threw them on the floor. Trying to help her was a lot harder than helping Angie.

According to family stories, my mother's mother had never been easy to live with. When she was seventeen, she'd gone from plain old Susan to Allie Belle, which would be her stage name. Allie Belle was driven to achieve and had grand dreams for her future. She was headstrong and obstinate. When she told her mother, our great-granny, that she wanted to change her long hair into a stylish bob, Granny would not allow it. Ignoring her mother's dictate, Damsy asked her father. He said, "Sure, you can get your hair bobbed. I hear it's quite popular."

When Granny saw her daughter's short new haircut, she was so enraged that she went a little nutty and purposely drowned their new baby kittens.

That story horrified me. I couldn't believe that Granny, who had once called me Little Mousie, could have committed such a grizzly act. I worried that whatever Granny, Damsy, and Mom had, I would someday inherit. I was terrified about my future and prayed that I would learn I'd been adopted. Then Bob and Patty could worry in my place.

With all that craziness in the family, how could we expect Damsy to change just because a little time had passed? She spent most days slumped in a chair with elbows on her knees and her head hung low. I found out that she was suffering from depression just as our grandad did. Heaven help me. That meant depression was on both sides of our family. My future did not look bright.

My grandmother often misinterpreted a situation or imagined things that weren't true. She once boarded the bus that I caught to ride home from school, but I didn't see her. Not until we got off at Sunset Ridge did I realize she was there. As we walked home together she was cranky, and I had no idea why.

As soon as she saw Mom, she said, "Waneta, Betty ignored me on the bus today."

"Why would she do that?"

"She's ashamed of me."

I was shocked. Her accusation wasn't true, but it made me sad that I had hurt her feelings. I was relieved that my mother believed me when I explained what had happened. I tried to apologize to Damsy for not seeing her when she was in plain sight.

"I was in plain sight all right. You looked right at me and paid no attention."

I was terribly confused because she sincerely believed I had rejected her, so I went back and forth between pity and anger. She was so unpredictable. We never knew what might set her off. It made me wonder if she was sick in the head or afflicted with some strange disease. My grandmother was a pitiful mystery. I was so distressed that I wrote another letter to Bob. He was the only family member too far away to be affected by her chronic bad moods.

> *Dear Bob,*
>
> *Be glad you're not here. You-know-who is driving us crazy. Don't tell anyone I wrote this letter or you'll be sorry.*
>
> *Betty*

Two months after she moved in, an unknown offense made her so mad that she exploded in fury and started throwing things into her suitcase. My mother asked, "Mama, what's wrong now?"

Apparently, it was a big secret. She replied, "Well, if you don't know, I'm sure not going to tell you." Patty hid in our bedroom because our grandmother sometimes scared the wits out of her.

Damsy yelled, "Bassle, take me to the train station right now!"

Dad jumped out of his chair as though he'd won first prize.

She dragged her suitcase to the top of the steps and yelled again, "Take me now! I'm going back to Cedar Rapids!"

Dad hollered up the stairs, "Hold your horses, Allie. I'm hurrying as fast as I can."

"That's not fast enough."

With that, she gave her bulging suitcase a hard shove and sent it hurtling down the steps. It crashed into the wall below, leaving a gaping crack. I couldn't believe what was happening, but I should not have been surprised.

Dad didn't say a word. He picked up the suitcase like nothing had happened and put it into the car. He was so glad to see Damsy go that he probably ran every stop sign on the way so he could get her to the station on time.

I didn't have to write Bob to tell him that "you-know-who" had gone back to Iowa because he found out for himself. After a year in private school, my brother had to come home because the expense was more than my parents could handle.

Mom said that one year away was better than nothing. Their son would start his young manhood on a straight and narrow path. What she didn't know was that Bob had learned more lessons from his classmates than from his teachers. And he was ready to pass them on. After returning to Sunset Ridge, he got together with his friends to drink beer, share off-color stories, and cuss like sailors.

I wasn't about to stick my nose in someone else's business again by tattling. I'd learned that lesson well. But I really wanted to say, "Mom, if Bob had learned about smoking, drinking, and cussing here at home with Dad, it would have been a lot cheaper."

The Actress

MISS HUDSON'S ENGLISH CLASS WAS FILLED WITH DRAMA CLUB students, and we were different from the rest of the kids in school. The girls weren't cheerleader material, and the boys were not the type who dated cheerleaders. But they were our kind of boys: fun, funny, smart, and talented. Because we liked them, they were handsome in our eyes.

I was the jester of the group. Every time I approached Miss Hudson's desk, they all watched to see what subtle new thing I might do to amuse them, such as imitating Charlie Chaplin's walk for a few steps. I loved the attention. I had always enjoyed making someone laugh, especially my mother when she was trying to stay mad at me. I never planned ahead of time to be funny. I just came alive in front of an audience, even when it was only Mom.

Miss Hudson was aware of my tendency to attract attention, and it bothered her a lot. She had planned for me to play the starring role in *Smilin'*

Through. The show required the two main actors to be singers. I sang and acted, but my reputation as a clown was growing. She worried that my fellow students would never take me seriously in a dramatic part.

Punctuating her comments with eloquent gestures, my favorite teacher told me how to prepare for the auditions. "Betty, in the future when you come to my desk, ignore those in class looking for a small performance. They expect you to make them laugh. But I want you to prove that you are more than just a funny girl and start preparing for a serious role." She stopped, straightened her shoulders, and said, "Now . . . if you can't stop being an entertainer for one semester, I will cast Marilyn Little as Moonyeen."

I would have promised Miss Hudson the stars, the sun, and the whole sky because I respected her. When I saw that Eddie Williams and Billy Ehly, two of my favorite boys, had signed up for tryouts, I started taking the assignment seriously and cleaned up my silly act.

Some of the kids in class noticed the change in my demeanor and said, "You're no fun anymore. Are you sick?"

"Nope. I'm getting into character for the auditions."

"Well, Eddie and Billy are going for important parts, too, and they're the same old guys."

It was too hard to explain, so I didn't even try. But my friends missed the laughing Betty so much that they thought the whole idea of changing my behavior was a pile of rubbish. Did I care? No sirree. Marilyn Little was my friend, but I did not want her to have the lead in *Smilin' Through*.

I was thrilled when I was awarded the part I'd worked so hard to win. Marilyn made the second cast, which was important because they acted for the student body during a special performance. She would also take my place if I broke a leg or came down with the measles.

My family decided to see the performance because Mom and Dad had loved the old movie version, which featured Jeannette McDonald and Gene Raymond. I was pleased they were coming. I hoped it meant that Mom was more comfortable with my after-school activities. But as much as I wanted them to see me shine, I was also self-conscious about acting in front of all four of them. I dreaded the possibility that Bob and Patty would say, "That's not what she's really like . . . she's just showing off."

In Cedar Rapids, we three kids had acted for each other in our one-man shows on the front porch at 32nd Street. But we weren't that close anymore since we attended different schools and had become involved in our own interests. Growing up was taking its toll on our relationship.

The night that Bob, Patty, Mom, and Dad attended, I got through the evening only by imagining they weren't there. Everything went well. We all remembered our lines, and the audience was responsive, especially during the scene when Billy Ehly, who played the priest, performed the wedding ceremony for Eddie and me. Right after I said, "I do," I was shot at the altar by a rejected suitor.

We waited for the audience to stop gasping before proceeding. Then Eddie slipped the ring on my finger and kissed me. Before dying in his arms, I coughed a few times and sang a whole verse of the song "Smilin' Through." When the curtain came down, people were crying and clapping at the same time.

We had the audience on the edge of their seats for the rest of the play and bowed our way through four curtain calls.

I was a real actress. It was breathtaking.

On the drive home, no one said anything. No "you were good," "you sang well," "you died well," or anything. I didn't expect them to gush, but I didn't expect them to say nothing. Finally, Patty whispered, "Were you nervous?"

I bent close to her ear and said, "Yeah, I was nervous because you guys were there."

After we reached home, Mom took me aside and told me that after my dramatic dying monologue, Dad nudged her and whispered, "That's my kid up there."

I couldn't believe it. We weren't used to giving or receiving compliments. It was too personal.

Dad's remark meant more to me than four standing ovations.

Dancing Girl

TO DANCE OR NOT TO DANCE? THAT WAS THE QUESTION.

When I was really young, long before Mom got serious about religion, she and Dad took me along when they danced the polka at Sokol Hall in Cedar Rapids. The polka was the wildest thing I had ever witnessed, with people flying all over the place without bumping into each other or falling down. I said, "Mama, I wanna do that."

Dad said, "Nope, you'd get trampled flat, so you sit here with your root beer and watch."

When I got tired of watching, I stretched out on the chairs that lined the walls and fell asleep. I could hear the German band playing as I dreamed of Dad and Mom holding me in their arms as though all three of us were dancing.

Years later, Mom and Damsy took us kids along whenever they attended revival meetings. The churches behind those meetings believed that dancing was not only wrong but a pagan practice enjoyed by heathens. I had no idea what heathens were, so Mom explained that they were primitive jungle people who wore rings in their noses and didn't know about God. They gyrated around a campfire, worshipping the moon, rain, trees, and animals of all kinds.

I longed to be a heathen because I loved music and relished the movement I felt in my bones when complex rhythms punctured the air. Most of the time I heard animated rhythms on the radio, but others came straight from Mom's piano playing where the Free Methodists worshipped. Even when I was a little kid, I'd felt the beat and couldn't keep my feet from gently tapping against the pew in front of me.

Damsy always said, "Keep your feet still."

Inside my shoes, I'd wiggled my toes to the music where no one could feel it but me. I was not a devil worshiper; I just wanted like the devil to bounce around to music.

In high school, I attended dances with the other students, but instead of doing the boogie, I talked to boys who didn't mind being wallflowers.

"Tom, why aren't you out there on the floor?" I asked a fellow classmate.

"I don't know how to dance. Why aren't you out there on the floor?" he asked.

"My religion doesn't allow it."

"Gosh, don't you hate that?"

"Naw, I don't mind."

It was a lie. I envied the kids who had permission to bump and grind and bounce and wiggle, and I wondered what church they went to.

312 *The* HOME *for the* FRIENDLESS ❖ *Betty Auchard*

In our house of God, there were many expectations and even more restrictions. Membership was dependent on endless study sessions and weekly catechism instruction. Eventually, we would be examined before the entire congregation and welcomed as members. We were not allowed to take communion in any other place of worship nor could any outsider take communion in ours. No one could be married at our altar unless both parties were members of our congregation. When couples were married, they were not allowed to kiss at the end of the ceremony. And we were never allowed to tap our feet during the service because it implied that we were dancing.

In our catechism class, the reverend reminded us of our church's position on the subject: "Dancing is a vertical substitution for a horizontal activity." We all knew what that meant.

But those rules confused me. If sex was not acceptable to God, did it mean that married people had to sin a few times to get a baby? And if you were going to do sinful things after you got married, why couldn't you do them before? Wouldn't it be better to just go dancing and get those urges out of your system?

Dancing might not have been a problem if I'd left my hair in long braids and stayed uninterested in the world around me. But I hadn't. When I cut my hair, I felt different, looked different, and acted different. I joined the crowd so I could do most of the things they were doing because it sure looked like fun.

Since our minister said that desiring to sin was the same as sinning, I was already a sinner. No one knew it but God and me, and I couldn't force myself to feel guilty enough to stop thinking about it. I invented dance moves in my mind whenever I heard music. It felt natural. My drama teacher had said, "Elizabeth, you have a gift for reading a crowd and responding to the moment." If grades had been based on dreaming stuff up, I would've been on the honor roll every semester.

It might have been easier if I had stayed away from activities that involved movement and music, but I liked being part of everything. School was my home away from home. So I mingled with the students at every sock hop, hustling around the edges like a person in charge, with no time to move my feet to the beat of whatever tune was playing. It was not easy. While I was obeying the rules, my muscles did the jitterbug without my permission.

Deep in my heart, I was a dancing girl. Being a church girl, too, made my life very complicated.

🔆

Sweet Sixteen

Birthdays were modest celebrations in my family, but my sixteenth was an exception. My father had been building bikes for all of us so we could take a family bike hike on my special day. He had grown fond of using the phrase "sweet sixteen and never been kissed" because he planned to be the first male to do so. That would be strange for two reasons: (1) he had never kissed me before and (2) another guy had already done the deed. I couldn't decide whether to pretend or tell the ugly truth.

After I blew out my candles and made a wish, I started opening presents real fast, hoping Dad would forget about his favorite saying, but it didn't work.

"Betty, now that you're sixteen, I'm gonna kiss you before any other fellow."

I tried to be funny. "Ha ha ha, Dad. I'm sorry, but Frankie Cordona beat you to it."

My father barely masked his disappointment, and the expression on his face made my heart ache. I was sure I'd hurt him terribly by not waiting until I was sixteen before letting a boy kiss me.

I prayed that his disappointment wouldn't spoil our outing since he'd been looking forward to christening the bikes. Patty had gotten a brand new pink bike for her eleventh birthday, so hers was the only one that was shiny. We packed a picnic and divided it among our baskets. Ginger must have sensed that she would be included because her tail whipped all over the place.

We lined up in our driveway with the menfolk in the lead, my sister and me in the middle, and Mom bringing up the rear. Dad yelled over his shoulder, "Okay, we're headin' northwest. Don't anyone fall behind!"

Our destination was the narrow entrance to the Platte River Canyon, which was near the Arapahoe County Water Plant. It was a beautiful day, as I pictured it would be, with all five of us peddling alongside each other and sometimes riding single file. Occasionally, we hit a smooth patch where the road had been covered with tar, but most of the trip was on gravel. Gravel wasn't so bad until our legs got tired. Then the road became more of a challenge. So we talked and laughed and admired the rolling foothills while trying to ignore how much work it was to make progress.

Just as I expected, Patty was the first to break down. "My legs feel like wood," she whined. Mom must have been too drained to talk because she said nothing. But I heard her panting real hard.

A lifetime later, we finally arrived at the county park, worn out and weary. We were so pooped that we lollygagged too long eating our sandwiches, which meant it would grow dark during the ride back. Dad snapped his fingers and said, "Dang, I forgot about lights." A little bit of fear crept into me as I wondered how safe we would be riding that far in the dark.

We had packed up to leave when Ginger dashed down the steep slope to get a drink of water from the fast-moving channel. I watched in horror as she tumbled in and was swept away.

"Ginger fell in!" Bob and I yelled at the same time.

Dad slammed his bike to the ground and ran downstream to get ahead of her, then sidestepped through tall weeds to grab her collar as she floated by. He barely managed to pull our dog to safety and get back up the slope. A soggy Ginger shook water all over us, but we were so relieved that we didn't care.

The return trip seemed three times longer than it should have. My sister couldn't stop repeating, "I'm tired."

Mom said, "It's easier to move than complain, so keep peddling."

Bob said, "Thank goodness the moon is bright." I agreed, but I was too exhausted to say so. Dad just kept peddling without comment. I could hear our dog and my mother huffing and puffing. Except for occasionally calling out to each other to make sure we were all there, we rode in silence.

Finally, a familiar downhill road came into sight. It led to Monahan's Tavern, where we planned to stop. By then Patty was so weak and uncoordinated that she lost control on the slope. I watched helplessly as she zigzagged into a crash, arms and legs spread like a large X. Her knees were raw and red where skin used to be. Poor Patty was so worn out that she couldn't stop crying. Her new pink bike took a beating, too.

We walked our bicycles to the tavern entrance and stumbled in to find a place to plop. While Mom cleaned and bandaged Patty's wounds, Ginger lapped up a bowl of water and collapsed like a wet mop near the bar. The rest of us claimed a table, ordered something cold to drink, and began pulling ourselves together.

The main attraction at Monahan's that night was the Peal family show and tell. We showed the audience our injuries, our sunburns, and our dog's swollen pads. And our father told the story of our adventure, embellishing the tale so richly that I hardly remembered the truth.

Then he said, "I have an announcement to make. Stand up, Betty. Today, my daughter turned sixteen." Everybody cheered and clapped and drank a toast to me.

A patron yelled out, "Butch, is she sweet sixteen and never been kissed?"

"Nope, someone beat me to it. But I'm gonna give her a kiss anyway while you folks sing 'Happy Birthday' to my oldest kid."

As instructed, those slightly inebriated folks sang the familiar song, in three different keys. It was so awful it was funny.

The day wasn't at all what I'd expected it to be. How many girls spend their sixteenth birthday on a family bike hike that ends in a tavern? In a weird way, it was nice. And since my father wasn't mad about the kissing thing, I didn't feel so bad.

It was very late by the time we limped into our apartment at Sunset Ridge. Right before stumbling through the front door, Dad looked at his odometer, and said, "Sonofagun. We rode twenty-six miles today and mostly on gravel roads!"

Mom said, "Butch, please don't remind us."

Unsuitable Suitors

I HAD A LOT OF GUY FRIENDS IN HIGH SCHOOL, BUT NONE WHO ENDED up as boyfriends. Three came close to being more than buddies, but something got in the way each time. Twice it was Dad's upbringing, his fear and bigotry. One young man had a last name that included "stein" and another was the wrong color. The third eliminated himself because he flunked an important test.

Abe

Abraham Steinberg's locker was next to mine. The inside of his door was lined with award ribbons. One day I asked, "Where did you get those?"

"From tennis tournaments," he replied. "Been playing since I was five."

Abe didn't boast; he just answered my questions, and I was at ease with his friendliness. What made my heart pound were his scruffy black hair and suntanned hide. He was outdoorsy and cute. He was keen on me, too. I could tell. He paid attention by joking around a lot, which made my funny side come alive. I made him laugh until he almost cried. Soon he started doing something new to get my attention. With no warning, he'd toss a ball in my direction and say, "Catch!" I had a feeling he was testing my reflexes to see if my coordination matched his. I was thrilled. His way of flirting was different and fun, and having a locker next to his meant staying alert.

He said, "You're well-coordinated, Betty."

Aha — I was right. "I play softball whenever I can," I replied.

"I'll bet you'd like tennis."

"I don't know that game."

"I'll teach you."

"I don't have a racket."

"I have extras," he said. "And we have a court in our backyard."

I was heady with excitement and eager to spend more time with Abe.

One Saturday he picked me up in his car to practice the game at his home. I'd never known anyone who was so privileged but down-to-earth. I introduced my spunky new friend to Dad in the backyard and, before we left for my private lesson, they had a nice chat. I was sure Dad would be impressed with Abe because he was genuinely good natured and easy to talk to.

But after I returned home, the first thing out of Dad's mouth was, "About that fellow today . . . he's a nice kid, but kinda dark-skinned, doncha think?" I explained that he was deeply tanned because he spent a lot of time outside in the sun. Dad said, "Deeply tanned, my foot. That kid's a Jew."

Even though I was getting better at standing up to my mother, I was never comfortable opposing Dad. My almost-boyfriend must have sensed Dad's prejudice because he didn't toss the tennis ball to me anymore and his flirting dropped several notches until it turned into plain old friendliness. I was so depressed that I dragged myself to school each day, hoping "that fellow" would get a crush on me again. But it didn't happen. Thanks to my father, Abe Steinberg and I were destined to be nothing more than locker pals.

Kenny

The only Negro in our entire student body was practically a celebrity because he stood out from all the rest of the guys. He was the blackest person I'd ever met. As an infant he'd been adopted by white parents who were the whitest folks I'd ever seen. When the family attended school functions, they were an unusual sight.

Kenny was friendly and fun and everyone loved him. He had a lot of girl friends as buddies, but no girlfriends for dating. He was also an honor student, outstanding football player, and a real joker. He made people laugh more easily than I did. And if that wasn't enough, he was the owner of an old pickup that actually ran. If he had asked me to go out with him, I would've been thrilled.

He saw me waiting for the bus once and yelled out of his jalopy window, "Hey, Betty, wanna ride home?"

What a buzz that was! But I didn't want to look eager.

"I live pretty far from here."

"How far?"

"Clear out by Fort Logan in Sunset Ridge."

"No problem. Hop in."

I had held back just the right amount and was honored to hook a ride with the famous Kenny because I had a crush on him.

The number of nifty young men in my class was a marvel to behold, and the fact that a few were interested in me was just too hard to believe. My life was really changing, and my heart was filled with yearning. I couldn't stop thinking about boys, even though I rarely dated any of them.

As we got closer to my house, my mood shifted. I was thinking that I should ask my new friend to slow down, let me jump out, and then keep on driving. I didn't want Mom to notice that his skin was so dark. But she noticed. As soon as I entered the kitchen, she asked, "Who was that boy?"

Before Mom's imagination kicked in, I tried to reveal Kenny's finest qualities. When she listened and said, "Okay," I was relieved.

But that was not the end of it. Mom told Dad I'd accepted a ride with a Negro, so Dad, acting nonchalant, asked, "Who's this kid that gave ya a lift?"

Dad had been born and raised in the South, and I guess prejudice sticks to your hide like a scar. His whole family was the same. I jabbered way too fast about "this kid's" fine qualities, and my brain and tongue got scrambled. Dad listened and then got quiet as though thinking it over. Finally, he said, "Well . . . okay. You can hitch a ride with him now and then, but don't be coming home with a little black package under your belt."

I couldn't believe what I had heard. I knew what Dad was hinting at, and I was humiliated and angry. But I was too embarrassed to thrash it out with him.

Thank goodness, Kenny didn't know about any of that. He still joked around at school, and we had a lot of fun seeing which of us could make the other laugh first. I tried really hard to forget about my crush on him. I wouldn't accept a ride again because I was scared to death that Dad might humiliate him as he must have done with Abe. If that happened, I might as well become a dropout because I could never look a dark-skinned kid in the eyes again.

I was not doing very well in the boyfriend department.

Helmut

Since my church did not approve of dancing, my time at social activities was spent flirting with fellows who didn't know how to dance. There were plenty of them, so I had lots of choices. One was a German kid who played classical piano better than anyone I knew. Helmut Becker was tall and slightly stooped from leaning close to his sheet music. His muddy blonde hair was longer in front than in back. When he attacked the keys, he jerked his head wildly to flip hair off his face. The effect was breathtaking.

But he was not spirited and rarely talked to anyone because he was too self-conscious about his accent. How could that be? I was in awe of his accent and burning to meet him up close. I had a serious crush on his piano playing.

I stopped him in the hall and said, "Hi. My name is Betty. And your name?"

"My name? Uh . . . Helmut."

That was it. There was nothing more to talk about.

But his piano playing, mysterious personality, and wild hair tossing continued to draw me closer. When I heard him practicing Rachmaninoff's "Concerto in D Minor" and watched him fling his hair about, I swooned without falling down. It was what I'd experienced whenever Don, my first love, played the violin. It was also how some of my girlfriends felt about the skinny singer named Frank Sinatra, but when they swooned, they hit the floor. I just swayed in place.

Without a doubt, classical music made me emotional, so any boy rendering it well could become the object of my affection. When Helmut played sonatas, I grew dizzy with desire as I watched his long, slim fingers create musical magic. During orchestra rehearsal, I made an effort to get his attention from the violin section. But he was shy. If he had ever looked around to see whose eyes were burning holes in the back of his head, he would have seen me. His eyes bounced only between the orchestra director and the sheet music.

Finally, the German boy found out that I liked him, so he gradually inched closer to the space I occupied. But he didn't have the nerve to say hello. Then, during a break between classes, we accidentally came face to face. He couldn't avoid me any longer. In broken English, he asked, "Beddy, vould you go to movie vit me?"

Too quickly, I said yes, almost stepping on his words before he'd finished asking.

Even though he was not dark-skinned, I was sure his accent would set off another of Dad's prejudice attacks. So Dad must never meet him. That would be easy because Helmut had no driver's license.

I met my date in Englewood at the bus stop. From there we transferred to a streetcar to reach a theater in nearby Denver. Conversation did not flow easily, but I tried.

"So, have you ever ridden the streetcar into Denver before?"

"No. I haf not."

I didn't know what to do with a person who didn't elaborate on a subject. Conversation was my strong point, but not his. He was a pianist; he didn't need to talk. When he played the piano, he set my heart on fire and it melted.

I stopped daydreaming about how talented he was so we could get popcorn and sodas. Then we settled in to watch John Garfield and Priscilla Lane in *Dust Be My Destiny*. It was an old black-and-white film that I hadn't seen before, a drama that I hoped would end happily. It was riveting. My heart and soul were glued to the screen.

After an hour, my date glanced at his watch and whispered, "Ve must leaf now."

"What? Leave? Why? We're getting to the good part."

"I must be home by tan o'clock."

Not in my lifetime had I left before the end of a show. I couldn't imagine such a thing. It was crazy. But that's what we did. We caught the streetcar to Englewood, and neither of us spoke a word until we parted.

I said, "Thanks for the evening."

"You are velcome."

"Good night."

"Goot night."

And that was that. I caught my bus to Fort Logan and assumed that he walked a few blocks to his house. I didn't care if he beat his curfew or not.

Leaving before the movie's end had a terrible effect on me. Since I couldn't shake off the disappointment, my German boy began to look different. Watching him flip hair off his face looked like a tic, and his concertos lost their luster. Word never got around that we were almost an item, which meant that my heart was still open and available.

Sixty years later on the classic film channel, I finally saw the ending of *Dust Be My Destiny*. Naturally, I thought about the talented German lad and wondered where he was and if he was still making beautiful music. Does he ever think of me? I hope so. I want to be remembered by all the people for whom I felt such passion. And I'd had as much passion for Abe, Kenny, and Helmut as any seventeen-year-old girl could feel.

But wherever Helmut is, he owes me a movie . . . and maybe dinner afterward.

Auntie Marge to the Rescue

I BLOSSOMED DURING THE ELEVENTH GRADE AT ENGLEWOOD HIGH. Living in the same neighborhood and settling down in one place allowed my roots to grow. I wasn't just passing through. My world was larger, and Auntie Marge had played a big part in that growth.

My aunt provided opportunities that exposed me to culture, which I would never have learned about if not for her. She was a little snooty and said, "Season tickets to the Denver Symphony will expose you to a cultured crowd." She also kept informed about my social life, not wanting me to be left out of special events because I didn't have the right clothes. When she learned that a boy had asked me to the junior prom, she said, "Waneta, Betty will need a ball gown. I'm sending a check right away." A ball gown was the same thing as a prom dress to Auntie Marge, and she loved playing fairy godmother.

While my head was in the clouds enjoying a social life, other students were submitting applications for college. I didn't realize you had to apply a whole year ahead of time. I thought kids chose a college the way I chose a movie, paid the admission price, and went.

But I would not be attending any institution of higher learning after graduation. Dad always said, "We have no money to send a girl to school so's she can find herself a husband."

I didn't want to go anyway. Ever since I was five, I had yearned to be an artist, so all I had to do after graduation was keep honing my skills in drawing, painting, singing, and acting. And there were plenty of opportunities to do that. Auditions for a community play were announced in the *Denver Post*, and they would take place at the university the next Saturday at 7:00 p.m. The first steps into my future meant taking a streetcar to the campus.

Mom said, "I hate seeing you go there alone at night. How will you find the right building after dark?"

I convinced her I would be fine by myself, although I wasn't sure I would be. I wanted the thrill of something new, to see what it felt like being on my own. Riding the streetcar toward uncharted territory gave me goose bumps, and it was thrilling to audition with adults. I didn't get the part, but I was not discouraged. I was doing it to become a better actor.

I also had music in my heart. I played violin in the orchestra and sang second soprano in the choir and the girls' trio. I even earned twenty-five dollars for singing at a wedding.

But Miss Hudson, my drama teacher, had a completely different idea of my future. "Betty, I think you're a natural raconteur." My feelings were a little hurt. I thought she'd said I was a natural racketeer. When she explained that I was a storyteller, I felt a whole lot better.

The only thing I dreaded about life after graduation was that I'd no longer be at Englewood High School. It was more than a place. It personified my passage into a new life, with the teachers as travel agents and my friends as fellow passengers. Mom complained endlessly about the amount of time I devoted to that tour.

"You're in that building so much you may as well take your bed and live there." I would have loved that, but I didn't have a bed of my own.

At seventeen, I had finally discovered my potential, and I liked it. I longed to do something special with my life, but had no idea how to approach it. The thought of being on my own excited and terrified me. No matter how much I fantasized about my prospects as an actor, musician, or storyteller, Dad made things perfectly clear. "After high school is over, you need to start helpin' out by findin' a job. Maybe they would rehire you at the potato chip factory." Of course, there was no future in potato chips, and the job would mean only that another paycheck was coming into our house.

My principal, Mr. Gullette, called me to his office and asked, "Betty, what's this rumor I'm hearing about you not going to college?"

"Mr. Gullette, I've never planned to attend because my parents can't afford it."

"Really?"

"Yes, really. After graduation, I'll find a job so I can help out at home."

He leaned on his elbows, chin resting in both hands, and said, "Hmm. This is not good." Then he swiveled his chair, picked up the phone, and said, "I've got an idea."

Without looking up the number, he dialed. "Hello, Grace? This is Eugene in Englewood. Yes, we're all fine. I have a situation here that needs your advice."

I sat with hands in my lap while Mr. Gullette talked with the dean of women fifty miles away at the Colorado State College of Education in Greeley. He told her about my potential and my poverty, and, before I could blink, he had arranged a tuition waiver that was mine as long as I kept a 3.0 grade average. I always had good grades, but I had never signed up for anything very hard. My first thought was *Oh, my gosh . . . what am I getting into? Maybe I'm not smart enough for this.*

Things happened so fast that I was in a state of confusion. I thanked Mr. Gullette so many times that he finally said, "Go! Go home and explain this to your parents." I couldn't wait to tell them, but it sounded too simple. Surely there was more to it than a tuition waiver.

Mom listened, wide eyed, to every word of my report, then picked up the phone and called Auntie Marge. Pretty soon Uncle Al was on the other end and all three of them talked for a long time. When she hung up, Mom was looking kind of glum. She said, "Betty, you still have to pay for room and board. If we can't come up with the money, this may not happen after all." I didn't dare think positive, so I just waited for the phone to ring. It seemed forever, but my aunt finally called back.

She said, "Waneta, we have a plan. During Betty's first year of college we'll pay her room and board, but only if we can claim her as a dependent."

My parents understood and agreed. Since I did not understand, I waited it out to see what was coming next. After they finished talking, I learned that I must dig up a summer job after graduation and save all the money I could for the extras I would need. And I was encouraged to find a part-time job as a freshman because no cash would be coming from anyone else. It was an awful lot of planning for something that wouldn't happen for such a long time. I usually made decisions at the last minute. I never even knew what I'd wear to school until I'd put it on.

Mom and Dad were swept away with the excitement of the moment because neither of them had been allowed to finish ninth grade. Their parents had been even poorer than we were. They made the kids drop out of school and get jobs to help support the family.

Very early in the new adventure, I had to declare an area of study, which would not be an easy decision. I was interested in so many things that I couldn't make up my mind. Would it be art, music, or drama? Thank God I had several months to decide.

A friend in my art class asked, "Betty, is it true that you're enrolling at Greeley after graduation?"

"You heard right."

"That's where I'm enrolling, too."

"No kidding?"

"Yeah, really."

"That's nifty."

"Shall we be roommates?"

"Sure, why not?"

My friend said, "I'll pick out some twin bedspreads and you can pay me back later."

"Shouldn't I shop with you?" I asked.

"No need. I'll find something that we'll both like."

I was a little disappointed, but thought, *Oh, heck. I'll be fine with whatever she buys.*

Then she asked, "What will your major be?"

"I think I'll study art."

"But I'm studying art."

"Can't we both study art?"

"Not a good idea. Art materials take up a lot of space and the rooms are small. And we'd be in competition with each other all the time."

That made sense, so I changed my field of concentration to theater. However, when Auntie Marge heard that I planned to study acting, she said, "I want you to focus on music. It's more respectable. Women in theater have to sleep with directors."

Since Auntie had paid for my violin, my lessons, my concert tickets, and my prom dress, I didn't argue. I declared music as my major and theater as my minor. But I was feeling a bit dejected and had a conversation with myself. *Now, look. It's not a bad thing to allow other people to help plan my future. I am so lucky to have this opportunity that I'll major in rubber tires if I have to.*

After the smoke cleared, I figured I could switch things around and take the classes I wanted in the first place. The only two people who would ever learn the truth were my advisor and me. So if I kept my chin up and my mouth shut, anything that started out wrong would turn out right. I'd learned that from experience.

Betty Peal for Head Girl

AFTER LEARNING THAT I WOULD SOON ATTEND COLLEGE, SELF-CONfidence flowed through my veins and filled my fantasies with all kinds of grand ideas. I could accomplish whatever I set my mind to — or at least try. That was my smug frame of mind when the upcoming school election was announced over the PA system:

Nominations are being accepted for the following seats on next year's Student Council: Secretary, Treasurer, Historian, and — most important of all — Head Girl and Head Boy.

Those last two positions were filled by a senior boy and girl who shared the job of student body president. They were coveted titles that were earned through lively campaigns. Becoming Head Boy or Head Girl was, in some circles, more highly regarded than being voted homecoming queen or elected captain of the football team.

Many esteemed members of my junior class were planning to compete for the positions. I had never considered taking part in something of that magnitude, but for a few minutes I pretended I was that kind of person. It felt so good that I asked myself, *Why not?* I wanted to experience life inside the action instead of outside, watching it happen.

My thoughts blossomed into a feeling of self-confidence that rushed through my mind and body. It reminded me of my old comic book heroes when they magically changed costumes and transformed into their other, more powerful, selves. My favorite was Wonder Woman, and a little playful imagination made it easy for me to zip down the stairs to the school office as my heroine would have done. I approached the desk with great poise and a big, fat smile and announced, "I am taking part in the upcoming election."

"Who are you nominating?" the receptionist asked.

"Myself."

"You're supposed to be nominated by somebody."

"But I am somebody and I want to nominate myself."

"Well . . . this is highly irregular."

I stood tall and said, "There was no announcement about having to be nominated by somebody."

"It's not written down. It's assumed that people know they have to be nominated by someone else."

It was time to use my golden lasso and tie her up with the truth. "Please put my name down. If I take time to find someone to nominate me, I'll change my mind."

She sighed and then gave in. "Oh . . . all right."

As I left the office, my smile was so big I was sure it would blind the first person who saw me. Nominating myself for such a high office was the most daring thing I'd ever done.

Later that day, I overheard one of the cheerleaders say to her friends, "You've got to be kidding. You mean she nominated herself for the election?"

I knew who they were talking about, and it was just the prod I needed to launch my campaign. I started making posters, each sign including a bold illustration in living color. It was a sneaky move to show off my artistic side. I added images of appropriate vegetables and kept the messages simple:

VOTE for BETTY [a drawing of potato peels]
BETTY CAN'T BE [a drawing of a beet]
IF YOU [a carrot] *ALL — VOTE for BETTY*

I also distributed mimeographed flyers with just the words *BETTY PEAL* in large print. Even if I didn't win, the entire student body would sure remember my name. I even composed a commercial jingle to the tune of "Turkey in the Straw" and sang it to small clusters of people during lunch hour:

> *She sure doesn't dance,*
> *But she does play the fiddle.*
> *She sings and she draws,*
> *And she is kinda little.*
> *But she's friendly and fine*
> *And oh so neat. So vote for*
> *Betty 'cause she can't be beat.*
> *Dum dudda da dum . . . dum dum!*

The whirlwind campaign lasted a week, and I was having so much fun that I got behind in homework. It was hard to concentrate on classes because I had never felt so wild and carefree. A friend asked, "Aren't you nervous about giving a speech?

"Oh, heck, no. It'll be fun." Privately, I thought, *I can't wait!*

At home, Mom started fretting. "If you win this election, I won't get any help from you in your senior year."

I didn't think that far ahead. I lived for what was going on in the moment and couldn't form a clear thought about any subject beyond the campaign.

In fact, I hated to see my running-for-office experience end. But in a few days it would all be over.

On the day of the election, the polls stayed open for twenty minutes after school was dismissed. A crush of kids hung around the reception office waiting for the election returns to come in. The place was packed with juniors eager to see who had won. After an hour, Mr. Gullette's door opened and the vote counters emerged to announce the winners for the following year. After the names of the newly-elected secretary, treasurer, and historian had been read, the announcer said, "I will now reveal the last two winners for 1948."

I looked around to see where my opponents were so I could congratulate the victor. Being a good sport was more important than winning.

"Next year's Head Girl will be . . . Betty Peal."

Cheers hit my ears when I heard my name. *I heard my name!* Goose bumps exploded down my left leg. Would I faint or cry? My mouth dropped open and got stuck. Someone said, "Close your mouth. They're taking your picture."

As a camera flashed, the voice announced, "And your Head Boy will be Bill Reddick." Another wall of cheers struck me, and I vaguely wondered who the heck Bill Reddick was.

I couldn't believe that I had just been elected to a prestigious post. I made a mental note to get acquainted with Bill since we would preside over the weekly assemblies and make announcements over the PA system. It was amazing. He and I would be governing the Student Council meetings just like a real president.

I'd won. What came next?

I was sure there was a mountain of stuff to understand, and I was not a fast learner. But winning that election made me realize I could do pretty much anything I set my mind to. Head Girl was only the beginning. If I wanted, I could become an actress, an artist, a teacher, a mother . . . or even a writer. The future was mine.

The Senior

As Head Boy and Head Girl, Bill Reddick and I were expected to be honorable examples for other students at all times. I rarely dated, Bill was squeaky clean, and we both had good reputations. So how could we possibly be anything but good role models?

Head Boy and Head Girl

Being in charge of Student Council meetings, assembly programs, the pep rally schedule, and daily announcements on the PA system kept us hopping. I loved doing the announcements because we were talking to every student, and all of them had to sit still and listen. Messages were supposed to be only five minutes long, which meant we had to speak fast, but clearly, with no time for joking around. That part took discipline.

Our positions were so public that everyone in the school knew who we were. Teachers and administrators monitored our behavior and attendance and occasionally reminded us of our obligations.

Soon after classes started, my reputation became important for another reason. Three older women interviewed five of us girls for the purpose of choosing one as a DAR representative. I learned that DAR stood for Daughters of the American Revolution, but no one explained the purpose of the award or told us what qualities would help us earn it. The others were petrified as though it was some kind of test. I loved being interviewed, so I switched on the conversation button that allowed me to smile, chat, and enjoy the attention. It was a lovely experience because I felt that I was auditioning for a part in a play. I probably won because I was relaxed. Winning got me a framed certificate and a nice gold pin that formed the letters D-A-R. I wore it for a while, but no one else knew what it meant either, so where was the glory?

I remained involved with the choir, a trio, and the orchestra. I missed a lot of football games and most of the Pep Club meetings because there was so much else to do. For that reason, the officers decided to kick me out of Pep Club whether I was Head Girl or not. It didn't surprise me at all. I was embarrassed because I could no longer sit with the Pep Club. But I was also relieved because I didn't have to feel guilty about missing sports events.

Just when I thought my senior year might fly by without problems, I slipped up as a good role model. Two of my friends and I were behind schedule in writing our final papers for Miss Hudson's English class. We all cut school together to cram our research into seven hours at the Denver Public Library. Debbie knew that her mom would cover for her. Norma was sure that her mom would not, so she planned to forge her own note. I assumed my mother would bail me out since I was doing homework, but when the time came, she refused to lie about where I'd been. Her note for the attendance clerk read:

> *Elizabeth Peal was at the Denver Public Library on Wednesday, March 17, writing an English paper at the last minute.*
>
> *Mrs. Bassle S. Peal*

I was so upset that I almost wrote my own excuse. But I had never forged a note in my life and couldn't bring myself to do it. I handed my mother's message to the attendance clerk, well aware that it meant a dreaded red slip for an unexcused absence.

The clerk was also the dean of girls, Miss Helen Grubbs. She frowned and said quietly, "Elizabeth, I think we'd better go to Mr. Gullette's office."

The principal was so surprised and disappointed that he slumped in his chair for a while, letting me sit in front of his desk with my hands in my lap. I wondered if he was going to fire me from my hard-earned position.

Eventually, he broke the silence. "Elizabeth, what in the world were you thinking?"

Hot tears burned my eyes, but I didn't say anything.

Then he said, "We cannot have a student leader going from class to class carrying a red excuse for teachers to sign. Your negligence sets a poor example for everyone."

I tried hard to keep from sniveling, but finally had to reach for a tissue in a box that must've been there for those occasions.

"A red excuse says that you do not take your position seriously. That would send a very bad message. So we're going to give you a white one." He handed me another Kleenex to mop up my new display of tears.

As I left the principal's office with a white excuse in hand, I tried to look honest, but the paper was burning a hole in my flesh. My guilt multiplied when my two friends found out about my mother's note. Since all three of us had been together that day, they were sure to be found guilty by association. What a mess I'd created.

It was pure luck that I avoided trouble the next time it arrived. A horde of seniors cut class to protest the food served in the cafeteria. The disgruntled students had staged their rebellion at the offices of the *Denver Post*. But the uprising did not include me because I was home sick that day. Mom discovered what had taken place when she opened the newspaper and said, "Good grief. Look at this!" The photo splashed across the front page showed my classmates pushing protest signs into the air as if it were a football rally.

The next day, the dissenters challenged me. "Betty, how come you didn't support us yesterday?"

I could have admitted that I was home sick that day, but I wanted to be a good role model who would never skip school and get involved in a protest. So I just said, "Because I love the cafeteria food." I was secretly relieved that I hadn't been forced to make the choice.

All twelfth graders had to take an IQ test. Although being Head Girl didn't mean I had to be the smartest person in school, I sure didn't want anyone thinking I was dumb either. So on the day of IQ testing, I was a little nervous.

The exam took a long time and when it was finally finished, I said to my best friend, "Joann, I'm glad that's over."

"Me, too," she said. "I thought the hardest questions were on the back, didn't you?"

My heart fell. On the back? There were questions on the back?

A week later the test results were ready and students rushed to the dean's office to discover their IQs. The next thing you knew everyone was buzzing about who had high scores and who had low ones. I thought to myself, *If I didn't even check for more questions, I must have a very low IQ.* I was so scared that I avoided the office for the rest of the week. Not knowing made me feel so normal that I decided I never needed to learn my IQ score.

When I'd won the election for Head Girl, I expected my last year in high school to be as fun-filled and exciting as the eleventh grade. In a way, it was fun, but being under scrutiny made my weaknesses and flaws more noticeable. Being a senior didn't seem quite as thrilling as the process of getting to that point.

My lack of enthusiasm baffled me. All my life I had yearned for a normal family life and to fit in at school, and I finally had both. Mom hadn't broken dishes for a long time, and I couldn't even remember the last time she ran away. By my senior year, she and I weren't arguing as much either. She seemed to accept that school was always going to take up my time. And she was thrilled about Auntie Marge sending me to college. Mom even helped me get ready.

Dad seemed pleased, too. "Dang," he said. "I think you're the first kid in the whole Peal family to get more than a high school education."

He still felt that college was wasted on girls and an expensive way to find a husband. But he couldn't object since someone else was paying for it. Even though he couldn't say the words, I knew darn well that he was proud of me.

I continued to feel restless as graduation approached. But when the big day finally arrived, it was like being plopped into a whirlwind. The ceremony was held in our auditorium, and several of my classmates were involved in the program, including me. In our caps and gowns, we dashed here and there, back and forth, to sing in the choir and also play "Pomp and Circumstance" in the orchestra. Our choir and orchestra were small, so we couldn't spare anyone from those groups just because they were graduating.

By the time the hoopla was over and families were leaving for parties, I was exhilarated and somewhat out of breath. I literally ran into Johnny Evans, my best buddy from the journalism class. He gave me a hug and said, "Well, no more newspaper deadlines for us, huh?"

"I know," I replied, "but I'll miss that class. We had so much fun, and now it's all over."

"The fun doesn't have to end. How about going out with me this summer?"

"But . . . what about your girlfriend?"

"We broke up."

"Well . . . okay then."

Johnny was high spirited. When he started laughing, he lost control and squealed until he got his breath back. I really liked him. We dated until the end of the summer, then he went off to the Navy and I left for the campus in Greeley. Whenever Johnny was home on leave, we got together. He was a salty swab in his tight-fitting navy blues and white sailor's cap set at a jaunty angle. Being with a handsome sailor in public made me feel older.

His mom thought we were made for each other. In a wistful moment, she grabbed her camera and said, "Son, put your arms around Betty and let me take your picture. Yeah, that's it. Awwww. You two look so cute together." Then she winked and said, "Someday I would sure love to have some grandkids."

That scared the livin' daylights out of me. As much as I liked Johnny, I wanted a husband who wanted a college education and Johnny didn't know what he wanted. But we continued to date since there was no reason to break up until that other man entered my life.

After the spring semester ended, a good friend got married and I was her wedding singer. A handsome older guy named Denny was the groom's best man. Denny had already earned an undergraduate degree in mathematics. He'd just started teaching at a small college in York, Nebraska, but that summer he would be a graduate student on my campus. We'd had several dates when my gut told me that he was the one I'd been waiting for.

But first I had to write a "Dear John" letter to Johnny Evans. I explained who my new beau was and that I had met him at a wedding where he was the best man.

My sailor was not happy about being dropped so suddenly and wrote back, "Just let me meet this Denny Dimwit on any corner, and I'll show you who the best man is!"

When I told my new boyfriend what Johnny had written, he smiled and said, "Like I'm really going to meet him on a corner to see who gets to date you."

Denny was five years older and more mature than any guy I'd ever met. When I was with him, I felt like a young woman instead of a girl. He was soft-spoken, modest, down to earth, and strikingly handsome.

We laughed a lot and talked about everything. I asked, "How many children are in your family?"

"I'm the fourth of five kids. How many in your family?"

I told him that I was the oldest of three children. When I shared that I was the first person in the entire Peal family to attend college, Denny said that all three of his older siblings attended college, but they had to work their way through. I found out that he'd held down three jobs so he could graduate because his family was poor, too.

I was thrilled to learn that and jumped in fast to say, "My family is so poor that my aunt and uncle are paying for my education."

"Betty, we have a lot in common," he said.

"Denny, we sure do."

I admired that Denny was ambitious and had set high goals for himself. It also helped that we both came from humble Midwestern roots. I was so at ease with him that I felt he might be more than a fling, and I could tell that he felt the same. By the middle of the summer, we knew that we wanted to be together and, quite naturally, started discussing our future.

We skipped the proposal part and moved right to the most important question on our minds: when to get married.

"Betty, let's have a Thanksgiving wedding."

"That's only six weeks away."

"Is that too soon?"

"No, but there's something I have to do first."

"What's that?"

"I have to get permission from my church to marry you."

"Oh, that's right. I'm an outsider. Do you think they'll relax their rules?"

"I'm sure they will."

But it wasn't that easy. After weeks of pleading my case and getting no-where, it was time to have a come-to-Jesus talk with my minister. I made it clear that I was going to be Denny's wife, and if he couldn't marry us, I would find someone who could.

He sighed, then said, "All right. I'll marry you on one condition."

"Yes?"

"You must do all in your power to convert him to our faith."

Except for the no-dancing rule, Denny and I believed the same things. So I wasn't really lying when I said, "Sure. No problem."

A few weeks later, I said, "I do," and my life as grownup began at last.

For more about Denny and our life together, read *Dancing in My Nightgown: The Rhythms of Widowhood* by Betty Auchard, published by Stephens Press, LLC, Las Vegas, Nevada.

Afterword

Waneta and Butch

WANETA WAS DRIVING WITH PURPOSE, FACE RIGID AND knuckles white, like the bicycle-riding witch in *The Wizard of Oz*. "Mom, what's going on with you?" my sister asked.

"I found out where your dad's girlfriend lives!"

Patty knew that big trouble was ahead.

I was married and gone by then, so I didn't witness the drama firsthand. But I was able to assemble the story after I heard about it from my sister, my dad, and my mother, all of whom played a part.

Hearing their accounts made me happy all over again that I lived far away. But I felt sorry for my younger sister. With our brother off on his own adventures, Patty had no one left to absorb the fallout from our parents' antics. I hoped the protective spells I'd cast over her before I left home would see her through until she could escape, too.

My parents had been each other's first loves. They wed young and embarked on a wacky love affair that spanned twenty-seven years. My mother's temper tantrums often launched her into reckless decisions, such as repeatedly filing for divorce. As a result, my parents ended their marriage three times before finally making the split permanent. It was a crazy way to exist, but that's how they did it. Their third marriage lasted the longest, and those eleven years were as filled with pandemonium as any of their shorter unions. When Mom threatened divorce once again, Dad went his own merry way and started dating a nice, calm lady named Lucille.

When my mother learned that her ex-husband was seeing someone else, she was beside herself. By the time she picked up my seventeen-year-old sister at school, her simmering anger was about to boil over into uncontrolled rage. Hunching forward with the steering wheel clutched in a death grip, she raced through the neighborhood, intent on locating the woman who had unknowingly become her archenemy.

Patty was worried sick about what was coming next. That feeling was all too familiar to me.

"Forget about it," Patty told Mom, hoping to divert disaster. It was like reasoning with a rock. Mom became deaf when she was enraged.

"I think he's there now!" Screeching to a stop in front of a house with Dad's car parked in front, she backed up a little, then sped forward to bash into his door.

Patty screamed, "Stop!"

Her plea had no effect. Our mother kept backing up and bashing, backing up and bashing, until she decided that hitting the vehicle straight on would do more damage. Ignoring my sister, who was nearly hysterical, Mom sped around the block and bashed the target of her rage at full speed. Patty's nose smashed into the dashboard, creating a bloody mess.

The police had arrived in time to witness the last big crunch. Reminiscent of the movies, one of them approached the window and said, "Ma'am, turn off the motor and step outta the car!" Dad and Lucille showed up about then and took my sister and her bloody nose inside the house.

"Ma'am," the officer explained, "we've gotta take you to jail."

Mom begged for mercy. "I'm not a criminal. I'm sick. I've been under a lot of pressure, and I need to be in a hospital, not jail. Here's my minister's phone number. He'll explain. He's been counseling me."

"Apparently it hasn't helped," the officer muttered before contacting the police dispatcher by radio.

Mom's minister suggested they contact her doctor. He even provided the phone number. The officer told the dispatcher to explain that Waneta Peal had been arrested for willfully damaging Mr. Peal's car. "Tell him she has to go somewhere and ask him if it should be the hospital or jail."

Mom later said to me, "My doctor told the police to lock me in jail overnight. Can you imagine?"

"Uh, yes, I can."

"Not me. I called him back the next day and dismissed him as my physician."

"Was he angry with you?"

"Nope. He thanked me. Can you believe that?"

I just smiled.

Eventually, Lucille became Dad's second wife, and my mother moved to California to be close to me. She never forgave the new Mrs. Peal for stealing her man, but she learned to live with it. And whenever she was in Iowa visiting relatives, she and my father met privately at their favorite tavern for a friendly chat and lots of laughs over cold beers.

After a few years, Dad and Lucille also divorced. My mother was triumphant. She and Butch soon had another friendly get-together, this time to talk seriously about becoming a couple again. Bob, Patty, and I were in three different states, so they called each of us separately to see what we thought of their plan. I was first on the list. It was evident that my father wanted to get remarried, but Mom did not. She wanted them to live together so their social security checks wouldn't change.

Waneta and Bassle, 1986

Dad said, "Betty, I wouldn't want my grandkids to find out that their grandparents were shackin' up, so we want your advice on what to do."

It was odd being asked for advice after all the times they remarried without caring what anyone thought. In the background, just like in the old days, Mom was yelling her opinion. "I don't mind living with your father, but I'm damn sure not going to marry him again!"

They were sixty-eight years old, and their grandkids were all mature adults. No one would have faulted them for sharing rent. But Dad must have felt it was more moral to wed and divorce repeatedly than to reside with a woman out of wedlock.

When Mom refused to change her mind, Dad reconciled with Lucille because he was not meant to be alone. My mother, on the other hand, got so used to being alone that she became a freer spirit than she had ever been. That's saying a lot because she had always been the queen of freedom.

Dad eventually ended up in a full care facility in Belle Plaine, Iowa. He was alert and active, read the daily paper front to back, and kept informed about current events. But his memory for some people had dimmed. While he was there, Lucille died. When someone gave him the newspaper clipping from the obituary column, he said, "Who's this?"

"Mr. Peal, that's your recently deceased wife."

"I don't think so. My wife's name is Waneta."

He tucked the clipping into his wallet and occasionally pulled it out to inquire of visitors who Lucille might be.

He didn't remember us kids either. When I visited, we had lovely conversations, but he couldn't recall if I was his sister or his daughter. However, his memory of my mother stayed as sharp and fresh as a glass of spring water. He said, "If you live in California, you must know Waneta."

"Yes, she's my mother."

"I'll never forget her."

Together or apart, my parents never lost touch. Mom stayed in California and drove her old Buick to Iowa every spring to stay with family for a month or two. During one of her annual Midwest road trips, she saw Dad at the convalescent home. After returning to California, she said, "Your father couldn't keep his hands off me."

"Really? What did he do?"

"He kept tweaking my titties."

"No kidding?"

Then she shared their conversation, which turned out to be their last.

"Waneta," he said, "you oughta move in here. The food ain't half bad."

"Butch, I can't move in here. I'm in California now."

"Dammit, Girl, listen to me. There's an empty room right down the hall."

"Butch, a person can't move in here because she wants to. A person has to be sick, and I'm not sick."

"Hell, Girl, I ain't either, but here I am. All you have to do is sign up at the front desk."

"It's not that simple."

"Oh, yes, it is. That's how I got my room."

Since he may have thought he was in a hotel, Mom considered telling him that she had inquired about vacancies and, sadly, there were none. But he had already switched to another subject.

"Waneta, I don't think they make beer or cigarettes anymore 'cause I can't get 'em anywhere."

Mom told me that when it was time to leave, she gave Butch a nice, long hug. "And you know what that devil did?" she asked.

"No. What?"

"He tweaked my titties again. Betty, if I did live there, your father would be in my bed every night. My God . . . the man is seventy-eight, and he still has the hots for me."

I had to laugh. Did she view that as a blessing or a curse?

For another story about Dad in the convalescent home and his true confessions about Mom, read "First Love: Conversation with Dad" in *Dancing in My Nightgown: The Rhythms of Widowhood* by Betty Auchard, published by Stephens Press, LLC, Las Vegas, Nevada.

Don

A FRIEND, CAROL WOOD, READ ABOUT MY CHILDHOOD CRUSH ON Don Johanos in the story titled "First Love." She enjoyed it so much that she was certain he would want to know the effect he'd had on a young girl's life. With great difficulty, Carol located him through a Google search and then presented me with a valentine card that included his address. I was stunned, and I was not sure I wanted to reveal my silly teenage secrets to him personally.

But I eventually did write to my childhood friend. I hadn't talked with him for more than fifty years. It was possible he wouldn't even remember the girl I used to be. After waiting for three weeks, I assumed he had chosen not to reply. Then the phone rang at 9:00 one morning. I answered and a warm, lively voice said, "Hi. Lizzie? This is Don Johanos."

I was so shocked that I squealed with delight. He explained that he had been away for three weeks visiting his daughter. "When I got back home and sorted my mail, I was delighted to read your letter."

"Did you actually remember who I was?" I asked.

"Of course I remembered you, Lizzie. You were the girl with long braids who followed me everywhere."

We had a memorable conversation, laughing and recalling the old days in Cedar Rapids when we were kids. We compared ages and he said, "You don't sound seventy." He didn't sound like a guy in his seventies either. He still had the upbeat, animated personality he'd had when he was seventeen. He said that he'd been widowed, but would soon propose marriage to his girlfriend.

Don and I stayed in touch by email and he shared the details of his romantic proposal aboard a cruise ship. He, his new wife, and I had hoped to meet in San Francisco the following July, but it didn't work out.

In August, 2007, my brother and I were doing research for this book at the History Center in Cedar Rapids, Iowa. The volunteers, Beverly Redford, Nova Dannels, and Ruth Darling were older than my brother and me and were dedicated history buffs. Two of the women were natives of Cedar Rapids. For two hours, those caring volunteers collected photos and articles and answered questions because they had known everyone we were asking about. Then I asked, "Do you have any information on Don Johanos, our town celebrity?"

A white-haired docent gushed, "Oh, wasn't he the handsomest young man you ever laid eyes on? We were saddened to lose him a few months ago."

It was like being kicked in the stomach. I hadn't heard from him for a long time and didn't know he'd been ill. I couldn't concentrate after hearing that Don was gone. I appeared busy, but I was just going through the motions. I picked up an old newspaper article, stared at it, and set it down. Then I picked up another one and did the same thing. I was in shock. I couldn't even cry. It took me the rest of the afternoon to absorb the bad news.

What eased me back to life was something my first love had shared during our initial telephone reunion. He'd told me that his daughter was so touched by the story "First Love" that she had read it aloud at a family barbeque when his grandchildren were there.

"Lizzie, I wish you could've seen my thirteen-year-old granddaughter's face when her mother was reading your story. It was obvious that you'd gotten inside her head and she knew exactly what you were talking about. She identified. It was written all over her face."

I had treasured hearing that. Love was being passed down from the older generation to their offspring through stories. Don had laughed and added, "My granddaughter probably thinks I was born this old because she seemed surprised that a girl her age would have a crush on her grandpa."

I wasn't the only one who'd had a crush on her grandpa.

EPILOGUE

PEOPLE USED TO SAY, "BETTY, YOU REMIND ME OF YOUR MOTHER." I would reply, "I am nothing like her because she's wacky, and I'm not wacky."

That was a long time ago. Now I know better. I've changed over the years, although I don't break dishes when I'm mad. I grind my teeth instead. I decided to look up the word that I've used so carelessly to describe my mother.

Wacky: crazy, madcap, weird, off the wall.

Since that's exactly how my friends describe me, I guess I've become as wacky as Mom.

This is not a sudden discovery. It started while I was revising a scene in the manuscript. It should have been dramatic, but it was anemic and flat because I had written it with my head and not my heart. In order to bring it to life, my writing coach told me to tap into my feelings as a teenager. It was not easy, but I finally remembered so much that it brought my characters back to life. My words weren't just descriptions anymore; they were real. I once more became that sixteen-year-old who stomped up the stairs during a quarrel with her mother as they yelled back and forth. Tears of anger almost strangled me, just as they had all those years ago. Dialogue leapt from my fingertips onto the screen so fast that I ignored the typos. When the argument with Mom was over, I felt drained and sat at the computer and cried.

That wasn't the end of it. I had finally learned how to go deep inside my memories so each character could take a turn at coming to life. I could almost feel what they felt. I was older and wiser and saw things more objectively. Gruff Damsy seemed more human, and I could understand why she begrudged taking us in each time my parents split up. I could feel my mother's panic when she ran away from home for a few days.

The Peal family, 1947

When several people appeared in a scene, I developed multiple personalities. I got in the "zone" and everyone seemed so real. I understood why they did what they did because I was in their heads. I had always cared about my family, but I cared about them ten times more when I was writing about them.

My mother and father were star-crossed lovers trying to live the American dream. Alongside their rocky relationship, we three kids managed to grow up as we adjusted to the endless family dramas. We learned how to survive in our unpredictable world. Mom and Dad's problems both hindered and helped us. You might think that no kid could possibly grow up normal in our erratic environment, but Bob, Patty, and I blossomed.

And that's what surprised me. All the time I'd been writing about my childhood, I thought we three kids were thriving in spite of our parents. Now I believe we thrived because of them. I can only support that statement by saying that I lived it, so I know it's true.

My siblings and I became three well-adjusted adults with close family relationships. The ways in which we were affected negatively by our unusual upbringing must have been so minor that it didn't mess us up. But

I sometimes wonder in what ways the oddities of our parents might have rubbed off on us. I would probably need deep hypnosis to find the answer.

But one small thing does come to mind. My parents traveled light. They owned very little and gave things away without much thought. They had to since we were always moving. Because we had so little when we were growing up, I am now the complete opposite. I hate letting go of things. I'm afraid of running out, so I keep it all while buying more. The result is that I have too much. My house is filled with flotsam and jetsam. Having stuff has become a burden that my parents never experienced.

Some of the things I save are good cardboard boxes with lids. I don't need them now, but I might in the future. They can be used for so many things. Saving them is in my genes, because boxes were the only possessions my mother hung onto.

While visiting Auntie Marge, Mom once saved cardboard containers of all sizes that my aunt had thrown out. My mother probably thought, *Good God, these are too good to throw away.* I once saw her bend over to pick up two giant-sized rubber bands from the sidewalk and say that very thing.

She stacked those nice boxes inside of each other with such mind-boggling accuracy that they looked like octuplets packed into a womb. Because the package was too large to fit in her car, she made my brother ship them to my address. He called to warn me that Mom and her box filled with boxes were heading my way, one by car and the other by UPS.

When the bulky delivery arrived at my home, the UPS man commented about the light weight of such a big package. I didn't have the nerve to explain that my mother had paid good money to ship empty space from Iowa to California.

So the pattern continues. If no one stopped me, I would probably save those boxes and mail them to myself just as my mother did.

No matter how many times I have declared that Mom was wacky and that I'm nothing like her, I now realize I was wrong. I believe the saying about the apple not falling far from the tree. So, if that makes me another wacky apple, it's okay with me.

Thank you, Mom.

BETTY'S HISTORY LESSONS

1946 Hit Parade — *Your Hit Parade* was a weekly radio program that played the most popular songs of the time. In 1946, the top ten songs included "The Gypsy" by the Ink Spots, "Oh! What It Seemed to Be" by Frankie Carle, "Rumors are Flying" by Frankie Carle, "The Gypsy" by Dinah Shore, "To Each His Own" by Eddy Howard, "Oh! What it Seemed to Be" by Frank Sinatra, "The Old Lamplighter" by Sammy Kaye, "For Sentimental Reasons" by Nat King Cole, "Let It Snow!" by Vaughn Monroe, and "Prisoner of Love" by Perry Como. [Part 7]

Baby, It's Cold Outside — Written as a duet in 1944 by Frank Loesser, "Baby, It's Cold Outside" was introduced by Loesser and his wife Lynn Garland at the housewarming of their Navarro Hotel. Garland was reportedly incensed when Loesser sold the rights to "their" song to MGM in 1948. MGM used the song in the film *Neptune's Daughter*, for which it won an Academy Award for Best Original Song. It was subsequently recorded by Dinah Shore and Buddy Clark, Margaret Whiting and Johnny Mercer, the Sammy Kaye Orchestra, Ella Fitzgerald and Louis Jordan, Esther Williams and Ricardo Montalban, Pearl Bailey and Hot Lips Page, and Louis Armstrong and Velma Middleton. [Part 7]

Baby Snooks — *The Baby Snooks Show* first aired on the radio on September 17, 1944, and starred comedienne Fanny Brice, who played a young girl whose impish pranks drove her daddy to distraction. Brice had originally played the Baby Snooks character in a vaudeville routine, beginning in 1912. During the 1940s, *The Baby Snooks Show* became one of the nation's most popular situation comedies. [Part 3]

Backstage Wife — The radio show *Backstage Wife* starred Vivian Fridell from 1935 through the early 1940s. Claire Niesen then played the lead role of Mary Noble until the series ended in 1959. The program detailed events in the life of a girl from small-town Iowa who traveled to New York and became the wife of a handsome actor. [Part 6]

Bank Night — Bank Night was a lottery game franchise popular during the Depression. Created and marketed by Charles U. Yaeger, the game was leased to theaters for five to fifty dollars per week, depending on their size. Anyone could enter his/her name in a book kept by the theater manager, and on Bank Night one name would be drawn at random. The person whose name was selected had to reach the stage within a set amount of time to claim the prize. [Part 5]

Betty Boop — Betty Boop was an animated cartoon character created by Grim Natwick. Her figure is said to have been modeled after Mae West. The character was featured in two different comic strips, one in the 1930s and another in the 1980s. She was rather risqué for the 1930s and, by 1934, public pressure resulted in Betty Boop showing far less leg. [Part 5]

Betty Grable — Betty Grable was the number one pinup girl during the World War II era. Her famous bathing suit photo was included in the *Life* magazine project "100 Photos that Changed the World." Grable was thought to have the most beautiful legs in Hollywood at the time because of their ideal proportions (according to hosiery specialists). The studio considered her legs so valuable that they insured them with Lloyds of London for one million dollars. [Part 5]

Blue Bells of Scotland— A traditional Scottish folk song, "Blue Bells of Scotland" was arranged for the trombone around 1899. The piece was known to pose technical challenges for trombonists, and it was said that only the most gifted musicians could do it justice. An orchestral arrangement was later written by American composer Leroy Anderson. [Part 7]

Bobby Socks — It's not clear where the "bobby" part of the name originated, but bobby socks (or bobby sox) have been around since 1927. They became fashionable in the 1940s and 1950s, and were often worn with skirts and saddle oxfords. The cuffs were thick and usually turned down. Sometimes the cuffs were decorated with lace or other materials, but the socks were almost always white. [Part 8]

Boogie Woogie — Boogie woogie is a piano-based blues style that originated around 1900, but became popular in the late 1930s and early 1940s. Boogie woogie style is often associated with dancing, and swing bands incorporated the beat into some of their music. One of the first bands to do so was the Will Bradley orchestra, beginning in 1939. The Andrews Sisters sang several boogies, and the Tommy Dorsey band landed a hit with an updated version of "Pine Top's Boogie Woogie" in 1938. The jitterbug and Lindy Hop both required a boogie beat. [Part 7]

Brownie Cameras— When Eastman Kodak launched the inexpensive Brownie camera line, they placed photography within the reach of the majority of Americans and introduced the concept of the snapshot. The first Brownie, a cardboard box camera with a simple lens, became available in 1900 at a cost of one dollar.

The Brownie slogan was "You push the button, we do the rest." The most popular model was the Brownie 127, a Bakelite version that sold between 1952 and 1967. [Part 7]

Buffalo Bob— Robert Emil Schmidt, aka Buffalo Bob Smith, began his career as a radio singer and musician. He gained national popularity when he was cast as the host of the *Howdy Doody Show* from 1947 to 1960. [Part 7]

Burma-Shave — The Burma-Vita company introduced Burma-Shave in 1925. It became the second-highest selling brushless shaving cream in the United States, but sales had declined by the 1950s. During its peak, Burma-Shave was best known for the road signs that appeared throughout most of the country between 1925 and 1963. Usually presented as a series of six small signs, the messages could be read sequentially by passing motorists. [Part 5]

Captain Cook — James Cook, born in 1728, was an English explorer, navigator, and cartographer who achieved the rank of captain in the Royal Navy. He made three voyages to the Pacific Ocean and established the first European contact with the eastern coastline of Australia and the Hawaiian Islands. He was also the first to circumnavigate New Zealand. [Part 2]

Captain Marvel (**comics**) — Comic book superhero *Captain Marvel* debuted in 1940. The brainchild of artist C.C. Beck and writer Bill Parker, *Captain Marvel* became the most popular superhero during the 1940s based on sales volume. It was the first comic book superhero to be adapted for film. [Part 6]

Captain Midnight — Created by Wilfred G. Moore and Robert M. Burtt, *Captain Midnight* was a radio program that aired from 1938 to 1949. The main character was Captain Jim "Red" Albright, a World War I Army pilot who was given the code name *Captain Midnight* when he returned from a high risk mission at the stroke of midnight. Initially, Midnight was a private pilot who helped people, but the character was later recruited to head the Secret Squadron to fight sabotage and espionage. After the United States joined World War II, the plots reflected more direct military encounters, and villains such as Baron von Karp, Admiral Himakito, and von Schrecker joined the cast of characters. [Part 6]

CBS Mercury Theater — In 1937, John Houseman and Orson Welles (who was just twenty-one years old at the time) formed their own theatrical production company and launched the Mercury Theatre with an initial investment of just one hundred dollars. In 1938, the company was converted to the *Mercury Theater on the Air* on the CBS radio network. By combining riveting performances by Mr. Welles with the inventive use of sound effects and music, it became one of the most unique programs on the radio. One of the most notable episodes was *The War of the Worlds*, broadcast on October 30, 1938. *Mercury Theater on the Air* continued until 1940. [Part 2]

Cedar Rapids Gazette — First published in Cedar Rapids, Iowa, as an evening journal called the *Evening Gazette* in 1883, the *Cedar Rapids Gazette* continues to be produced today. The daily publication is distributed throughout northeast and east central Iowa. [Part 1]

Celluloid — Celluloid is considered the first thermoplastic to be created. Before 1870, when the compound was registered under the name "celluloid," it had been known as Parkesine (so named for its creator, Alexander Parkes) and then as Zylonite. Its use in photography began in 1888 when John Carbutt created celluloid strips coated with a photosensitive gelatin emulsion. The next year,

more flexible celluloids were developed for photographic film. Celluloid is in limited use today, primarily employed in the manufacture of guitar picks and table tennis balls. [Part 5]

Chameleon — In 1940, Target Comics debuted a character called the Chameleon (aka Pete Stockbridge), who had the uncanny ability to impersonate just about anyone. He used his talent for disguise to solve crimes until World War II, when he served in Europe as a spy for the allies. The Chameleon comic strip ran from July 1940 to January 1949. [Part 2]

Charles Lindbergh — Lindbergh made aviation history when, in 1927, he flew nonstop from New York to Paris, France, in his single-engine plane, the Spirit of St. Louis. In 1932, Lindbergh's twenty-month-old son Charles II was kidnapped from their Hopewell, New Jersey, home and then murdered in what became known as the Crime of the Century. [Part 1]

City of Denver — The City of Denver was a passenger train that operated between Chicago, Illinois, and Denver, Colorado. When it began operations in 1936, it was the fastest long-distance passenger train in the world, traveling at an average of sixty-five miles per hour. [Part 6]

Colorado State College of Education in Greeley — In 1890, the Colorado State Normal School began training teachers for the state's public schools, offering certification after completion of a two-year course. In 1911, the name was changed to Colorado State Teachers College and four-year bachelor degrees were offered. In 1913, graduate degrees were added and, in 1935, the school became The Colorado State College of Education. Another name change took place in 1957, when the school became Colorado State College. Since 1970, the institution has been known as the University of Northern Colorado. [Part 8]

Cubs Stadium (Wrigley Field) — Originally built by Charlie Weeghman for the Chicago Federals, the stadium was first called Weeghman Park. It was purchased two years later by a syndicate that included William Wrigley, Jr., who purchased the Cubs. By 1919, Wrigley had bought out the shares of the other members of the syndicate. The name of the stadium was changed to Cubs Park in 1920 and renamed Wrigley Field in 1926. [Part 5]

DAR — The Daughters of the American Revolution, founded in 1890, is a volunteer women's service organization that promotes patriotism, the preservation of American history, and better education for children. [Part 8]

Day of Infamy — On December 8, 1941, President Franklin D. Roosevelt gave the Presidential Address to a joint session of Congress at 12:30 p.m. to address Japan's attack on the Pearl Harbor Naval Base in Hawaii. In the speech, which ran only six and one-half minutes, Roosevelt referred to December 7th as "a date which will live in infamy." Within an hour of the President's remarks, Congress formally declared war against Japan, officially taking the United States into World War II. [Part 4]

D-Day— D-Day is the term given to the Normandy Landings during World War II. On June 6, 1944, an air assault landing of 24,000 American, British, Canadian, and Free French troops was launched shortly after midnight, followed by an amphibious landing of Allied infantry and armored troops on the coast of France at 6:30 a.m. By the end of the day, Allied troops had gained a foothold in Hitler's "fortress Europe." [Part 6]

Dear John Letter — The term "Dear John letter" is believed to have been

initially used by Americans in World War II. While the wives and girlfriends waited for many months or years for their soldiers to return home, some of them began relationships with new men. It became common for a woman to inform the serviceman of her change of heart by beginning a letter with "Dear John." [Part 8]

Debussy — Achille-Claude Debussy was a French composer born in 1862. He was prominent in the field of impressionist music, although he disliked having the term applied to his own compositions. His music defined the transition from late Romantic to modernist music. [Part 7]

Denver City Park — The Colorado state legislature passed a bill in 1878 to allow Denver to purchase state land for the purpose of building parks. The Denver City Park was the largest. It was initially designed by Henry Meryweather in 1882, blending the tradition of English pastoral gardens with the casual design of Central Park in New York City. In 1908, the Denver Museum of Nature and Science was built on the eastern edge of the park. [Part 6]

Denver Post — The *Denver Post* is a daily newspaper first published in 1892. It was founded by supporters of Grover Cleveland to publicize political ideals and slow the number of Colorado Democrats leaving the party. The newspaper now ranks among the top fifty papers in the United States in terms of circulation. [Part 6]

Ding Dong School — Called "the nursery school of the air," *Ding Dong School* was a half-hour children's television show that aired from 1952 to 1956 on NBC. It was hosted by Dr. Frances Horwich, known as Miss Frances. [Part 7]

Dionne Quintuplets — On May 28, 1934, near the village of Corbeil, Ontario, five babies were born two months prematurely. They were the first quintuplets known to have survived infancy and the only identical set of five female quintuplets ever recorded. After living with their birth family for four months, the children were made wards of the King for the next nine years. They became a profitable tourist attraction in Ontario, with nearly three million visitors between 1936 and 1943. [Part 1]

Dorothy Lamour — Born Mary Leta Dorothy Slaton in New Orleans, Dorothy Lamour was of French Louisianan, Spanish, and Irish descent. She adopted her stepfather's last name and became Dorothy Lambour, which was later changed to the more glamorous Dorothy Lamour. After attending secretarial school, she moved to Hollywood in 1936 and soon began appearing in films for Paramount Pictures. She continued to be one of the most popular screen actresses in the 1950s. Lamour was instrumental in starting the World War II war bond tours and personally promoted the sale of more than $21 million in bonds. [Part 7]

Dream When You're Feelin' Blue — Also known by the shortened title "Dream," this jazz and pop standard was written by Johnny Mercer in 1944. It has been performed by numerous artists, including Frank Sinatra, The Pied Pipers, and Roy Orbison. [Part 7]

Dust Be My Destiny — The film drama *Dust Be My Destiny*, released in 1939, starred John Garfield as a prisoner and Priscilla Lane as the daughter of the prison foreman. The original ending had the lovers dying as fugitives, but audience reaction at the preview prompted the studio to create a happy ending. [Part 8]

Enrico Caruso — Born in Naples in 1873, Enrico Caruso became one of the most famous male opera singers in history. The Italian tenor was noted for his technique and the power of his voice and richness of its tone. He was said to be able to reach high C. Caruso sang for audiences in Europe, North America, and South America from 1895 to 1920, performing at the New York Metropolitan Opera 863 times. He made more than 250 recordings for the Victor Talking Machine Company and earned millions of dollars in royalties from the resulting discs. He died at the age of forty-eight after a year-long illness. [Part 4]

Ferdinand Magellan — Portuguese explorer Ferdinand Magellan was born in 1480. He obtained Spanish nationality to serve the Spanish crown by searching for a westward route to the Spice Islands. Magellan became the first European to lead an expedition across the Pacific Ocean. He spearheaded the first successful attempt to circumnavigate the earth, but was killed in the Battle of Mactan in the Philippines before the voyage was completed. [Part 2]

Fireside Chats — Franklin D. Roosevelt initially presented fireside chats in 1929 during his first term as governor of New York to address the citizens directly to help get his agenda passed. His first fireside chat as president of the United States took place on March 12, 1933, using the radio to share his messages. FDR presented thirty fireside chats between 1933 and 1944. [Part 4]

Florence Nightingale — Born in 1820, Florence Nightingale was dubbed "The Lady with the Lamp" for her habit of making rounds at night to tend injured soldiers during the Crimean War. Her pioneering work in nursing, along with her book, *Notes on Nursing,* became the foundation for professional nursing. [Part 6]

Flour-Sack Underwear — Beginning in the mid 1800s, flour and other foodstuffs were packaged in sacks made of cotton that were often imprinted with the company's logo. Emptied and washed, the sacks were ready to be sewn into underwear, nightgowns, and little girls' dresses. By 1925, companies realized this practice presented a terrific marketing opportunity, and they added colorful prints to the fabric and pasted their labels on the sacks for easy removal. The marketing ploy worked, as women selected brands of flour, sugar, rice, and other commodities based on the design of the sacks. If a housewife had more sacks than she could use herself, she could sell them back to the store. [Part 1]

Fort Logan — In 1887, an Army post was authorized near Denver, and 640 acres of land south of Denver's Union Station were purchased with contributions from citizens and businesses. Soldiers from Fort Hays and Leavenworth, Kansas, officially occupied the fort on October 31, 1887. Construction began on the permanent facilities in July of 1888. The fort was named for John Alexander Logan, a Union Army officer during the Civil War. To honor the Civil War casualties, he established May 30 as Decoration Day, which later became the national holiday called Memorial Day. During the 1940s, as many as 5,500 individuals were stationed at Fort Logan. The fort was closed in May of 1946. In 1960, 308 acres of fort land were deeded to the state of Colorado to establish the Fort Logan Mental Health Center, now known as the Colorado Mental Health Institute at Fort Logan. [Part 7]

Frank Sinatra — Francis Albert Sinatra began his musical career in the swing era, becoming a successful soloist in the early to mid 1940s when he was the idol of many bobby soxers. His career stalled in the early 1950s, but gained momentum when he won the Academy Award for Best Supporting Actor for his role in *From Here to Eternity*. Throughout his life, he was at the center of several controversies, and his career was marked by a rollercoaster of highs and lows. [Part 7]

Franklin D. Roosevelt — Franklin D. Roosevelt, often referred to as FDR, served as the thirty-second president of the United States. He was the only American president elected to more than two terms, serving for a total of twelve years. He shepherded the United States through most of World War II and died in office from a cerebral hemorrhage on April 12, 1945, just before the end of the war. [Part 4]

Game of Authors — The first Game of Authors was published in 1861 by G.M. Whipple and A.A. Smith of Salem, Massachusetts. It was also published in 1897 by Parker Brothers. Several versions of the game have been produced, including American Authors, Children's Authors, and Composers. [Part 3]

Gettysburg Address — Abraham Lincoln presented the Gettysburg Address at the dedication of the Soldiers' National Cemetery in Gettysburg, Pennsylvania, on November 19, 1863, four and one-half months after the Union armies defeated the Confederates at the Battle of Gettysburg. The address, which began with the now-famous words, "Four score and seven years ago," advocated the struggle to ensure that "government of the people, by the people, for the people, shall not perish from the earth." [Part 5]

Gone With the Wind — *Gone with the Wind* was the only novel Margaret Mitchell wrote during her lifetime. Published in 1936, it was set in the south during the Civil War and Reconstruction and follows the life of southern belle Scarlett O'Hara. The romantic novel won the 1937 Pulitzer Prize and came to fame as an Academy Award-winning film in 1939. [Part 6]

Governor Hickenlooper — Republican Bourke Hickenlooper was elected lieutenant governor of Iowa in 1939 and became the twenty-ninth governor of Iowa in 1943. In 1944, he was elected to the U.S. Senate, where he served until 1969. Hickenlooper was born in Blockton, Iowa, in 1896, and earned a law degree from the University of Iowa College of Law in 1922. Before becoming a politician, he practiced law in Cedar Rapids, Iowa. He died in 1971 and is buried in Cedar Rapids. [Part 4]

Grand Central Station (**radio show**) — The radio series *Grand Central Station* aired from 1937 to 1953. The stories, ranging from romantic comedies to lightweight dramas, all began in Grand Central Station in New York City. Different characters met in the station each week, and the plot centered around their experiences after they left the station. Actors included Jim Ameche and Hume Cronyn, and the programs were narrated by Jack Arthur, Alexander Scourby, and Stuart Metz. [Part 6]

Hopalong Cassidy — A cowboy hero created in 1904 by Clarence Mulford, Hopalong Cassidy appeared in a series of stories and novels. Beginning in 1935, the character was played by William Boyd in a series of popular films. Mulford later rewrote several of his earlier stories to fit the movie version, which led to a comic book series. [Part 2]

Hungarian Rhapsody — Composer Franz Liszt wrote a set of nineteen Hungarian Rhapsodies, of which "Hungarian Rhapsody No. 2" is the most popular. Composed in 1847, No. 2 is considered one of the most technically challenging pieces for solo piano. It has become an unofficial standard for pianists to demonstrate their proficiency. The composition

has also gained some notoriety through its appearance as a soundtrack in many cartoons. [Part 7]

I Love a Mystery — Scripted by Carlton E. Morse, radio drama *I Love a Mystery* featured three friends who come together in San Francisco and form a detective agency after first meeting as mercenaries. The motto of their A-1 Detective Agency was "No job too tough, no adventure too baffling." The program aired from 1939 to 1944. In 1948, the characters returned to radio in *I Love Adventure* and continued until that series ended in 1952. [Part 3]

Inner Sanctum — The radio series *Inner Sanctum Mysteries* first aired in 1941. The program was memorable for its opening sequence, designed to establish an air of mystery and intrigue. Each weekly episode began when an organist struck a chord, a doorknob turned, and a creaking door slowly opened. The stories involved ghosts, murderers, and lunatics. Film stars Boris Karloff, Peter Lorre, and Claude Rains were occasional guest stars on the program. A total of 526 episodes had aired by the time the show ended in 1952. [Part 4]

Jack Armstrong, All American Boy — The radio adventure program *Jack Armstrong, the All-American Boy* ran from 1933 to 1951. Armstrong was portrayed as a popular athlete at Hudson High School whose uncle, James Fairfield, was a wealthy industrialist. Jack and his siblings often traveled with their uncle when he visited exotic parts of the world, and the program described their globe-trotting adventures. [Part 4]

Jane Arden Comic Strip — The syndicated Jane Arden comic strip ran from 1927 to 1968. Featuring a "spunky girl reporter" who attempted to expose criminal activity instead of just reporting it, the series inspired later comic book characters such as Lois Lane and Brenda Starr. Jane Arden was more popular in Canada and Australia than in the United States, but the storyline was eventually adapted for film and radio. The comic strip was created by Monte Barrett and Frank Ellis. After Barrett's death in 1949, Walt Graham took over as the scriptwriter. Five artists drew Jane Arden throughout the forty-one years it was in production. Along with the comic strip, newspapers sometimes printed a paper doll version (including several outfits) of Jane Arden for readers to cut out. [Part 4]

Japanese Surrender World War II — The United States dropped an atomic bomb on Hiroshima on August 6, 1945, and on Nagasaki on August 9. About the same time, the Soviet Union launched a surprise invasion of the Japanese colony in Manchuria. As a result, Emperor Hirohito ordered the leaders of the Supreme Council for the Direction of the War (the "Big Six") to accept the terms offered by the Allies in the Potsdam Declaration. The surrender ceremony was held on September 2, 1945, aboard the United States battleship Missouri. [Part 7]

Johnny Mercer — John Herndon Mercer was a lyricist, songwriter, and singer who recorded his own tunes as well as those written by others. Many of the songs Mercer wrote and performed were wildly popular from the 1930s through the 1950s. A prolific songwriter, he penned the lyrics to more than 1,500 songs, including compositions for films and Broadway shows. During his career, Mercer was nominated for nineteen Academy Awards and won four of them. [Part 7]

Jon Hall — Jon Hall, born Charles Felix Locher, was a nephew of James Norman Hall, one of the authors of *Mutiny on the Bounty*. Jon Hall's acting career began in 1935, but his breakthrough film came in 1937 when he was cast with Dorothy Lamour in *The Hurricane*, which was also written by James Norman Hall. He continued to play leads in adventure films until the end of the 1940s, but Jon Hall is remembered by later audiences as the star of the 1950s television series *Ramar of the Jungle*. [Part 7]

Jumping Jehosaphat — According to the *Oxford English Dictionary*, the expression "Jumping Jehosaphat" dates back to 1847 and is of American origin. It's thought that "Jehosaphat" refers to the King of Judah and that the expression "Jumping Jehosaphat" was used as a euphemism for Jehovah or Jesus. [Part 4]

Kid Curlers — Kid Curlers were a popular hair styling product from the early 1900s that were made from kid leather sewn over thin, flexible metal rods. Sections of damp hair were wrapped around the leather rods, and the ends were bent inward to hold them in place. Once the hair had been allowed to dry, curls resulted. [Part 1]

Lake Michigan — One of the five Great Lakes of North America, Lake Michigan is the only one located entirely within the United States. It is bounded by the states of Wisconsin, Illinois, Indiana, and Michigan. With a surface area of 22,300 square miles, it is the largest freshwater lake in the United States and the fifth largest lake in the world. [Part 5]

Let's Pretend — The long-running children's radio series was created and directed by Nila Mack. It began as *Aunt Jymmie and Her Tots in Tottyville* in 1928, featuring fantasy and fairytales with a cast of children. It was replaced by *The Children's Club Hour* in 1929, which was later replaced by *Land O' Make Believe*. In 1934, Nila Mack took over as director and changed the title to *Let's Pretend*, "radio's outstanding children's theater." The program ran for two decades, ending in 1954. [Part 3, 6]

Lights Out— Various versions of *Lights Out* aired on several different networks from 1934 to 1947 before the series was converted to a television format. The programs focused on horror and the supernatural. The original conception was the brainchild of writer Wyllis Cooper whose idea was to create a "midnight mystery serial to catch the attention of the listeners at the witching hour." The stories were grisly in nature, seasoned with dark humor and realistic sound effects. Cooper left the program in 1936 and Arch Oboler took over. Oboler added stream of consciousness narratives and, occasionally, social and political themes. [Part 3]

Lowry Air Force Base, Colorado — Lowry Air Force Base, located in Aurora and Denver, Colorado, was in operation from 1938 to 1994. The base conducted Air Force technical training, including the training of US Air Force bomber crews during World War II. The base served as the home of the United States Air Force Academy from 1954 to 1958, when the academy's permanent site in Colorado Springs was completed. [Part 7]

Lux Radio Theater — The long-running radio program known as *Lux Radio Theater* premiered on October 14, 1934, on the NBC Blue Network with a production of *Seventh Heaven*. The hour-long programs were performed live before studio audiences and featured the stars of stage and film who were popular at the time. They were broadcast on radio for more than twenty years and continued as the *Lux Video Theater* television show through the 1950s. [Part 3]

Ma Perkins — Radio soap opera *Ma Perkins* was on the air from 1933 to 1960, with a total of 7,065 episodes. The lead character, known as "America's mother of the air," was portrayed by Virginia Payne. She began the role at twenty-three and didn't miss a single performance during the twenty-seven years that the show aired. Ma Perkins, the main character, was a kindly widow with a big heart who operated a lumber yard in the small town of Rushville Center. The plot revolved around her interactions with the townspeople and her three children. [Part 6]

Mason Jar — The Mason jar was invented and patented by John L. Mason in 1858. The glass jars were created for use in canning and have also been called Ball jars, named for the Ball Corporation, an early manufacturer of the jars. They continue to be widely used for canning and preserving food today. [Part 3]

Merle Travis — Country and western singer Merle Travis was born in Rosewood, Kentucky. His lyrics, including those in "Sixteen Tons" and "Dark as a Dungeon," often reflected the exploitation of coal miners. He was renowned for his masterful guitar playing. "Travis picking," a syncopated style of finger-picking, was named for him. Travis was inducted into the Nashville Songwriters Hall of Fame in 1970 and elected to the Country Music Hall of Fame in 1977. [Part 7]

Movietone News — The Movietone News, known in the United States as the Fox Movietone News, was a newsreel that ran in movie theaters between 1927 and 1963. Topics included sports, Hollywood happenings, World War II, and natural disasters. Fox's first news event was on May 20, 1927, and featured Charles Lindbergh's takeoff from Roosevelt Field for his historic flight. [Part 4]

Mr. District Attorney — A radio crime drama that aired from 1939 to 1952, *Mr. District Attorney* featured a crusading D.A. known only as "Mr. District Attorney" or "Chief" until the final year, when he was dubbed Paul Garrett. A key player in the series was the District Attorney's secretary Edith Miller, who was played throughout the series by Vicki Vola. The scripts were written by former law student Ed Byron, who was inspired by the early years of New York governor Thomas E. Dewey. The series debuted as a television show in 1951. [Part 3]

My Dreams are Gettin' Better All the Time — The song "My Dreams are Gettin' Better All the Time" was written by Manny Curtis and Vic Mizzy and published in 1945. One version was recorded by the Les Brown Orchestra, featuring Doris Day, and another by Johnny Long and Dick Robertson. [Part 7]

Oh Bury Me Not on the Lone Prairie — A cowboy folk song also known as "The Cowboy's Lament" and "The Dying Cowboy," "Bury Me Not on the Lone Prairie" was based on an old sailors' song. It first appeared in print with the present melody in 1932. It has been recorded by many country stars including Johnny Cash, Tex Ritter, and Roy Rogers. [Part 2]

Oleomargarine — Margarine was first created in 1807 by a Frenchman in response to Napoleon's request for a satisfactory butter substitute. He used margaric acid, which prompted the name "margarine," and won the emperor's prize. In 1871, the U.S. Dairy Company in New York City began the production of "artificial butter." By 1902, in a move to protect the dairy industry, thirty-two states had passed laws that prohibited the manufacture and sale of yellow-colored margarine. To get around the ban, manufacturers sold margarine with capsules of food coloring to be kneaded into the margarine by the purchaser. The practice continued through World War II, and the ban on yellow margarine was lifted shortly after the war ended. [Part 4]

Orson Welles — Born in 1915, George Orson Wells was a writer, actor, producer, and director who became known for his innovative dramatic productions and distinctive voice. He first came to fame as the director and narrator of a radio adaptation of *The War of the Worlds*, a novel written by H.G. Wells. The radio program was presented on October 30, 1938, as if it were a live news broadcast, leading listeners to believe they were truly in the midst of an extraterrestrial invasion. [Part 2]

Our Gal Sunday — Radio show *Our Gal Sunday* was based on a 1904 Broadway play titled *Sunday*, starring Ethel Barrymore. The radio version aired from 1937 to 1959. The question posed in each program was, "Can this girl from the little mining town in the West find happiness as the wife of a wealthy and titled Englishman?" [Part 6]

Over the Rainbow — The song, sometimes referred to as "Somewhere Over the Rainbow," was created by Harold Arlen and E.Y. Harburg for the film, *The Wizard of Oz*. The song almost didn't make the cut when MGM CEO Louis B. Mayer deleted it because it slowed down the movie. Arlen persuaded MGM to keep it in the movie, and it eventually became Judy Garland's signature song. "Over the Rainbow" was named the number one song by the Recording Industry Association of America and the National Endowment for the Arts. During World War II, the song was adopted as a symbol of the United States. [Part 5]

Palmer Method Penmanship — The Palmer Method of instruction for penmanship was created by Austin Palmer in 1888. It encouraged a uniform system of cursive writing that used rhythmic motions, and children who were left-handed were forced to write with their right hands. In 1894, *Palmer's Guide to Business Writing* was introduced. Eventually, Palmer's style became less popular as the emphasis on teaching proper handwriting declined. [Part 2]

Pearl Harbor — Pearl Harbor is located on the island of Oahu west of Honolulu. A deep-water naval base was established in the harbor in 1887 and serves as headquarters for the U.S. Pacific Fleet. On the morning of December 7, 1941, the Japanese navy conducted an unannounced military strike against the Pearl Harbor Naval Base. Two aerial attacks involving 353 aircraft were launched, sinking four U.S. Navy battleships, three cruisers, three destroyers, and one minelayer. Also destroyed were 188 aircraft. American casualties totaled 2,402, with 1,282 individuals wounded. The Japanese lost twenty-nine aircraft and five midget submarines. Sixty-five Japanese servicemen were killed or wounded and one was captured. [Part 4]

Penny loafers — Loafers became popular as a shoe style in the 1930s. George Henry Bass put his own unique stamp on them when he produced a style called Weejuns that had a strap across the shoe with a split design. The resulting opening was soon used as a way to add a decorative touch, including pennies. [Part 8]

Pepper Young's Family — A popular radio drama that ran from 1932 to 1959, *Pepper Young's Family* starred Burgess Meredith as Pepper. The series was created by author and playwright Elaine Sterne Carrington and initially aired as *Red Adams*. The title was changed to *Red Davis* until 1935, when it became *Forever Young*. In 1936, the show was dubbed *Pepper Young's Family*, a title the series retained for the rest of its long run. The stories revolved around Larry "Pepper"

Young and his family in the town of Elmwood. [Part 6]

Pinky Lee — Born Pincus Leff in 1907, the comedian became known as Pinky Lee, a "baggy pants" comic. He excelled in slapstick, comic dancing, and rapid-fire jokes. His costume was typically a plaid suit, baggy checkered pants, and an undersized hat. He had his own children's television program, *The Pinky Lee Show*, in the 1950s. In 1957, he hosted *The Gumby Show*. [Part 7]

Point Sublime — From 1940 to 1948, radio show *Point Sublime* entertained listeners with tales of life in a small seaport village "located in the quiet reaches of anybody's imagination." Actors included Cliff Arquette as a storekeeper and mayor of Point Sublime and Mel Blanc as the mayor's sidekick. Jane Morgan played a paleontologist, while Earle Ross portrayed a Texas businessman and the owner of the local golf course. The comedy series was sponsored by John Hancock Mutual Life Insurance throughout most of its run. [Part 6]

Portia Faces Life — In 1940, radio soap opera *Portia Faces Life* debuted on CBS. Lucille Wall portrayed Portia Blake, an attorney who fought corruption in the small town of Parkersburg. The series continued until 1953. [Part 4]

Rath Packing Company — George John Rath emigrated from Germany to the United States in the late 1940s and settled in Dubuque, Iowa. In addition to other endeavors, he started a pork packing operation. His son joined the business in 1873, and the company became George Rath and Son. After the business was destroyed by fire in 1891, the Raths were approached by the Waterloo, Iowa, Board of Trade and enticed to rebuild in that community with promised capital of $10,000, land, and tax concessions. George Rath elected to resume his mercantile business in Dubuque, but his son E.F. Rath and a cousin, John Rath, accepted the Waterloo offer and opened the new Rath Packing Company in 1891. By 1908, they added beef and eventually lamb to the products. During both world wars, they had lucrative contracts to supply meat to the armed forces. By 1941, the Rath Packing Company was the nation's largest meatpacking facility, with branches in twelve states. Despite problems with labor relations after World War II, the company continued to thrive until the 1970s, when workforce and facility problems challenged profitability. After a series of financial setbacks, the Rath Packing Company ceased operations in 1985. [Part 5]

Rinso White — Rinso laundry soap was created in 1908 by Hudson's Soap, which was sold to Lever Brothers. Lever Brothers began to manufacture Rinso in the United States in 1918. Rinso sponsored many radio programs from 1936 to 1946, including *Big Sister, Big Town, Mayor of the Town,* and *Amos 'n Andy.* Their slogan, "Rinso white, Rinso bright. Happy little washday song!" first aired in 1973. It was sung by twelve-year-old Belle Sullivan, who became the famous opera singer Beverly Sills. [Part 3]

Saddle Oxfords — Saddle oxfords are shoes that feature a separate saddle-shaped piece of leather at the instep. The color of the saddle may match or contrast with the color of the rest of the shoe. Spalding originally introduced them in 1906 as a racquet sport shoe. Eventually, the style became popular with teens. [Part 8]

Sam Hill — "Sam Hill" is a slang phrase that serves as a euphemism for "the devil" or "hell." Some etymologists date the expression back to the late 1830s, while others consider it of unknown origin. Millionaire Samuel Hill was sometimes associated with the phrase in the 1920s,

but the expression had been in use long before he was born. [Part 1]

Sears Roebuck Catalogue — Richard Sears announced on the 1894 cover of the Sears, Roebuck and Co. catalog that it was the "Book of Bargains: A Money Saver for Everyone." Every year, more goods were added to the "Big Book Catalog," which continued to be published until 1993. [Part 3]

Shirley Temple — Born April 23, 1928, Shirley Temple began acting in 1932 at the age of three with bit parts in feature films. In 1934, her career took off and she quickly became a star, becoming the youngest person (at age six) to be awarded an Oscar. She starred in twenty-four films for Twentieth Century-Fox during her career. [Part 1]

Sloppy Joe Sweater — In the 1940s, high school and college age girls turned to casual fashions. One of the popular items of the time was the sloppy joe sweater, a long, baggy pullover sweater. It was worn with both skirts and blue jeans. [Part 8]

Smilin' Through — Written in 1919, the play *Smilin' Through* was filmed in 1922, 1932, and 1941. The 1941 movie featured film stars Jeanette McDonald and Gene Raymond. It was the only film the couple, who were married, made together. [Part 8]

Snow White and the Seven Dwarfs — The Disney movie, *Snow White and the Seven Dwarfs* premiered on December 21, 1937. It was not only the first film produced by Walt Disney, but the first animated feature film produced in America. It has received numerous awards over the years and made the American Film Institute's list of the 100 greatest American films of all time in 1997. [Part 5]

Someday My Prince Will Come — This popular song was written by Larry Morey and Frank Churchill and appeared in the 1937 Disney movie, *Snow White and the Seven Dwarfs*. In their list of the 100 greatest songs in movie history, the American Film Institute listed "Someday My Prince Will Come" as number nineteen. [Part 5]

Stereoscopic Viewer — Also called stereograms, stereoviews, and stereocards, these instruments presented three-dimensional views of pictures. They were first created in the 1840s and remained popular until the 1930s, when movies took center stage. Then, in 1939, the View-Master was introduced at the New York World's Fair as an alternative to postcards. At the time, the primary subjects for viewing with the View-Master were scenic attractions. [Part 1]

Terry and the Pirates — The radio series *Terry and the Pirates* was a spinoff from the comic strip created in 1934 by Milton Caniff. The action adventure first aired from 1937 to 1939. It returned shortly before the attack on Pearl Harbor and continued until 1948. [Part 6]

The Ancient Mariner — "The Rime of the Ancient Mariner," written in 1797 by Samuel Taylor Coleridge, is his longest poem. It was published in the first edition of *Lyrical Ballads* in 1798. [Part 8]

The Great Depression — In 1929, the first effects of a severe worldwide economic depression began to surface. It started in the United States with the stock market crash known as Black Tuesday. But the Depression soon spread to almost every country in the world. Income, tax revenue, and profits plummeted, along with international trade. Unemployment in the United States reached 25 percent. The devastating economic effects continued until the start of World War II. [Part 1]

The Home for the Friendless — Established by Episcopal Bishop William Stevens Perry in 1884, the Home for the Friendless in Cedar Rapids, Iowa, was charged with providing residential care for dependent children. The name was changed to The Children's Home in 1940. It remained in operation into the 1970s. [Part 2]

The "L" — The "L" is a rapid transit system in the City of Chicago, Illinois. The oldest section of the rail system began operating in 1892. The "L" currently consists of eight lines totaling 106.1 miles. 57.1 miles of the line are elevated. [Part 5]

The Lone Ranger — The first episode of the radio program *The Lone Ranger* aired in 1933. The musical theme, which became inextricably linked to the Lone Ranger, was "March of the Swiss Soldiers," the finale of the "William Tell Overture." Numerous radio premiums were developed around the masked Western hero, including a Lone Ranger Six-Shooter Ring and Lone Ranger Deputy Badge. The radio series ended in 1954. [Part 6]

The Roosevelt Hotel — The Roosevelt Hotel in Cedar Rapids, Iowa, was built in 1927. In its heyday, the hotel boasted 241 guest rooms, a ballroom, and a restaurant. The interior was designed in the Italian Renaissance style. After undergoing bankruptcy in 1932, the Roosevelt was purchased by the First Avenue Company. That company operated the Roosevelt as a hotel until 1975. Eventually, the hotel rooms were converted into apartments. The twelve-story colonial revival style building was placed on the National Register of Historic Places in 1991. [Part 4]

The Shadow — The Shadow debuted in 1930 as the narrator of the *Detective Story Hour*. In 1931, the narrator became the star of *The Shadow Magazine*. It wasn't until 1937 that the radio drama *The Shadow* aired. The lead character was a crime fighter with "the power to cloud

men's minds so they cannot see him."
At the beginning of every show, actor
Frank Readick, Jr., said, "Who knows
what evil lurks in the hearts of men? The
Shadow knows!" He ended each episode
with, "The weed of crime bears bitter
fruit. Crime does not pay . . . The Shadow
knows!" [Part 3]

The Taming of the Shrew — *The Taming of the Shrew* is a comedy written in
the late 1590s by William Shakespeare.
It features a stubborn, headstrong
woman named Katherine who eventually
becomes an obedient wife to Petruchio.
[Part 8]

Tube Radios — In 1914, AT&T bought
the rights to manufacture vacuum tube
radios from inventor Lee DeForest. The
vacuum tube was used to create and
amplify the electric signals. Most radios
used tubes until transistors replaced them
in the early 1960s. [Part 4]

Vasco da Gama — Born in the 1460s,
Vasco da Gama was a Portuguese explorer
who commanded the first ships to sail
directly from Europe to India. In 1524,
he served as the governor of Portuguese
India. [Part 2]

Victory Gardens — During World
War I and World War II, residents of
the United States, the United Kingdom,
Canada, and Germany were encouraged
to plant vegetable, fruit, and herb gardens
at homes and public parks to reduce the
pressure on the public food supply. Planting Victory Gardens gave people a means
of contributing to the war effort on the
home front. Victory Gardens were also
called war gardens or food gardens for
defense. [Part 4]

Victrola — The Victor Talking Machine
Company, based in Camden, New Jersey,
was the leading American producer of
phonographs in the early 1900s. Their
trademark image of the terrier listening to a Berliner Gramophone was an
adaptation of an 1893 painting by Francis
Barraud. In 1906, the Victor Company
released a line of phonographs with the
turntable and amplifying horn inside a
wooden cabinet so that the instrument
became a beautiful piece of furniture. The
units were trademarked with the name
Victrola. They continued to be sold under
that name until the early 1970s. [Part 4]

Virginia Reel — The folk dance referred to as the Virginia Reel dates from
the seventeenth century. Generally considered to be an English country dance,
it was popular in the United States in
the 1800s. It is danced in a line with the
partners facing each other and often uses
a caller to announce the steps. [Part 5]

Wizard of Oz — The film, *The Wizard of Oz,* was first released in 1939. It
was based on the children's novel, *The
Wonderful Wizard of Oz,* by L. Frank
Baum and starred Judy Garland, Ray
Bolger, Jack Haley, Bert Lahr, and Frank
Morgan. At the time, the movie was not
financially successful due to the large
budget required to produce the film. But
The Wizard of Oz did win two Oscars
and eventually became one of the most
well-known films in history. The Library
of Congress named it the most-watched
film in history. [Part 5]

Wonder Woman — The DC Comics
superheroine Wonder Woman was created by Dr. William Moulton Marston
and first appeared in print in All Star
Comics number eight in 1941. [Part 8]